The Psychology
and
Biology
of Emotion

The Psychology
and
Biology
of Emotion

Robert Plutchik
Albert Einstein College of Medicine

HarperCollins*CollegePublishers*

Acquisitions Editor: Catherine Woods
Project Coordination and Text Design: Proof Positive/Farrowlyne
    Associates, Inc.
Cover Design: Kay Petronio
Production Manager: Kewal Sharma
Compositor: Proof Positive/Farrowlyne Associates, Inc.
Printer and Binder: R. R. Donnelley & Sons Company
Cover Printer: Phoenix Color Corporation

For permission to use copyrighted material, grateful acknowledgment is made to the copyright holders on pp. 383–387, which are hereby made part of this copyright page.

The Psychology and Biology of Emotion, First Edition
Copyright © 1994 by HarperCollins College Publishers

Library of Congress Cataloging-in-Publication Data
Plutchik, Robert.
    The psychology and biology of emotion / Robert Plutchik. — 1st ed.
        p.   cm.
    Includes bibliographical references and indexes.
    ISBN 0-06-045236-6
        1. Emotions.   2. Emotions—Physiological aspects.   I. Title.
BF531.P595 1994
152.4—dc20   93-32729
                                                         CIP

93 94 95 96 9 8 7 6 5 4 3 2 1

"If you can conceive yourself, if possible, suddenly stripped of all the emotion with which our world now inspires you . . . no one portion of the universe would then have importance beyond another; and the whole character of its things and series of its events would be without significance, character, expression, or perspective."

—William James

Table of Contents

Preface

Most people believe they know what emotions are. They think of emotions as special kinds of feelings that they label with such words as *happy, sad, angry,* and *surprised.* They would also probably say that emotions occur frequently in daily life and can be seen at football games, on the television news reports, in the daily newspapers, and in ordinary encounters with friends, lovers, or family members. Sometimes they see homeless or mentally ill people wandering the streets showing evidence of depression, apathy, or anger. Emotions pervade life. They are a central theme in works of history and in the Bible, and are described in novels, in poetry, and in paintings.

Given the obvious importance of emotions in daily life, one would think that psychologists would study this topic systematically, and that it would be a focal point in textbooks and teaching. Suprisingly, this is not so. Very few universities in the United States or in other countries offer a course on emotions. When it is offered it is usually part of a course on motivation and emotion. Introductory textbooks in psychology typically have one chapter on emotions that usually contains a discussion of a theory psychologist-philosopher William James proposed over 100 years ago, followed by a discussion of a theory physiologist-physician Walter Cannon proposed around the time of World War I. Sometimes the chapter includes information on emotional development in young children, and information on the lie detector and its possible relation to emotion. All in all, it is meager fare for such a potentially rich topic as emotions!

The reasons for this situation are many and they will be described in detail in the first two chapters of this book. However, in brief, some of the bases for the confusions involved in studying emotions have been: ambiguities in the language of emotion, reluctance of many psychologists to study so subjective an experience, ethical limitations on laboratory research on emotions, existence of different historical traditions, and lack of well-articulated theories in the field. There was even a period during the 1950s when some psychologists proposed that the concept of emotion was so ambiguous that psychology would be better off without it. For a while, some writers eliminated the word *emotion* from their textbooks and tried to ignore the topic. It is no surprise, however, that the concept (but not the word) appeared in disguise in books under such heading as stress, frustration, aggression, avoidance responses, conflict, and the like.

However, in the 1960s a greatly heightened interest began in the topic of emotions with a concomitant increase in research and theory. Contributors to this new interest in emotions are not only psychologists but biologists, ethologists, psychiatrists, and psychoanalysts. This diversity of interest implies that the concept of emotions applies not only to human adults who are capable of verbalizing their feelings, but also to infants, children, the mentally retarded, the mentally ill, higher primates, and lower animals.

In the past 30 years, much information has been amassed about emotions in all these diverse settings, and sufficient theory has been generated to now enable some degree of integration of ideas. That is one of the reasons this textbook was written. It attempts to present to the interested student a broad summary of research and theory, based on the assumption that the subject of emotions is not merely a branch of clinical psychology, social psychology, ethology, psychiatry, or psychoanalysis. Emotions are ultimately related to each of these fields, but have, in fact, identities of their own, just as the subjects of learning, development, and motivation are related to all aspects of psychology and yet have identities of their own. Given this belief, another reason for this text is to demonstrate the integrated identity of the topic of emotions, at the same time that they are recognized to be part of diverse areas of investigation.

I have undertaken this difficult task because I have been concerned with the study of emotions for over 30 years and have contributed many articles, chapters, and books to this subject. My recurrent discoveries of how emotions enter our lives, sometimes disguised and indirect, and sometimes powerfully present, have endlessly fascinated me. I have wanted to convey my own enthusiasm about the study of emotion, and wanting to share insights into new ways of thinking about emotions in terms of their deep structure as well as their transient aspects, I hope this textbook will successfully express to the reader these various reasons for its existence.

Acknowledgments

Every work is a reflection of countless influences, and I should like to add a few words of thanks to some of those people who have had a direct or indirect effect on the outcome of this endeavor. At an early stage of my thinking about emotion, Dr. H. Enger Rosvold and Dr. Mortimer Mishkin invited me to assist in brain stimulation research on primates at the National Institute of Mental Health. The two years I spent with them broadened my knowledge and appreciation of brain models in relation to emotions.

My friend, Dr. Henry Kellerman, a psychoanalyst, shared with me over a long period of time the excitement of discovering the multiple masks of emotions as well as their multiple derivatives. Psychiatrists with whom I have worked closely over the years have also helped me recognize the manifold expressions of emotions in everyday life and in clinical practice. The three people who have been most influential in this regard are Dr. Jack Wilder, Dr. Byram Karasu, and Dr. Herman van Praag. To all these men I am indebted for providing me with a congenial, supportive working environment at the Albert Einstein College of Medicine for many years, as well as the pleasure and value of their personal friendship.

A number of people who have read part or all of this book in manuscript form have given me the benefit of their expertise and suggestions. Among these colleagues are Dr. Hope Conte, Dr. Elliot Gardner, Dr. David Kemper, and Dr. Detlev Ploog. I am especially indebted to Dr. Jaak Panksepp, who made useful suggestions about all parts of the book, and was especially helpful with the chapters on emotions and the brain. I would also like to thank the many reviewers who advised me on the manuscript. They include:

James Averill, University of Massachusetts
Irving Benig, McGill University
Ross Buck, University of Connecticut
Linda Camras, DePaul University
Margaret Clark, Carnegie Mellon University
Victor Denenberg, University of Connecticut
Paul Ekman, University of California—San Francisco
William Morris, Dartmouth University
Craig Smith, Vanderbilt University
Robert Stern, Penn State University

I should also like to thank several secretaries who worked long and tirelessly in preparing the manuscript in esthetically pleasing form. These are Shirley Kreitman, Laurie Hillman, and Teresa Cannella. Thanks for your patience, your kind tolerance, and your skills.

Finally, I should like to express my deepest appreciation to my family members, who have educated me more than all my research about emotions: my wife Anita, my daughter Lisa and her husband Steve, my daughter Lori, my son Roy, and my granddaughter, Lauren Beth. They represent for me the cycle and the wisdom of life.

ROBERT PLUTCHIK

Introduction

What should a textbook on emotions be about? What are the domains of inquiry that define emotion as a separate field of psychological study?

At the present stage of the history of psychology, these are difficult questions to answer; little codification of the field has taken place, unlike areas such as learning, motivation, and development. Research and theorizing about emotions have covered a huge and diverse universe of ideas. They include social psychological studies of the antecedent conditions and cognitive attributions associated with particular emotions such as jealousy, pity, and envy. They include psychophysiological studies of autonomic changes under conditions of stress and induced emotions. They include observational studies of human and animal behavior under a variety of conditions that elicit anger, aggression, fear, and anxiety. They include studies of the brain systems involved in emotion during aversive conditioning, during self-stimulation, and during drug intake. And they include studies of patients suffering from emotional disorders, patients who are said to be neurotic, psychotic, depressed, stressed, suicidal, or violent. Somehow, the study of emotions should enable us to incorporate all these ideas and issues within the general rubric of *emotions.*

Because there is now a ferment among psychologist and other investigators form other disciplines concerning emotions, many new ideas have entered the field, and a new textbook of emotions should attempt to embrace many of them. The fact that there have been few previous textbooks on emotions provides much flexibility to the present endeavor. One is not hampered by tradition as to what is or is not appropriate to include in such a book.

I have therefore included in this text a wide variety of ideas and studies. For example, along with newer developments, traditional thinking about facial expressions receives extensive coverage. The issue of identifying emotions in early life is carefully examined along with the question of how emotions change with maturation. The biological aspects of emotions and the brain are covered extensively, as are the clinical conditions resulting from disorders of emotions. Ethological ideas about emotions in animals are also covered, as well as descriptions of many important new theories on ways to conceptualize emotions.

A brief description of the sequence of chapters follows, along with a few important ideas in each one. Every chapter begins with a statement of the goals of the chapter, followed by a list of important questions addressed in the chapter. At the end of each, there is a summary statement.

Chapter 1   The Study of Emotions. Some of the reasons for the difficulties in studying emotions are given. These reasons include the fact that both behaviorism and psychoanalysis have raised questions about the validity of self-reports as measures of inner states, the belief that emotions occur in blind and deaf children as well as lower animals, and the diversity of opinion about what words in our language describe emotions. A preliminary definition of the word *emotion* is given as a first approximation to a more adequate definition.

Chapter 2   Major Historical Traditions in the Study of Emotions. Five major traditions concerned with emotions are described. The evolutionary tradition has emphasized the adaptive significance of emotional expressions as communications that tend to increase the chances of individual survival, but has little to say about subjective feelings. The psychophysiological tradition has been largely concerned with the relations among autonomic changes, facial expressions, and subjective feelings. The neurological tradition has stimulated the search for the brain structures and systems that organize all the information we use in feeling or expressing our emotions. The psychodynamic tradition has stimulated the thinking of clinicians to recognize the complexity of emotional states and the general presence of mixed emotions or blends. The cognitive tradition has focused largely on the role of cognitions, assessments, and appraisals, all crucial aspects of the emotional process.

Chapter 3   The Language of Emotions. Although many investigators have attempted to identify the words that describe emotions, there is surprising disagreement on many terms. This situation suggests the need to conceptualize emotions in broader, theoretical ways. As one important approach to defining emotions, the history of the concept of primary and derived emotions is presented. A contemporary version of these ideas is seen in the efforts to describe emotions in terms of a circle or circumplex model, and in terms of the concept of prototypes, and fuzzy categories.

Chapter 4   Theories of Emotions. Theories reviewed in this chapter are grouped under a few main categories: motivational theories, cognitive theories, psychoanalytic theories, and evolutionary theories. In recent years, the thinking of theorists representing these different types of theories has overlapped. It is likely that increasing interpenetration of ideas will occur as time goes on.

Chapter 5   The Measurement of Emotions. Because emotions are complex states involving feelings, behavior, impulses, physiological changes, and efforts at control, the measurement of emotions is also a complex process. This chapter describes the use of adjective checklists, structured and unstructured questionnaries, behavioral rating techniques, projective techniques, and physiological indices. No one method is necessarily better than any other, and all have sources of bias connected with them.

Chapter 6 Facial Expressions and Emotions. Judgments of emotion from facial expressions have not always been consistent. Explanations for these findings are given, and a review of cross-cultural studies of emotion-recognition is presented. These studies tend to support the idea that certain emotional expressions are universal and based on genetic codes. Further evidence for innateness of certain expressions is found in observations of children born blind and deaf. It is concluded that facial expressions are only one kind of nonverbal behavior, all of which function to communicate information.

Chapter 7 Neurophysiology and Theories of Facial Expression. Evidence is presented that suggests that many facial expressions are based on genetically determined brain programs that are activated by significant stimuli in the life of an individual. However, in many situations, facial expressions are deceptions that individuals control in their desires for power and acceptance. Thus, facial expressions represent compromises between innate tendencies and socially determined desires. Three general types of theories of facial expressions are described: peripheral theories, central theories, and functional theories. Some ideas about the evolutionary origins of emotional expressions are also presented.

Chapter 8 Emotional Development. Studies of infants have led to the conclusion that emotional expressions are forms of communication that indicate the need for nourishment and protection. Emotional signals increase the probability of contact with the mother. Loss of attachment leads to certain strategies that have survival value. Since it is evident that children learn to use the language of emotions as they mature, many studies have attempted to assess the sequence of language changes that typically occur. It is also possible to identify the prototype elicitors for particular emotions as well as typical types of reactions.

Chapter 9 Emotions and Evolution. This chapter presents an evolutionary perspective on the nature of emotions. This viewpoint suggests that basic survival issues in all living organisms require certain types of adaptive reactions that are ubiquitous and may be interpreted as the prototypes of emotions in humans. Other topics covered in this chapter concern how to make meaningful inferences about subjective states in animals, and how to find evidence of self-consciousness in lower animals.

Chapter 10 Emotional Communication in Animals. Display behaviors related to emotions have several functions: they are related to important life events, they communicate information, they are genetically based, species characteristics, they often conflict to produce blends, and the meanings of such displays must be deciphered. Emotions appear to be complex patterns of action, in response to environmental emergencies, that attempt to restore a stable, functioning state.

Chapter 11   Emotions and the Brain. A review is provided of the development of the nervous system from amphibia to humans. The major brain structures and their interrelations are described with particular emphasis on the concept of the limbic system. Mild electrical stimulation of the brain of conscious human patients has been shown to produce, depending on the location of electrodes, reports of fear, anxiety, anger, disgust, surprise, joy, and pleasure.

Chapter 12   Theories of Brain Function in Emotion. The work of seven theorists who have developed theories about emotions and brain function is described. The role of limbic system structures and circuits in emotion is elaborated as well as that of neurotransmitters and endocrine changes. Because emotional reactions such as fear can be conditioned to previously neutral stimuli, it is evident that emotion circuits in the brain must interact with the neural systems related to sensation, assessment, memory, decision-making, and consciousness.

Chapter 13   Love and Sadness in Everyday Life. Current research reveals that love can be considered to be a complex state having a variety of components such as respect, attraction, and attachment. Attachment theory suggests that love results from an interaction of the attachment, the caregiving, and the mating systems. Sadness is typically associated with the loss of an important attachment. When sadness is chronic, a psychiatric condition called depression exists. Various methods of treatment for depression are described.

Chapter 14   Understanding Emotional Disorders. A true understanding of emotions should provide insight into disorders of emotion. Two of the most troubling emotions seen in clinical practice are anxiety and anger. These emotions may be expressed in the form of anxiety disorders, as well as in suicide and violence risk. Despite their troublesome nature when fear and anger occur in extreme or persistent forms, there is evidence that both have certain adaptive functions. Some descriptions are given of therapeutic methods to modify or control the expression of fear and anger.

The Study of Emotions

*The obvious need for a term is a sure
indication that a concept which
corresponds to something
very real does exist.*
—Konrad Lorenz

▌ Goals of This Chapter

Emotions are so much a part of our lives that one would think that psychologists should be able to define the field and systematically study the problems within it. You may be surprised to learn that psychologists have long considered the study of emotions one of the most confused and difficult topics in all of psychology, and that there is relatively little agreement on how to define the term and on how to go about studying the topic.

As an introduction to the field, the present chapter will examine a number of proposed definitions of emotion and will provide a preliminary first approximation to a general definition. It will be preliminary because many important facts and theories will be presented in the following chapters that may influence how you begin to think about the subject; a fully adequate definition may have to wait until much more is known.

This chapter will also examine the question of why the study of emotions seems to be so difficult. It will indicate that one of the problems relates to the inherent ambiguity of our language, particularly our introspective language. Another problem concerns the type of individual to whom the concept may

1

be said to apply. Should the word *emotion* be applicable only to normal adults, or should it apply to mentally ill or mentally handicapped persons as well? Should it apply to children, infants, and even animals? The answers to these questions influence the kinds of definitions and theories that we chose.

Still another issue relates to the impact that certain schools of psychology have had on our thinking. Behaviorism has maintained the philosophy that inner states, such as emotions are thought to be, are not appropriate subjects of study for a scientific psychology. This attitude greatly inhibited research in the field. Similarly, the philosophy of psychoanalysis implied that an individual's verbal reports were often not to be trusted, and that inner feelings were sometimes distorted or repressed, and in any case, exceedingly complex. These beliefs also raised questions about the validity of self-reports of inner feelings. Finally, it is noted that different historical traditions have influenced the ways that contemporary psychologists and biologists study and conceptualize emotions.

Important Questions Addressed In This Chapter

- How have theorists defined the word *emotion?*
- Why is the study of emotion so difficult?
- Can we make inferences about emotions in children who are blind and deaf?
- Is there reason to believe that animals have emotions?
- What have been the effects of behaviorism and psychoanalysis in shaping our ideas about emotions?
- To what extent can we trust verbal reports of emotions?

■   ■   ■   ■   ■   ■   ■   ■   ■

▌The Diversity of Definitions of Emotion

Despite the fact that emotions are part of daily life and have been described in the literature of all cultures, there is still, at present, considerable confusion about their nature. Examination of published papers and books shows that many definitions of the word *emotion* have been proposed over the past 100 years. Although no list can be complete, it is possible to provide a sense of the way psychologists and others have thought about the topic by examining a few of the more influential definitions.

In 1884, William James, one of the most influential figures in the history of psychology, defined emotion in the following way: "My theory is that the bodily changes follow directly the perception of the exciting fact, and that our feeling of the same changes as they occur *is* the emotion." This definition was basically concerned with the question of sequence, that is, which comes first, the feeling of an emotion or the bodily changes associated with a strong emotion. James believed that for the "coarser" emotions such as fear and anger, the bodily changes (that is, the increased beating of the heart, the increased blood pressure, the increased sugar in the blood) came first, and the feeling of emotion was based largely on a person's recognition of these changes. This definition or some version of it is still found in many textbooks, and it has influenced the thinking of many generations of psychologists.

John Watson was the founder of behaviorism as a psychological movement. He defined emotion in one of his publications in 1924 where he wrote: "An emotion is an hereditary 'pattern–reaction' involving profound changes of the bodily mechanisms as a whole, but particularly of the visceral and glandular systems." In this definition Watson introduced the idea that an emotion involved changes in the whole body, that these changes showed different patterns for different emotions, and that all these reactions were based on innate hereditary systems.

As an extension of this idea, and in contrast with the views of William James, the neurophysiologist Walter Cannon in 1929 declared that "The peculiar quality of the emotion is added to simple sensation when the thalamic processes are roused." In writing this, Cannon was summarizing his many studies with cats that seemed to reveal that a certain part of the brain, the thalamus and hypothalamus, were the integrating centers for emotional feelings as well as emotional behaviors. This idea was important in that it stimulated many psychologists to become interested in brain functions and led to studies that have taught us a great deal about the roles that different parts of the brain play in determining emotional feelings and displays.

In 1963, another neurophysiologist, Paul MacLean, who has studied the behavior of squirrel monkeys for many years, came to the conclusion that "Emotional feelings guide our behavior with respect to the two basic life principles of self-preservation and the preservation of the species." This statement introduces a new idea toward our understanding of emotions. It suggests that emotions have biological functions and that these functions are related to the survival of the individual as well as survival of the group of which the individual is a part. This implies that emotions have something to do with evolution, an idea that Charles Darwin first described in a book he wrote in 1872.

A British psychiatrist, John Bowlby, in 1969 proposed still another definition of emotion. He wrote that "Emotions are phases of an individual's intuitive appraisals either of his own organismic states and urges to act or of the succession of environmental situations in which he finds himself. . . . At the same time, because they are usually accompanied by distinctive facial expressions, bodily postures and incipient movements, they usually provide valuable information to his companions." This definition of emotion introduces several new ideas. It implies that emotions are related to appraisals or interpretations of events going on within an individual's own body, as well as to events that are occurring around the individual. It indicates that the signs of emotion can be found in facial expressions, postures, and urges to act. And finally, the definition implies that the expressive behavior of an emotion provides information from one individual to another. These ideas are consistent with Darwin's descriptions of emotional expressions wherein he stated that emotions communicate intentions.

Psychologist Richard Lazarus proposed another definition of emotion in 1975. He suggests that "Emotion is a complex disturbance that includes three main components: subjective affect, physiological changes related to species-specific forms of mobilization for adaptive action, and action impulses having both instrumental and expressive qualities." This definition brings up the idea that emotion is a disturbance; yet despite the notion that emotion is a kind of disruption, it is also said to be a form of readiness for adaptive action. In other words, emotions change an ongoing situation and help the individual prepare for appropriate action. The final point made is that the action helps the individual achieve his or her goals (i.e., is instrumental), and at the same time shows expressive displays such as changes of facial expression that are characteristic of each specific emotion.

Dutch psychologist Nico Frijda, who has contributed many important ideas to the study of emotion, defined emotion in 1986 in the following way: "Emotions are tendencies to establish, maintain, or disrupt a relationship with the environment. . . . Emotion might be defined as action readiness change in response to emergencies or interruptions." One important idea this definition represents is that emotions are ways that individuals interact with the people and events around them. If the interactions are unpleasant, emotions are attempts to decrease or interrupt the relationship. The other important idea this definition expresses is that the triggers of emotions are emergencies in the life of the individual, and that emotions are responses to these emergencies.

Still another definition of emotion that reflects the so-called cognitive orientation of some psychologists has been provided by Andrew Ortony in 1988. He suggests that "Emotions are valenced reactions to events, agents or objects, with their particular nature being determined by the way in which the eliciting situation is construed." The term *valence* is used in the sense of positive or negative, and therefore the definition implies that an emotion involves a pleasant or unpleasant feeling. In addition, the special nature of each emotion is determined by the way that each event is interpreted. This definition thus focuses upon the issue of interpretation of events. Other theorists have mentioned the same idea in terms of concepts of appraisal, evaluation, or cognitive assessment as the basis for emotion.

Finally, let us examine what Webster's unabridged dictionary says about emotion. The word *emotion* comes from a Latin word which means *to move* or *to stir up*. It now has several meanings. It can mean excitement, or agitation, or feelings of pain or pleasure. It is also described as "a physiological departure from homeostasis that is subjectively experienced as strong feeling (as of love, hate, desire or fear) and manifests itself in neuro-muscular, respiratory, cardiovascular, hormonal or other bodily changes preparatory to overt acts which may or may not be performed." This defin-ition emphasizes the point that an emotion is a change from a normal or baseline level of activity. It does not say what brings this change about, but it does indicate that the changes are extensive and involve most of the systems of the body. The other interesting point this definition makes is that an emotion could, but need not, be expressed in the form of overt action. It could, by implication, simply be a state of mind or a state of preparation for action.

As mentioned earlier, the definitions given here, are a sample from a larger group of definitions, but they are useful in that they cover many (although not all) of the ideas about emotion that psychologists and others have proposed over the years. It is evident that there is some agreement and some disagreement. On the basis of these definitions, it may be said that emotions are triggered by our interpretations of events, that they involve strong reactions of most, if not all, of our bodily systems, that they can be disruptive of ongoing activity, and yet somehow adaptive. Emotions communicate information from one person to another, and they may express different feeling states. They may have something to do with survival of the individual and the species, and they may be based on hereditary or genetic processes that influence the way the brain works. In some way, emotions may even have something to do with influencing or regulating the relations between people. All in all, these statements describe a large set of complex ideas.

Two psychologists seeking to create a consensus on how emotions should be defined have already summarized some of these ideas. They identified 92 definitions found in various textbooks, dictionaries, and other sources (Kleinginna & Kleinginna, 1981). Their review indicated that certain ideas or themes were frequently repeated, a fact that led them to propose the following integrated definition:

> Emotion is a complex set of interactions among subjective and objective factors, mediated by neural/hormonal systems, which can (a) give rise to affective experi-ences such as feelings of arousal, pleasure/displeasure; (b) generate cognitive processes such as emotionally relevant perceptual effects, appraisals, labeling processes; (c) activate widespread physiological adjustments to the arousing con-ditions; and (d) lead to behavior that is often, but not always, expressive, goal-directed, and adaptive.

This definition is useful because it includes many of the diverse ideas found in the literature about emotions. However, it should be considered as a first approximation to this complex category. Later chapters will pro-vide additional ideas to help elaborate and refine this definition.

It should be evident by now that the definitions of emotions are not isolated and arbitrary, but that they tend to imply some broader issues or questions. In other words, a definition is in a sense, a kind of mini–theory. It is a way in which the proponent of the definition has decided to describe an area of study. Each definition has, or should have, implications about what one should study or measure.

The existence of multiple definitions of the word *emotion* is paralleled by the existence of many different *theories* of emotion. In a review of theories, Plutchik (1980) describes 24 approaches to an understanding of emotions. In a similar overview, Strongman (1988) describes 30 approaches. Most of these theories tend to be somewhat narrow in focus and are usually concerned with one or two major issues; for example, what parts of the brain are involved in emotional reactions; or how the autonomic nervous system changes during emotions; or what kind of stimulus events trigger what kinds of emotion. Each of these questions is important, but a theory that is broad and general should attempt to deal with all of them.

▋Why Is the Study of Emotions So Difficult?

Most people believe that emotions are such feelings as joy and anger, fear and sadness, surprise and happiness, feelings that people tell us about or that we recognize in ourselves. This is a reasonable way to think about emotions but it does create certain problems. One problem is that the language of emotions is often ambiguous, vague, or obscure. An example of this point may be seen in the work of Davitz (1970), who asked college students to write brief reports about emotional experiences they had had. From these reports he compiled a list of 556 words and phrases they used to describe emotions. To illustrate the complexity of these ideas, consider the terms these college students used to describe depression.

> "I feel empty, drained, hollow, understimulated, undercharged, heavy, loggy, sluggish; I feel let down, tired, sleepy; it's an effort to do anything, I have no desire, no motivations, no interest."
>
> "I feel sorry for myself; there is simply no place to go; I lose all confidence in myself and doubt myself; I feel vulnerable and totally helpless; I feel insignificant."
>
> "I want to withdraw, disappear, draw back, be alone, away from others; crawl into myself; everything seems useless, absurd, meaningless; I feel as if I'm out of touch, can't reach others; my body wants to contract."
>
> "I have no appetite; there is a lump in my throat; I can't smile or laugh; it's as if I'm suffocating" (Davitz, 1970).

Looking at these descriptions of depression it is obvious that they present a picture of a complex internal state having many elements. There are physical symptoms (*tired, sleepy*), attitudes about self (*feel vulnerable*), impulses to action (*want to withdraw*), and physiological changes (*no appetite*). Any one class of descriptions is clearly only a partial image of the total state called depression. Similarly, any one set of descriptions is only a partial description of the complex states of emotion.

Where Do People Locate Emotional Sensations?

Another example of the complexity of our ideas about emotions is in a report by Lyman and Waters (1986). They asked students to describe the sensations and the locations of these sensations associated with 34 emotions. Grouping of the data by means of a statistical procedure called factor analysis suggested that the face was strongly associated with feelings of embarrassment, amusement, and resentment, while the stomach was strongly associated with feelings of guilt, anxiety, and jealousy. The emotion most associated with the eyes was sorrow. Lyman and Waters also found overlap. Worry, for example, was associated with both the face and the stomach, joy with both the head and the heart, and anger with both the face and hands.

These overlappings of feelings and associations connected with different emotions have led some investigators to suggest that emotions are actually *fuzzy* categories and that the best way to describe them is to give a good example of each *basic* emotion. (The good example is called a *prototype*). Other emotions are then considered to be members of the same family depending on how similar they are to the prototype.

In a study Shaver and his associates (1987) designed to identify prototypes of some emotions, they asked college students to describe the typical features of a number of emotions. When asked to describe anger, for example, the students used such words as the following:

Loud voice, yelling, screaming
Unfairness
Real or threatened pain
Thinking "I'm right"
Red, flushed face
Violation of expectation
Reversal or loss of power, status

When asked to describe joy, the students used the following kinds of descriptions:

Smiling
Seeing bright side of things
Getting what was wanted
Physically active
Saying positive things
Not easily worried

These descriptions are said to define the prototypes for particular emotions and to some degree can be duplicated in different cultures (Lutz, 1982). They suggest how complex is our implicit knowledge of emotions.

Emotions in Nonverbal Individuals

Researchers have carried out a great many studies of emotion with the help of college students who are generally intelligent and verbal. But most people believe that young children and even infants have emotions, too. We accept this idea even though children and infants cannot report their inner feelings with familiar words. Similarly, anyone who has observed severely ill psychiatric patients will admit that they seem to show emotions even though their words may be confusing. Mentally retarded individuals also show emotions, even though their verbal statements of feelings are often limited or absent.

We may see an example of this phenomenon in the research of Eibl-Eibesfeldt (1973), a German ethologist. He took extensive motion pictures of six children who had been born severely handicapped because their mothers had taken the drug thalidomide during pregnancy. As a result, five of the six children had slight to extensive brain damage and all were born deaf and blind. All showed retarded development to varying degrees, and all showed some stereotyped behaviors such as teeth grinding, head or body swaying, and kicking.

Despite the fact that these children could neither see nor hear the world around them and were also greatly impaired in cognitive capacity, they showed many normal emotional reactions. Eibl-Eibesfeldt wrote:

> Smiling was observed in all deaf-and-blind-born studied so far. It occurred spontaneously during play, and in Sabine when she sat by herself in the sun patting her face with the palms of her hands. Smiling could be released by patting, mild tickling, and engaging in social play. The smiling started with an upward movement of the corners of the mouth. At higher intensities the lips opened wide in front, exposing the teeth in the way sighted people do; the eye slits were narrowed, and finally the head was raised and tilted back.

In addition to smiling, the children all showed laughter, generally during rough social play such as wrestling as well as during tickling. The children cried when hurt or when left in an unfamiliar environment. In such cases the corners of the mouth usually turned down and opened, the eyelids pressed together, and tears were shed. Sometimes the children raised the eyebrows and furrowed the brow at the same time that frown lines appeared between the eyes. Occasionally, when someone persistently offered a child a disliked object, the child cried in anger. The children also spontaneously embraced, caressed, and kissed other people on some occasions. At times they showed expressions of smiling, laughing, crying in distress, crying in anger, frowning, pouting, surprise, and others that clearly denote emotions. Figure 1.1 shows a photograph of one of these children.

Another reason for doubting the idea that verbal reports of feelings are the only way to recognize feelings is that emotions are believed to occur in animals. From prehistoric times, people have used observations of an ani-

| Figure 1.1 | Photograph of Sabine Laughing |

Sabine was born blind and deaf because her mother had taken the drug thalidomide during pregnancy.

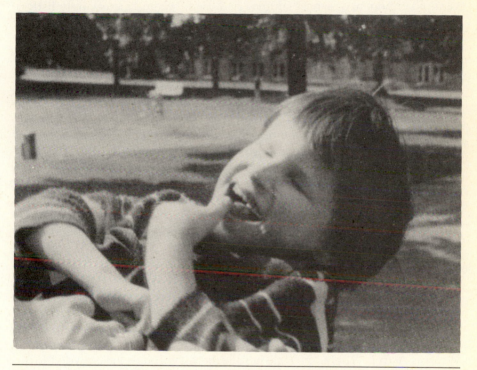

mal's behavior and expressions to judge the existence of emotions in animals. The belief in animal emotions is the basis for the many studies that researchers have conducted on animals to determine the factors that produce and modify such emotions as fear and anger.

Most people, particularly those who have had experience with pets, will agree that animals show emotions. Observers have reported dogs to show depression when their owners have died or gone away. Dogs also show signs of jealousy. When scolded, their tails droop, their activity slows, and they slink away.

In the chimpanzee, we see signs of anger in the form of sulking and temper tantrums. Young chimps may hold their heads on the floor, and pull at their hair when they are restrained from getting something they apparently want. In laboratory research, chimpanzees have expressed signs of terror on being shown a plastic model of a chimpanzee's head.

Observers in the wild have seen chimpanzees and gorillas giving help to youngsters in trouble even though it meant going into dangerous areas.

The ethologist Jane Goodall, who has spent over 20 years studying chimpanzee behavior under relatively natural conditions in Africa, has often described emotional behavior in the chimpanzees. Merlin, a three-year-old chimpanzee whose mother had died, became increasingly listless, stopped playing with other chimpanzees, and developed a number of stereotyped patterns of behavior such as rocking back and forth. Figure 1.2 illustrates this behavior. A human observer would probably describe Merlin as depressed. A later chapter will discuss in more detail how observers make inferences about emotions in animals. It is worth noting, however, that over the years, researchers have raised a number of chimpanzees in homes and treated them very much like children. In all such cases, the chimpanzees' behavior has been remarkably human-like, and their expressions of emotion are indistinguishable from those of young children of roughly comparable age.

Harry Raven, a curator at the American Museum of Natural History, made one of the earliest attempts to raise a chimpanzee. In 1930 he bought a baby chimp from two hunters in Africa who had just killed its mother. He took the chimp, whom some African children named Meshie Mungkut, and raised it with his family in his Long Island, New York, home. Raven often took Meshie to the Museum where she would ride around the halls on a tricycle. She ate in the staff dining room with a knife and fork.

Raven also made motion pictures showing Meshie picking up a baby in the family, carefully carrying her to a high chair, taking her food in a bowl, and feeding her with a spoon. In 1933, Meshie was a guest of the president of the American Museum of Natural History at a formal banquet at the Waldorf Astoria. There, she rode her kiddie car through the crowded foyer, and took her place at the table with the rest of the guests. She politely ate some of each course, and sat quietly while the speeches were made.

When Meshie became sexually mature at about six years of age, the Raven family had difficulty dealing with her and reluctantly sold her to a zoo in Chicago. About a year later, Raven was passing through Chicago and decided to visit Meshie. Although the zookeeper said that Meshie had become wild and dangerous, Raven insisted on going into the cage. According to a later report of this event, when he went in, Meshie rushed into his arms and clung to him tightly. Meshie died in childbirth a year later.

We see another example of the belief that animals show emotion in *The Bestiary: A Book of Beasts.* This book was widely distributed in the Middle Ages when it was almost as popular as the Bible. Meant as a serious work of natural history first written down around the second century A.D., it was based on a variety of sources. It was probably written first in Greek and then translated into Syrian, Armenian, Ethiopian, and eventually Latin in the eighth century. The Greek original describes 49 beasts, while the later Latin version includes 150.

Figure 1.2   Merlin, One Year After His Mother's Death

Merlin, a chimpanzee aged about three years old, whose mother died. He became increasingly listless, stopped playing with other chimpanzees, and developed a number of stereotyped patterns of behavior such as rocking back and forth.

Source: J. van Lawick-Goodall, 1973.

The Bestiary is a cross between an encyclopedia and a work of religion. Each animal is said to have human characteristics that provide insights into its moral nature. For example:

> Lions . . . are called beasts because of the violence with which they rage, and are known as "wild" because they are accustomed to freedom by nature and are governed by their own wishes. . . . So far as their relations with men are concerned, the nature of lions is that they do not get angry unless they are wounded.
>
> Any decent human ought to pay attention to this. For men do get angry when they are not wounded, and they oppress the innocent although the law of Christ bids them to let even the guilty go free.
>
> The compassion of lions, on the contrary, is clear from innumerable examples— for they spare the prostrate; they allow such captives as they come across to go back to their own country; they prey on men rather than on women, and they do not kill children except when they are very hungry.

Figure 1.3 is an illustration taken from *The Bestiary* showing the lion having homage paid to him.

Figure 1.3	The Lion as the King of the Beasts

*A medieval drawing pub-
lished originally in the
Middle Ages.*

Source: T. H. White, ed., 1960

These examples illustrate the point that most people believe that at least higher animals can experience and show emotions. The existence of the Society for the Prevention of Cruelty to Animals and the widespread existence of animal rights groups attest to the belief that animals can feel pain, and, by implication, pleasure. Subjective feelings of pain and pleasure are clearly aspects of what people call emotions. This belief in animal emotions creates the problem of how to make meaningful inferences about such emotions. A later chapter will discuss this issue in detail. Let us now consider some other reasons for the difficulties involved in studying emotions in humans.

Problems of Verbal Reports

Most of us have learned to be cautious about accepting at face value other people's comments about their feelings. One important reason for the distrust we may feel is that we suspect that others censor their verbalizations. This conclusion stems directly from the fact that we are aware of the fact that we often censor our own thoughts and feelings. We learn to grin and bear it in embarrassing situations. We learn to smile even when we are angry, and we learn to keep a poker face when necessary. We place these controls upon the expression of our feelings to avoid embarrassment or criticism from others, and help us get the things we want from other people, such as good will, respect, acceptance, and acknowledgment. Since we recognize the fact that we censor our own expressions of our feelings, we assume that other people do it as well. This censorship contributes to the difficulty in studying emotions.

The Effect of Behaviorism

Another reason for the distrust of verbal reports is the powerful effect that behaviorism has had on the thinking of psychologists. The early behaviorists such as Watson and Skinner were dissatisfied with the introspective tradition in psychology. They believed that the only truly reliable, objective information obtainable about living creatures was information about their behavior, and preferably, behavior as simple as possible. This attitude reduced psychology to the study of behavior and not mind, and led to a preoccupation with conditioned responses, simple habits, automatic reactions to stimuli called tropisms, and simple on-off responses to stimuli. Emotions were considered to be inner states that could not be reliably observed and were therefore outside the realm of scientific psychology.

The Effect of Psychoanalysis

Interestingly enough, another quite different tradition led to almost the same conclusion. This was the psychoanalytic tradition. Psychoanalysts have made us aware of the fact that subjective reports of emotions cannot always be accepted at face value. Not only are some emotions totally repressed, and thus unavailable to introspection, but others are frequently modified or distorted as a result of partial repressions. Brenner (1974), a psychoanalyst, presents a case history to illustrate these points.

A patient recalled that once, when he returned home at the end of a college term, he had a daydream in which he imagined his mother and younger sister had been killed. He had this idea without "feeling anything" about it. The patient was not conscious of any of the thoughts that would be expected to accompany the daydream; of a wish to kill, of joy in revenge, or of horror, sadness, or remorse (guilt) at having, in fantasy, done the deed.

Analysis makes it possible to understand in some detail the psychological determinants of such an experience. In the case in point, they were in essence as follows. The patient was alone in the house after his return from college. His father had died a few years before, his older brother was about to be married, and his mother and sister were off on a holiday. These and other circumstances forcibly reminded the patient of the time when his sister was born–a time when his mother had gone to the hospital for delivery and when the patient had felt very alone. What had happened after mother's return had been even worse. She had turned from the patient and focused her affection on her new baby, a girl. From that time on, the patient felt unwanted and unloved. But rage was dangerous, since being a "bad" boy, he learned, would lead all the more to being abandoned by mother, who used to punish him by putting him in a dark closet when he had an angry outburst or, later on, by refusing to talk to him. Even more, jealousy was terrifying, because to be jealous of his sister meant wanting to be a girl himself, which meant wanting to be castrated, while to be jealous of his father threatened him both with retribution and with loss of the only member of his family who he felt still loved him and cared for him after his sister's birth.

When the patient came home to an empty house, he reacted with memories of that earlier time when his sister was born and when he was overcome by jealousy, longing, and rage. He could not banish completely all of his frightening and guilt-laden reactions. He did imagine that his mother and sister had been killed. At the same time, however, he denied that it was his own wish to kill them—in his fantasy, the deed had been done by others—and he did ward off any feeling of either pleasure or unpleasure at the idea that they had been killed. There was no conscious trace of either, any more than there was a conscious trace of sexual wishes toward his mother, or of memories of such wishes and of the past experiences connected with them."

This case history illustrates the presence of emotions of which the patient is unaware, and which can be identified only through a long and complex process of analysis. From the psychoanalytic point of view, emotions are inferences or interpretations based upon various kinds of indirect evidence.

The Problem of Ethical Research

Another problem that limits the extent to which we may study emotions concerns the ethics of laboratory research. In other branches of psychology concerned with learning and memory, for example, it is possible to create highly controlled situations in which researchers can know and measure the stimulus conditions, and can equally measure responses precisely.

In the study of emotions, ethical considerations greatly limit the extent to which researchers can create emotions such as grief, rage, and fear in the laboratory. Almost all academic and research institutions now have review committees that must decide whether research conducted there adequately protects the rights of the subjects and whether the potential benefits are commensurate with the potential risks. Studies that were once acceptable, such as giving strong electric shocks to subjects, or deceiving them into believing they have low intelligence or an abnormal personality trait, would probably not be acceptable today in many research settings. As a result, researchers in the field of emotions are frequently forced to study existing clinical conditions such as bereavement, depression, suicidality, and violence. Important as such studies are, they seldom allow causal statements to be made, nor do they permit detailed knowledge of the sources of the observed behavior.

Are Verbal Reports the Best Measure of Emotions?

The issues that have been raised so far in this chapter suggest that verbal reports of feeling states are sometimes not wholly adequate ways to describe emotions. Some of the reasons for this conclusion are:

1. Verbal reports of emotions may be deliberate attempts to deceive another person.
2. Verbal reports of emotions may be distortions or partial truths for conscious or unconscious reasons.
3. Reports of emotions depend on an individual's particular conditioning history, as well as his or her facility with words.
4. Reports of inner emotional states usually are retrospective and depend on memory. Remembered events are notoriously subject to distortions.
5. Requests for a report of one's immediate emotional state creates the problem that the process of observing may change the thing observed.
6. Emotions are generally believed to occur in infants and young children as well as adults. Young children have not yet acquired the ability to use language to express their emotions. Therefore, the belief is based on other classes of evidence.
7. Emotions are generally believed to occur in mentally defective and in mentally deranged humans. In many such cases, the patient is unable to provide any direct verbal reports on his or her emotional states.
8. The inherent ambiguity of language creates the problem of the *true* meaning of emotion terms. The importance of context in determining meaning implies that the same verbal report of an emotion will have a different referent in another setting.

9. Repression may create false negatives; that is, an observer may erroneously assume that no emotion exists because the subject has reported none.
10. Emotions are rarely, if ever, experienced in a pure state. More typically, any given situation creates mixed emotions that are difficult to describe in any simple or unequivocal way.

For these various reasons, it seems reasonable to conclude that a verbal report of an inner emotional state is only a rough approximation of whatever that state is. One should not consider an emotion as synonymous with a presumed inner-feeling state. Instead, it appears that the emotion refers to a complex theoretical term whose characteristics can only be inferred on the basis of a congruence of various classes of evidence. One of these classes of evidence consists of verbal reports of supposed inner states, but such evidence has no greater logical priority than do the other classes of evidence. This approach is exactly analogous to that taken in other parts of psychology or the physical sciences. Such terms as memory, perceptions, traits, atoms, genes, and DNA molecules are theoretical constructs whose properties one infers on the basis of various kinds of evidence. Emotions, too, are inferred from a complex variety of observations.

The Influence of Different Historical Traditions

We have seen that there are a number of reasons why the study of emotions is difficult. Among them is the fact that the language of emotion is complex and often ambiguous, that people are aware of the fact that they, and probably others, disguise or hide their feelings for various social reasons, that the philosophy of behaviorism distrusted introspective reports because of their presumed unreliability, and because laboratory research on emotions created ethical dilemmas. Important as these reasons are, there is another major factor to consider when trying to understand why the study of emotions is so difficult. This factor concerns the different historical traditions that have directly or indirectly influenced the way scientists and laypeople alike think about emotions. These historical traditions will be described in some detail in the following chapter.

Summary ■

During the past 100 years, psychologists and other scientists have proposed dozens of definitions of the word *emotion*. Although the definitions vary widely, some key ideas tend to be repeated. These include the notion that our interpretations of events usually trigger emotions, that emotions involve strong reactions of many bodily systems, that expressions are based on genetic mechanisms, that they communicate information from one person to another, and that they help the individual adapt to changing environmental situations. Such adaptation contributes in some way to the chances of survival, and to the regulation of social interactions between people.

Some of the reasons for the difficulties in studying emotions are given. These include such things as the diverse descriptions that people give of the same emotion terms, as well as the belief that emotions occur in blind and deaf children as well as lower animals. These observations require inferences from various sources of evidence. In addition, the behavioristic and psychoanalytic movements in psychology have raised questions about the validity of self-reports as measures of presumed inner states called emotions. There also are questions about the extent to which it is appropriate or ethical to subject people to laboratory stresses designed to produce emotional states. Finally, it is necessary to emphasize that we base our ideas about emotions on a number of diverse historical traditions that have conceptualized and studied emotions in quite different ways.

Chapter

2

Major Historical Traditions in the Study of Emotions

Thought is deeper than all speech;
feeling deeper than all thought.
—Christopher Cranch

▌Goals of This Chapter

Although science generally advances by small steps, there are times when exceptional individuals provide important new ways of thinking about the world. This was true, for example, of Newton and Einstein in physics, of Darwin in biology, and of Freud in psychiatry. In relation to the study of emotion, a few historical figures have had a major influence on the way contemporary scientists think about emotions. These individuals are Charles Darwin, William James, Walter Cannon, and Sigmund Freud. Each of them began traditions which are still conceptually powerful today. Three of these individuals were trained as physicians, and Darwin, who was a biologist, also had some medical training. Despite their similarity of educational background, the thinking of each went in different directions.

In the middle of the nineteenth century, Charles Darwin, a British biologist, proposed the theory of evolution as a way to explain the diversity of living things. He came to recognize that biological diversity was also associated with behavioral diversity, and one aspect of such diversity was the variation in the forms of emotional expression we see in all animals. Darwin came to believe that emotional expressions have an evolutionary history as well as a

19

survival function in the life of animals. His writing on this subject led to the *evolutionary tradition* in the study of emotions.

William James was an American psychologist writing mainly during the latter half of the nineteenth century. Among his many writings about both psychology and philosophy was a paper on the nature of emotions. In it, James proposed a new way to consider the sequence problem, that is, the issue of how subjective feelings were temporally related to changes in autonomic physiology. His views led to a host of studies on the autonomic nervous system and how its activation influences emotional experience. These ideas led to the *psychophysiological tradition.*

Walter Cannon was an American physician working during the early part of the twentieth century who studied the physiological changes that occurred in animals under stress. He used his findings to challenge the hypotheses of William James and then proceeded to try to identify the part of the brain that might be called the "seat of the emotions." He also believed that most emotions could be considered to be either "fight or flight" emotions. His work had a major influence in stimulating studies of the role of the brain in emotional experience and behavior, and might be called the *neurological tradition.*

Early in the twentieth century, Sigmund Freud, a Viennese psychiatrist, formulated a new way of thinking about the mind. Based on his studies of hysterical patients, which he later extended to other types of patients, he concluded that a large part of mental life is unknown to the individual. Emotions, he believed, are not simple feelings, but complex inner states subject to repression, distortion, and modification for conscious or unconscious reasons. Emotions are not obvious feeling states that each of us has access to, but rather are complex events with many historical elements, whose existence and form we must infer on the basis of limited evidence. Of great importance was his point that we need to infer emotions in ourselves just as we do with other people. These ideas led to the *psychodynamic tradition.*

These four traditions led to research that individuals pursued in very different academic settings. The evolutionary tradition stimulated the work, mainly with animals, of zoologists, ethologists, and sociobiologists. The psychophysiological tradition influenced the work of psychologists interested in autonomic physiology. The neurological tradition stimulated research on the brain carried out, for the most part, by physiological psychologists and neurologists. The psychodynamic tradition had a major impact on twentieth century psychiatry and led to major innovations in treatment approaches.

If we assume that each tradition has something useful to contribute to our thinking about emotions, then an ideal solution to the problem of what is emotion might be a synthesis of the best ideas from each approach.

Important Questions Addressed In This Chapter

- How did Charles Darwin relate his theory of evolution to emotions?
- What does the apparent enlargement of body size that many animals

manifest have to do with emotions?
- What do scientists mean by a functional view of expressive behavior?
- What contemporary group of scientists has been strongly influenced by Darwin's views about emotions?
- Why has William James's theory had such an impact on contemporary psychologists?
- What were Cannon's five major criticisms of James's theory?
- What evidence did Cannon use for his belief that the hypothalamus is the "seat" of the emotions?
- What are the symptoms of hysteria?
- How did the study of hysterical patients lead Freud to the theory that individuals can repress emotions?
- What are Freud's three theories about the nature of anxiety?
- What is meant by a *cognitive tradition?*

Almost everyone who has written about emotions during the past century has considered them from one of four points of view. Each of these these views was associated initially with the work of a particular individual, and each has influenced the thinking and research of scientists to the present day. This chapter will examine the major ideas of these four pioneers in the study of emotion: Charles Darwin, William James, Walter Cannon, and Sigmund Freud. A brief introduction will also be given to a more recent set of ideas, sometimes referred to as the *cognitive tradition,* associated with the writings of Fritz Heider.

■ ■ ■ ■ ■ ■ ■ ■

▮ Charles Darwin and the Evolutionary Tradition

Charles Darwin's great work describing his theory of evolution, *On the Origin of Species,* appeared in 1859. In it, he tried to explain how different groups of animals gradually appeared on the earth in response to changing environments. He interpreted the changes that took place in animals' size and shape of organs, body parts, and life styles as their attempts to adapt to changes in the conditions of life. Those adaptations that were successful led to survival of the group. Inadequate adaptations left traces of groups only in fossil records.

Darwin tried to show that anatomical structures such as fins, wings, hands, and eyes represented successful adjustments of different species to different types of environments. However, Darwin recognized that the process of evolution applied not only to anatomical structures, but to an animal's "mind" and expressive behavior as well. He assumed that

Charles Darwin
(1809–1882)

In his autobiography written a few years before he died, Charles Darwin described his good qualities while at school in the following way: "I had strong and diversified tastes, much zeal for whatever interested me, and a keen pleasure in understanding any complex subject or thing." Despite these qualities, he did not consider himself a particularly outstanding student. For two years he studied medicine at Edinburgh, but after he decided he did not want to become a physician, his father sent him to Cambridge to become a clergyman. While at Cambridge, he studied botany and geology and developed a passion for collecting beetles. After graduation, one of his professors recommended that he join a ship called the *Beagle* as its scientific observer, since it was about to sail around the world on a scientific expedition.

Darwin considered this trip as the most important event of his life in that it sharpened his powers of observation and provided him with a tremendous range of experiences that led eventually to his theory of evolution. As a result of his voyage on the *Beagle,* Darwin developed a theory of the formation of coral reefs, wrote two books on geological topics, another on barnacles, and then his most famous work, *On the Origin of Species.* This book was published in 1859, twenty years after he had first conceived of the idea of evolution.

Darwin's book, *The Descent of Man* was published in 1871 and represented an attempt to apply the concepts of evolution to human beings. Although an entire chapter was devoted to emotions, Darwin recognized that the subject would require a separate treatise. The following year, his book *The Expression of the Emotions in Man and Animals* was published. This work has been a major source of ideas and a stimulus to research for scientists in many different disciplines who are concerned with the nature of emotions. Darwin made these contributions despite a long illness and a state of near-invalidism that continued for many years. In his autobiography, Darwin concluded by pointing out that whatever success he had was based on four qualities of mind: "The love of science—unbounded patience in long reflecting over any subject—industry in observing and collecting facts—and a share of invention as well as of common sense."

intelligence, reasoning ability, memory, and emotions all had an evolutionary history, and that all could be identified at different phylogenetic levels. Darwin began to collect evidence for this point of view and, in 1872, his classic book, *The Expression of the Emotions in Man and Animals,* was published. This book has profoundly influenced contemporary thinking on the subject of emotion, and is the source of the *evolutionary tradition.*

Darwin was not concerned with subjective feelings in lower animals; he focused his attention entirely upon expressive behavior such as postures, gestures, and facial expressions. For data he relied upon his own observations, and on descriptions given him by zookeepers, explorers, and missionaries concerning the behavior of animals and the expressive behaviors of individuals in primitive human groups. His data also included a number of studies of facial expressions produced artificially by electrical stimulations of facial muscles in humans.

In his effort to explain the various expressions observed in humans and lower animals, Darwin suggested three hypotheses, or "principles." The first principle was that some expressions or actions are of value in gratifying desires. The second principle (of antithesis) claimed that since certain states of mind lead to certain useful actions, then opposite states of mind lead to the performance of movements of a directly opposite nature (e.g., an animal's expressions preparatory to attack are often opposite in appearance to those shown in submission). The third principle (of direct action of the nervous system) stated that strong excitation of the nervous system affects various systems of the body (e.g., sweating, trembling of the muscles, color changes in the skin, voiding of the bladder, fainting, etc.). Darwin used his various sources of information and these principles to try to account for the particular forms taken by expressions of pain, anxiety, grief, love, hatred, anger, contempt, disgust, guilt, pride, surprise, fear, shame, shyness, and other emotions. The evidence he presented was designed to illustrate the basic continuity of emotional expressions from lower animals to humans. He suggested that the baring of the fangs of the dog or wolf is related to the sneer of the human adult. He noted that flushing of the face in anger has been reported in widely diverse human races, as well as in certain species of monkeys. Defecation and urination in association with fear has been observed in rats, cats, dogs, monkeys, and humans.

Some of the flavor of Darwin's descriptions appears through his discussion of one of the expressive signs of fear and anger; namely, apparent enlargement of body size. He wrote, "Hardly any expressive movement is so general as the involuntary erection of the hairs, feathers and other dermal appendages; for it is common throughout three of the great vertebrate classes. These appendages were erected under the excitement of anger or terror; more especially when these emotions are combined, or quickly succeed each other. The action serves to make the animal appear larger and more frightful to its enemies or rivals, and is generally accompanied by various voluntary movements adapted for the same purpose, and by the utterance of savage sounds."

To support these generalizations, Darwin cited observations of chimpanzees, orangutans, and gorillas in a zoo. He also pointed to the bristling of the mane in lions and the erection of hairs in hyenas, dogs, cats, horses, cattle, pigs, elk, goats, antelope, anteaters, rats, and bats. Figure 2.1, from *The Expression of the Emotions in Man and Animals,* is a sketch of a cat terrified by a dog showing the erected hairs of the cat's body and the apparent increase in its body size.

Individuals have observed this kind of adaptive behavior in many different species of animal. Birds ruffle their feathers when other animals threaten them; Darwin cited similar observations made of chickens, roosters, swans, owls, hawks, parrots, finches, warblers, and quail. Some reptiles have been observed during courtship to expand their throat pouches or frills, and erect their dorsal crests. Toads, frogs, and chameleons take in air and swell up in size, and it has been reported that when a frog is seized by a snake, the swelling of the frog's body sometimes allows escape. In humans, a somewhat parallel expansion of apparent body size occurs in anger as reflected by expansion of the chest, thrusting the head forward, standing more erect, and sometimes by erection of body hair.

On the basis of these kinds of evidence it is clear that Darwin's view of expressive behavior is a *functional* one. Emotional expressions serve some functions in the lives of animals. They act as signals and as preparations for action. They communicate information from one animal to another about what is likely to happen. Therefore, they affect the chances of survival.

The expressive behavior of a cat when confronted by an attacking dog illustrates these points. The cat opens its mouth showing its long incisors, pulls back its ears, erects the hair of its body, arches its back, and hisses. This pattern of emotional expression associated with mixed fear and anger has definite signal value to the attacker. It signals the possibility of an attack in return. It makes the cat look larger and more ferocious and decreases the chances of a direct confrontation. This, in turn, increases survival possibilities for the cat, and anything that increases the chances of survival tends to be maintained during the course of evolution.

Darwin considered another important problem in his book, namely, the question of the innateness of emotional expressions. He believed that many, but not all, emotional expressions are unlearned. He used four kinds of evidence for his conclusions about the innate basis of emotional expressions: (1) some emotional expressions appear in similar form in many lower animals; (2) some emotional expressions appear in very young children in the same form as in adults, before much opportunity for learning has occurred; (3) some emotional expressions appear identical in those born blind as well as in those who are normally sighted; and (4) some emotional expressions appear in similar form in widely distinct races and groups of humans.

Figure 2.1 Drawing of a Cat Reacting to a Threatening Dog

Source: Darwin, 1872.

However, despite his strong belief in the unlearned nature of many emotional expressions, Darwin clearly understood that some expressions are simply gestures that have been learned like the words of a language. This would be true, for example, of joining the hands in reverent prayer, kissing as a mark of affection, or nodding the head as a sign of acceptance. He also pointed out that even though many expressions are unlearned, once they have occurred, they may be voluntarily and consciously used as a means of communication. They also may be voluntarily inhibited except under the most extreme conditions.

Another important question that Darwin considered concerns the issue of whether animals have the innate capacity to recognize emotional expressions in others. He believed that it was likely that they did; otherwise the communication effects of an emotional expression would be dependent on the chances of accidental learning having taken place. He admitted that evidence on this question was very scant and speculated that recognition that does occur might be limited only to within each species. In other words, cats may recognize emotional expressions in other cats, but probably do not recognize them in humans. Darwin implied that intraspecies recognition of emotion was probably innate and had adaptive significance.

Finally, in the last chapter of his book, Darwin presented some hypotheses about the relative primitiveness of different emotional expression. Based on the similarity of expressions in lower animals and humans, he suggested that fear and rage expressions, and laughter, are quite primitive. Signs of grief and weeping are late evolutionary developments. Frowning and blushing are also relatively recent evolutionary acquisitions. In a parallel way, although vomiting reactions of disgust are quite primitive, some of the more "refined" ways of showing disgust, such as lowering the eyelids, or turning away, are more recently evolved expressions.

What are some implications of Darwin's views? One is simply the idea that "behavior patterns are just as conservatively and reliably characters of species as are the forms of bones, teeth, or any other bodily structures. Similarities in inherited behavior unite the members of a species, of a genus, and of even the largest taxonomic units in exactly the same way in which bodily characters do so" (Lorenz, 1965). A second implication is that the story of emotional expressions, in Darwin's own words, "confirms to a certain limited extent the conclusion that man is derived from some lower animal form, and supports the belief in the specific or subspecific unity of the several races" (Darwin, 1872). A third implication is that the study of emotion was expanded from the study of subjective feelings to the study of behavior within a biological, evolutionary context. It became scientifically legitimate to ask the question: "In what way does a particular emotion or behavior pattern function in aiding survival?" Finally, and of equal importance, Darwin produced a series of hypotheses and theoretical issues that have guided research in animal behavior, particularly by the ethologists, to the present time.

▎ William James and the Psychophysiological Tradition

Twelve years after Darwin had published his book on emotions, the American psychologist-philosopher William James published an article in which he presented a new way of looking at emotion, and at the same time founded a second major tradition in the psychology of emotion (James, 1884). In his article and in an expanded chapter in his book published in 1890, William James pointed out that the commonsense way to think about the sequence of events when an emotion occurs is that the *perception* of a situation gives rise to a *feeling* of emotion, which is then followed by various *bodily changes,* both inner and outer. His theory was that this sequence is incorrect. Instead, he proposed that bodily changes directly follow a perception of an exciting event and that the feeling of these bodily changes is the emotion. James illustrated this idea by saying: "Common sense says we lose our fortune, are sorry and weep; . . . (My) hypothesis . . . is that we feel sorry because we cry, angry because we strike, afraid because we tremble . . ." (James, 1890).

James then proceeded to justify his theory and answer possible criticism. But first, he began with a qualification. His theory was to apply only to what he labeled as the "coarser emotions" such as grief, fear, rage, and love, and not to the "subtler" emotions which he described as "cerebral forms of pleasure and displeasure . . . [associated with] certain pure sensations and harmonious combinations of them . . . [in short] moral, intellectual, and aesthetic feelings" (James, 1890).

The first argument in support of his theory is that it is impossible to imagine feeling an emotion if we do not at the same time experience our bodily symptoms. Emotion disconnected from all bodily feeling is not conceivable, he believed. He then stated that his theory would be challenged if a person could be found who experienced no inner sensations but who otherwise could function normally. James then described one such case, "a shoemaker's apprentice of 15, entirely anesthetic, inside and out, with the exception of one eye and one ear, who had shown shame . . . grief . . . surprise, fear and anger" according to a physician who attended him. Despite this apparent contradiction with his theory, James dismissed the case as not studied thoroughly enough.

Another type of evidence relevant to his theory is found in cases of objectless emotions; that is, when people report feeling anxious, angry, or melancholy without knowing why. James's interpretation of such events is that such persons are unusually sensitive to their own labile bodily changes and that the emotion felt is simply the feeling of their bodily states. He failed to discuss the question of how such bodily states arise in the first place, or why they are often episodic.

In a footnote, James did mention that the opposite may occur; that is, a person may report strong emotional feelings and not show any obvious

William James
(1842–1910)

As a young man, William James wanted to become a painter, but eventually decided that he did not have sufficient talent. He entered Harvard and began training as a physician, but in the middle of his education, he left Harvard and went to Germany to study. While there, he became physically ill as well as emotionally depressed, and at one time considered suicide.

After returning to the United States, he completed his medical education but never practiced medicine. He began his career by teaching anatomy and physiology at Harvard. Later he identified himself with psychology and wrote the highly influential textbook *Principles of Psychology* in 1890. In it he presented his views on all aspects of psychology and elaborated on his theory of emotion. He considered emotions to be a kind of "native" or "instinctive" reaction that could also be modified by training and habit.

James became increasingly interested in philosophical issues and began to teach philosophy at Harvard. In the last dozen years of his life he published a number of books dealing with philosophy: *The Will to Believe* (1897), *The Varieties of Religious Experience* (1902), and *Pragmatism* (1907), among others.

Although James's philosophy of pragmatism was often interpreted as emphasizing the practical aspects of life, William James, the man, had a great respect for imagination and its role in human life. Throughout his life, William James had a strong belief in individuality and in the doctrine of live and let live.

bodily changes. This may happen in dreaming, for example. He provides no explanation of this possibility.

Another criticism of his theory is that actors often simulate an emotion without feeling it. James's reply is simply that the visceral and organic parts of an emotion are not present even when the facial expressions or gestures are.

His theory raises two basic questions. The first is, what bodily changes, inner and outer, are associated with emotions? The second is, what is the source of these associations? In his brief discussion of these questions,

James describes Darwin's views approvingly, but adds that the functional significance of many bodily changes in emotion such as dryness of the mouth, diarrhea, and nausea, are simply not known.

Unfortunately, James never examined other basic questions that his theory implied; for example: how does a perception produce a bodily change in the first place? To follow this line of reasoning further: of all the kinds of perceptions that are possible, why do some lead to emotions and not others; and why do emotions seem to have fairly similar patterns of expression in diverse individuals, groups, or races?

Given these unanswered questions and conceptual ambiguities, it is reasonable to ask why the James theory has persisted and influenced both writers of textbooks and researchers. (Parenthetically, it should be added that a couple of years after James proposed his viewpoint about emotion, a Danish physiologist named Lange independently suggested a similar idea; the conceptualization has since become known as the James-Lange theory.)

William James was a major figure in nineteenth-century American psychology. He was educated as a physician, taught in the philosophy department at Harvard, and was a prolific writer of influential books on psychology. Whatever he wrote was taken seriously, and other psychologists almost immediately became concerned with either proving or disproving his ideas.

The James-Lange theory is hardly what we would call a theory today. It was concerned primarily with a kind of chicken-and-egg question: Which came first, the subjective feeling of an emotion, or the bodily changes that are associated with it? Its importance obviously did not lie in the narrowness of the issue it posed, but rather in emphasizing what was, in fact, a common sense idea. It reiterated the notion that an emotion is a feeling state, an introspective, subjective, personal, idiosyncratic feeling state. And this was an idea that most psychologists were willing to accept.

The second reason for the importance of his ideas is that they gave a strong impetus to investigators to begin examining autonomic changes in relation to emotion. Gradually, a substantial literature developed in these areas, one that is increasingly active and important to this day. It includes studies of autonomic physiology, lie detectors, and physiological measures of arousal. Because James and many who have followed him have been concerned with the relations between introspective states and physiological changes, this approach may be described as the *psychophysiological tradition*.

▌Walter B. Cannon and the Neurological Tradition

A few years after William James died, another Harvard professor, Walter Cannon, working in the Physiology Department, began to publish a series of studies concerned with testing and modifying the James-Lange theory. These studies led Cannon to reject the basic elements of this theory and to propose an alternative one. In his book *Bodily Changes in Pain, Hunger, Fear and Rage,* first published in 1915 and revised in 1929, he presented evidence that raised serious questions about the James-Lange theory. The evidence consisted of five major points.

First, Cannon pointed out that the British physiologist Charles Sherrington had cut the spinal cord and vague nerves of dogs so that no sensory impulse could reach the brain of the animal from the heart, lungs, stomach, bowels, spleen, liver, and other abdominal organs. In addition, Cannon and his associates had removed the entire sympathetic divisions of the autonomic nervous system in several cats so that "all vascular reactions controlled by the vasomotor center were abolished; secretion from the adrenal medulla could no longer be evoked; the action of the stomach and intestines could not be inhibited, the hairs could not be erected, and the liver could not be called upon to liberate sugar into the blood stream" (Cannon, 1929). Under these conditions, both Sherrington and Cannon found that their experimental animals showed typical emotional reactions of anger, fear, and pleasure to handling and exposure to other animals. The lack of feedback of visceral changes apparently had no effect on emotional expression, as the James-Lange theory would have predicted.

Cannon's second criticism was based on the fact that stressful stimuli of any type tend to produce pretty much the same physiological reactions. For example, fear, rage, fever, exposure to cold, and asphyxia all tend to produce an increase in heart rate, blood sugar, adrenalin excretion, pupil size, and erection of body hair; and a decrease in size of arterioles, activity of digestive glands, and amount of gastrointestinal peristalsis. These visceral responses seem to be too uniform to provide a basis for distinguishing among strong emotions, or among emotions and other nonemotional stresses such as exercise.

Cannon's third criticism simply pointed out that the viscera are relatively insensitive structures and may be cut, torn, crushed, or burned in operations on unanesthetized humans without producing discomfort. In addition, people are normally unaware of the contractions and relaxations of the stomach, intestines, diaphragm, spleen, or liver. Therefore, it appears unlikely that such visceral events could contribute to an individual's recognition of his or her own emotional states.

The fourth criticism that Cannon offered concerns the slow reaction time of visceral organs to stimulation. A number of investigators had reported that the speed of reaction of smooth muscle and glands was anywhere from one-quarter of a second to several minutes. Other studies have apparently shown that emotional reactions to pictures or odors typically occurred within three-quarters of a second. It therefore seemed unlikely that visceral events could provide information to the brain quickly enough to help the individual decide what emotional state he or she was experiencing.

Walter B. Cannon
(1871–1945)

Walter Cannon was raised in a small town in Wisconsin. At the age of fourteen he left high school because of a lack of interest in his studies. After working for two years in a railroad office, he returned to school, graduated with honors, and won a scholarship to Harvard. Cannon completed both his undergraduate and medical degrees at Harvard and was immediately offered an instructorship in physiology at the medical school where he remained as a teacher and researcher until he retired in 1942.

Cannon was among the first to use the newly discovered X-rays for research on digestion, but because of a lack of awareness of the dangers of radiation, received severe burns and eventually developed the radiation-related disease from which he died. By 1911 he had begun to study endocrine secretions in relation to the autonomic nervous system and was impressed by evidence that emotional states could influence bodily processes. He wrote many papers in this topic and a general summary of his conclusions appeared in 1929 in his book *Bodily Changes in Pain, Hunger, Fear and Rage*. In this book he presented evidence which he believed refuted William James's theory of emotion. He also included evidence for his own theory, which attempted to relate emotional states to brain structures.

In 1932, Cannon's book *The Wisdom of the Body* was published. He pointed out that the stability of the organism is of prime importance for survival and that the many internal and external adjustments and adaptations that organisms make are the basis for stability. He concluded that social institutions are basically in the service of maintaining biological integrity. In his own words, "The main service of social homeostasis would be to support bodily homestasis."

Finally, Cannon pointed out that artificial attempts to induce visceral changes typical of strong emotions did not produce emotional feelings. For example, injections of adrenalin into normal or abnormal persons produced such extensive bodily change as palpitations, tightness in the chest and throat, trembling, chills, dryness of the mouth, and feelings of weakness, yet did not induce feelings of fear or any other emotion. These people were therefore able to report their bodily changes without interpreting them as indicating an emotional experience. On the basis of all this evidence, Cannon concluded that visceral feedback is faint and at best plays a minor role in the feelings of emotion.

If Cannon had simply presented these cogent criticisms of the James-Lange theory, it would have been a useful contribution. He did, however, much more. Cannon went on to present an alternative theory of what bodily changes were related to emotion, and also provided an alternative interpretation of the role of visceral changes. Let us consider these ideas.

Surgeons have long known that patients sometimes show strong emotional reactions—sobbing, laughter, or aggression—while under early stages of ether anesthesia. Dentists sometimes see a similar phenomenon when they give their patients nitrous oxide (or *laughing gas*). These observations suggest that the temporary abolition of cortical control "releases" those lower brain centers that presumably determine emotional reactions. Similarly, in certain types of hemiplegia (i.e., paralysis of half the body), a patient may be unable to move his or her face on the paralyzed side. However, if the patient hears a joke or learns of the death of a family member, the very muscles that could not be voluntarily controlled may suddenly act to give the face the normal expression of pleasure or sadness. Patients with total facial paralysis have likewise reported their ability to experience emotional feelings, despite the lack of feedback from facial muscles.

Cannon and his associates carried out a series of experiments with cats in which different parts of the brain were removed. They found that the cortex could be removed without affecting the animal's capacity to show emotional behavior. However, when the cerebral hemispheres were removed leaving the other brain structures intact, an interesting effect occurred.

> As soon as recovery from anesthesia was complete a remarkable group of activities appeared, such as are usually seen in an infuriated animal—a sort of sham rage. These quasi-emotional phenomena included lashing of the tail, arching of the trunk, thrusting and jerking of the restrained limbs, display of the claws and clawing motions, snarling and attempts to bite. These were all actions due to skeletal muscles. Besides these, and more typical and permanent, were effects on the viscera, produced by impulses discharged over the sympathetic nerve fibers. They included erection of the tail hairs, sweating of the toe pads, dilation of the pupil, micturition, a high blood pressure, a very rapid heartbeat, an abundant outpouring of adrenalin, and an increase of blood sugar up to five times the normal concentration. This play of a "pseudoaffective" state or sham rage might continue for two or three hours (Cannon, 1929).

Further studies showed that the neural structure associated with the display of rage is located in a part of the brain called the optic thalamus. In his words, "The peculiar quality of the emotion is added to simple sensation when the thalamic processes are roused." Instead of assuming that there is a linear sequence of events relating perception to feeling as proposed by William James, Cannon proposed that the thalamic discharge simultaneously produces both an emotional experience and a series of bodily changes. This hypothesis is sometimes called the Cannon-Bard theory because of the empirical studies of Bard dealing with these issues. Diagrammatically, the two views might be shown schematically as in Figure 2.2, where they are contrasted with the commonsense one.

Several points are worth noting about the diagrams. First, all views include the idea that a perception is necessary to start an emotional process. Second, none of the theories makes any attempt to explain how a perception can directly produce an emotional feeling, a motor reaction, or a

Figure 2.2	The Sequence Problem

Three different ways to think about the problem of what sequence of events occurs in connection with the appearance of an emotion.

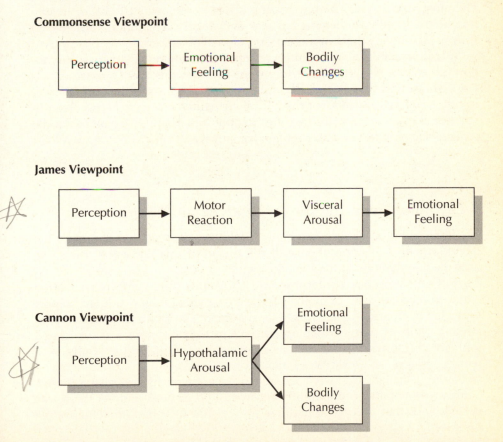

hypothalamic arousal. Third, all the theories are concerned fundamentally with conscious, reportable, subjective emotional experience. Even when the subjects of experiments are cats and dogs, the assumption is that their emotional behavior directly reflects emotional feelings. Cannon, for example, never seemed to question this relationship. However, whereas William James found the sources of emotional feelings in the viscera, Cannon found them in the thalamus. Both men accepted at face value the subjective reports of patients or subjects as valid expressions of emotional feelings.

Before we leave the work of Cannon, we should consider one last point. He had extensive biological training and was well acquainted with the work of Charles Darwin. He was accustomed to asking functional questions about biological events. He therefore asked the following question: What is the function of the extensive internal changes that occur during emotional excitement?

Cannon answered this question by concluding that visceral changes did not tell us anything about emotions; rather, they were homeostatic adjustments that helped the body prepare for action. When events occur that create emergencies, if the individual is to survive, he or she must take action. The most appropriate action in most cases is to run away (flight) or to stay and attack (fight). The feelings of fear and anger (or emotions in general) simply accompany these organic preparations for action.

Some writers have called this conception an emergency theory of emotion. However, it is important to emphasize that this theory represents a view of emotions that is logically quite independent of the thalamic theory. In other words, regardless of the neural structures that may be involved in emotional expression or feeling, the function of emotion may be to handle emergencies connected with problems of survival.

▍Sigmund Freud and the Psychodynamic Tradition

In 1895, Freud published a book, *Studies on Hysteria*, that described the development of his new theory of the origin of this illness. At the same time, he laid the foundation for a theory of emotion.

Patients who had hysteria would show puzzling symptoms, related either to sensory losses or motor paralysis. A patient might suddenly report that a leg or an arm was paralyzed, or that he or she had lost all sensation in a hand. Quite often, the initial appearance of the symptoms was associated with some traumatic event such as an accident, a death in the family, or a war experience. In World War I, many of the soldiers who were diagnosed as having "shell shock," were actually suffering with hysterical symptoms. Some of these patients apparently became blind or deaf, and yet there was no evidence that they were malingering or that they had an actual nerve disease.

Even more interesting was the fact that the use of hypnotic suggestion could temporarily create or eliminate every one of the symptoms of hysteria in normal people. A number of physicians had already demonstrated this phenomenon. Sometimes they used hypnosis to eliminate the symptoms in patients with hysteria.

Freud's book, *Studies on Hysteria*, which he wrote with another physician, Joseph Breuer, is basically a description of a number of patients with hysteria whom they had successfully treated. One chapter described the now famous case of a young female patient named "Anna," who developed a number of hysterical symptoms during a period when she was helping to care for her dying father. These symptoms included paralysis of one arm, partial paralysis of neck muscles influencing the swallowing reflex, and occasional periods of "absences" or "fits."

Dr. Breuer treated Anna successfully during a two year period. Through the use of hypnosis, all the symptoms were gradually eliminated. Freud and Breuer observed a similar pattern in the other cases, and as a result came to the conclusion that their patients were suffering from memories that they had actively forgotten or repressed. The kinds of memories to which this happened were those that had a strong emotion attached to them, even though the patient might not be aware of the emotion. The hysterical symptom, Freud suggested, acts as a kind of disguised representation of the repressed emotion. At first, Freud believed that the patient could eliminate the symptoms only by an intense expression of the repressed emotion, a process he called abreaction, or catharsis. The need for such catharses was often suggested to the patient during hypnosis.

However, Freud finally changed his mind about the need for catharsis as well as the need for hypnosis after he found that there were some patients he could not hypnotize. He began to think that his cures based on hypnosis were unreliable, but he continued to believe in his theory of the origin of the symptom. In fact, as his experience with patients increased, he came to the conclusion that repression of emotionally charged memories was the basis for all neurotic symptoms, and not only those associated with hysteria.

When Freud gave up hypnosis as a technique of therapy, he substituted free association as the method for patients to help identify their repressed memories and emotions. The aim of therapy was no longer to "abreact" an emotion that had got onto the wrong lines, but to uncover repressions and replace them by acts of judgment which might result either in the acceptance or rejection of what had formerly been repudiated. Freud then stopped calling his method of investigation and treatment *catharsis*, and substituted the term *psychoanalysis*. Gradually over a period of many years, Freud and his associates built up a very elaborate and complex theory of the origin and development of neuroses and aberrant mental states. Explicit or implicit in psychoanalytic writing is a theory of "instincts" or drives, affects, stages of emotional development, fixations or aberrations of development, conflict, mind, and personality. The ramifications are so extensive that they are clearly beyond the scope of this brief introduction. However, we can consider in somewhat more detail some of Freud's ideas on emotions, or, as psychoanalysts prefer to call them, affects. Freud bases his ideas about affects on his theory of drives.

Fairly early in the development of his thinking, Freud assumed that there were two classes of instincts: sexual instincts and ego instincts. (Although most translations of Freud's writings use the word *instinct*, the German term Freud used could have been translated by the more acceptable current term, *drive*. In all further discussion, the word *drive* will therefore be used instead of the word *instinct*.) These drives were thought of as internal stimuli that affected the behavior of each individual by regulating direction and type of action. Each drive was assumed to have a source, an aim, and an object. The source of each drive was to be found in some biological or biochemical internal process; the aim was discharge and pleasure. The object of each drive could vary greatly and was dependent on experience, learning, and the vicissitudes of conditioning. An important characteristic of drives was their lability; they could be displaced, localized, or transformed.

The ego drives included hunger, thirst, and aggression, although Freud was not always consistent on how he classified aggression. Also included in the ego drives were impulses to control others, to wield power, to attack, and to flee from danger. Freud did not assume that aggressiveness was always present and striving for expression; he assumed that aggressiveness appeared only when something threatened a person's survival (Bibring, 1941). Also part of the aggressive drive were feelings of hate and destructiveness. In his later writings, Freud modified the theory of sexual and ego drives into the confusing notion of *life* and *death* instincts.

Freud's concept of drives was not a theory of emotion, but it did provide some basis for psychoanalytic interpretations of two major affects, anxiety and depression. Let us consider Freud's views of anxiety as an example of his thinking about affects.

The concept of anxiety took a number of different forms in Freud's writings, and they were not all consistent. One view of anxiety that Freud proposed was that it represented a reaction due to an inability to cope with an overwhelming stress. Such a condition first occurs in every individual's life at the time of birth when the sudden massive stimulation of the environment creates a *birth trauma*. This trauma produces an *archaic discharge syndrome*, which Freud referred to as *primary objective anxiety*, the prototype for the occurrence of secondary anxiety reactions later in a person's life.

Freud presented a second hypothesis about anxiety in 1915. He proposed that affects were primarily a form of energy that required some kind of direct or indirect expression. If repression or inhibition of affect existed, then the energy of the emotion had to be expressed in the form of neurotic *overflow* mechanisms such as phobias, obsessions, or compulsive rituals.

Sigmund Freud
(1856–1939)

Sigmund Freud lived most of his life in Vienna, Austria. While he was in medical school at the Univeristy of Vienna, his special interests were physiology and comparative anatomy. Upon graduation in 1881, he hoped to devote his life to research in neurology, but lack of financial means led him into clinical practice. He studied hypnosis with Charcot, an eminent French neurologist, and then returned to Vienna to enter a medical collaboration with Joseph Breuer.

Together, Breuer and Freud evolved a method for treating hysterical patients based upon the use of hypnosis. They called their method "catharsis" and it required the patient to strongly express emotions connected with traumatic experiences that had apparently been forgotten. *Studies on Hysteria,* their book describing their theories, was published in 1895.

At about this time, Breuer withdrew from the collaboration, and Freud went on to develop a complex theory, which he called psychoanalysis, about the mind, about child development, and about psychological treatment. Key elements of this theory included the concepts of repression and resistance, infantile sexuality, stages of development, and dream interpretations for the understanding of the unconscious.

Among Freud's earlier works are *The Interpretation of Dreams* (1900), *The Psychopathology of Everyday Life* (1904), *Three Contributions to the Theory of Sex* (1905), *A General Introduction to Psychoanalysis* (1910), and *The Ego and the Id* (1923). Gradually, Freud became increasingly interested in broad social or cultural implications of his theories and he wrote such works as *Totem and Tabu* (1913), *The Future of an Illusion* (1928), *Civilization and Its Discontents* (1930), and *Moses and Monotheism* (1939). Freud developed cancer of the mouth in 1924, but, despite much pain and repeated operations, he continued to write until he died.

Freud's ideas were often bitterly attacked, but in spite of the opposition, they gradually became widely known. In addition to becoming an accepted part of psychology and psychiatry, they have influenced anthropology, education, art, and literature. Freud summarized his view of why he was able to withstand the many attacks on him by writing, "Men are strong so long as they represent a strong idea."

From this point of view, Freud saw anxiety as the consequence of repression of emotion. He also assumed that the emotions involved were always related to conflicts over the sexual drive.

However, in 1926, in his book *Inhibitions, Symptoms and Anxiety*, Freud formulated a new conception of the nature of anxiety. Instead of anxiety being the result of a conversion of the energy of the affect, he now interpreted it to be the result of the ego's evaluation of dangerous aspects of the external or internal environment. Examples of dangerous types of events that psychoanalysis has been primarily concerned with include birth, hunger, absence of mother, loss of love, castration, conscience, and death. In terms of Freud's later formulation, anxiety was not the result of repression but the reason for repression. Evaluations by the ego determine whether internal impulses or external events are to be considered dangerous. This decision, in turn, determines the subsequent emotional response. "All affects consist, on the one hand, of a cognitive process, and on the other of a response to this process" (Schur, 1968).

This psychoanalytic interpretation of emotion, as exemplified by anxiety, had several implications. It raised the question of whether an emotion could be unconscious; that is, whether an individual could experience an emotion and not be aware of it. Although Freud wrote about unconscious guilt and unconscious anxiety, he was dissatisfied with this idea, since he considered an emotion to be a response process. In his paper *The Unconscious* (1915), he wrote: "It is surely of the essence of an emotion that it should enter consciousness. So for emotion, feelings, and affects to be unconscious would be quite out of the question. But in psychoanalytic practice we are accustomed to speak of unconscious love, hate, anger, etc., and find it impossible to avoid even the strange conjunction, 'unconscious consciousness of guilt'. . . . Strictly speaking . . . there are no unconscious affects in the sense in which there are unconscious ideas. . . ." Only when he developed his later interpretation of anxiety did he resolve the the dilemma. He finally concluded that the *evaluation* of an event can be unconscious even though the *response* process is not. For example, a free-floating anxiety is evident, but the source of it (the evaluation) is not recognized.

A second implication concerns the question of how to recognize emotion in others. If it is true that emotions may be repressed, how can the analyst identify something that even the patient cannot identify?

Freud made the assumption that various displacements and transformations may occur in the expression of an emotion, but indirect signs of its presence are always noticeable. For example, if someone continually frowns, grinds his teeth, and has dreams in which people are being murdered, we might conclude that this person is angry even if he or she denies it. Freud relied heavily upon dreams, free associations, slips of the tongue, postures, facial expressions, and voice quality in order to arrive at judgments about a person's repressed emotions. In other words, in the Freudian psychodynamic tradition, an emotion is a complex state of the individual which one infers on the basis of various classes of behavior. Although subjective feelings may provide a clue to a person's emotions, they are only one type of evidence among many others. An emotion is not synonymous with a verbal report of a supposed introspective state.

A third implication of the psychodynamic tradition is that emotions are seldom if ever found in a *pure* state. Any emotion has a complex history that has elements that go as far back as infancy. An emotion may have several different drive sources and may include a mixture of feelings and reactions. The very idea of *psychoanalysis* implies an attempt to determine what the elements of the complex states are.

The psychoanalyst David Rapaport (1950) has summarized these ideas by saying that the psychoanalytic view of emotions assumes (1) that an unconscious process occurs between the perception of the stimulus evoking an emotion and the peripheral physiological or visceral change; (2) that the peripheral autonomic change and the feeling of the emotion are both discharge processes of the same drive source of energy; and (3) that all emotions are mixed in that they are expressions of conflicts. Figure 2.3 schematically represents these ideas.

The psychoanalytic theory of emotion that these views represent contains some interesting ideas. It eliminates the sequence problem (i.e., which came first, the feeling or the bodily change) by claiming that they both result from an unconscious evaluation. It emphasizes the idea that some aspects of an emotion are unconscious and, therefore, cannot be examined by introspection alone. We must infer these emotional processes in humans, just as we do in lower animals. Finally, psychoanalytic theory suggests that conflicts are involved in all emotions.

Despite these views, Freud never developed a general theory of emotion. He directed most of his attention toward anxiety, aggression, depression, and their various mixtures. The theory tends to be vague in spots and not entirely consistent, and it relies heavily on metaphorical thinking. In spite of these limitations, psychoanalytic theory has stimulated research and has been a major theoretical source in the development of the field of psychosomatic medicine.

A Recent Development

The fact that these four historical figures have had a major impact on contemporary thinking about emotions does not mean that many other people have not contributed important ideas. For example, another tradi-

| Figure 2.3 | A Psychoanalytic Conception of an Emotion |

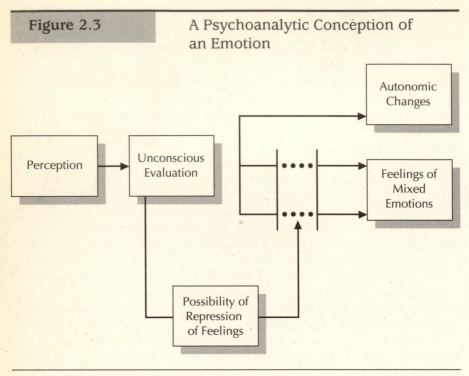

Source: Based on Rapaport, 1950.

tion that has gradually developed during the past thirty years or so has stemmed from the work of social psychologists who have been concerned about the expression of emotions in social relationships.

▍Fritz Heider and the Cognitive Tradition

One of the most important contributors in this context is a psychologist named Fritz Heider (1896–1988), who wrote an influential book entitled *The Psychology of Interpersonal Relations* in 1958. Although he did not try to present a general theory of emotions, he emphasized the relation between emotions and cognitions. He pointed out that if one can influence someone's beliefs, one can thereby influence his or her emotions. He wrote descriptions of the beliefs that people have about such emotions as pity, vengeance, gratitude, envy, and jealousy. He pointed out that different cognitive processes such as our causal attributions, our sense of what "ought" to be, and our aspirations and goals all influence our emotions. For example, he said that the violation of our ideas about what ought to be tends to

Fritz Heider
(1896–1988)

Fritz Heider was born and educated in Austria. For many years he considered writing and painting as possible careers, but finally, at the age of thirty, he decided to become a psychologist. Some time after World War I, he immigrated to the United States and began teaching at Smith College in Massachusetts. There he spent a number of years of discouragement and frustration because his daily responsibilities prevented the long periods of uninterrupted thought he felt were needed to do his theoretical analyses.

Feeling hemmed in, he began to experience attacks of anxiety. In his attempts to cope with his emotions, he tried to analyze the sources of his feelings of unhappiness and anger. Gradually he found that he could control his feelings by means of his thoughts. He also came to the belief that the study of commonsense psychology has two values for understanding interpersonal relations. First, commonsense psychology guides our behavior toward other people. We use it to interpret their actions and to predict what they will do under various circumstances. Second, commonsense psychology may contain truths that need to be discovered. For example, the way people think about such concepts as *cause, expect, belong,* and *ought* influences how they deal with one another. Although Heider believed that such cognitions have a major effect on our emotions, he also recognized that emotions may influence cognitions.

In 1958, at the age of 62, Heider published his book *The Psychology of Interpersonal Relations.* In it, he attempts to analyze the conventional language people use to describe their motivations, their beliefs, and their feelings. This book has had a major impact on the thinking of contemporary social psychologists.

lead to feelings of anger. Conversely, we feel gratitude if someone intentionally tries to benefit us out of benevolent motives. Envy involves a social comparison between what one has and what someone else has who is a member of one's own group.

Through such analyses and many anecdotes, Heider tried to relate everyday situations and beliefs to emotional feelings, and to show connections between cognitive states and emotions. However, he also recognized that sometimes the presence of an emotion alters our cognitions. If one feels anger toward someone, for example, one may exaggerate the faults of this person, blame him or her for shortcomings, and plan to get revenge. Thus, cognition and emotion may be related to one another through a kind of circular feedback system.

Heider's concepts have stimulated many social psychologists to pursue the path of trying to identify the cognitive states associated with different specific emotions. In recent years, many so-called cognitive theories of emotion have been formulated and they too have had an important influence on the thinking of many contemporary psychologists. Some of these ideas will be described in later chapters.

Summary ■

This chapter has described the major historical traditions that have influenced the thinking of most contemporary psychologists concerned with the study of emotion. The evolutionary tradition has emphasized the adaptive significance of emotional expressions as communications that tend to increase the chances of individual survival, but has had little to say about subjective feelings. The psychophysiological tradition has stimulated the extensive contemporary research and thinking on the relations between autonomic changes, facial expressions, and subjective feelings. The question posed in current terms is, are our feelings an expression of autonomic changes or changes in facial expressions, or are our feelings independent of such changes? We will consider this issue more extensively in the chapter on facial expressions.

The neurological tradition has stimulated the search for the brain structures and systems that organize all the information we use in feeling or expressing our emotions. Numerous researchers in recent years have revealed the complex and subtle interactions of information flow from critical sensory receiving areas to hypothalamic and limbic system structures to brain stem and even spinal levels of integration. Many of these developments will be described in the chapter on brain mechanisms and emotions.

The psychodynamic tradition has stimulated the thinking of countless clinicians to recognize the complexity of emotional states and the ubiquitous presence of mixed states of emotions or blends. Researchers have become aware of the difficulty of relying on only one source of information about emotions such as introspective reports of feelings. Consequently, they have emphasized the need to integrate multiple sources of information in order to make meaningful *inferences* about the presence of emotions. Psychoanalysts have also emphasized the connection between memory and emotions, a subject of increasing interest to contemporary psychologists. In addition, they have recognized the many ways that humans can hide, disguise, manipulate, and distort emotions.

The cognitive tradition is less clearly related to the work of a single person; however, most contemporary psychologists recognize and accept the role of cognitions, assessments, appraisals, and interpretations as important if not crucial aspects of the total emotional process. Social psychologists have particularly emphasized cognitions as important, while practitioners in other disciplines have focused much of their attention on different aspects of the emotional process: dynamics in the case of clinicians; neurology in the case of physiological psychologists; autonomic physiology in the case of psychophysiologists; and biology and adaptation in the case of zoologists and ethologists. As time goes on, increasing degrees of overlap occur in the thinking of these different disciplines about the subject of emotions, and practitioners freely borrow ideas from one discipline to another. Despite the different concerns and emphases that characterize these various approaches, it is reasonable to assume that each theory contains some truth. Any adequate integration of emotion theories should have something to say about the adaptive implications of emotions, about autonomic and brain mechanisms in relation to feeling states, about dynamic sources and complexities of emotional states, and about the role of cognitions.

The Language of Emotions

*Verbal responses are another, albeit highly
sophisticated, type of behavior; they are not
a direct window to the emotions.*
—Neal E. Miller

Goals of This Chapter

Most people believe they know what an emotion is. Despite this belief
they do not always agree on which words in the English language are emotion words and which are not. Psychologists have published many studies
that have tried to establish a kind of dictionary of emotion terms by asking
college students which words are descriptive of emotional states. The results
have been surprisingly inconsistent.

This chapter reviews some of the studies that have used this approach
and describes what they found. Also included in this chapter is a review of
the many historical and contemporary attempts that have been made to
describe certain emotions as primary, basic, or fundamental. It appears that
such attempts have a long history and that most contemporary psychologists
believe that there is a relatively small number of basic emotions. How much
agreement there is on this issue will also be discussed.

This chapter will also examine the question of how the words of the language of emotion are related to one another. It will be evident that emotion
words vary in terms of their degree of similarity to one another, and that one
can recognize families of emotion terms. Different ways of conceptualizing
this idea will be described.

Important Questions Addressed In This Chapter

- How well do college students agree on which words in English describe emotions?
- According to most contemporary psychologists, how many basic emotions are there?
- How does the concept of analysis and synthesis apply to the problem of identifying the language of emotions?
- How might one develop a dictionary of emotion words?
- What is the *semantic differential,* and how was it used in the study of emotions?
- What is meant by the concept of a circumplex as applied to emotions?
- Is *startle* an emotion?
- What are the differences among emotions, affects, and moods?

■　■　■　■　■　■　■　■　■

▎How Can We Identify the Language of Emotion?

One way to attempt to answer the question of how to identify the language of emotion is to ask people to list the words of our language that describe emotions. For example, in an effort to find out how consistent people are in identifying emotions, Shields (1984) gave a group of college students a list of 60 words that described subjective states (feelings) and asked them to distinguish the emotion words from the nonemotion words. The list included words like ashamed, bored, happy, sleepy, hungry, and sad.

The results showed that there was considerable agreement on certain words and relatively little on others. For example, more than 80 percent of the judges considered the following words to be emotions: angry, happy, sad, loving, jealous, joyful, depressed, embarrassed, frightened, terrified, and humiliated. More than 80 percent of the judges considered the following words as not referring to emotions: cold, hungry, thirsty, sleepy, tired, healthy, alert, nauseated, fidgety, and strong. At the same time, about half the judges considered many words to be emotions while the other half considered them not to be emotions. Examples of these ambiguous words are *startled, curious, confused, astonished, revolted, surprised,* and *scornful.* The author of this study concludes that there is no good agreement for many words that refer to feeling states as to whether or not they represent emotions. When researchers asked the judges to describe their reasons for identifying a state as emotion or nonemotion, they had difficulty in doing so. It appears that "emotion" is an ambiguous category for many college students.

Storm and Storm (1987) used a somewhat different procedure to see if they could develop a list of emotion words. They gave a group of college students a list of 72 words that they believed were probably emotions, and asked the judges to sort the words into nonoverlapping groups according to similarity of meaning. The researchers then used a sophisticated statistical technique called multidimensional scaling to identify clusters of terms. The results suggested 18 clusters with each cluster containing 2 to 5 terms. Examples of the clusters are: (1) anger, rage; (2) disgust, loathing, revulsion, contempt, hatred; (3) sadness, grief, melancholy, remorse; (4) panic, terror, fear; and (5) elation, jubilation, joy, ecstasy.

In order to expand this study, the researchers then asked several hundred children and adults to list every emotion word they could think of. They were also asked to label the feelings of characters in clips from commercial television shows. This exercise resulted in a list of over 500 terms for further study. In this phase of the research, four college professors placed the various words into clusters representing similar meanings, resulting in 61 separate groups. Table 3.1 shows an example of the group of words relating to shame, sadness, and pain.

The terms shown in this table generally represent what most people would agree are unpleasant feelings. Some of the words, such as shame and embarrassment, imply a social disadvantage or a feeling of submission. Some of the terms imply a general mood without a specific cause, such as shy or self-conscious. Others, such as humiliated or disappointed, imply that a specific external event caused a change, while a third subgroup of terms implies an absence of something desired (lonely, yearning).

The authors of this study note that only adults produced many of the terms in the list. Young children typically have a small vocabulary of emotion terms that tend to consist of the words *happy, sad, mad*, and *scared*. These observations suggest that children develop a few broad categories of emotion concepts and that these concepts are gradually refined, differentiated, and added to as a result of social development and experience.

One other point of great interest these researchers made is that many of the terms in the list refer to words commonly used to describe personality. Thus, words such as gloomy, resentful, or calm can describe personality traits as well as emotional feelings. This important observation will be discussed in more detail in a later chapter.

Another investigation concerned with identifying emotion words was reported by Clore, Ortony, and Foss (1987). In this study, small groups of about 20 students each rated lists of words taken from the writings of other psychologists. A total of 585 words were rated, some in adjective form (angry), some in verb form (reject), and some in noun form (sadness). The students used a four-point scale to indicate their degree of certainty that each word was or was not an emotion word.

The ratings for degree of certainty were subjected to statistical analyses that found considerable disagreement concerning which terms were and were not emotion words. For example, it appeared that intense states such as *astonished, bewildered, flabbergasted*, and *amazed* were all considered emo-

Table 3.1	Terms Related to Shame, Sadness, and Pain

Group	Term
1.0.0	Bad, Awful, Dreadful, Horrible, Horrid, Not good, Rotten Terrible, Frightful
1.1.1	Humiliated, Inferior, Intimidated, Oppressed, Put down, Ridiculous, Sheepish, Dumb, Silly, Small, Stupid, Ugly
1.1.3	Shy, Bashful, Self-conscious, Defensive
1.2.0	Sad
1.2.1	Melancholy, Blue, Down, Forlorn, Gloomy, Low, Moping, Unhappy, Unsatisfied, Woeful, Crying
1.2.2	Disappointed, Deflated, Discouraged, Disenchantment, Dismayed, Let down, Subdued
1.2.3	Wistful, Lonely, Longing, Homesick, Nostalgic, Wanting, Yearning
1.2.4	Guilty, Apologetic, Regretful, Remorseful, Repentant, Sorry
1.2.5	Hurt, Betrayed, Let down, Misunderstood, Neglected, Rejected, Reproachful, Self-pitying, Unwanted, Unwelcome, Different, Isolated
1.2.6	Sorrowful, Depressed, Dejected, Despairing, Despondent, Drained, Empty, Hollow, Hopeless, Resigned, Failure, Useless
1.2.7	Grief stricken, Desolated, Devastated, Distraught, Heartbroken, Lost, Mournful
1.3.0	Pained
1.3.1	Agony, Anguish, Distress, Misery, Suffering, Tormented

Source: C. Storm and T. Storm, 1987.

tional states, even though the authors preferred to think of them as "cognitive conditions." Other examples of words that the students rated as emotion words, contrary to the authors' expectations, were the terms *determined, disillusioned,* and *lively.* One of the reasons for the inconsistencies in the students' judgments is that the simple presentation of a word does not identify a linguistic context. Thus, for example, the word *good* on the list can be interpreted as *feeling* good or pleasant, or *being* a good person. If someone interpreted the word as in the first case, it would probably be rated as an emotion word, whereas if it was interpreted as a state of being, it might not. Here again, the same term might be used to describe an emotional state or a personality trait.

Another example of the confusion the data revealed is the fact that the word *courage* (or *courageous*) was considered an emotion word, while its opposite *cowardly* was not. Similarly, *optimistic* was considered an emotion word while its opposite *pessimistic* was not. It thus appears that simply asking people to identify emotion words from long lists does not result in much agreement nor is it a satisfactory solution to the problem of defining the language of emotion.

A study carried out by Averill (1975) provides another possible reason for the discrepant ratings among the subjects. Averill was interested in developing a relatively complete list of emotion words in the English language, and in describing some of their linguistic properties. In order to do this, he and four graduate students read through the list of 18,000 psychological terms compiled by Allport and Odbert in 1936. Any term that was considered to be an emotion word by at least two of the five judges was kept in the list. This resulted in a preliminary list of 717 words. These words were then given in random order to a group of college students who were asked to rate on a seven-point scale whether they believed that the average person would consider each term as referring to an emotion. They were also asked to rate whether each word was familiar to them or not.

The results showed that more than half of the words in the list were not familiar to many of the college students. The relatively unfamiliar terms included such words as *bedeviled, beguiled, bewailing, cantankerous, contrite, crestfallen, disconsolate, doleful, droll, enamored, galled, harried, macabre, panged, quaky, scoffing, smitten, testy,* and *volatile.* Only 351 words were rated as *familiar* by all the students, and it is likely that the final sample of familiar words would be much less if each student was asked to define each term. It is thus likely that the inherent ambiguity of the words of our language, the general lack of a context when words are presented in isolation, and the lack of familiarity with certain words may help account for the highly varied judgments that raters give concerning the question of which words are emotion words and which are not.

What may we conclude about the question being considered, "How can we identify the language of emotion?" The methods described that ask children, college students, or professors to select emotion words from long lists of terms do not seem to provide any clearcut answers. It appears that there is inconsistency among the judges in deciding which words are emotion words and which are not. These findings are probably due to several reasons: (1) The lists of words used come from diverse sources and contain many different types of words; (2) The words are often presented in different grammatical forms (adjectives, nouns, verbs), thus creating confusion due to the judges' having to change expectations or sets; (3) Many words on the lists are obsolete, obscure, or uncommon, and large numbers of judges admit to being unfamiliar with these words; (4) The words are presented out of context, thus adding to the ambiguity of the terms; (5) The different experiences of the judges with language in general and emotion words in particular add to the variability in the ratings.

The Multiplicity of Meanings of Words

To provide a parallel example of the multiplicity of words and phrases that describe a basic underlying state, we may examine the vocabulary of drunkenness. Drunkenness is a universal experience in the sense that it can be found in all cultures; most people have experienced some degree of it in their own lives; and many different words and expressions are used to describe the experience of drunkenness.

In 1737, Benjamin Franklin compiled a list of 228 terms for being drunk. *The Dictionary of American Slang* (1975) lists 353 terms, and the *American Thesaurus of Slang* (1953) lists almost 900 terms. Examples of synonyms for drunkenness include the following: *crashed, bombed, crocked, gassed, plastered, tanked, looped, floating, glassy eyed, gone, juiced, lit, loaded, mellow, pickled, potted, smashed, soused, stewed, tight, high,* and *zonked.*

Many of the terms are forceful or even violent words, while others suggest a pleasant state (e.g., floating, mellow). Levine (1981) has interpreted this variance to reflect different stages of drunkenness. The initial relaxed feeling is expressed by words like *high* and *lit,* the second stage by words like *tipsy,* and *bleary-eyed,* and the third stage by words like *clobbered, smashed,* and *stewed.* There seems to be considerable overlap between words for the effects of alcohol and for the effects of other drugs. Levine suggests that the underlying common element in all forms of intoxication is a break with ordinary consciousness, and that part of the pleasure of drunkenness is the pleasure involved in losing some level of conscious awareness. Emotion terms are similar in their expression of different levels of intensity of feeling, in their partial expression of complex inner states, and in that a limited class of stimuli trigger them.

Language is a complex structure that has evolved over a period of thousands of years. Within each language there are many different historical elements. The words of the English language, for example, stem from Latin, Greek, German, and French roots, and, to lesser degrees, from various other sources. Over the centuries, a multiplicity of meanings may become attached to a word. In addition, if a word becomes used in a scientific or technical context, it is often given a new or modified meaning.

To illustrate this last point, consider the word *anxiety.* Most people would agree that this is an emotion word; yet the definitions of the term are diverse. *Webster's International Unabridged Dictionary* states that the word *anxiety* comes from a Latin root which means "to cause pain or to choke." It then provides three different definitions. The first definition of anxiety is "a painful uneasiness of the mind respecting an impending or anticipated ill." The second definition describes anxiety as "a pathological state of restlessness and agitation with a distressing sense of oppression about the heart." The third definition is based on psychoanalytic theory and it describes anxiety as "an expectancy of evil or of danger without adequate ground, explained as a transformed emotion derived from repressed libido." This last definition is evidently based on theory and not on subjective experience. There is no possible way that a group of college students would ever define anxiety in those terms based solely on their experiences. Therefore, the use of judges to select emotion from nonemotion words is only a limited way to begin to identify the language of emotions. It is likely that scientists must define emotions as part of a body of theory, and the definitions they choose will undoubtedly influence the kind of information that researchers collect.

This general way of defining words is used in all the other sciences as well. The word *mass*, for example, is defined as a sequence of prayers and ceremonies used in the Catholic Church; as a musical setting for the parts of the mass that do not vary from day to day; as a quantity of matter; as a group of people in a limited area; as an indicator of the majority of people compared with the elite; and in physics, as a property of a body that is a measure of its inertia. In order to understand what mass is in physics one must know something about the theory of gravitation and what the concept of inertia is. Theories thus help define the meanings of words used in science, and this is as true for the language of emotion as it is for any other scientific language.

One last point is that the meanings of words are given not only by explicit definitions, but also by listing related words or synonyms. Thus, to understand a word like *anxiety*, it is useful to list such related words as *fear, worry, foreboding, concern, dread, uneasiness,* and *apprehension.* However, the dictionary adds one other important way to help understand emotions, and that is by listing antonyms as well as synonyms. In this case, words such as *bold, calm,* and *confident* are given as antonyms for *anxiety.* This practice implies that the concept of opposites (antonyms) or bipolarity is a useful way to describe at least one aspect of emotions.

How Do People Learn the Language of Emotions?

It must be difficult for a child to acquire appropriate verbal labels for his or her own internal states. Such states are private events, which are only loosely coupled to events in the environment. Skinner poses the problem in the following way: "So far as we know. . . differential reinforcement is required if a child is to distinguish among events within his own skin. . . .

Because the community cannot reinforce self-descriptive responses consistently, a person cannot describe or otherwise 'know' events occurring within his own skin as subtly and precisely as he knows events in the world at large" (Skinner, 1963). Reports of private states are thus likely to be subject to greater variability than reports of other types of events.

How does a young child learn to use emotion words correctly? Although there are undoubtedly a number of different avenues, let us consider some possible sequences of events.

Scenario I. If a mother punishes her son by slapping him, he is likely to develop a series of inner feelings (which may be a combination of pain, embarrassment, and anger), and he is likely to act (or have an impulse to act) in a certain way (kick his little brother). If the mother sees the kicking behavior, she may label the child as angry. There is, however, an ambiguity, since the child may connect the word *angry* with his *behavior* of hitting his brother, or with his *feeling* of pain or embarrassment. Only after repeated experiences with this sequence of events might he develop a reasonably clear connection between a supposedly unique feeling called *anger* and a certain type of behavior or situation.

Scenario II. A little girl tracks mud into her house and gets it on the rug. Her mother pulls her out of the room and yells, "You make me very angry." The child does not feel angry, and the behavior of tracking mud into a house has no intrinsic connection with anger. The child will probably be confused, and may learn that the word *angry* is connected with a loud voice and brusque behavior of her mother.

Scenario III. A boy sees another child throw a temper tantrum, kicking the wall, crying, and screaming at the top of his voice. He hears the other child's mother say quietly, "Why are you angry?" Thus, he may learn that the word angry is connected with this complex of active behaviors.

It is apparent that adults may use the word *anger* in a variety of different situations, therefore confusing and making it difficult for a child to learn this new concept to describe an inner state. It must take repeated exposures to these kinds of scenarios for a child to begin to use the word *angry* in a way roughly similar to the way others in the community use the word. However, there will always be some idiosyncratic ways in which each person uses emotion labels.

The preliminary analysis of verbal labeling suggested above has an important limitation. It is relevant only to a few relatively common, easily recognizable states, such as fear, anger, sadness, and joy. The analysis probably does not apply very well to more subtle mixed emotions, such as hope, curiosity, hostility, and optimism. The reason for this statement is simple. In order for a child to learn to identify his or her own private events as examples of socially meaningful interactions, the feelings must be relatively unambiguous, the behaviors must be consistent, and the outcomes specific and predictable. For a great many emotions, excepting only a few basic ones, these conditions do not obtain. The result is that people must learn many complex emotions later in life through verbal exchanges, dictionaries, and various kinds of descriptive accounts.

A Note on the Evolution of Languages

Archaeologists and linguists have long been interested in the origins of language. They believe that human vocal-auditory language is probably only about 50,000 years old. The evidence used for this conclusion relates to the sudden increase in tool use and technological diversification that occurred about this time. In addition, the structure of the mandibles of the jaw had to reach a certain form before subtle articulations became possible (Harnard, Steklis, & Lancaster, 1977).

It is estimated that about 40,000 years passed before a written mode of language expression developed about 8,000 years ago. Such written language passed through a recognized series of stages, beginning with pictographs, or actual sketches of objects, and moving to more and more abstract forms.

With a limited number of signs available, people had to express a great many different ideas with the same sign. For example, "the sign for foot meant 'foot,' but it meant also 'to go,' 'to stand,' etc. However, while the sign was always the same, the picture of a foot when it was to be read 'to go' was read with the special sound which meant 'to go,' and when it was intended to indicate the idea of 'standing,' it was read in an entirely different way. We thus find that every one of the pictures came to be associated with three or four ideas and therefore with three or four sounds" (Chiera, 1938).

What was true of the early origins of language is true to some degree today. Words are not precise symbols that have a single, unequivocal meaning. They are inherently ambiguous and depend on context to help establish meanings. Because of this inherent ambiguity, words help to create meanings by influencing the conceptual content of often poorly defined and diffuse inner-feeling states. Thus, the statements one makes about one's own inner emotional states are partially dependent upon the kinds of words available to the individual and the kind of linguistic community he or she is in. The point is simply that many factors influence verbal reports of inner, private, emotional states and, therefore, the nature of the inner states will always remain an inference that requires confirmation by independent sources of evidence.

▌How Many Basic Emotions Are There?

From a historical point of view, there is an alternative, and much older, way of trying to understand emotions than by examining lists of emotion words. This alternative approach makes the assumption that a small number of emotions are considered primary or fundamental or basic, and that all other emotions are secondary, derived mixtures, or blends of the primary ones. From this perspective, one needs to identify the basic emotions and then explain which mixed emotions or blends are derived from them. Over the centuries, many philosophers and psychologists have proposed lists of basic emotions. This section will review some of these proposals.

The French philosopher Descartes (1596–1650), assumed that there were only six primary emotions or, as he called them, passions, and that all others were composed of mixtures of these six or derived from them. He suggested that love, hatred, desire, joy, sadness, and admiration were primary emotions but gave no justification for his choice.

A more extensive attempt to develop a system of the emotions was presented by Spinoza (1632–1677), who assumed only three primary affects: "joy, sorrow, and desire"; all others were assumed to spring from these. For example, he wrote, "Love is nothing but joy accompanied with the idea of an external cause." Fear was described as "an unsteady sorrow, arising from the image of a doubtful thing. If the doubt be removed . . . then . . . fear becomes despair. . . . Remorse is the sorrow which is opposed to gladness. . . . Pride is that joy which arises from a man's thinking too much of himself." Spinoza attempted to analyze a number of common emotions using this procedure but gave no justification for his choice of primaries; nor is it evident how he decided on the components of a particular complex emotion. Later, the British philosopher Hobbes (1588–1679), suggested that there were seven simple passions: "appetite, desire, love, aversion, hate, joy, and grief," and several English philosophers of the nineteenth century continued making distinctions of a similar kind.

Darwin's book on the expression of emotions does not explicitly say which emotions are primary and which are mixed. However, his chapters deal with seven clusters of emotions that he believed can be identified both in animals and humans. These chapters are titled: "Low Spirits, Anxiety, Grief, Dejection, Despair"; "Joy, High Spirits, Love, Tender Feelings, Devotion"; "Reflection, Meditation, Ill-Temper, Sulkiness, Determination"; "Hatred and Anger"; "Disdain, Contempt, Disgust, Guilt, Pride, Helplessness, Patience, Affirmation and Negation"; "Surprise, Astonishment, Fear, Horror"; "Self-Attention, Shame, Shyness, Modesty, Blushing." These clusters presumably reflect the more basic emotions, rather than the derived ones.

Early in the twentieth century, McDougall, a British psychologist, gave the concept of primary and secondary emotions an extensive analysis. He described his views in his textbook of social psychology, published in 1921. There, he pointed out that all animals including humans have "instincts" or "propensities" and that when these are activated, an affective quality that we call emotion is associated with each. For example, the instinct to flee from danger is associated with the emotion of fear; the instinct of pugnacity is associated with the emotion of anger, and so on. In all, he assumes seven important, clearly defined instincts and five more obscure, less differentiated ones, as follows:

Instinct	Emotion
flight	fear
repulsion	disgust
curiosity	wonder
pugnacity	anger
self-abasement	subjection
self-assertion	elation
parental	tender

The five less clearly defined instincts are the gregarious instinct, the acquisitive instinct, the constructive instinct, the reproductive instinct, and an instinct connected with the desire for food.

The secondary or complex emotions are illustrated by such things as hate, which McDougall defines as a mixture of anger and disgust; or loathing, which results from the combination of fear and disgust. He analyzes relatively few other emotions in this way. No specific criterion is given for arriving at the components in any mixed emotion.

McDougall, however, is one of the few writers on this subject who makes some attempt to explain the methods used to decide which emotions are primary. He suggests three criteria: (1) A similar emotion and impulse are clearly shown in the behavior of the higher animals; (2) the emotion and impulse occasionally appear in humans with "morbidly exaggerated intensity" (which presumably indicates its relatively independent functioning in the mind); and (3) most of the complex emotions can be conceived of as mixtures of the primaries. Unfortunately, McDougall does not apply these criteria consistently. He refuses to accept joy and sorrow as primary emotions, even though they are occasionally expressed in the morbidly exaggerated forms of mania and depression; he arrives at components of mixtures strictly on the basis of his own introspections. In addition, his utilization of the concept of instinct, a concept that has fallen into disrepute in contemporary writing, has left many psychologists highly skeptical of the general scheme. This result is unfortunate since many interesting and perceptive observations are found in his work.

McDougall's attempt to describe behavior in terms of primary emotions is by no means the most recent such attempt. In the 1928 Wittenberg Symposium on Feelings and Emotions, Jorgensen proposed his own scheme. He suggested six primary emotions: "fear, happiness, sorrow, want, anger, and shyness," with the possibility that *loathing* might also be one. He noted the very important point that the naming of these primaries is partly fortuitous because they each may vary in intensity. Thus, *fear* might also be called *dread, terror, anxiety,* or *apprehension* and *sorrow* might be called *grief, despair, pain,* or *despondency.* Using this scheme, he interprets *hope* as a mixture of *want, sorrow* and *happiness,* and *envy* as a mixture of *sorrow and want.* Here again, no meaningful criterion is given for deciding on the units within each mixture.

Several more recent attempts have been made to identify basic emotions. For example, Cattell has factor-analyzed a variety of descriptive items related to the objective expression of emotions and motivations (1957). He reports ten factors that he defines as basic emotions. He proposes that each emotion has a particular goal or aim, and when he combines these two ideas, his resulting list looks very much like McDougall's. His list follows:

Emotion	Goal
sex-lust	mating
fear	escape
loneliness	gregariousness
pity, succorance	protectiveness
curiosity	exploration
pride	self-assertion
sensuous comfort	narcissism
despair	appeal
sleepiness	rest seeking
anger	pugnacity

Tomkins (1962) has proposed still another list of basic emotions. He assumes that there are eight basic emotions or affects. The positive affects are *interest, surprise,* and *joy.* The negative affects are *anguish, fear, shame, disgust,* and *rage.* These basic emotions are "innately patterned responses" to certain types of stimuli and may be expressed by means of a wide variety of bodily reactions. Tomkins, however, emphasizes the importance of the face as the primary mode for the expression of emotions. He also assumes that there is a genetic, species-related basis for the expression of the basic emotions.

Izard has worked closely with Tomkins and has provided experimental evidence that these emotions can be reliably distinguished from one another on the basis of posed facial expressions (Izard, 1971). The following list is Izard's way of describing these eight emotions; he also provides some defining adjectives for each emotion.

Emotions	Defining Adjectives
interest: excitement	attending, curious
enjoyment: joy	glad, merry
surprise: startle	astonished
distress: anguish	sad, unhappy
disgust: contempt	sneering, scornful
anger: rage	hostile, furious
shame: humiliation	shy, embarrassed
fear: terror	scared, panicked

In the same year that Tomkins published his book, Plutchik also published a theory of emotion based upon the idea that certain emotions are primary, or prototypes, and all others are derived (Plutchik, 1962). He assumed that primary emotions are identifiable, in some form, at all phylogenetic levels and that they have adaptive significance in the individual's struggle for survival. Plutchik conceptualized eight such prototypical emotion dimensions, but also emphasized that they could be described in several different *languages*—for example, a subjective language, a behavioral language, a functional language, and so on. Using only the subjective language of introspective feelings, the eight basic emotion dimensions could be described by such names as joy, sadness, acceptance, disgust, fear, anger, expectation, and surprise, or other synonymous terms reflecting differences in intensity, terms such as ecstasy, grief, trust, revulsion, panic, and so on.

These examples show that the idea that some emotions are more primary or basic than others is an old one. Although there have been different conceptions of just which emotions are primary and which secondary, there has been considerable agreement on the belief that there is a small number of such primaries.

In the last three decades numerous investigators have embraced the concept of basic emotions. In a review of this recent literature, Kemper (1987) provides a table listing the primary emotions that have been proposed; Table 3.2 is based on his review.

These theorists all agree that a small number of emotions qualify as primary emotions. The smallest number is three and the largest number is eleven, while most proposals list five to nine emotions. Also of interest is the fact that certain emotions such as fear and anger appear on every list. Sadness (or its synonym grief, distress, or loneliness) appears on all but two lists. And joy (or near equivalents such as love, pleasure, elation, happiness, or satisfaction) appears on every list. Less commonly cited as primary emotions are surprise, disgust, curiosity, expectancy, shame, and guilt.

Kemper (1987) believes that there are at least four physiologically based primary emotions: fear, anger, sadness, and satisfaction. He argues that the rationale for considering them as primary is that they can be observed (or inferred) in most animals, that they are universally found in all cultures, that they appear early in the course of human development, that they are outcomes of power and status interactions, and that they are associated with distinct autonomic patterns of physiological changes. These are important points in that they represent an explicit justification for considering certain emotions as primary.

Similarly, Ortony and Turner (1990) point out that the usual reasons that theorists give for assuming the existence of primary emotions is that: (1) some emotions appear to exist in all cultures; (2) some can be identified in higher animals; (3) some have characteristic facial expressions; and (4)

Table 3.2	Primary Emotions Proposed in Recent Theories
Theory	**Emotions**
Evolutionary approaches	
Plutchik (1962, 1980)	fear, anger, sadness, joy, acceptance, disgust, anticipation, surprise
Scott (1980)	fear, anger, loneliness, pleasure, love, anxiety, curiosity
Epstein (1984)	fear, anger, sadness, joy, love
Neural approaches	
Tomkins (1962, 1963)	fear, anger, enjoyment, interest, disgust, surprise, shame, contempt, distress
Izard (1972, 1977)	fear, anger, enjoyment, interest, disgust, surprise, shame/shyness, contempt, distress, guilt
Panksepp (1982)	fear, rage, panic,[*] expectancy[+]
Psychoanalytic approach	
Arieti (1970)	fear, rage, satisfaction, tension, appetite
Autonomic approach	
Fromme and O'Brien (1982)	fear, anger, grief/resignation, joy, elation, satisfaction, shock
Facial expressions approaches	
Ekman (1973)	fear, anger, sadness, happiness, disgust, surprise
Osgood (1966)	fear, anger, anxiety-sorrow, joy, quiet pleasure, interest/expectancy, amazement, boredom, disgust
Empirical classification approaches	
Shaver and Schwartz (1984)	fear, anger, sadness, happiness, love
Fehr and Russell (1985)	fear, anger, sadness, happiness, love
Developmental approaches	
Sroufe (1979)	fear, anger, pleasure
Trevarthen (1984)	fear, anger, sadness, happiness
Malatesta and Haviland (1982)	fear, anger, sadness, joy, interest, pain
Emde (1980)	fear, anger, sadness, joy, interest, surprise, distress, shame, shyness, disgust, guilt

[*]Panic is associated with "sorrow, loneliness, and grief" (Panksepp, 1982, p. 410).
[+]Expectancy is understood as "joyful anticipation" (Panksepp, 1982, p. 414).
Source: T. D. Kemper, 1987.

some seem to increase the chances of survival. These points are very similar to those Darwin made.

Is the Startle Reaction a Basic Emotion?

Despite agreement on criteria that one may use to decide which emotions are basic, there has been controversy over the status of a particular pattern of behavior, the *startle reaction*. Some theorists have considered it an emotion, while others have considered it to be a reflex reaction of the whole body. How can we decide between these two alternatives?

Ekman, Friesen, and Simons (1985) carried out a series of studies that threw light on this controversy. They took high speed motion pictures of subject's reactions to the sound of a blank pistol being shot off behind the subject's chair. Subjects went through several conditions. The first involved measurement of the startle reactions without knowledge of when the pistol would be fired. The second measured the startle reaction when the subject anticipated the moment of firing. The third measured the startle pattern when the subjects tried to inhibit it. And the fourth condition asked the subjects to simulate the startle pattern voluntarily.

The results showed that the startle reaction was like other basic emotions in that it had a quite uniform facial expression associated with it. "However, startle differs from other emotions in four ways: (a) Startle is very easy to elicit; (b) it is shown reliably as the initial response by every subject; (c) the startle response cannot be totally inhibited; and (d) no one seems able to simulate it with the correct latency." Startle does not seem to require a cognitive evaluation, nor does it seem to exist with different levels of intensity. Ekman and his colleagues therefore conclude that startle is probably not a basic emotion. Unfortunately, because it is not possible to apply a similar test to other emotions, more general and less clear-cut criteria must be used.

The Relation of Basic Emotions to Secondary Ones

The problem remains, however, of explaining how secondary emotions relate to the primary ones. In connection with this point, Kemper (1987) suggests that the secondary emotions result from the attachment of new labels to various aspects of social interaction. For example, he considers guilt to result from a feeling of fear of punishment associated with the expression of forbidden acts. Pride, he believes, is a feeling of satisfaction that the self is worthy. Shame is supposedly a feeling of anger directed toward oneself because of an unworthy action. Other examples of secondary emotions are hate, jealousy, and envy, supposedly mixtures of fear and anger; anxiety, supposedly a mixture of fear and depression; and vengeance, presumably a mixture of anger and happiness. While these are interesting ideas, Kemper does not make evident how he decided the components of the different emotions.

In contrast, Plutchik (1980) has made some effort to provide an empirical basis for naming mixtures of primary emotions. He suggests that there are at least two possible approaches to the problem of naming emotion mixtures.

1. Present a group of judges with all possible pairs of primary emotions and ask them to suggest an appropriate name for the resulting mixture.
2. Present a group of judges with a long list of emotion-names taken from our language and ask them to indicate which of the primaries are present.

It was discovered that the first procedure listed above—that is, the introspective *synthesis* of primary emotions—is a difficult task that produces more variability than the method of *analysis*. Consequently, Plutchik has relied more heavily on the second procedure. In this connection, he asked a group of judges to examine a long list of emotion terms in our language and to indicate which two or three of the eight primaries are components. In some cases, there was great consistency; in others, less. Table 3.3 indicates those mixed emotions on which there was the most agreement (Plutchik, 1962/1990).

Examination of this table suggests that the judges sometimes found a single word to represent a mixture, and sometimes a group of words. However, it is evident that when a group of terms is listed they all share a common meaning; they tend to be synonyms (e.g., contempt, hatred, hostility, or anxiety and caution). This phenomenon implies that emotion terms are grouped into certain families or clusters. Is there any definitive way to label these mixtures or clusters? Shall one word be chosen from a list of related terms and be arbitrarily used to define the mixture?

The problem of establishing names for emotion mixtures is not easily solved. Interestingly enough, it is somewhat like the problem of naming colors. In 1955, the National Bureau of Standards published a *Dictionary of Color Names* and a standard method for designating colors. In the preface the authors stated:

> Ever since the language of man began to develop, words or expressions have been used first to indicate and then to describe colors. Some of these have persisted throughout the centuries and are those which refer to the simple colors or ranges such as red or yellow. As the language developed, more and more color names were invented to describe the colors used by art and industry and in late years in the rapidly expanding field of sales promotion. Some of these refer to the pigment or dye used, or a geographical location of its source. Later when it became clear that most colors are bought by or for women, many color names indicative of the beauties and wiles of the fair sex were introduced, such as

Table 3.3	Judges' Attributions of Words Appropriate to the Description of Mixed Emotions

Primary Emotion Components		Labels for Mixed Emotions
Joy + Acceptance	=	Love, Friendliness
Fear + Surprise	=	Alarm, Awe
Sadness + Disgust	=	Remorse
Disgust + Anger	=	Contempt, Hatred, Hostility
Joy + Fear	=	Guilt
Anger + Joy	=	Pride
Fear + Disgust	=	Shame, Prudishness
Anticipation + Fear	=	Anxiety, Caution

Source: R. Plutchik, 1980.

French Nude, Heart's Desire, Intimate Mood, or Vamp. . . . The dictionary will serve not only as a record of the meaning of the 7,500 individual color names listed but it will also enable anyone to translate from one color vocabulary to another (Kelly & Judd, 1955).

The development of an appropriate and standard color language is called *colorimetry*, and its presence enables people working in a number of different fields such as color television, paint and dye development, advertising, minerology, and physics to speak a common language. It is hoped that one day standards will be established for the description of emotions and their mixtures—a science of emotionimetry.

We see another analogue to this problem of naming emotion mixtures in the periodic table of the elements used in physics and chemistry. In the periodic table combinations of a limited number of basic elements result in the millions of compounds we see in nature. The basic elements can be grouped into a few major classes. Within each major class are a number of related families (e.g., the rare gases; the alkali metals, the halogens, and so forth). It is not always easy to name all compounds or mixtures; even in the periodic table, scientists discovered gaps, although subsequent research identified the substance on the basis of its familial properties. In relation to emotion, it is possible that our language may not contain emotion words for certain combinations, although other languages might. Certain combinations may not occur at all in human experience, just as chemical compounds can be formed only in certain limited ways. It is thus evident that the naming of emotions and their mixtures is not a simple task. The widespread existence of emotional blends with subtle variations in the degree of each component is probably one of the major reasons for the inconsistencies in the naming and identification of emotions in the general vocabulary.

A Dictionary of Emotions

Given the problems described above, is it possible to prepare a definitive list of emotion words in the English (or any other) language? As already noted, researchers have made various attempts in the past to prepare this type of list, although agreement on the contents of the list is limited.

Whissell (1989) has made the most recent attempt to establish a dictionary of emotions. She selected words different investigators of emotions used and added a great many words she obtained from dictionaries. College students rated each word on degree of pleasantness associated with the term and on degree of activation or arousal associated with the term. This procedure yielded a final list of 4,000 English words that Whissell calls a *Dictionary of Affect.* Many of the words, however, are clearly not emotion words as ordinarily used. Examples are bank, bear, cream, dive, full, limp,

Table 3.4			A Sample of 107 Words from the *Dictionary of Affect* with Scores Along the Dimensions of Evaluation and Activation		

Word	Activation	Evaluation	Word	Activation	Evaluation
Adventurous	4.2	5.9	Anxious	6.0	2.3
Affectionate	4.7	5.4	Apathetic	3.0	4.3
Afraid	4.9	3.4	Ashamed	3.2	2.3
Aggressive	5.9	2.9	Astonished	5.9	4.7
Agreeable	4.3	5.2	Attentive	5.3	4.3
Amazed	5.9	5.5	Bashful	2.0	2.7
Ambivalent	3.2	4.2	Bewildered	3.1	2.3
Amused	4.9	5.0	Bitter	6.6	4.0
Angry	4.2	2.7	Boastful	3.7	3.0
Annoyed	4.4	2.5	Bored	2.7	3.2
Antagonistic	5.3	2.5	Calm	2.5	5.5
Anticipatory	3.9	4.7	Cautious	3.3	4.9

Word	Activation	Evaluation	Word	Activation	Evaluation
Cheerful	5.2	5.0	Irritated	5.5	3.3
Confused	4.8	3.0	Jealous	6.1	3.4
Contemptuous	3.8	2.4	Joyful	5.4	6.1
Content	4.8	5.5	Loathful	3.5	2.9
Contrary	2.9	3.7	Lonely	3.9	3.3
Cooperative	3.1	5.1	Meek	3.0	4.3
Critical	4.9	2.8	Nervous	5.9	3.1
Curious	5.2	4.2	Obedient	3.1	4.7
Daring	5.3	4.4	Obliging	2.7	3.0
Defiant	4.4	2.8	Outraged	4.3	3.2
Delighted	4.2	6.4	Panicky	5.4	3.6
Demanding	5.3	4.0	Patient	3.3	3.8
Depressed	4.2	3.1	Pensive	3.2	5.0
Despairing	4.1	2.0	Pleased	5.3	5.1
Disagreeable	5.0	3.7	Possessive	4.7	2.8
Disappointed	5.2	2.4	Proud	4.7	5.3
Discouraged	4.2	2.9	Puzzled	2.6	3.8
Disgusted	5.0	3.2	Quarrelsome	4.6	2.6
Disinterested	2.1	2.4	Rebellious	5.2	4.0
Dissatisfied	4.6	2.7	Rejected	5.0	2.9
Distrustful	3.8	2.8	Remorseful	3.1	2.2
Eager	5.0	5.1	Resentful	5.1	3.0
Ecstatic	5.2	5.5	Sad	3.8	2.4
Embarrassed	4.4	3.1	Sarcastic	4.8	2.7
Empty	3.1	3.8	Satisfied	4.1	4.9
Enthusiastic	5.1	4.8	Scornful	5.4	4.9
Envious	5.3	2.0	Self-controlled	4.4	5.5
Furious	5.6	3.7	Serene	4.3	4.4
Gleeful	5.3	4.8	Sociable	4.8	5.3
Gloomy	2.4	3.2	Sorrowful	4.5	3.1
Greedy	4.9	3.4	Stubborn	4.9	3.1
Grouchy	4.4	2.9	Submissive	3.4	3.1
Guilty	4.0	1.1	Surprised	6.5	5.2
Happy	5.3	5.3	Suspicious	4.4	3.0
Helpless	3.5	2.8	Sympathetic	3.6	3.2
Hopeful	4.7	5.2	Terrified	6.3	3.4
Hopeless	4.0	3.1	Trusting	3.4	5.2
Hostile	4.0	1.7	Unaffectionate	3.6	2.1
Impatient	3.4	3.2	Unfriendly	4.3	1.6
Impulsive	3.1	4.8	Wondering	3.3	5.2
Indecisive	3.4	2.7	Worried	3.9	2.9
Intolerant	3.1	2.7			

Source: C. M. Whissell, 1989.

me, profit, and test. In addition, different forms of words with the same root (e.g., wish, wishful) were included, as well as plural forms and conjugations. After eliminating many of these irrelevant or overlapping terms, Whissell provided a sample of 107 words from her *Dictionary* along with their scores on the arousal and pleasantness (evaluation) dimension. The possible range of scores is 1 to 7, standardized in such a way that the mean for each dimension is 4.0 and the standard deviation is 1.0. This list is shown in Table 3.4.

It is worth noting that although the possible range of scores is 1 to 7, the average scores range from a low of 1.1 on pleasantness for the term *guilty* to a high of 6.4 for *delighted,* thus covering most of the range of pleasantness or evaluation. The ratings also indicate that *surprised, wondering, amazed,* and *pensive* are all judged to be fairly pleasant.

The *Dictionary* has been used to rate the intensity and pleasantness of verbal reports of short duration such as brief mood changes, as well as personality descriptions. It can also be used to quantify certain aspects of the stimulus materials that researchers use.

One other study might be briefly mentioned with regard to the question of whether investigators can develop a dictionary of emotion. Gehm and Scherer (1988) were interested in examining the degree of similarity of emotion terms. To carry out this study, they first obtained a list of as many terms as they could find in the literature on this topic. They then eliminated synonyms and terms that expressed only slight differences in the intensity of a particular emotional state, resulting in a list of 235 terms mostly in adjective form. They also identified equivalent words in French, Spanish, Italian, and German. It turned out that their list was quite similar to the one Whissell developed, shown in Table 3.4. Examples of additional words included: courageous, distressed, elated, frightened, grief-stricken, horrified, passionate, scared, shy, and vengeful.

What can we conclude in relation to the question asked earlier, "How many basic emotions are there?" Most researchers agree that a small number of emotions are basic, primary, or in some sense prototypic. The existence of the various lists of derived or mixed emotions that have been described implies little agreement on how long these lists should be. Kemper (1987) believes that the number of possible emotions is limitless, because society distinguishes new social situations, labels them, and socializes individuals to experience them. Another possible reason for the lack of a defined number of emotion terms is that words take on different meanings over time or in different situations in terms of the connotations we attach to them. For example, is aggressive an emotion, a motivation, or a personality trait? Is it good or bad? Does it represent *forceful energy and initiative, offensive action,* or *self-confidence in expression of opinion?* Depending upon what choices one makes, the term may or may not appear on a list of emotion words. Fortunately, research on emotion is not hampered by the lack of a final answer to this question.

▌How Are Emotions Related to One Another?

Three Characteristics of Emotion: Intensity, Similarity, and Polarity

Most people who have studied emotions have recognized that the language of emotions has an implicit intensity dimension. For most words in the emotion lexicon, it is usually possible to find other words that suggest either a more intense or a weaker version of that emotion. For example, more intense versions of anger would be rage and fury, while less intense forms of anger would be annoyance and irritation. Similarly, we might recognize the intensity differences between pensiveness, sadness, and grief. The implication of these examples is that most (perhaps all) emotions exist at points along implicit intensity dimensions.

A second point worth noting is that emotions vary in how similar they are to one another. This characteristic is clearly evident in the case of synonyms such as fear and fright (which may simply reflect close points along the intensity dimension), but it is also true for the major dimensions themselves. The dimension of anger, for example, is more similar to the dimension of disgust (dislike, loathing) than it is to the dimension of joy (cheerfulness, elation). It is, in fact, possible to study systematically the degree of similarity of the various emotion dimensions, or primary emotions, as will be shown shortly.

A third important characteristic that is part of our experience of emotions is their bipolar nature. In our everyday experience we tend to think about emotions in terms of opposition; we talk about happiness and sadness, love and hate, fear and anger. William James once pointed out that we can use self-control to influence our own emotional tendencies by practicing opposite emotions; we can deal with our own feelings of hate by trying to love our enemies. Thus, we may conclude that the language of emotions implies at least three characteristics of emotions: (1) they vary in intensity; (2) they vary in degree of similarity to one another; and (3) they express opposite or bipolar feelings or actions.

Several attempts have been made to study these characteristics in a systematic way. Block carried out one of the earliest of these studies in 1957. He was interested in determining some of the connotative meanings of emotions in contrast to the dictionary or denotative meanings. Connotative meanings refer to the ideas and images that people associate with a word but that do not necessarily define it. Thus, for example, most people tend to associate the color red with anger and blue with sadness. Similarly, the expression *gave me the chills* tends to be associated with fear, while the expression *made my skin crawl* suggests disgust or horror.

This approach to understanding a word by finding out its connotations is called the *semantic differential* and was developed by Osgood and his associates in the mid-fifties (Osgood, Suci & Tannenbaum, 1957). When Block adapted this method, he asked a group of male college students and

Figure 3.1	A Two-Dimensional Graph of Emotions

The similarity relations among emotions, based on a plotting of Block's factor analytic data.

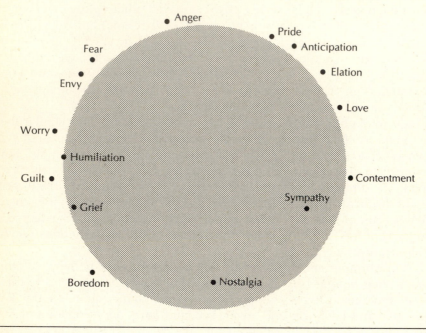

Source: J. Block, 1957.

a group of female college students to describe a series of 15 emotions using 20 semantic differential scales applied to each emotion. The scales were 7-point bipolar scales defined at each end by such terms as good-bad, high-low, active-passive, and tense-relaxed. The mean rating for each emotion was obtained on each scale to produce a kind of verbal profile for each emotion. Researchers then computed correlations between each pair of profiles to produce a matrix of all possible pairs of correlations. These correlations were then subjected to a statistical technique called factor analysis, which identifies clusters of terms or ideas. It was possible to plot the data on a two-dimensional graph, which produced the results shown in Figure 3.1.

Although the emotion terms were not picked in any systematic way, they fell into a circular order. The circle indicates the relative similarity of the emotions as reflected by their connotative meanings. At the same time they reveal certain polarities; for example, elation vs. grief, contentment vs. worry, and love vs. boredom. It is worth noting that the results obtained from the males and females were almost identical, and similar results were obtained from a group of Norwegian students.

In an effort to study further this apparent circular ordering of emotion concepts in terms of similarity, Plutchik (1980) used an alternative procedure. The basic procedure was as follows. Three emotion words were chosen as *reference* words. The words, *accepting, angry,* and *sad,* were selected because they seemed to be quite different, and were clearly not synonyms of each other. Any other diverse set of three such terms could just as well have been used. This point has been demonstrated by Conte (1975) in her analysis of the relative similarity of personality traits. The judges were then asked to rate the relative similarity of 146 emotion words to each of the three reference words. The ratings were made on an 11-point bipolar scale ranging from *opposite* (-5) to *the same* (+5).

The mean similarity ratings were converted to angular locations on a circle by procedures Conte and Plutchik (1981) described more fully. On the basis of this method, they obtained angular placements for every emotion in the list. This information is presented in Table 3.5 and a sample of the terms is presented in Figure 3.2 on page 70.

The first thing to notice about Table 3.5 is that the emotion terms are distributed around the entire circle and there are no gaps. Nothing about the method for locating the angular placements would guarantee such a result, and this finding is not, therefore, an artifact of the method.

Additional support for this point is the fact that many terms that are linguistically opposite fall at opposite parts of the circle. For example, the terms *interested* and *disinterested* are almost 180° apart. This is also true for *affectionate* and *unaffectionate,* and *obedient* and *disobedient.* Similarly, words that are clearly opposite in meaning are also found on opposite sides of the circle. To take just a few examples, the words *accepting, agreeable,* and *tolerant* are opposite *resentful, displeased,* and *revolted;* emotions such as *joyful, happy,* and *enthusiastic* are opposite the emotions of *gloomy, unhappy,* and *grief-stricken.*

A second important observation the table and the figure reveal is the particular sequence of terms. It is evident that emotions with similar meanings tend to cluster. For example, the terms *lonely, apathetic, meek, guilty, sad, sorrowful, empty, remorseful, hopeless,* and *depressed* are located in consecutive positions covering a range of 88.3 to 125.3°. We find similar clusters for the fear dimension, the anger dimension, and for other basic dimensions.

A third interesting implication of this empirical emotion circle is its possibility for helping to define the sometimes ambiguous language of emotions. For example, the term *worried* is often thought of in the context of fear; however, it was empirically located in the cluster of depression words. Similarly, *scornful,* which has a definite element of rejection or disgust in it, was found to be located in the cluster of anger words. This finding suggests that dictionary definitions may not always correspond to the way people actually use emotion terms.

Table 3.5		Angular Placement for a Population of Emotion Terms	
Emotion	**Angular Placement**	**Emotion**	**Angular Placement**
Accepting	0.0	Unhappy	129.0
Agreeable	5.0	Gloomy	132.7
Serene	12.3	Despairing	133.0
Cheerful	25.7	Watchful	133.3
Receptive	32.3	Hesitant	134.0
Calm	37.0	Indecisive	134.0
Patient	39.7	Rejected	136.0
Obliging	43.3	Bored	136.0
Affectionate	52.3	Disappointed	136.7
Obedient	57.7	Vascillating	137.3
Timid	65.0	Discouraged	138.0
Scared	66.7	Puzzled	138.3
Panicky	67.7	Uncertain	139.3
Afraid	70.3	Bewildered	140.3
Shy	72.0	Confused	141.3
Submissive	73.0	Perplexed	142.3
Bashful	74.7	Ambivalent	144.7
Embarrassed	75.3	Surprised	146.7
Terrified	75.7	Astonished	148.0
Pensive	76.7	Amazed	152.0
Cautious	77.7	Awed	156.7
Anxious	78.3	Envious	160.3
Helpless	80.0	Disgusted	161.3
Apprehensive	83.3	Unsympathetic	165.6
Self-conscious	83.3	Unreceptive	170.0
Ashamed	83.3	Indignant	175.0
Humiliated	84.0	Disagreeable	176.4
Forlorn	85.0	Resentful	176.7
Nervous	86.0	Revolted	181.3
Lonely	88.3	Displeased	181.5
Apathetic	90.0	Suspicious	182.7
Meek	91.0	Dissatisfied	183.0
Guilty	102.3	Contrary	184.3
Sad	108.5	Jealous	184.7
Sorrowful	112.7	Intolerant	185.0
Empty	120.3	Distrustful	185.0
Remorseful	123.3	Vengeful	186.0
Hopeless	124.7	Bitter	186.0
Depressed	125.3	Unfriendly	188.0
Worried	126.0	Stubborn	190.4
Disinterested	127.3	Uncooperative	191.7
Grief-stricken	127.3	Contemptuous	192.0

Emotion	Angular Placement	Emotion	Angular Placement
Loathful	193.0	Curious	261.0
Critical	193.7	Reckless	261.0
Annoyed	200.6	Proud	262.0
Irritated	202.3	Inquisitive	267.7
Angry	212.0	Planful	269.7
Antagonistic	220.0	Adventurous	270.7
Furious	221.3	Ecstatic	286.0
Hostile	222.0	Sociable	296.7
Outraged	225.3	Hopeful	298.0
Scornful	227.0	Gleeful	307.0
Unaffectionate	227.3	Elated	311.0
Quarrelsome	229.7	Eager	311.0
Grouchy	230.0	Enthusiastic	313.7
Impatient	230.3	Interested	315.7
Defiant	230.7	Delighted	318.6
Aggressive	232.0	Amused	321.0
Sarcastic	235.3	Attentive	322.4
Rebellious	237.0	Joyful	323.4
Exasperated	239.7	Happy	323.7
Disobedient	242.7	Self-controlled	326.3
Demanding	244.0	Satisfied	326.7
Possessive	247.7	Pleased	328.0
Greedy	249.0	Generous	328.0
Wondering	249.7	Ready	329.3
Impulsive	255.0	Sympathetic	331.3
Anticipatory	257.0	Content	338.3
Boastful	257.3	Cooperative	340.7
Expectant	257.3	Trusting	345.3
Daring	260.1	Tolerant	350.7

Source: R. Plutchik, 1980.

In order to determine the validity of this emotion circle, an independent method was used to locate the positions of various emotions on the circle. This alternate method involved a factor analysis of semantic differential ratings as described in connection with Block's study. In this validation, a subset of 40 emotions was selected and five judges rated the connotative meanings of each term on twenty 7-point semantic differential scales.

The correlations among emotions were factor-analyzed and the data were plotted on a graph. After it was found that the placements of emotion words formed a circular ordering, the angular position of each of these 40 emotion words was calculated. These angular placements were then compared with the angular placements obtained with the first method of direct

---

Figure 3.2   Angular Locations of Emotions Based upon Similarity Judgments

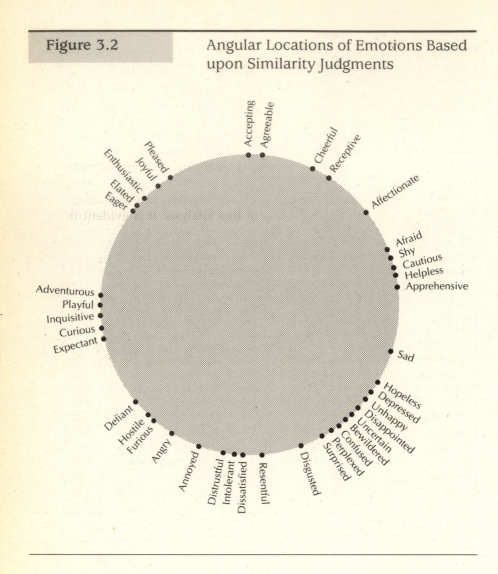

---

similarity scaling. The product-moment correlation was found to be +.90, indicating that the two sets of orderings on the circle were almost identical. This outcome strongly supports the validity of a circular similarity structure for emotions.

One final example illustrates still another method for studying the similarity of emotions. Russell (1983, 1989) has contributed a number of investigations on this issue. In one, he selected 28 emotion terms and obtained translations of these terms into Chinese, Japanese, Croatian, and Gujarati. Subjects were people who were fluent in each of these languages.

Each subject was given a deck of 28 cards with one emotion term on each, and asked to sort the cards into 4, 7, 10, and 13 groups on successive trials. The subjects were to make groupings in terms of similar emotional states. The number of sorts in which the rater placed the pair in the same group determined the similarity of pairs of words. Minimum similarity would be scored as 1 while maximum possible similarity would be $1 + 4 + 7 + 10 + 13 = 35$, which would occur if the rater placed the pair in the same group on all trials.

The various ratings were analyzed by means of a multidimensional scaling procedure. In this statistical method, the degree of similarity between two words is represented by their closeness in a two-dimensional space. Figure 3.3 shows the results of this analysis. It is evident that the

Figure 3.3   A Circumplex for Emotions Based on Multidimensional Scaling

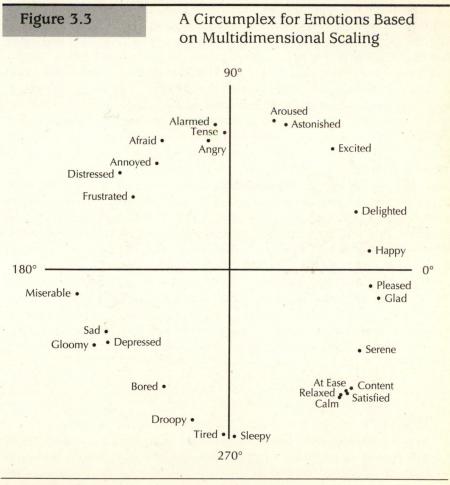

Source: J. Russell, 1989.

words fall in a circular pattern, a pattern which has been called a circum-plex. In a circumplex, the categories blend into one another in a continuous form without beginning or end. Terms that are close together (e.g., calm and relaxed) tend to be synonyms, while opposite terms on the circle tend to be antonyms (e.g., excited vs. bored; annoyed vs. calm; sad vs. delight-ed). Russell also found a circumplex pattern for the other four languages, although some variation in the positions of certain terms existed. Variations in the exact placement of terms in different studies are probably due to dif-ferent samples of emotion terms, different methods of statistical analysis, and different samples of subjects. Despite these factors, the consistency among the different circumplexes is reasonable.

Emotions, Affects, and Moods: Are They the Same?

In reading the literature on emotion, it becomes apparent that certain words are often used more-or-less interchangeably with the word *emotion*. The two most common stand-ins for *emotion* are the words *affect* and *mood*. Are they really synonyms or do they carry special meanings of their own?

A review by Watson and Tellegen (1985) of studies of self-rated mood includes frequent interchange of terms. For example, they write, "We began by noting that *mood* assessment and *mood* research should reflect the struc-ture of *emotional experience*. Now that we have demonstrated that a highly replicable structure exists, what implications can we draw to guide future *affect* research?" This example illustrates the idea that the three terms are often used interchangeably. *Emotions* are often described as transient feeling states that manifest themselves in bodily changes related to action or antici-pated action. *Moods* are usually defined as states of mind predisposing to action; or sometimes as a prevailing attitude. Moods are often said to be emotions that last longer than expected, perhaps even weeks or months, although no one has provided definitive guidelines on what is an expected duration of any particular emotion. The term *affect* stems largely from the psychoanalytic tradition, and clinicians often use it to describe the so-called hedonic tone of an emotional state; that is, whether it has a positive (plea-surable) or negative (unpleasurable) quality. However, it must be empha-sized that there are no fixed, universally accepted definitions for these terms, so that, in practice, most psychologists will go on using them inter-changeably.

Summary ■

When researchers ask college students to identify emotion terms from various lists of words, there is good agreement on some words and poor agreement on others. It is likely that the reasons for the discrepancies include the ambiguity of some of the terms, the fact that many college students are not familiar with the terms, and the different experiences of the judges with language in general and emotions in particular. These findings suggest that the identification and meaning of emotion concepts should not depend entirely on naive judgments, but should, as in other sciences, depend upon their place within a theory.

An alternative approach to identifying the language of emotions, having a long history, is to assume the existence of a small number of basic or primary emotions, somewhat like the primary colors. Almost all theorists who have written on this subject agree that anger, fear, joy, and sadness should be considered to be basic emotions, while fair agreement exists on such emotions as disgust (contempt), surprise, and perhaps shame. The assumption of primary emotions implies the existence of secondary ones, or mixed emotions or blends, in order to explain the large number of emotion terms that exist in our language. However, identifying the components of the blends is not an easy task and more work needs to be done on this problem.

If one accepts the concept of primary emotions, the question arises of their relations to each other. Over the years, investigators have carried out a number of studies that indicate that a circle or a circumplex can best represent the relative similarity of the primary emotions. The emotion circumplex implies that certain emotions are relatively alike and others are quite dissimilar, and that certain emotions are bipolar. Perhaps the emotions can be thought of as fuzzy concepts separated by vague rather than sharp boundaries. Despite the lack of sharp boundaries, the prototypes underlying the basic emotions, at least, are well known. We may conclude that subjective experience is a useful guide to emotions, but not an infallible one.

Theories of Emotions

It is the great beauty of science that advancement in it, whether in a degree great or small, instead of exhausting the subject of research, opens the doors to further and more abundant knowledge, overflowing with beauty and utility.
—Michael Faraday

Goals of This Chapter

The first three chapters have examined a number of important issues. They have illustrated the many difficulties that beset the study of emotions, and have emphasized the need to consider emotion from a number of different vantage points. A preliminary review of definitions of emotion revealed the need to consider self-reports, behavior, and physiology, recognizing that any one of these domains is not a complete description of an emotion.

We saw too that a number of different historical traditions have focused attention on different ways to think about and study emotions. Adherents to each of these views have tended to go their own ways so that until fairly recently there has been relatively little cross-fertilization of ideas.

Despite these divergences, with few exceptions, there has been general agreement that some emotions are more basic or fundamental than others. There is also reasonably strong evidence that emotions have certain systematic relations to one another, and that a circumplex is at least a reasonable description of these relations.

Enough information has been given to enable us to begin to consider a number of contemporary perspectives on emotion. Such perspectives are often referred to as "theories," although that is perhaps too grandiose a term to use. In most cases, they refer to different ways of looking at the different aspects of emotion, and thus, in some cases at least, tend to be narrow in focus rather than broad.

A previous review of theories by Strongman (1988) has identified 30 different but overlapping approaches to understanding emotions. To attempt to cover all such approaches would be a difficult task and one that might end up producing more confusion than enlightenment. I have therefore selected those theories that I believe have had the most impact on the thinking of contemporary psychologists and/or those that have been most fully elaborated in publications. This does not mean that other theoretical contributions are not important; in fact, I will describe several other theories in the chapters that deal with the study of facial expressions and the study of brain function in emotion.

Important Questions Addressed In This Chapter

- What are some general characteristics of theories?
- What is the role of analysis and synthesis in theory construction?
- What does Tomkins mean by the expression *affects as amplifiers?*
- What is *differential emotions theory?*
- What is the evidence for the view that emotions are verbal labels given to states of arousal?
- In what sense is Lazarus's theory a cognitive theory of emotion?
- Why does the psychoanalyst Brenner consider subjective reports of affects unreliable?
- What is meant by Plutchik's concept of derivatives of emotion?
- What is the basic purpose of Ortony's cognitive theory of emotions?
- What is meant by the idea of emotion as a form of *action-readiness?*
- What is meant by the concept of emotion as a *readout* mechanism?

■   ■   ■   ■   ■   ■   ■

▌The Function of Theories

Some of the reasons for the difficulties in understanding emotions have already been discussed in an earlier chapter. These include the reluctance of behavioristic thinking to find a place for subjective feelings; the idiosyncratic nature of verbal reports of introspective states; the ethical problems of creating unpleasant emotion states in subjects in research settings; the problem of deception of self and others; the problem of relating research carried out with lower animals to humans; and the influence of tradition in stifling innovation.

Perhaps another reason for the confusions in the field is a lack of agreement on just what a theory of emotion is, or should be, and what a theory is not. A definition of emotion is important, but it is not a theory. Thus, when Skinner (1953) defines an emotion "as a particular state of strength or weakness in one or more responses induced by any one of a class of operations," this may or may not be a useful definition of emotions, but it is not a theory of emotion. When Izard (1972) says that "Emotion is a complex process that has neurophysiological, motor-expressive, and phenomenological aspects," this may be true, but it does not distinguish emotion from many other bodily processes—exercise, for example. Similarly, when neurophysiologists identify particular brain structures as being involved in emotion, the facts may be true or false, but knowing something about brain systems does not make a theory.

If we use the experience of other sciences as a guide, we recognize that a theory is generally a complex system of interrelated ideas. They involve multiple statements, assumptions, postulates, and hypotheses that deal with a certain range of observations and have at least four functions.

First, a theory should attempt to provide answers to a series of questions that scientists and laypeople alike ask about emotions, questions such as the following:

1. What is an emotion?
2. What produces emotions?
3. What functions do emotions have?
4. Can there be emotions without awareness?
5. How many emotions are there?
6. How can emotions be measured?
7. How universal are emotions?
8. Are emotions learned or innate?
9. Do infants have emotions?
10. What are the relations among emotions, cognitions, motivations, and personality?

The list is obviously incomplete, but an adequate theory attempts to provide answers to these and related questions.

Second, a theory should be a stimulator of research. It should suggest which questions are the most interesting or the most fundamental, and which variables are worth measuring. The data that research finds, even if surprising or unexpected, can be related to the key ideas of the theory. William James's theory, for example, stimulated considerable research on autonomic activity in humans and animals, and Cannon's theory stimulated research on brain systems involved in emotions.

The third function of theory is to predict new observations, things that no one thought of before or looked for. It is likely that this purpose of theory has been overstated. Theories in any field of science rarely predict entirely new observations. New facts come primarily from new experiments and new observations. Einstein's theory of relativity, when first formulated, predicted only two or three new possibilities (for example, the apparent displacement of the positions of certain stars as a result of the sun's gravitational field), but its value was great in accounting for known and puzzling phenomena in terms of a small number of new ideas.

A fourth function of theory sometimes overlooked is to show connections between apparently diverse areas. One example is the attempt to relate the psychophysics of color vision to the properties of retinal and brain neural systems. Another example is the attempt to relate autonomic physiology and brain chemistry to the states of pleasure and displeasure. To summarize these points, good theories should be sets of interrelated concepts that provide insight or understanding of existing facts, that stimulate research, that predict new observations, and that suggest connections between diverse areas of scientific research.

Theories in general try to account for a large number of observations in terms of a small number of basic concepts. These basic concepts usually refer to states or events whose properties are known only indirectly through a series of inferences. In psychoanalytic theory, concepts like libido, fixation, repression, or superego refer to hypothetical states whose properties are gradually derived on the basis of increasing evidence. In learning theory, such notions as reaction potential, and cognitive maps are also hypothetical constructs whose properties are inferred.

One other important aspect of theory construction is that the basic terms or constructs of a theory do not necessarily have to accord with common sense, so long as the experiences of common sense can ultimately be derived from them. To most scholars of the Middle Ages, Galileo's principle of inertia, that bodies will move in a straight line with constant speed unless a force is applied, seemed incomprehensible. The development of quantum physics at the turn of the century involved assumptions contrary to both common sense and well-established laws of mechanics. Yet the ultimate justification was the new-found ability to predict observed phenomena and to relate diverse observations.

Analysis and Synthesis

In most theories there is an attempt to conceive of a complex phenomenon as the result of the interaction of a variety of simple causes or units. In chemistry, the millions of naturally occurring substances are shown to result from the mixture of a relatively few kinds of elements, and these in turn result from the interaction of an even smaller number of units of matter. This process of reducing a compound or mixture to its elements is called analysis.

Freud (1935) has written that in psychiatry, "Our path has been like that of chemistry; the great qualitative differences between substances were traced back to quantitative variations in the proportions in which the same elements were combined." This idea of analyzing complex mixtures into simpler units is at the core of attempts by psychologists to find basic personality dimensions and basic personality types. The same path has been taken in trying to understand the phenomena of color mixture; the manifold colors of daily experience can be analyzed into combinations of a few basic primaries or pure colors. This process of analysis, however, is only part of the process of achieving understanding. If the analysis is an adequate one, it should be possible to recombine the units in suitable proportions and thereby reconstruct the original complex mixture.

This process of synthesis is illustrated by the mixture of three primary colors to match any other given color, or by chemists' combination of carbon, hydrogen, oxygen, and a few other elements to produce almost any organic substance. The same should be true of any psychological theory as well.

Analogy

In understanding any relatively unexplored area or one in which much disagreement prevails, it is often useful to proceed by analogy. Thus we use the known as a model to guide our thinking about the unknown. Physicist Robert Oppenheimer elaborated on this idea in the following way (1956):

> Whether or not we talk of discovery or of invention, analogy is inevitable in human thought, because we come to new things in science with what equipment we have, which is how we have learned to think, and above all how we have learned to think about the relatedness of things. We cannot, coming into something new, deal with it except on the basis of the familiar and the old-fashioned. . . . This is not to say that analogy is the criterion of truth. . . . But truth is not the whole thing; certitude is not the whole of science. Science is an immensely creative and enriching experience; and it is full of novelty and exploration; and it is in order to get to these that analogy is an indispensable instrument.

Reasoning by analogy was an important part of the development of the theory of evolution; and in chemistry, before the periodic table was developed, a very similar scheme called the law of octaves was proposed, based on analogy with musical scales.

Given these various proposals about what a theory is, and what its functions are, let us now consider a number of different theories of emotion.

▌Motivational Approaches to Emotion

Sylvan S. Tomkins: Affects as Amplifiers

Tomkins (1962, 1970) assumes that there are eight basic emotions (or affects, as he prefers to call them). The positive ones are *interest, surprise,* and *joy.* The negative ones are *anguish, fear, shame, disgust,* and *rage.* These basic emotions are "innately patterned responses" to certain types of stimuli and we express them through a wide variety of bodily reactions, particularly through facial responses. For each distinct affect, there are assumed to be specific *programs* stored in subcortical areas of the brain. There is therefore a genetic, species-related basis for the expression of the basic emotions.

Much of the theory's emphasis is on the distinctions between the affect system and the motivational system. Most psychologists take for granted the idea that motives, such as hunger and sex, strongly drive a person to action. In contrast, Tomkins believes that motives are primarily signals of bodily need and that emotions then amplify these signals. As an illustration, he points out that oxygen deprivation (anoxia) creates a need for oxygen, but the affect of fear creates the sense of urgency or panic. In World War II, pilots who neglected to wear oxygen masks at 30,000 feet suffered gradual oxygen deprivation. Although the need was present, the slow process of deprivation did not produce an awareness of the need, and no panic occurred. Without the emotion being present, the pilots took no action and lost their lives.

The affect system is more general than the drive system. Drives are primarily concerned with getting certain objects into or out of the body and tend to have a rhythmic pattern. Affects can become associated with almost any stimuli (through learning) and can exist for long or short periods of time. Affects are stronger than drives, according to Tomkins, since in order to get a person to act, all we need do is create an emotional state (for example, joy, anger, or shame), regardless of his or her state of drive. A person who is frightened by a car will run, regardless of whether he or she is hungry or thirsty.

Carroll E. Izard: Differential Emotions Theory

One of Tomkins's close collaborators has been Carroll Izard. In recent years, particularly in relation to the role of facial expressions in emotions, he has extended the theory that Tomkins first proposed.

Izard argues that theorists have directed too much attention to feedback from the autonomic nervous system as a major determinant of emotion. Instead, he proposes that affects are primarily facial responses. Patterns of facial reaction that we call emotional are assumed to have a neurological basis in subcortical *programs* for each emotion. Such programs are genetically based. "One does not learn to be afraid, or to cry, or to startle, any more than one learns to feel pain or to gasp for air. Of course, one does learn to fear specific things, to be angry or ashamed or excited under certain conditions" (Izard & Tomkins, 1966). Similarly, the idea of learned anxiety or learned depression is misleading. People do not learn to feel afraid or depressed; they only learn the cues that trigger reactions of anxiety or depression (Izard, 1972).

Following Tomkins, Izard states that there are several fundamental emotions from which all others can be combined. Sometimes he lists eight fundamental emotions, and sometimes ten. His longer list includes interest, joy, surprise, distress, anger, disgust, contempt, shame, guilt, and fear. Although many investigators have assumed that they have studied one or another of these emotions in isolation, Izard argues that this is unlikely. Discrete fundamental emotions probably occur rarely in the life of an individual.

To illustrate his ideas about the mixing or patterning of emotions, Izard examines the concept of anxiety. In 1966, he and Tomkins described *anxiety* as a disruptive affect that should simply be identified as fear. By 1972, however, Izard concluded that "anxiety" was a multidimensional concept that included the emotions of fear and two or more of the following emotions: distress, anger, shame, guilt, and interest (Izard, 1972). In addition, he claimed that love, hostility, and depression were also complex emotions.

Izard suggests that from an evolutionary point of view, it does not seem likely that an animal had to *think* before it could *feel.* In fact, in order to survive, an animal had to have emotional responses (such as fleeing or attacking) triggered by innate releasers, drives, or perceptions, as well as by cognitions. For example, the appearance of a certain color on the underside of the female will trigger the mating dance of the male stickleback fish. Izard would argue that no cognitive process is involved in this emotional reaction. Another illustration, frequently noted in clinical practice, is free-floating anxiety or objectless fear, which Izard interprets as emotion without a cognitive signal. In brief, "emotion (is) an experience defined not by a stimulus but by evolutionary-hereditary processes" (Izard, 1972).

Izard also has some important ideas about the appearance and development of emotions in infants (Buechler and Izard, 1983). What he calls basic or discrete emotions develop very early in infancy, and they each have a specific function; that is, they signal the infant's urgent needs for a caretaker. These emotional states are signaled by facial expressions, which Izard believes are tightly linked to emotional experience.

From Izard's point of view, emotions are only one part of the organization of personality. The other subsystems of personality include the homeostatic, the perceptual, the cognitive, and the motor systems. Although each system has some degree of independence, they are all complexly related.

In order to justify the idea of fundamental emotions, Izard lists a number of criteria which include the following: Fundamental emotions have: a specific neural basis; a specific facial expression; a distinct feeling; an origin in evolutionary-biologic processes; and a motivating property that serves adaptive functions (Izard, 1991).

No doubt, Izard has made some important contributions. He has reported experiments dealing with factors related to the matching of facial expressions and verbal labels, cross-cultural variables in emotion descriptions, and physiological indices of muscular patterns in the face, among others. He has developed a simple self-report adjective checklist that clinicians have used with various psychiatric populations. And he has stimulated a number of his colleagues to pursue research in this area.

▋Cognitive Approaches to Emotion

Stanley S. Schachter: Emotions as Verbal Labels of Arousal

In 1962, Stanley Schachter and his colleague Jerome Singer published a paper describing a cognitive approach to emotions that has had a major impact on the thinking of many psychologists. William James's view of emotions stated that our feelings of emotion were largely based upon the experiences we have of autonomic changes in our bodies. An implication of this view is that we base our experience of different emotions, such as sadness and anger, on different patterns of autonomic arousal for each emotion.

Since there is little evidence for such patterns, Schachter and Singer decided to try to identify the basis for the labeling of an emotional state in terms of the interpretation one makes of the situation he or she is in. However, still influenced by James, they added the assumption that a state of physiological arousal must also be present. According to these authors, one could interpret the same state of physiological arousal as joy or anger or any other emotional state, depending on his or her interpretation of the situation. This view assumes only one kind of physical excitement or arousal. For example, in this view, a man aroused because he was playing football would be in the same physiological state as one aroused because he was kissing his girlfriend.

What is the evidence for these views? The major study purporting to confirm them, published in 1962, described a rather complex deception experiment using college students as subjects. Since this study has been widely cited as providing proof of the theory, it will be instructive to describe it in some detail.

Several groups of college students were told during their participation in the experiment that they were given an injection of a new vitamin to determine its effects on vision. In reality, they were injected with adrenaline, which tends to produce an increase in heart rate as well as palpitations. The experimenter then exposed subjects in one group to a "euphoria" condition—that is, one in which a confederate of the experimenter ran around the room, played with paper airplanes, and acted silly. A rating was made of the extent to which the subject joined in the activity. In addition, subjects made self-ratings on their degree of *happiness* and *anger*. Subjects in another group were asked to complete an embarrassing questionnaire and were joined by a stooge instructed to act in an angry fashion. Behavior ratings of anger and self-ratings of *happiness* and *anger* were repeated. In some additional groups, experimenters told subjects to expect physical symptoms that in fact would never occur as a result of an injection of adrenaline. Some subjects were given an injection of saline (a placebo), which has no physical effects.

One surprising finding of the study was that the students' self-ratings showed that they were more *happy* in the anger situation than *angry*. Later, experimenters learned that this was because the students had been promised two extra points on their final exam for participating in the experiment, and they feared that if they reported their feelings of anger they would lose this credit. In this study, the subjects' self-ratings did not accurately reflect their emotional feelings.

When observers' behavior ratings were analyzed, no significant differences were found between the groups that received the injection of adrenaline and those that did not (placebo groups). Since this result was inconsistent with the expectations of the authors, they performed some further *internal analyses,* which consisted of eliminating certain subjects from the groups who had a tendency to explain away their physical reactions, the so-called *self-informed* subjects. With the groups thus changed, some significant differences were found.

Considering the number of subjects who were dropped from the experiment, it is interesting to look at this issue in more detail. Of the 185 original subjects, one refused to accept the injection, and 11 were so suspicious that their data were discarded. Twenty placebo subjects were found to have a decreased pulse rate and were dropped from the study. Sixteen subjects in the experimental conditions were considered to be *self-informed* and were dropped. One subject was dropped when the sound system went dead. Therefore, out of the original 185 subjects, only 136 were included in the final analyses, meaning the data from almost one out of every four subjects were not used.

Another questionable aspect of the experiment concerns the authors' use of heart rate as a measure of arousal. It has been shown by many authors (e.g., Lacey & Lacey, 1962) that heart rate has little correlation with other measures of arousal, such as blood pressure or skin resistance. It is also well known that certain stimulants (e.g., amphetamine) produce a decrease in pulse rate, whereas certain tranquilizers (e.g., chlorpromazine) produce an increase in heart rate (Goodman & Gilman, 1960). Therefore, heart rate is a poor measure of general bodily levels of arousal.

Harris and Katkin (1975) reached a similar conclusion after reviewing the literature on false feedback of autonomic information as factors in producing emotion. The evidence was equivocal but is at least consistent with the idea that "emotion is primarily a cognitive state, not dependent upon autonomic arousal." In other words, it is possible that emotions can be reported without evidence of arousal; conversely, it is also known that arousal can occur without evidence of emotions.

Despite the importance of the Schachter-Singer study in terms of the influence it has had on subsequent research, there are, apparently, no reports of its replication (Marshall and Zimbardo, 1979; Maslach, 1979; Reisenzein, 1983). However, the study is important in bringing attention to the role of cognitive factors—that is, a person's interpretations—in determining emotional states. In the real life of humans and animals, cognitive assessments of situations occur before the nervous system acts to release hormones into the blood. From the point of view of the chances for survival, it is highly unlikely that emotional behavior must await an evaluation of the echoes of arousal from the viscera.

George Mandler: Emotion as Cognition-Arousal Interaction

Another version of a cognition-arousal theory, similar in many respects to Schachter's views, was proposed by Mandler in his book *Mind and Emotion* (1975). In it he states that he is concerned with presenting a psychological concept of arousal as a basic explanatory term. A good deal of the book is concerned with the Jamesian chicken-and-egg problem of which comes first—the feeling of emotion or the state of autonomic arousal —and, like all the people who have tackled this problem, he arrives at no definitive conclusions.

Mandler's major assumption is that autonomic arousal "is a signal to the mental organization for attention, alertness, and scanning of the environment." Furthermore, arousal may be produced either as a result of a "preprogrammed automatic release of the autonomic nervous system" by stimulation or as a result of a "meaning analysis," that is, an appraisal or an interpretation of the situation. In one place, Mandler's views seem to echo those of William James, in that perception of arousal is assumed to produce emotional experience. In another, he appears to accept the alternative position that "cognitive evaluations and arousal . . . are necessarily contemporaneous."

One of Cannon's important criticisms of James is that autonomic responses are very much slower than introspective responses of emotional states. Mandler admits that this implies that emotional responses can occur in the absence of arousal, which is contrary to his theory. In order to deal with this problem he tentatively suggests the possibility of the existence of *autonomic images,* which provide some kind of temporal bridge between the onset of the environmental event and the feeling of the emotion.

Mandler argues that the autonomic nervous system is a signal system that enters into the evaluation of situations. This is of doubtful relevance to emotion since autonomic changes are slow, diffuse, fairly generalized, and often not available to introspection. There is evidence that many autonomic responses such as skin resistance, blood pressure, or muscle tension cannot even be subjectively discriminated.

Mandler himself cites evidence that individuals may easily be misled about their own levels of arousal. People can be led to believe that arousal exists when in fact it does not. Conversely, they can believe that arousal has not occurred when objective measurements of the autonomic nervous system show that it has. The studies of false feedback of autonomic indices indicate the extent to which reports of arousal may be manipulated. In addition, studies of placebo effects have provided reports of emotional states in the absence of autonomic arousal. Finally, the extensive psychopharmacological literature indicates that many drugs that can pass the blood/brain barrier can have profound effects on emotional feelings and behaviors without having any effects on the autonomic nervous system. Therefore, it is unlikely that variations in the level of arousal of the autonomic nervous system play an important role in the subjective report of an emotional state of a human, or in the appearance of emotional behavior in a lower organism.

Andrew Ortony, Gerald Clore, and Allan Collins: The Cognitive Structure of Emotions

Every theorist recognizes that emotions are typically triggered by events, but relatively little attention has been given to a precise analysis of the triggers of emotion, and of the interpretations or cognitions associated with these triggers. In the book by Ortony, Clore, and Collins called *The Cognitive Structure of Emotions*, the authors attempt to evaluate the contribution that cognition makes to emotion. They pay no attention to the role of physiology, behavior, or expressions not because they consider these facets of emotion unimportant, but because they wish to study an earlier point in the emotion chain, the cognitions. They "seek to bring some semblance of order to what remains a very confused and confusing field of study."

The authors base their approach on the assumption that emotions arise as a result of certain cognitions or interpretations. The emotion itself is a subjective feeling or experience that human adults can report in words. In other words, the theory the writers propose assumes that emotions are reportable feelings, expressed by language and self-reports.

Ortony, Clore, and Collins point out that we use four kinds of evidence to understand emotions. First is the language of emotion as recorded in dictionaries; but a theory of emotion is not the same as a theory of the language of emotion. The emotion language is often ambiguous and metaphorical, a function of history and culture. The second is self-report, which, although subject to many pressures to avoid revealing true inner states, is still assumed to be the best way to get at them. The third is behavior or expressive displays, which have been a central focus of many psychologists and ethologists. And the last kind of evidence is physiological reactions. Ortony, Clore, and Collins are interested in only the first two types of evidence for their cognitive theory.

In the theory itself, these authors distinguish between an *emotion type* and *emotion tokens*. An emotion type is a distinct family of closely related emotions that have the same basic eliciting conditions. Thus, for example, *fear* is an emotion type, while words like *happy, hate, pity,* and *remorse* are tokens representing different types. Fear is presumably a type because it is dependent on the interpretation of certain events as having undesirable consequences for oneself.

The theory assumes that three aspects of the world determine our cognitions: *events, agents,* and *objects*. Events are people's interpretations of things that happen. Objects are simply objects, while agents are things (usually people) that can cause or contribute to events. Emotions are considered to be a kind of chain reaction, which always begins with a strong positive or negative reaction to the consequences of events, or the actions of agents, or some aspect of objects. Thus, one may feel pleased or displeased about the consequences of some event; one can approve or disapprove the action of a person; and one can like or dislike an object. To carry the illustration further, if one approves the action of an agent, and if the agent were oneself, one's emotional feeling or attribution would be pride. If the agent were someone else, one might feel admiration. If one disapproved of oneself, one would feel shame, while if one disapproved of someone else, one would feel reproach. Similar kinds of analyses are given for terms like gloating, relief, disappointment, and anger. In this connection, love is simply described as liking some aspect of an object. Other examples are:

joy = pleased about a desirable event
distress = displeased about an undesirable event
pity = displeased about an event presumed to be undesirable for someone else
resentment = displeased about an event presumed to be desirable for
    someone else

These authors add the following ideas. The fundamental description of emotion is based on subjective experience or feeling. The cognitive or appraisal mechanism does not have to be conscious. In other words, a person may have a feeling of fear without knowing what cognitions this fear is based on. From a functional point of view, these authors suggest that one function of emotion is to focus attention on the emotion-inducing event and to prepare the individual for action, should action be necessary.

The type of study this theory generates has been described in Chapter 2. Concerned in part with the types of labels students give to certain types of cognitive events, the theory seems to imply that emotions require a high level of abstract thinking such as is found in adults. Whether the theory could apply to children or animals is simply not discussed.

Richard S. Lazarus: A Cognitive-Motivational-Relational Theory of Emotion

Lazarus has been concerned during much of his career (Lazarus, 1966; Lazarus and Folkman, 1984) with the relations between stress and coping in adults. This research gradually led him to realize that stress and coping are part of a larger area of study—the emotions. In 1991, he published a book, *Emotion and Adaptation*, that describes his beliefs about the relations among all these domains.

He points out that the study of emotion must include the study of cognition, motivation, adaptation, and physiological activity. Emotions involve appraisals of the environment and of the individual's relationships with others, and attempts at coping with them. Lazarus therefore refers to his theory as a "cognitive-motivational-relational system of explanation," with the focus being on the person-environment relationship.

The central idea of the theory is the concept of *appraisal*, which refers to a decision-making process that evaluates the personal harms and benefits existing in each person-environment interaction. *Primary appraisals* concern the relevance of the interaction for one's goals, the extent to which the situation is goal congruent (that is, thwarting or facilitating of personal goals), and the extent of one's own ego-involvement (or degree of commitment). *Secondary appraisals* decide on blame or credit, one's own coping potential, and future expectations. This view sees emotions as discrete categories, each of which can be placed on a dimension from weak to strong. It recognizes that several emotions can occur at the same time, because of the multiple motivations and goals involved in any particular encounter. It also implies that each emotion involves a specific action tendency such as anger with attack, fear with escape, shame with hiding and so forth.

A key ingredient of his concept of *secondary appraisal* is the idea of *coping*, which refers to ways to manage and interpret conflicts and emotions. According to Lazarus, there are two general types of coping processes. The first is called problem-focused coping, which deals with conflicts by direct action designed to change the relationship (e.g., fighting if threatened). The second is called emotion-focused (or cognitive) coping, which deals with conflicts by reinterpreting the situation (e.g., denial in the face of threat). The concept of appraisal implies nothing about rationality, deliberateness, or consciousness.

Another important aspect of Lazarus's theory is the concept of *core relational themes*. A core relational theme is defined as the central harm or benefit that occurs in each emotional encounter. For example, the core relational theme for anger is "a demeaning offense against me and mine;" for guilt it is "having transgressed a moral imperative;" and for hope it is "fearing the worst but yearning for better." One implication of these ideas is that emotion always involves cognition. As Shakespeare said, "There is nothing either good or bad but thinking makes it so."

A question sometimes raised is whether appraisal is necessary for all emotional reactions, or whether emotions can occur without appraisal. Lazarus discusses this at some length and concludes that "appraisal is a necessary and sufficient cause of the emotions, and that the emergence of different emotions in infants and young children at different ages reflects the growth of understanding about self and world." This argument, he believes, applies to lower animals as well.

Another issue that sometimes arises is whether we need to understand the brain in order to be able to understand emotions. Lazarus believes that a case can be made for the opposite view; that is, that we need to understand how people and animals act and react (the mind), in order to understand the functioning of the brain.

A third issue that has been raised about emotions is whether cultural groups can experience an emotion that they do not have a specific word for. For example, because the Tahitians have few words for sadness or loneliness, does it imply that they do not experience these emotions? Lazarus believes that cultures experience the key relationships underlying all emotions whether or not they have a word for them. In other words, emotions are primarily psychobiological and not so much linguistic phenomena.

Lazarus tries to show the relevance of his ideas about emotions to child development, health psychology and psychopathology. He concludes by saying, "Although everyone seems to assume that emotion is irrational, quite the contrary [is true]; emotion depends on reason." His fundamental premise is that "in order to survive and flourish, animals (especially humans) are constructed biologically so that they are constantly engaged in evaluations (appraisals) of their changing relationships with the environment." Appraisals involve detection and evaluation of the relevant adaptational conditions of living that require action. These appraisals determine the emotional state.

Lazarus's theory is important because it directs attention to an aspect of emotion, the cognition, that others have overlooked or minimized. No one has ever explicitly denied that a perception or a cognition is necessary to trigger the sequence of events that result in emotion; few however, have tried to manipulate stimulus conditions systematically as he has done in his research, in order to identify variables that affect the cognition. Strictly speaking, there is no such thing as a cognitive psychology, any more than there is such a thing as an autonomic nervous system psychology or a feeling state psychology. All these types of variables or measures enter into the complex state called an emotion, and one can ignore any aspect only at the risk of losing the phenomenon entirely. An important value of Lazarus's theory is that it does not present an oversimplified view of emotions but points to many of the complex issues that require research and new theory.

Psychoanalytic Approaches to Emotions

Almost all psychoanalysts are clinicians engaged in the private practice of psychoanalysis. Their writings are not concerned with experimental evidence, but with theoretical consistency and relevance to therapeutic practice. Although the case histories that analysts describe in their writings are filled with references to emotions, there have been relatively few attempts to develop a psychoanalytic theory of the emotions (or the *affects* as they prefer to call them). Several of the more recent contributions will be described.

Sandor Rado: A Theory of Emergency Affects

Sandor Rado was trained in Europe as a psychoanalyst but spent many years of his life as director of a major psychoanalytic training center in the United States. Although his background of training in psychoanalysis is orthodox, he has made innovative contributions to analytic theory, particularly in the area of affects.

Like most other analysts, Rado emphasizes the idea that emotions are states of the individual that are inferred on the basis of various kinds of evidence. These include overt behavior in the therapy situation, free associations, dreams, and life history. He points out, however, that making inferences about another person's feelings depends in part, at least, on empathy and emotional resonance. It is often possible to infer the existence of an emotion in another individual, even though that person cannot report its existence. The nonreporting of affect is due, presumably, to the process of repression, but even in such a case the repressed emotion may continue to exert an influence on the patient's actions and thoughts.

Rado says that at least seven important affect patterns may be identified. These patterns include escape, combat, submission, defiance, brooding, expiation, and self-damage, among others (Rado, 1956).

Rado then proceeds to develop a multilevel theory of emotion based on evolutionary considerations. He hypothesizes that there are four psychological levels of integration or control. The first, called the hedonic level, refers simply to the effects of pleasure and pain in organizing and selecting forms of behavior. We find this primitive mode of control in all organisms, even the very lowest. Its effect is to move an individual toward a source of pleasure and away from a cause of pain. In primitive organisms with limited sensory capacities, signals of pleasure or pain result only from direct contact. Contact with a *good* object, such as food, leads to absorption or incorporation of the source of pleasure with a consequent engorgement or swelling of the organism. He writes, "The most primitive manifestation of this tendency of the organism is to absorb literally the cause or source of pleasure by incorporation. Think of the one-celled animal engulfing food and of the baby trying to put everything it can into its mouth. In the human being, this expression of the tendency to absorb pleasure changes into a tendency to absorb pleasure by holding onto the source of the pleasure. Yet another aspect of the pleasure-absorption principle is the reaction of the organism when the pleasure is lost or taken away from him. The deprivation elicits a readily discernible behavior tendency, the need to recapture the lost source" (Rado, 1969).

Contact with a *bad* or dangerous object usually leads to pain, which is simply a primitive, emergency signal indicating that injury has already occurred. "This signal arrangement, developed at an early stage of evolutionary history, is the very basis upon which the entire organization of emergency behavior has evolved" (Rado, 1969).

Just as the effect of pleasure is to produce an *incorporation* response, the effect of pain is to produce a *riddance* response. These responses are illustrated by primitive reflexes designed to eliminate pain-causing agents already incorporated. For example, spitting, vomiting, or diarrhea have the effect of eliminating foreign bodies from the gastrointestinal system. Other examples of riddance reflexes are sneezing, coughing, and shedding tears.

Rado assumes that *mental pain* or anticipated pain may precipitate riddance behavior just as readily as does bodily pain, but the attempts at riddance are less effective and may even be pathological. For example, the defense mechanism of repression is a form of riddance response and acts to exclude painful thoughts or emotions from awareness. Some psychotic patients in delusional states have been known to suddenly remove a vital organ (e.g., eye or genital organ) through self-multilation but have perceived this riddance as a way of avoiding painful sights or feelings. Rado concludes his thesis about pleasure and pain in the following words: "Hedonic self-regulation, which may have appeared already in the organization of the protozoan, has remained basic to the life process at all subsequent stages of evolutionary history, including man. Despite the complications introduced through the emergence and development of higher levels of integration, the human organism, like all other animal organisms, is a biologic system that operates under hedonic regulation. . . . All behavior is probably guided by the sensations or feelings of pleasure and pain" (Rado, 1969).

Rado calls the second level of integration the brute-emotional level. As organisms evolved distance receptors with a corresponding development of the central nervous system, they also evolved new ways to organize and select patterns of behavior. These new methods of control are the basic emotions of fear, rage, love, and grief. Just as pleasure and pain move the organism toward or away from stimuli in the environment, these emotions provide a more controlled way to do the same thing. For example, fear will organize patterns of combat or attack. These emotions create the possibility of anticipation of future events, since an animal that evaluates an environmental event as threatening may fearfully run away or angrily attack. In a sense, the overt behavior amplifies whatever feeling states exist in the organism.

Rado calls the third level of integration the emotional-thought level, and it is associated with a notable increase in encephalization of the brain. In this level of control, emotions are more restrained and more mixed. Derivative emotions appear, such as apprehension, annoyance, jealousy, and envy. The goal of ruling and exploiting replaces the goal of destruction associated with anger. Defense mechanisms such as repression become used more frequently. The number of emotions exhibited is much greater than four basic ones.

The fourth level of regulation of action Rado calls the unemotional-thought level. This level involves the mastery of events by rational, intellectual means alone. The key elements of such mastery are foresight and postponement of reaction. Reason can overrule the evaluation of events that immediate feelings of pleasure or pain determine, and can lead an individual to engage in painful means designed to achieve pleasurable goals. We see this, for example, when adults tolerate painful dental surgery for the purpose of having healthy or beautiful teeth. However, Rado explicitly makes the point that "an unemotional human being has never existed and cannot exist. Control of emotion is another matter. . . ." Rado then defines emotion as "the preparatory signal that prepares the organism for emergency behavior. . . . The goal of this behavior is to restore the organism to safety" (Rado, 1969).

As a practicing psychoanalyst, Rado sees these ideas as meaningful only in relation to their role in the treatment of patients. He therefore writes at some length about the practical implications of his views and claims that disordered behavior is fundamentally an overreaction. A person who experiences pain, fear, rage, or other emergency emotions tries to get rid of the cause by withdrawal, submission, or combat. These emergency reactions often do not work, and instead create an extreme, somewhat rigid style of behavior.

Rado's conceptions of emotions are original and thought-provoking, evidently influenced by Cannon's ideas on fight and flight as emergency reactions. Some of Rado's ideas are like those of Darwin's, as when Rado writes about the social communication value of emotions. But fundamentally he writes within the Freudian tradition that acknowledges the existence of unconscious and mixed emotions whose characteristics can only be inferred on the basis of indirect evidence.

Charles Brenner: Affect as Hedonic State Plus Idea

Charles Brenner is a well-known psychoanalyst and a former president of the American Psychoanalytic Association. His work is strongly based on classical psychoanalytic thinking, and his theoretical proposals have only cautiously moved away from this traditional body of concepts.

Brenner points out that Freud's theory of affects was largely limited to anxiety and that Freud's focus was on emotions as processes of motor discharge. In recent years, psychoanalysts have become increasingly concerned with so-called "ego psychology" and have tried to clarify the role of ideas in relation to action. Brenner's aim is to develop a theory of affects that is congruent with contemporary ego psychology.

Like all psychoanalysts, Brenner believes that conscious, subjective reports of emotions (affects) are often unreliable. This is simply because most affect states are characterized by mixtures of both pleasant and unpleasant feelings, as well as expectations or memories of both good and bad events. Such ambivalences are the rule rather than the exception. In addition, part or all of these affects may be repressed or modified, and thus a conscious report is seldom what it seems. As an example, Brenner states that the idea of overcoming a rival may produce a feeling of pleasure and triumph, but may also involve a feeling of pity or compassion for the rival and an expectation of punishment for having defeated him or her (Brenner, 1974). The only way these complex mixtures can be unraveled, according to Brenner, is by the analytic method; that is, by the observation of the patient's behavior in the treatment setting, by his or her free associations, by his or her dreams, and by his or her past history.

In order to relate affects to ego psychology, Brenner defines an affect as "a sensation of pleasure, unpleasure, or both, plus the ideas, both conscious and unconscious, associated with that sensation" (Brenner, 1974). From this point of view, anxiety is a feeling of unpleasure associated with certain specific ideas of danger. He distinguishes between the different words related to anxiety in terms of the intensity of the unpleasure or the degree of certainty of the danger. For example, if the danger is imminent, the affect is called *fear*. If the unpleasure is intense, the affect is labeled as *panic*. If the unpleasure is mild and the danger uncertain, the affect is described as *worry*. These ideas are summarized in Table 4.1, which is based on Brenner's descriptions.

Once an individual develops an unpleasant affect such as anxiety, for whatever reason, certain consequences follow. In accord with the operation of the so-called pleasure principle, he or she attempts to reduce the degree of unpleasure either by actions such as withdrawal from the situation or by unconscious mental operations called *ego defenses*. Examples of ego defenses are repression, by which the individual becomes unaware of the unpleasant feelings; denial, which essentially ignores the existence of the event; and displacement, which deflects the affect toward nonthreatening objects.

Brenner goes on to point out that the theory that applies to anxiety as an affect also applies to the affect of depression. Whereas anxiety is defined as feelings of unpleasure connected with the idea that something bad is about to happen, depression is defined as feelings of unpleasure associated

Table 4.1	Labeling of Affects in Terms of Hedonic Tone and Idea	
Label	**Hedonic Tone**	**Idea**
Anxiety	Unpleasure	Danger
Fear	Unpleasure	Imminent danger
Panic	Intense unpleasure	Imminent danger
Worry	Mild unpleasure	Uncertain danger
Sadness	Unpleasure	Object loss or physical injury
Loneliness	Unpleasure	Longing for lost object
Despair	Unpleasure	No hope of relief from loss
Misery	Intense unpleasure	No hope of relief from loss
Discontent	Mild unpleasure	No hope of relief from loss
Shame	Unpleasure	Public defeat or failure
Embarrassment	Mild unpleasure	Public defeat or failure
Happiness	Pleasure	Fantasy or experience of gratification
Ecstasy	Intense pleasure	Fantasy or experience of instinctual gratification
Triumph	Pleasure	Defeat of rival

Source: C. Brenner, 1974.

with the idea that something bad has already happened. The something bad "may be a narcissistic injury or humiliation; it may be a person or other object one has lost; it may be a bad deed one has committed or a brutal punishment one is suffering; it may involve physical pain, mental anguish or both" (Brenner, 1975). Brenner does state that the experience of loss need not be based upon a real loss; even a fantasied loss may bring about the affect of depression.

In regard to depression as well as anxiety, the appearance of the affect triggers some kind of ego defense such as repression, denial , or projection. These defenses function to reduce the feelings of unpleasure. However, since ego defenses are seldom completely efficient in reducing a danger or a loss, the final result is always a compromise between the affect and the reaction to the affect (the defense). A symptom, such as a phobia, or a personality trait, such as submissiveness, may express the compromise.

These ideas are represented schematically in Figure 4.1. The perception of a situation as dangerous or as implying a personal loss leads to the development of the affects of anxiety or depression or both. Because these affects are unpleasant, various ego defenses (depending on the individual's personal history) then begin to act, to reduce the feelings of unpleasure. Since most defenses are not entirely successful, a compromise results. The compromise involves the formation either of a symptom or of a character trait.

What are some of the practical, clinical implications of these views? For one thing, Brenner insists that there is no such thing as free-floating, or contentless, anxiety. "When a patient complains of anxiety, but has no conscious knowledge of what it is that he fears, analysts assume that the nature of his fear, the 'something bad' that is about to happen, as well as all the other associated ideas are unconscious. They assume that it is repression and other defenses that are responsible for the fact that the patient himself is unable to say what it is he fears, to give any content to his anxiety" (Brenner, 1975). Second, in line with the theory that affects trigger ego defenses that function to minimize the unpleasant affect, the presence of overt anxiety or depression indicates a failure of defense. It means that the individual has been unsuccessful in reducing the unpleasant affect. This condition implies that the therapist should examine the problem of why

Figure 4.1

A Psychoanalytic Point of View of the Sequence of Events Involving Affects and Their Consequences

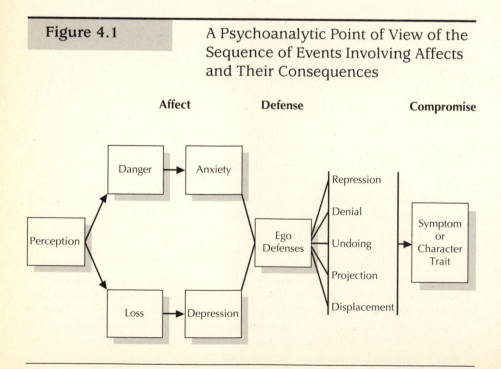

the ego defenses are not working. Such an examination may provide insights into personality dynamics that the therapist may not otherwise recognize. A third implication of Brenner's views relates to the use of the term depression. He points out that it has been used in two different senses: (1) as an affect state and (2) as a diagnostic label. The diagnostic label of depression refers to a heterogenous group of symptoms, conflicts, and origins. The therapist should try to separate the role of danger from that of object loss and should try to identify the defenses and personality traits that reflect the compromises individuals make in handling the vicissitudes of life.

Brenner's concept of affects as hedonic states plus ideas is an important addition to the psychoanalytic literature. It leads to new insights about the role of ego defenses, as well as some practical therapeutic ideas.

▌Evolutionary Approaches to Emotions

The theory of evolution has been described as one of the most important ideas in biology. It has had a major impact on the thinking not only of biologists but on investigators in the physical and social sciences as well. As Darwin recognized, evolution implied changes in both physical structures and mental (or behavioral) systems. This is why Darwin began observations of emotional expressions in lower animals and humans and why he wrote his classic book, *The Expression of the Emotions in Man and Animals*, after writing *On the Origin of Species* and *The Descent of Man*.

Evolutionary ideas have gradually entered the thinking of psychologists concerning the nature of emotions. These include the idea that emotions are forms of communication signals that have adaptive or survival value. It also includes the notion that certain basic or primary emotions may interact to produce the great varieties we see in social encounters. The implications of these and other ideas are apparent in several contemporary theories of emotion. In this context, three theories will be reviewed.

Ross Buck: Emotion as Communication and Readout

Buck has tried to understand emotions from the point of view of communication theory. He describes his views most fully in *The Communication of Emotion*, published in 1984. Communication theory implies that emotions are meaningful primarily in the context of a system involving the interaction between a sender and a receiver. When emotions occur, an emotional state is encoded in the central nervous system and expressed or sent by means of facial expressions, sounds, or gestures. The receiver attends to these signals, decodes them, and uses the information received in accord with his or her own motivational or emotional state.

Buck considers motivation and emotion to be two aspects of the same underlying processes. Both are concerned with bodily adaptation and maintenance of homeostasis, both involve some external expression of inner states, and both can be directly accessed by subjective experience. The purpose of the motivational/emotional system is to facilitate social coordination through communication of states and intentions. Contrary to the theory of William James, and consistent with that of Walter Cannon, Buck believes that subjective experience is not based on feedback from the autonomic system, but is based largely on a *readout* of neurochemical activity in certain regions of the brain. This idea is derived from the evolutionary argument "that it is useful for a creature with significant cognitive capacities to have direct knowledge of the state of certain of its own neurochemical systems associated with motivational/emotional states, just as it is useful for a social animal to have knowledge of certain of the motivational/emotional states of its fellows."

Social animals need to be able to communicate states of fear, anger, and sexual interest in order to accomplish their goals. And if the social system is to run smoothly, the individuals toward whom these communications are directed must be able to understand them correctly most of the time. In the course of evolution, certain displays become ritualized as a way of sending information in an easily recognized way. For example, some ethologists believe that the evolution of eyebrows in primates functions to accentuate the eyebrow-raise associated with surprise or interest . It has also been suggested that the complex set of facial muscles has evolved to increase the effectiveness of emotional communication.

Buck proposes that there are three types or aspects of emotion. The first is the maintenance of homeostasis; the second is the expression of displays; and the third is the subjective experience. He suggests that each aspect of emotion should be interpreted as an ongoing progress report or readout of the state of certain brain systems. These readouts make the individual aware of needs for food, water, or air, and of his or her impulses toward fight or flight. Such awareness allows a person to anticipate homeostatic problems before they occur.

This communication theory of emotion assumes that cognitive processes are clearly involved in all emotional interactions. Individuals label or appraise stimuli on the basis of past experience and present circumstances, which in turn affects the quality of the subjective feelings that result. Display rules, defined by a given culture or subgroup, influence the extent to which subjective feelings become expressed in overt behavior.

The basic model that Buck proposes follows: External stimuli interact with the motivational/emotional system and with relevant previous learning. The cognitive system of the brain appraises and labels the emotional state. The appraisal process is also influenced by one's homeostatic states, one's expressive tendencies, and one's subjective experience. Display rules then determine to what extent the emotional/motivational state becomes expressed in terms of self-reports, goal-directed behavior, and bodily expressions. Experimental work based on the theory has been concerned mainly with the communication and recognition of emotional displays.

Nico H. Frijda: Emotion as Action Readiness Change

In a book called *The Emotions* (1980), Nico Frijda, a Dutch psychologist, has presented a theory of emotion. He begins with a number of principles:

1. Emotions have a biological basis; emotions involve both bodily activity and impulses; and emotions occur in animals as well as humans.
2. Emotions in humans are influenced to various degrees by cognitive factors that may not operate in animals; such factors are norms, values, and self-awareness.
3. The presence of emotions in both humans and animals is invariably associated with efforts at inhibition and control, or, more generally, with regulation.
4. Emotions differ in terms of mode of activation, in terms of kind of action tendency, and in terms of autonomic response.
5. Different emotions—that is, different action tendencies— are initiated by different stimulus configurations, as an individual interprets them.
6. Emotions are evoked by events that are of significance to the life of an individual.

Although Frijda's theory has these diverse aspects, he tends to think of it as a cognitive theory because of the emphasis placed on his analysis of the cognitive emotion process. He points out that when an individual is confronted with a stimulus event, an internal *analyzer* codes the event in terms of known events. A *comparator* then judges whether the event is relevant to the individual's interests. A *diagnoser* then appraises the situation in terms of what the individual can or cannot do about it. An *evaluator* then judges the urgency or seriousness of the situation. This is followed by an *action proposer*, which generates a plan for action, or action tendency. Depending upon the nature of the action tendency, a physiological change generator produces bodily changes of an appropriate sort. Finally, in the last step, overt action is selected. It should be evident that this sequence is a list of hypothetical cognitive process, for which little direct evidence exists.

From Frijda's perspective, emotions are defined as changes in readiness for action, or changes in readiness for modifying or establishing relationships with the environment. Emotions deal with concerns related to the satisfactions of the individual.

Where does emotional experience enter this theory? Frijda proposes that emotional experience consists mainly of an awareness of action readiness, such as impulses to run, attack, or embrace. Although learning has a major effect on the connection among stimuli and emotional experience and behavior, in many instances there is an innate stimulus-response connection that is based on neural programs within the brain.

Frijda offers several other ideas about emotions. One idea is that the change in action readiness that defines an emotional state generally occurs in response to emergencies or interruptions. Another is that *flexibility* of reaction pattern and ability to *inhibit or control* behavior are essential features of emotion. These factors are what help distinguish between the emotions of a human being and the more limited emotions of an ant. However, since flexibility and inhibitory control are not all-or-none attributes, we cannot clearly say just where in evolution emotions begin.

Frijda's account of emotions is a functionalist theory. Emotions have a purpose; they act to deal with emergency issues related to life's satisfactions, and they do this by evaluating the relevance of events and organizing appropriate action. When emotions appear not to be functional, as in drug addiction or suicide, Frijda's interpretation is that such disturbances reflect the limits of capacity of the emotion system. Finally, Frijda points out that because emotions evolved to deal with emergencies, it is a fast-reacting system based on a minimum amount of information processing. Consequently, the emotion system occasionally makes mistakes and generates emotion when none is required or generates an emotion that is inappropriate for a given situation. However, in the long run, considering the size of the risks, there is reasonably successful adaptation.

Robert Plutchik: A Psychoevolutionary Theory of Emotions

The psychoevolutionary theory of emotions was first described in a paper in 1958 (Plutchik, 1958). It has been further elaborated in *The Emotions: Fact, Theories and a New Model* (1962), and in *Emotion: A Psychoevolutionary Synthesis* (1980), as well as in many papers. The theory has at least six fundamental postulates as described in Table 4.2.

Table 4.2	Basic Propositons of a Psychoevolutionary Theory of Emotions

1. Emotions are communication and survival mechanisms based on evolutionary adaptations.

2. Emotions have a genetic basis.

3. Emotions are hypothetical constructs based on various classes of evidence.

4. Emotions are complex chains of events with stabilizing feedback loops that produce some kind of behavioral homeostasis.

5. The relation among emotions can be represented by a three-dimensional structural model.

6. Emotions are related to a number of derivative conceptual domains.

Source: R. Plutchik, 1983.

The first postulate, that emotions are communication and survival mechanisms, is a direct reflection of the Darwinian, ethological tradition. Darwin (1872/1965) pointed out that emotions have two functions for all animals. First, they increase the chances of individual survival through appropriate reactions to emergency events in the environment (by flight, for example). Second, they act as signals of intentions of future action through display behaviors of various kinds (Enquist, 1985).

Evolutionary theory assumes that the natural environment creates survival problems for all organisms that must be successfully dealt with if they are to survive. These problems include, for example, differentially responding to prey and predators, food and mates, and care givers and care solicitors. Emotions can be conceptualized as basic adaptive patterns that can be identified at all phylogenetic levels that deal with these basic survival issues. Emotions are the ultraconservative evolutionary behavioral adaptations (such as amino acids, DNA, and genes) that have been successful in increasing the chances of survival of organisms. They have therefore been maintained in functionally equivalent forms through all phylogenetic levels (Plutchik, 1962, 1970, 1980a, 1980b, 1991).

The second postulate, that emotions have a genetic basis, stems directly from the psychoevolutionary context. Darwin (1872/1965) first suggested at least four types of evidence one can use for establishing a genetic basis for emotions. First, he noted that some emotional expressions appear in similar form in many lower animals (for example, the apparent increase in body size during rage or agonistic interactions due to erection of body hair or feathers, changes in postures, or expansion of air pouches). Second, some emotional expressions appear in infants in the same form as in adults (smiling and frowning, for example). Third, some emotional expressions are shown in identical ways by those born blind as by those who are normally sighted (pouting and laughter, for example). And fourth, some emotional expressions appear in similar form in widely separated races and groups of humans (Eibl-Eibesfeldt, 1975; Ekman & Friesen, 1971).

Recent genetic studies comparing monozygotic (i.e., twins resulting from a single fertilized egg) and dizygotic twins (twins resulting from two separately fertilized eggs), cross-adoption studies, and other methods have revealed hereditary contributions to such temperamental (emotional) qualities as aggressiveness (Fuller, 1986; Wimer & Wimer, 1985), timidity or fearfulness (Goddard &Beilharz, 1985), assertiveness (Loehlin, Horn, & Williams, 1981), and shyness (Stevenson-Hinde & Simpson, 1982), as well as many others.

Genetic theory indicates that individuals do not inherit behavior per se but only the structural and physiological mechanisms that mediate behavior. Genes influence thresholds of sensitivity, perceptual inclinations, cellular structures, and biochemical events. They determine epigenetic rules that act as filters limiting the kind of information allowed into the system and how that information is to be processed. For example, most animals appear to have auditory detectors tuned to signals that are of special significance for their survival (Lumsden & Wilson, 1981). Most, but not all, emotional expressions are based on genetic templates or schemata that determine the generality of emotional development and reactions to probable events in the environment (Plutchik, 1983).

The third basic postulate of the psychoevolutionary theory of emotion is that emotions are hypothetical constructs or inferences based on various classes of evidence. The kinds of evidence we use to infer the existence of emotions include (1) knowledge of stimulus conditions, (2) knowledge of an organism's behavior in a variety of settings, (3) knowledge of what species' typical behavior is, (4) knowledge of how an organism's peers react to it, and (5) knowledge of the effect of an individual's behavior on others (Plutchik,1980a). One of the more important reasons that emotional states are difficult to define unequivocally is that more than one emotion can occur at the same time. Any given overt display of emotion can reflect such complex states as approach and avoidance, attack and flight, sex and aggression, or fear and pleasure.

The fourth basic postulate of the theory is that emotions are complex chains of events with stabilizing loops that tend to produce some kind of behavioral homeostasis. Figure 4.2 illustrates this idea. Emotions are triggered by various events. These events must be cognitively evaluated as being of significance to the well-being or integrity of the individual. If such a determination is made, various feelings as well as a pattern of physiological changes will result. These physiological changes have the character of anticipatory reactions associated with various types of exertions or impulses, such as the urge to explore, to attack, to retreat, or to mate. Depending on the relative strengths of these various impulses, a final vectorial resultant will occur in the form of overt action that is designed to have an effect on the stimulus that triggered this chain of events in the first place. For example, distress signals by a puppy or the crying of an infant will increase the probability that the mother or a mother-substitute will arrive on the scene. The overall effect of this complex feedback system is to reduce the threat or to change the emergency situation in such a way as to achieve a temporary behavioral homeostatic balance.

The fifth postulate of the theory suggests that the relations among emotions can be represented by a three-dimensional structural model shaped like a cone as shown in Figure 4.3. The vertical dimension represents the intensity of emotions, the circle defines degree of similarity of emotions, and polarity is represented by the opposite emotions on the circle. This postulate also includes the idea that some emotions are primary and others are derivatives or blends, in the same sense that some colors are primary and others are mixed. A number of studies have been published showing that the language of emotions can be represented by means of a circle or circumplex (Conte & Plutchik, 1981; Fisher, Heise, Bohrnstedt & Lucke, 1985; Plutchik, 1980a; Russell, 1989; Wiggins & Broughton, 1985).

Figure 4.2 — Illustrations of the Complex Chain of Events Defining an Emotion

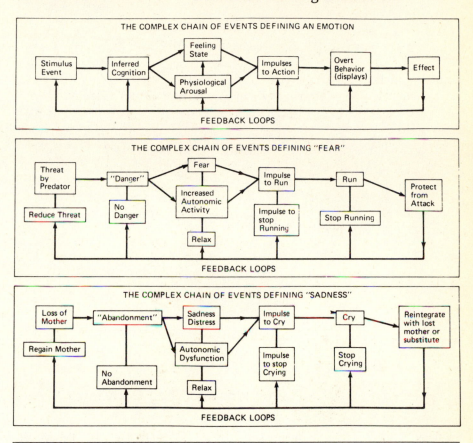

Source: J. van Lawick-Goodall, 1973.

The concept of primary and derived emotions leads to the sixth basic postulate of the theory, which states that emotions are related to a number of derivative conceptual domains. This idea has been explored in a number of different ways. For example, it has been shown that the language of mixed emotions is identical to the language of personality traits. Hostility has been judged to be composed of anger and disgust, sociability is a blend of joy and acceptance, and guilt is a combination of pleasure plus fear. Emotional components have been identified for hundreds of personality traits. In addition, there is now clear-cut evidence that personality traits also exhibit a circumplex structure just as do emotions (Conte & Plutchik, 1981; Russell, 1989; Wiggins & Broughton, 1985).

Figure 4.3   A Multidimensional Model of
                        the Emotions

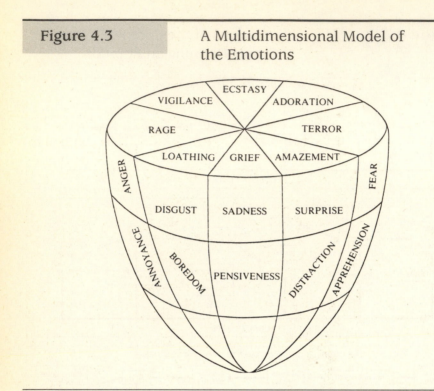

Source: R. Plutchik, 1980.

Table 4.3   Emotions and Their Derivatives

Stimulus Event	Inferred Cognition	Subjective Language	Behavioral Language
Threat	"Danger"	Fear	Escape
Obstacle	"Enemy"	Anger	Attack
Potential mate	"Possess"	Joy	Mate
Loss of valued individual	"Abandonment"	Sadness	Cry
Member of one's group	"Friend"	Acceptance	Groom
Unpalatable object	"Poison"	Disgust	Vomit
New territory	"What's out there?"	Expectation	Map
Unexpected object	"What is it?"	Surprise	Stop

One can extend the idea of derivatives further. Diagnostic terms such as *depressed, manic,* and *paranoid* can be conceived as extreme expression of such basic emotions as sadness, joy, and disgust. Several studies have also revealed that the language of diagnoses also shares a circumplex structure with emotions (Plutchik & Platman, 1977; Schaefer & Plutchik, 1966).

Carrying the notion of derivatives still another step, our research has shown that the language of ego defenses can also be conceptualized as being related to emotions. For example, displacement can be conceptualized as an unconscious way to deal with anger that cannot be directly expressed without punishment. Similarly, projections can be conceptualized as an unconscious way to deal with a feeling of disgust for (or rejection of) oneself by attributing this feeling to outsiders. Parallels of this sort have been drawn for each of the primary emotions and are described in detail by Kellerman (1979), Plutchik et al. (1979) and Plutchik (1989). Table 4.3 more fully illustrates the concept of derivatives, showing the conceptual links among affects, behavior, functions, personality traits, diagnoses, and ego defenses. Also added is the domain of coping styles, which can be hypothesized to be the conscious derivatives of the unconscious ego-defenses. Thus, fault finding corresponds to projection, reversal to reaction-formation, and mapping to intellectualization. Other derivative domains have also been proposed (Plutchik, 1984b, 1989).

Functional Language	Trait Language	Diagnostic Language	Ego-defense Language	Coping-style Language
Protection	Timid	Passive	Repression	Suppression
Destruction	Quarrelsome	Antisocial	Displacement	Substitution
Reproduction	Sociable	Manic	Reaction-formation	Reversal
Reintegration	Gloomy	Depressed	Compensation	Replacement
Incorporation	Trusting	Histrionic	Denial	Minimization
Rejection	Hostile	Paranoid	Projection	Fault finding
Exploration	Demanding	Obsessive Compulsive	Intellectualization	Mapping
Orientation	Indecisive	Borderline	Regression	Help seeking

Source: R. Plutchik, 1989.

The psychoevolutionary theory of emotion has been useful in a number of ways. It has provided a general approach to emotions that is relevant to lower animals as well as to humans. It is parsimonious in that the same set of assumptions has relevance and explanatory value for a number of conceptual domains (affects, personality, defenses, diagnoses). It has predicted some new observations that have been empirically confirmed (the circumplex structure of affects, personality traits, diagnoses, and defenses). It has also provided some new insights into specific issues such as the relations between emotions and motivations (Plutchik, 1980a), emotions and cognitions (Plutchik, 1977, 1985), emotions and empathy (Plutchik, 1987), emotions and dreams (Kellerman, 1987), and emotions and primary processes (Kellerman, 1990). And also of great importance, it has provided a theoretical rationale for the constructions of a number of new test instruments designed to measure affects (Plutchik, 1966, 1971, 1989), personality (Plutchik & Kellerman, 1974), ego defenses (Plutchik et al., 1979), coping styles (Buckley, Conte, Plutchik, Wild, & Karasu, 1984; Wilder & Plutchik, 1982; Conte, Plutchik, et al., 1989), and psychotherapy (Kellerman, 1979; Plutchik, 1990).

The various ideas outlined above clearly draw on aspects of genetics and evolutionary theory. They imply that emotions represent fundamental adaptive mechanisms that can be identified at all evolutionary levels, and that there are genetic underpinnings to emotional states. The generality of this approach to emotions is a direct reflection of the generality and value of evolutionary theory.

Summary ■

Although the study of emotion has been considered one of the most confusing chapters in psychology for almost a century, a new surge of interest in the field has occurred during the past two or three decades. Concomitant with this interest, researchers have made a number of attempts to provide general approaches to understanding emotions. Some of these approaches may be thought of as theories.

For the most part we may distinguish between approaches and theories in that theories tend to be broad rather than narrow, tend to have many interrelated postulates or assumptions rather than one or two, tend to stimulate research and new measurement ideas, and sometime predict new or unexpected findings. Very few of the theories that currently exist meet all these challenges, but they do attempt to deal with such issues, at least to some degree.

The selection of theorists who are described in this chapter is based on the belief that they have had the most influence on the thinking of contemporary psychologists. Other important theoretical contributions are described in later chapters. The contributions of those theoreticians are not less well known or important, but they tend to be more narrowly focused on one major aspect of emotions, so that their contributions are more readily understood in these other contexts. This characteristic is particularly true of the work of Ekman, Le Doux, and Panksepp, whose ideas will be described elsewhere.

The theories reviewed in the present chapter have been grouped somewhat loosely under a few main categories: Motivational theories, cognitive theories, psychoanalytic theories, and evolutionary theories. These categories are only approximate, since increasing overlap of ideas has occurred in recent years. Thus, for example, Lazarus is placed under the general rubric of cognitive theories; yet he describes his views as a *cognitive-motivational-relational* theory of emotions. Similarly, even though Izard is described under the heading of motivational theories, he has always emphasized the importance of cognitions in understanding emotions. The narrowest theoreticians in the cognitive group are Ortony, Clore, and Collins, who clearly indicate that the entire focus of their theory is on the cognitive conditions that elicit emotions, with emotions being considered as subjective states most readily accessed by verbal reports. They have no expressed interest in behavior, physiology, brain states, or issues of adaptation.

Within the psychoanalytic tradition, Rado describes emotions as emergency reactions designed to regulate feelings of pain and pleasure. In developing his ideas he uses concepts from evolutionary biology including images related to incorporation, riddance, and escape. He also tries, in a general way, to relate the development of the central nervous system to changes in the capacity of organisms to integrate sensory signals, cognitions, emergency reactions, and coping behavior. Rado also recognizes, as do many of the other theorists, the social communication value of emotions.

In the section on evolutionary approaches to emotions, all three of the theories described emphasize the communication role of emotions. All emphasize the idea, that emotions are adaptive reactions and thus have survival value. And all recognize that the concept of emotions applies to lower animals as well as to higher ones.

It thus becomes evident that ideas that stem from different historical traditions now infuse the thinking of psychologists who represent different approaches to the understanding of emotions. It is likely that increasing interpenetration of ideas will occur as time goes on, and that the textbooks of the future will present perhaps one or two broad theories that include the best ideas taken from the many views currently in existence.

Chapter

5

The Measurement of Emotions

Were any man to keep minutes of his feelings
from youth to age, what a table of varieties
they would present—how numerous, how
diverse, how strange.
                              —August W. Hare

▮ Goals of This Chapter

How we measure emotions depends on how we define them as well as on the theories we have about them. The different theories of emotion described in the previous chapter each have some implications for assessment of emotions. For example, cognitive theories usually try to find ways to describe the situational and conceptual triggers of emotional reactions at the same time that such reactions are assessed by means of self-reports. Motivational theories are likely to direct the researcher's attention to autonomic changes that occur within the body, and are also likely to use facial expressions as key indicators of emotion. Evolution-based theories are likely to focus attention on the measurement of expressive behavior of humans and animals, while psychoanalytic theories imply that measures of emotion that best reflect the unconscious, mixed-states typical of humans are projective and drawing techniques.

However, because of the increasing overlap of theoretical ideas, we see overlap of measurement techniques as well. Thus, we find four general approaches to measuring emotions, most of which tend to be used by proponents of all viewpoints.

107

One method involves the use of self-reports of subjective feelings, a procedure that is useful mainly with human adults. A second method for judging emotions is through ratings made of the behavior of an individual. Such ratings can be used with adults, children, mentally retarded persons, and with lower animals. A third way to evaluate emotions is through a rating of the product of someone's behavior; for example, an individual's handwriting or figure drawings. Finally, emotions may be assessed through the use of recordings of physiological or neural changes. Each of these methods will be described in this chapter.

Important Questions Addressed In This Chapter

- What are some problems with the use of adjective checklists?
- Can all emotions be grouped into either positive or negative affects?
- What is the difference between a state and a trait?
- What advantages, if any, does a forced-choice emotion test such as the *Emotions Profile Index,* have?
- How much consistency of emotional antecedents has been revealed by cross-cultural questionnaires?
- What advantages and disadvantages do rating scales for measuring emotions have?
- What aspects of infant behavior are considered to reveal emotions?
- What was learned about sex differences in chimpanzees through the use of rating scales for emotions?
- What is meant by the idea of measuring emotions by the products of behavior?
- What are some reasons for the difficulties in measuring emotions by means of physiological recordings?

■   ■   ■   ■   ■   ■   ■   ■

▌Self-Report Measures of Emotions

One of the most common, and deceptively simple, ways to measure emotional states in human adults is by means of adjective checklists. Such lists consist of a series of adjectives such as calm, nervous, fearful, or bored that individuals identify as reflections of their current feelings. Although this seems like a simple enough idea, there are problems with it. One concerns the question of which words we should use that are descriptive of current feelings. The second concerns the question of how best to group terms to represent scales or dimensions, and the third concerns the question of how long an emotion lasts.

One of the earliest adjective checklists was developed by Gough and his associates (1960). They selected 300 words that included such terms as affectionate, charming, deceitful, absent-minded, prudish, sexy, slow, weak, quiet, relaxed, and gloomy. Other authors have included words like droopy, tired, sleepy, and aroused (Russell, 1989). The problem with these choices is that people do not always agree on which words are emotion words and which are not. Some students, for example, believe that hunger and thirst, as inner states, are emotions, and that states of fatigue or excitement are also emotions. Many do not agree with these judgments. Fortunately, there is good agreement that words like fearful, sad, angry, and happy describe emotions, and such terms or their synonyms are generally found on every checklist.

The second question concerns the issue of how to group emotion words to form scales or dimensions. For example, a common practice is to group emotion words into two broad categories called *positive affect* and *negative affect*. (The word affect is often used interchangeably with the word emotion). In a recent study, Watson, Clark, and Tellegen (1988) described the development of brief measures of positive and negative affect. They started with 60 emotion words and through use of factor analysis reduced this list to 10 words that strongly reflected positive affect and 10 that expressed negative affect, with relatively little overlap. Examples of positive emotions are: interested, excited, strong, proud, alert and active. Examples of negative emotions are distressed, upset, guilty, hostile, nervous and afraid.

One of the problems with these lists is that many of the words are vague and it is not clear just what they imply. For example, the word *excited* could be associated with rage. Similarly, the word *upset* could mean that one feels bad, sick, uncomfortable, or depressed. One of the puzzling things about emotion words is that we sometimes find unexpected associations. Watson and others reported that the two positive sounding words "delighted" and "healthy" were omitted from their list of positive affects because they had "relatively high secondary loadings on negative affect."

Researchers have made some attempts to identify groups of words that express clusters of related feelings. One such list is called the Multiple Affect Adjective Check List (MAACL) (Zuckerman & Lubin, 1965). It consists of 132 adjectives, 90 of which are scored for the affects of *anxiety*, *depression*, and *hostility*; the rest are not scored for any particular affect. Some of the words are considered *plus* words and some are *minus* words for each affect; for example, shaky is a plus word for anxiety whereas calm is a minus word for anxiety. The scoring system for the MAACL subtracts minus from plus scores (according to a simple formula) to produce a single index for each of the three affects.

Although the MAACL has been reported to be useful in several studies, there are a number of problems with it. The basis for the grouping of words within the three scales is sometimes puzzling. For example, the words hostility and aggression, though present in the checklist, are not scored on the hostility dimension. Similarly, words with obvious face validity for hostility, such as indignant, incensed, and sullen, are not scored on the hostility dimension. It has also been shown that all three scales of the MAACL are highly correlated (Russell, 1989).

Lorr and his colleagues made another attempt to develop an adjective checklist with different clusters of words, called The Profile of Mood States, or POMS (1984). This test consists of 65 words representing six emotion dimensions that have been labeled Anger-Hostility, Depression-Dejection, Vigor-Activity, Fatigue-Inertia, Tension-Confusion, and Friendliness. Examples of the words used on the scales are friendly, tense, angry, and worthless. Subjects make intensity of feeling judgments on a 5-point scale ranging from *not at all* to *extremely*. The POMS has been useful in a number of investigations concerned with the effects of drugs and antidepressants on mood states.

Let us consider one additional example of a brief adjective checklist (Plutchik, 1980). The rating scales consist of eight emotion words that sample a wide range of emotions. These words, listed in Table 5.1, are rated for intensity on a 5–point scale ranging from *not at all* to *very strongly*. In order to test the usefulness of such a simple instrument, a group of 40 college students was asked to complete it at the beginning of each Monday, Wednesday, and Friday class during one week. This sample represented the control condition. The emotion scale was then given just prior to an examination and just after the exams were returned to the students. Analysis of the emotion ratings showed that all eight moods remained quite stable during the control week. Ratings made just before the examination showed highly significant increases in ratings of *fearful* and *interested* and highly significant decreases in ratings of *happy* and *agreeable*. The other four emotions did not show any significant changes.

On the day that the test was returned, the students were given their examination papers and allowed to see their grades. Emotion ratings were then obtained again. Under these conditions, seven of the eight emotions showed highly significant changes in mean self-ratings. There were significant decreases in *happy*, *agreeable*, and *interested*, and significant increases in *angry*, *disgusted*, *sad*, and *surprised*. These findings suggest that these simple adjective scales are sensitive to stresses, and cover a wide range of affect states. This same mood rating scale has been used as part of a battery of tests designed to identify changes in elderly (mostly welfare) tenants in a single-room-occupancy hotel in New York City (Plutchik, McCarthy, & Hall,1975). These tenants were assessed just after a new medical social service program was introduced directly into the hotel and again assessed one year later. Among the changes that took place during that period was a significant increase in feelings of *anger* and *sadness*. No significant changes occurred in the other emotions. One hypotheses to account for these results might be an increase in feelings of frustration associated with rising expec-

| Table 5.1 | | | Illustration of a Mood Rating Scale | | |

Please describe the way you feel right now by circling the appropriate number next to each word:

Right Now Do You Feel	Not at All	Slightly	Moderately	Strongly	Very Strongly
Happy	1	2	3	4	5
Fearful	1	2	3	4	5
Agreeable	1	2	3	4	5
Angry	1	2	3	4	5
Interested	1	2	3	4	5
Disgusted	1	2	3	4	5
Sad	1	2	3	4	5
Surprised	1	2	3	4	5

Source: R. Plutchik, 1980.

tations. Despite the concerns of the staff, relatively few improvements in living conditions were noted during the first year.

Table 5.2 provides information on the range of emotions covered by the various adjective checklists that have been described in the literature. Ten different instruments are listed. The number of adjectives per test ranges from 8 to 132 while the number of dimensions or subscales varies from 3 to 10.

Adjective checklists for the measurement of emotional states have come into wide use in recent years. Their advantage is that they are usually brief, have obvious face validity, and can be easily self-administered. They can also be used to provide indices of transient states of emotion as well as long-term emotional dispositions. Their disadvantages include the facts that they are easy to fake and that relatively little validation has been done on clinical populations. In addition, many of the checklists have no theoretical justification for the particular dimensions or scales that are scored. Despite these problems, such checklists have been widely used.

How Long Do Emotions Last? States Versus Traits

One of the confusing problems connected with the study of emotions concerns the distinctions we tend to make between emotions that last a

Table 5.2		Dimensions Measured by Various Adjective Checklists	
Checklist	**Adjectives**	**Checklist**	**Adjectives**
Borgatta (1961) 40 adjectives	Lonely (depressed); warmhearted; tired; thoughtful; defiant (aggressive); startled (anxious)	Izard (1972) 30 adjectives	Interest; joy; surprise; distress; disgust; anger; shame; fear; contempt; guilt
Clyde (1963) 132 adjectives	Friendly; aggressive; clear thinking; sleepy; unhappy; dizzy	Plutchik and Kellerman (1974) 66 adjectives	Sociable; trusting; dyscontrolled; timid; depressed; distrustful; controlled; aggressive
Zuckerman and Lubin (1965) 89 adjectives	Depression; hostility; anxiety	Curran and Cattell (1975) 96 adjectives	Anxiety; stress; depression; regression; fatigue; guilt; extraversion; arousal
Plutchik (1966) 8 adjectives	Happy; agreeable; fearful; angry; interested; disgusted; sad; surprised	Howarth (1977) 60 adjectives	Concentration; anxiety; anger; depression; potency; sleep; control; cooperation; optimism; scepticism
McNair, Lorr, Dropleman (1971) 57 adjectives	Anger–hostility; depression–dejection; vigor–activity; fatigue inertia; friendliness; confusion	Lorr and McNair (1984) 72 adjectives	Composed; anxious; agreeable; hostile; elated; depressed; confident; unsure; energetic; tired; clearheaded; confused

Source: R. Plutchik, 1989.

short time and those that last a long time. For example, we may use the word *angry* to describe a transient feeling associated with someone accidentally stepping on your toe. We may also use the same word to describe a person who seems to be irritable much of the time; that is, we think of this person as an angry person. In the first case, the word *angry* refers to a brief state; in the second the word *angry* refers to a long-term trait, the kind that we usually think of as a personality trait. Somewhere in the middle are words like *moods* and *affects* that suggest emotional states that may last for days, weeks, or even months.

In general, we assume that emotional states are feelings evoked by immediate changes in a situation (e.g., winning a lottery, threats, losing a job), or by temporary physiological changes (e.g., being very hungry, having a bad headache, being massaged). Traits, in contrast, are usually considered to be stable patterns of behavior that are manifested in a variety of situations. Thus, for example, someone may feel *anxious* in anticipation of an examination. At the other end of the continuum are people for whom *anxiety* is a constant part of their lives, and they are said to have an *anxiety disorder* or *anxiety neurosis*.

Although the two ends of the continuum are fairly obvious, it has often been pointed out that the distinction between states and traits is largely arbitrary (Allen and Potkay, 1981). Often the same adjective checklist, or another emotion test, can be used to measure both states and traits by a simple change in instructions. If the subjects are asked to describe how they feel *now*, or within the past few days or so, we are asking about emotional states or moods. If, however, subjects are asked to describe how they *usually* feel, we are dealing with long-term traits. This obvious point implies that the distinctions between emotions and personality traits are not sharp, and that these two domains may represent extremes of the same underlying dimensions. Thus, there is no simple or single answer to the question of how long emotions last. Whether we call a condition an emotion or a personality trait is a matter of degree.

Self-Report Questionnaire-Type Scales for Emotion

In addition to adjective checklists, self-report questionnaire-type scales have been extensively used to assess emotions. Such questionnaires or scales usually ask the subject or respondent to answer questions of the following kind:

Are you afraid of snakes?
Do you lack self-confidence?
Do you feel lonely and blue?
Are you able to tell other people what is on your mind?
Do you easily lose your temper?

The answers to such questions presumably reflect emotional states or emotional traits in a person, depending on the nature of the instructions. If the question refers to the present moment or recent past only, the answers probably reflect emotional states, moods, or feelings that may be relatively transient. If the question refers to typical or long-term behaviors or feelings, then the answers reflect emotional traits or dispositions.

Some of the tests used to measure anxiety illustrate the use of questionnaire-type emotion scales.

The Taylor Manifest Anxiety Scale

In the early 1950s, Janet Taylor, an experimental psychologist, developed a test that purported to measure manifest anxiety (Taylor, 1953). It was originally constructed by having five clinical psychologists select items from the Minnesota Multiphasic Personality Inventory that the judges agreed had face validity for measuring manifest anxiety. The final version of the scale that was used in many researches had 50 items.

Several studies then compared groups of subjects rated high on anxiety with those rated low. Using such extreme groups, it was found that fewer than 20 of the 50 Taylor Manifest Anxiety Scale (MAS) items discriminated between the high- and low-anxiety subjects (Hoyl & Magoun, 1954). Based on these findings, Bendig (1956) then developed a short form of the MAS, using only as below 20 of the items, that had approximately the same internal reliability as the long version. Some of the items of the 20-item version follow:

> I work under a great deal of tension.
> I frequently find myself worrying about something.
> I certainly feel useless at times.
> I am a high-strung person.
> I sometimes feel that I am about to go to pieces.

The person taking the test is asked to indicate whether each statement is true or false for him or her. It is also evident that the statements imply the existence of persisting characteristics and are thus meant to measure trait anxiety. However, the same statements can be used with instructions to respond in terms of recent events (e.g., a one-week period); the resulting scores would then presumably reflect the existence of a current state of anxiety.

The State-Trait Anxiety Inventory

Another scale for measuring anxiety was developed by Spielberger, Gorsuch, and Lushene (1970). The respondent is presented with 20 statements and is to indicate on a four-point scale to what extent each statement describes his or her feelings at the present moment. Some of the items are:

I feel tense.
I feel upset.
I feel nervous.
I am worried.

A second scale tries to measure trait anxiety; the subjects are asked how they generally feel. Examples of items are:

I wish I could be as happy as others seem to be.
I lack self-confidence.
I try to avoid facing a crisis or difficulty.
I am inclined to take things hard.

The authors of these scales have found that the reliability of the state anxiety questionnaire is much lower than is that of the trait anxiety questionnaire. This finding is reasonable in that the trait represents a kind of average of many states over time.

The Emotions Profile Index

The anxiety scales that have thus far been described are essentially empirical in origin. They stem from daily observations or clinical experience and may have some practical value in research. However, none stem from a theoretical framework that postulates relations among emotions, nor do any show how anxiety is related to anger, joy, or depression. In contrast, the *Emotions Profile Index* (Plutchik & Kellerman, 1974) was developed directly on the basis of a theory of emotion and has wide use both as a measure of emotion and as a measure of personality. Not only does it provide an index of fear and anxiety, but also of other emotions and their combinations as well.

The *Emotions Profile Index (EPI)* provides measures of the eight basic emotions that Plutchik first postulated in 1958, and described more fully in subsequent publications (1962, 1970, 1980, 1990). It is based on the idea that all interpersonal personality traits can be conceptualized as resulting from the mixture of two or more primary or basic emotions. This means that those who describe themselves as shy or gloomy are implicitly telling us something about the primary emotions that go to make up these traits. Shyness, for example, implies frequent feelings of fear, whereas gloominess implies frequent feelings of sadness.

The *EPI* was developed initially by having ten clinical psychologists rate the primary emotion components of a large number of traits. Twelve trait terms were finally selected on the grounds of high interjudge consistency on the components and a wide sampling of the trait universe that factor analytic studies described. These twelve terms were then paired in all possible combinations, yielding 66 pairs. Clinicians found that four of the pairs had identical scoring categories and so were dropped, thus leaving 62 pairs of trait terms for the final form of the test.

The *EPI* is a forced-choice test. The person taking it is simply asked to indicate which of two paired words is more descriptive of him or her; for example, is he or she more quarrelsome or shy? The choices are scored in terms of the primary emotions implied by the trait word. Each time the respondent makes a choice between two trait words, he or she adds to the score on one or more of the eight basic emotion dimensions. Thus, rather than measure only anxiety, the test also simultaneously measures anger, sadness, joy, and so on. Because the implications of the choices are not always clear to the respondent, the test has something of a projective quality since the subject does not usually recognize the implicit scoring system. Finally, because of the forced-choice format of the *EPI*, it tends to reduce response bias associated with a set to choose socially desirable traits. This is true because many of the choices must be made between two equally undesirable or two equally desirable traits. In addition, a bias score is built into the test as a measure of the respondent's tendency to choose socially desirable (or undesirable) traits in those cases where the items are not matched.

The twelve terms used in the *EPI* follow: adventurous, affectionate, brooding, cautious, gloomy, impulsive, obedient, quarrelsome, resentful, self-conscious, shy, and sociable. A brief definition is provided in the test for each term. The total score for each of the eight primary emotion dimensions is converted into a percentile score based on normative data. Investigators then plot the percentile scores on a circular diagram, as illustrated in Figure 5.1 for a group of severely depressed patients. The center of the circle represents zero percentile and the outer circumference of the circle is the 100th percentile. The larger the dark wedge-shaped area, the stronger the emotional disposition that is revealed.

Figure 5.1 shows that the depressed patients are highest on the Depression scale and moderately high on Timidity (anxiety), Distrust (rejection), Aggression (anger), and Control (expectation). They tend to be low on Dyscontrol (interest in novelty), and Gregariousness (socializing with others). High scores on opposite emotions on the circle reveal areas of conflict. Accordingly, with this group of patients a major conflict seems to be between Aggression (anger) and Timidity (anxiety).

Thus far this chapter has discussed the use of subjective reports of feeling states as measures of emotion. Although several different approaches to such measurement have been developed, the most common is based on the use of adjective checklists of various kinds. Many studies have tried to reduce such checklists to a small number of basic dimension, but at present there is no general agreement. Various investigations have revealed that self-report emotion measures can be reasonably stable and can be valid

| Figure 5.1 | Depression Profile Obtained From A Group of Manic-Depressive Patients |

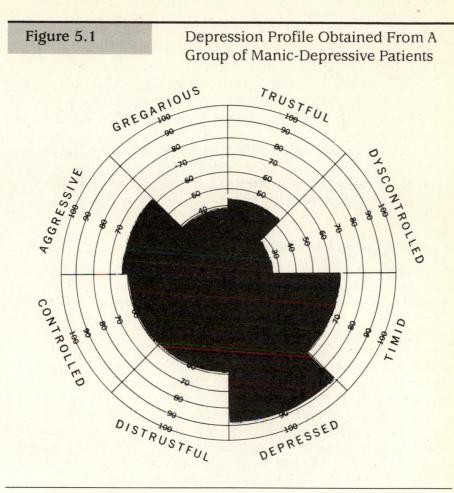

Source: Platman, Plutchik, Fieve, and Lawlor, 1969.

indices of life stresses or other conditions. Such measures thus appear to be useful measures of emotion. However, those that are based upon a formal theory of emotion are more likely to reveal important interconnections among variables and to be of general use.

With regard to possible biases in self-report checklists, a recent study has shown that such lists are susceptible to various response biases related to scale type, instructions, and format (Green, Goldman, & Salovey, 1992). When such biases are corrected, mood studies show good evidence of bipolarity of positive and negative terms (e.g., happy vs. sad) rather than independence. According to Green et al. (1992), the best way to correct biases is to use a series of short-questions of different format and to combine the responses. For example:

1. Select the adjectives that describe your feelings.
2. Indicate the degree to which you agree or disagree with each statement (5-point scale) (e.g., "For some reason, I've been feeling sort of nervous").
3. Indicate the extent to which each statement describes you (4-point scale) (e.g., "I have felt rather distressed").
4. Rate on a 7-point scale the extent to which each term describes you (e.g., scared-not scared).

A Cross-Cultural Questionnaire Study of Emotions

During the past few years, Scherer and his associates (1986; 1989) have been engaged in an extensive cross-cultural study of emotions using questionnaires. These investigators recognized that it is extremely difficult (and unethical) to try to create strong emotions in the laboratory. They therefore decided to rely on the recall of real-life experiences.

The questionnaire they constructed asked for information about the situations that aroused each particular emotion, how the individual felt during the emotion, and how strongly an attempt was made to control the emotion. Initially, four emotions were studied—joy, sadness, fear, and anger—on the grounds that nearly all theories agree that these emotions are basic or fundamental. Later, the emotions of disgust, shame and guilt were added. So far, data have been obtained on about 2,500 college students, ranging in age from 18 to 35 years, in eight countries: Germany, France, Switzerland, Great Britain, Italy, Israel, Belgium, and Spain.

Table 5.3 lists some of the general categories that have relatively strong effects in generating emotional experiences. For example, personal relationships (such as falling in love) and temporary meetings are the most frequent antecedents of pleasurable experiences. Achievement in college as well as body-related experiences (such as food, drink and sex) also are relatively frequent antecedents of joy. For *sadness*, the major eliciting situation is also personal relationships (deterioration of a marriage), followed closely by death of close persons. For anger, personal relationships (usually negligence of close friends or relatives) were the most important elicitor.

In contrast, fear seems to be elicited most often by nonsocial situations (the brakes of a car fail, a fog impairs vision). Interactions with strangers also tend to elicit fear, as do novel situations and failures of achievement.

The questionnaire study also threw light on the kinds of physiological nonverbal changes that are likely to occur with different emotions. Table 5.4 (on page 120) summarizes these results.

Measures of Emotions   119

Table 5.3	Percentage Frequency of Antecedent Elicitors of Different Emotions[a]			
Factor	**Joy**	**Sadness**	**Fear**	**Anger**
News	9.9	9.5	2.4	4.6
Relationships	29.4	27.1	4.6	38.5
Social institutions	4.7	3.1	1.5	1.8
Temporary meeting/separation	19.6	6.5	1.0	.6
Permanent separation	—	8.9	.8	.4
Death/birth	8.3	22.2	6.5	.8
Body/mind centered	12.8	10.1	7.2	2.1
Interactions with strangers	2.3	.9	14.9	19.9
Achievement	16.0	7.2	11.7	6.7
Supernatural	—	—	3.9	—
Risky situations/natural forces	—	—	11.2	—
Traffic	—	—	20.0	—
Unknown, novel situations	—	—	14.5	—
Injustice	—	—	—	20.9
Inconvenience	—	—	—	8.5

[a]Based on 779 subjects; data do not add up exactly to 100% because of some "uncodeable" situation descriptions and double coding.
Source: Wallbott and Scherer, 1989.

Subjective experiences of temperature changes in the body appear to be an important discriminator of some emotions. Feeling warm, for example, is exclusively associated with joy, while feeling hot is mostly associated with anger; feeling cold is associated primarily with both fear and sadness. Bodily changes such as a faster heartbeat appear to occur in a wide variety of emotions. The fact that silence is often reported for most of the emotions suggests that many individuals exercise self-control over the expression of their emotions. In all, however, it is evident that different patterns of physiological symptoms, nonverbal reactions, and verbal behavior exist for different emotions. It should be emphasized that these patterns are verbal descriptions and are not based upon actual observations or measurements of physiology or behavior. Thus, social expectations and stereotypes may have some degree of influence on the reported results.

Table 5.4	Symptoms/Reactions Described in N Samples[a]

Symptom/Reaction	Joy	Fear	Anger	Sadness	Disgust	Shame	Guilt
Physiological symptoms							
Lump in throat	2	17	10	26	9	15	17
Change in breathing	9	26	24	15	4	7	3
Stomach trouble	—	7	—	2	6	—	—
Feeling cold	—	22	—	16	3	—	1
Feeling warm	27	—	—	—	—	—	—
Feeling hot	3	1	23	—	—	20	4
Heartbeat faster	26	27	26	19	12	23	19
Muscles tensing	—	27	24	17	12	12	13
Muscles relaxing	15	—	—	—	—	—	—
Perspiring	1	27	9	2	2	12	2
Other symptoms	1	2	2	6	6	2	3
Nonverbal reactions							
Laughing, smiling	27	—	—	—	—	—	—
Crying, sobbing	—	1	2	27	—	—	—
Changed facial expression	2	21	24	16	22	21	16
Screaming	—	—	14	—	—	—	—
Changes in voice	2	8	20	11	7	5	3
Change in gesturing	5	3	16	2	3	4	1
Abrupt movements	—	7	11	—	—	—	—
Moving toward	25	—	—	3	—	—	—
Withdrawing	—	4	2	22	11	17	14
Moving against	—	—	16	1	1	—	—
Other reactions	2	8	2	4	6	1	1
Verbal behavior							
Silence	—	27	15	27	25	27	27
Short utterance	3	10	5	6	7	9	5
One/two sentences	—	—	1	—	1	1	—
Lengthy utterance	21	—	20	—	3	—	1
Speech melody change	18	1	13	4	1	1	2
Speech disturbances	18	1	3	2	—	3	3
Speech tempo change	11	—	16	1	—	—	1
Other verbal reactions	3	—	1	—	1	—	—

[a]Based on 27 country samples with 2235 subjects; criterion was that 25% of the subjects in the sample mention symptom/reaction for a specific emotion.

Source: Wallbott and Scherer, 1989.

■ Measuring Emotions by Rating Behavior

It is obvious that self-reports of emotional states are not possible for certain types of populations. These include severely ill psychiatric patients; mentally retarded patients; young children and infants; and animals. In this section, a description will be given of some of the types of rating scales that have been developed for use with these populations. Such scales usually require detailed observations by experienced judges of the behavior of an individual. For some scales the rater is expected to identify the presence of certain classes of behavior assumed to reflect emotions. For other scales the judge is expected to make an inference about the presence of emotions without necessarily specifying what behavior is being observed. Interjudge reliability is obviously important in all such ratings. The following sections will illustrate the types of scales used with these various populations.

Scales for Rating Psychiatric Patients

The psychiatric literature contains many examples of rating scales used to assess emotional states in psychiatric patients. This abundance of rating scales reflects the fact that psychiatrists are usually not inclined to accept a patient's self-descriptions at face value; they assume that repression, denial, and lack of insight often prevent an accurate self-description. Therefore, psychiatrists typically make ratings after an interview with a patient or after ward observation. The use of rating scales may be illustrated by a study reported by two psychiatrists (Clancy and Noyes, 1976) that was designed to identify the behavioral correlates of anxiety. They reviewed the records of over 4,000 patients referred for psychiatric consultation over a five-year period. Of this total, 82 patients were given a primary or secondary diagnosis of anxiety neurosis, had complete records, and had no other medical condition. From these records researchers determined the frequency of report of various symptoms; Table 5.5 presents the list. This list represents symptoms found in patients diagnosed as suffering from persistent anxieties. It provides a way of identifying the relative importance, as measured by frequency of occurrence, of many symptoms. It is evident that anxiety states include a large number of physiological symptoms that can be determined only by observation or examination.

Scales for Rating Mentally Retarded Patients

A number of scales have been developed for rating the behavior of mentally retarded persons. Although the focus of these scales is usually on cognitive or functional skills, some include items that relate to emotions. In

Table 5.5		Symptoms of Anxiety Obtained from the Records of 71 Patients	
Symptom	**Percentage of Patients**	**Symptom**	**Percentage of Patients**
1. Chronic nervousness	97	16. Dizziness	44
2. Attacks of nervousness	92	17. Abdominal pain or	
3. Shortness of breath	70	discomfort	44
4. Muscle aching or tension	65	18. Depressed mood	41
5. Sweating, flushing, or		19. Crying spells	37
chills	61	20. Anorexia	31
6. Chest pain or discomfort	56	21. Fear of death or dying	24
7. Fatigue or tiredness	56	22. Difficulty swallowing	23
8. Insomnia	52	23. Blurred vision	21
9. Numbness or tingling	52	24. Restlessness	20
10. Trembling	52	25. Weight loss	15
11. Headaches	51	26. Poor concentration	14
12. Palpitations	48	27. Irritability	10
13. Nausea or vomiting	46	28. Dry mouth	8
14. Weakness	45	29. Fear of insanity	8
15. Fainting or light-		30. Urinary frequency	8
headedness	45	31. Nightmares	7

Source: J. Clancy and R. Noyes, Jr., 1976.

one of the more widely used scales (Nihira et al., 1970) there are a number of ratings to be made about the emotional behavior of the mentally retarded patient. Here are two examples:

Item 1: *Select all statements that are true of the person.*
   1. Uses threatening gestures
   2. Indirectly causes injury to others
   3. Spits on others
   4. Scratches or pinches others
   5. Pulls others' hair, ears, etc.
   6. Bites others
   7. Kicks, strikes, or steps on others
   8. Throws objects at others
   9. Uses objects as weapons against others
   10. Chokes others
   11. Hurts animals

Item 2: *Select all statements that are true of the person.*
   1. Is timid and shy in social situations

2. Hides face in group situations
3. Does not mix well with others
4. Always prefers to be alone

It is evident that the first group of behaviors is designed to measure the emotion of anger or the trait of aggressiveness, while the second group attempts to provide an index of timidity. Interjudge reliability is reported to be high.

Scales for Rating Children

The fact that young children cannot be expected to articulate their feelings clearly has led developmental psychologists to rely heavily on behavior-rating scales to evaluate emotions in children. Of the well known standardized scales, one of the earliest introduced into general use was the Fels Child Behavior Scales (Richard & Simons, 1941), developed at the Fels Institute at Antioch College. There are 30 Fels scales suitable for children in the first few grades as well as for preschool children. Judges are asked to make a rating along a line that represents different degrees of a trait. Such emotions or traits as aggressiveness, affectionateness, emotional control, and vigor of activity are rated. Interjudge reliability is reported to be high.

Another example of rating scales used to measure emotions in children was reported by Brody and others (1973). In this study, they attempted to determine the relations between personality traits of third-grade children and the extent to which the children showed problem behavior in the classroom. In addition, they determined relations among personality traits, IQ, and absence records.

A random sample of 60 children was selected from the 600 children in the third grade of a school district. The homeroom teacher for each of these 60 children was asked to rate each designated child on 12 personality traits using a 9-point scale of intensity. The 12 traits were the same ones used in the Emotions Profile Index described in the previous chapter; some of the descriptions follow:

Someone who often tries new activities for excitement
Someone who starts arguments
Someone who feels timid with other people and in new situations

A second measure, called the Problem Inventory, simply listed 10 problems that children have been reported to show in a school setting. These include reading problems, speech problems, being withdrawn, temper tantrums, stealing, hyperactivity, fighting, can't get along with other children, disruptiveness, and daydreaming. Each designated student was rated on a 3-point scale that ranged from *not a problem* through *slight problem* to *serious problem.*

Results showed that the girls were significantly more sociable and affectionate than the boys, and that the boys were significantly more quarrelsome than the girls. No other sex differences were found in personality. Results also determined that children who were rated high on the traits cautious, self-conscious, quarrelsome, or impulsive tended to have more problems, and children rated high on sociable had fewer. In terms of the frequency of problems, 8% of the children were described as having a serious problem in getting along with other children, 6% were seriously withdrawn, and 3% had severe temper tantrums or severe hyperactivity. One of the conclusions of the study emphasized the point that there are different kinds of emotional difficulties that children have and that each type has its own spectrum of problems associated with it. Such a conclusion would not have been possible without a set of rating scales that covered a wide range of emotional states.

Scales for Rating Infants

In what many consider to be a classic study of this type, Birch and his colleagues (1962) studied temperament in infants and the changes that occur over time. For this purpose they obtained information on 95 infants from age 2 months to age 24 months at 3-month intervals for the first year and 6-month intervals during the second year. Information on each child was based upon each mother's reports, plus direct observations of the child in the home, in a playroom, and in nursery school.

From a content analysis of the records of the first 22 children, 9 categories were defined as *primary reaction characteristics* and labeled as follows: (1) activity level; (2) rhythmicity (predictability of behavior over time); (3) approach or withdrawal to new stimuli; (4) adaptability to altered situations; (5) intensity of reaction; (6) threshold of responsiveness; (7) quality of mood (pleasant vs. unfriendly); (8) distractibility; and (9) attention span and persistence.

Analysis of the data showed that "some children respond quietly and placidly to a new situation, approach it at once and adapt quickly and smoothly. At the other extreme are those children who withdraw sharply and violently, persist tenaciously in their old behavior, and adapt irregularly and slowly to a new situation." The hypothesis was presented that these reaction patterns are the bases for later emotional and personality development or, in other words, the sources of temperamental differences among individuals. A follow-up study by Scarr and Salapatek (1970) examined these ideas in greater detail. They explored the development of a variety of fears in infants during the first two years of life, and tried to relate these fears to the primary reaction characteristics Birch and his colleagues described. Ninety-one infants between the ages of 2 and 23 months were exposed to a series of 6 stimuli that have been reported to produce fear reactions in infants and young children. The stimuli were strangers, heights, a jack-in-the-box, a mechanical dog, loud noises, and masks. The child's fear reaction to each stimulus was rated on a 3-point scale. 1 = no evidence of fear; 2 = sober, cautious, stops ongoing activity; 3 = fretting, crying, fleeing to mother. The nine temperamental characteristics were rated after a structured 3-hour interview with the child's mother.

The results showed that the fear of heights tended to increase linearly up to the age of about 18 months, but that the fears of the mechanical dog, noise, and the jack-in-the-box remained fairly constant over the 7- to 24-month age range. Fears of strangers and masks increased to a maximum at about age 10 months and then remained constant. It was also found that a particular temperament pattern correlated with fear behavior. "Infants who had generally negative quality of mood, low threshold of response, poor adaptability, and low rhythmicity were more likely to show fear across situations." Finally there appeared to be a fair amount of stability of fear reactions over a 2-month period when the same infant was tested twice. The authors concluded that these findings suggest a possible genetic role in the development of fear during infancy. These studies also indicate that it is perfectly possible to study emotions in young infants, and, by implication, it should be possible to also study organisms that are lower on the phylogenetic scale.

Scales for Rating Emotions in Animals

Comparative psychologists and ethologists have been rating the emotional behavior of animals for a long time. In fact, all those who have followed the Darwinian tradition have no difficulty with the idea that animals show emotional behavior and that such behavior can reliably be rated. This section will provide some appropriate illustrations.

The identification of emotions in animals requires careful observation of the animal's behavior, some knowledge of its history, observations of the consequences of its behavior, and knowledge of how other animals react to the animal under observation. Using this framework, one of the most detailed studies of social behavior and emotions in animals was carried out by Van Hooff (1973) on a chimpanzee colony of 25 animals at a research laboratory in New Mexico. He spent more than 200 hours in direct observation of these animals, and developed a catalog of observed behaviors, keeping a record of the relative frequency of each behavior. He noted interactions among animals and the effects of each action.

From these observations, Van Hooff identified 53 behavior elements that were scored as frequently preceding or succeeding other elements, thus creating a list of behaviors in their typical sequential context. He then used a type of factor analysis to identify clusters of behaviors that tended to occur together. The results of this analysis are summarized in Table 5.6.

Most of the behaviors tend to fall into five groups, which Van Hooff calls: the *affinitive* system, the *play* system, the *aggressive* system, the *submissive* system, and the *excitement* system. These terms clearly relate to emo-

Table 5.6	Cluster Analysis of Chimpanzee Behaviors

Group I   **The Affinitive System**

Examples: Touch, cling, hold out hand, smooth approach, silent pout, groom, embrace, pant, mount

Group II   **The Play System**

Examples: Relaxed open mouth, grasp, poke, gnaw wrestle, gnaw, pull limb, gymnastics, hand-wrestle

Group III   **The Aggressive System**

Examples: Trample, tug, brusque rush, bite, grunt-bark, sway-walk, hit, stamp, shrill bark

Group IV   **The Submissive System**

Examples: Flight, crouch, avoid, bared-teeth scream, bared-teeth yelps, parry, shrink-flinch, hesitant approach

Group V   **The Excitement System**

Examples: Squat-bobbing, rapid "ohoh," rising hoot, upsway

Source: van Hooff, 1973.

tional states, and it is evident that animal social behaviors do not occur in isolation, but always as part of a complex emotional interaction. It is interesting that Jane Goodall, after years of observations of chimpanzees in Africa, arrived at a fairly similar classification of their social-emotional behaviors. Her list includes the following terms: flight and avoidance; frustration; aggressive behavior; submissive behavior; reassurance behavior; greeting behavior; communications related to sex, play, and mothering. It is thus evident that emotions enter into the basic fabric of all social encounters.

The Rating of Emotions in Baboons and Chimpanzees

Another interesting way to assess emotions in animals has been described by Buirski and others (1973). These investigators selected and defined a set of 10 terms descriptive of emotional behavior: belligerent, fearful, inquisitive, irritable, defiant, depressed, dominant, playful, sociable, and submissive. The emotion components of each of these states was determined by consensus of a group of judges. The terms were then paired in all possible combinations, and the resulting form was used in a study of baboons at the Nairobi National Park in Kenya, Africa.

Three observers watched a small troop of 7 baboons for 35 hours over a 3-week period. They noted every incident of grooming in terms of who groomed whom, ad the length of time of the act. At the end of the 35 hours of observation, the baboons in the troop were independently ranked on dominance. Each rater simply picked one word from each pair that best described the behavior of the baboon being observed. Interrater reliability for most of the scales was high.

Among the many interesting findings of this investigation is an almost perfect correlation among the dominance rank and some of the indices of grooming. The most dominant animal, "Big Harry," was groomed most. In general, the higher dominance animals had briefer but more frequent grooms by others, and they did less grooming of others. This investigation also found that the animals rated lowest on the fearfulness dimension of the rating scale and highest on the aggressiveness dimension were groomed the most by the other baboons.

Buirski and his colleagues adapted this same measurement technique for use with chimpanzees. They observed 23 free-living chimpanzees, 13 males and 10 females, at the Gombe Stream Research Centre in Tanzania, East Africa, established by Jane Goodall. Ratings were made by 7 graduate students living at the camp, who were quite familiar with the day-to-day behavior of most of the chimps. Asked to rate those chimps whose behavior they were most familiar with, in terms of the defined scales, they picked one word from each of the 45 pairs that best described the behavior of the chimp under observation. Most of the interjudge reliabilities were greater than +.70.

The dominance rank of each male was independently estimated from brief biographies of the animals. Investigators then correlated the rank position with each of the 8 emotion dimensions. The set of correlations suggested a profile: Dominant animals tend to be aggressive and distrustful, whereas nondominant animals tend to be timid, impulsive, and trustful.

Investigators also found sex differences, rating the female chimpanzees more timid, more depressed, and more trustful than the males, who were judged more gregarious and more distrustful.

There are a number of implications of this study of chimpanzees. In terms of emotions, chimpanzees have been reported to show depression, curiosity, aggression, jealousy, affection, timidity, and other states (Goodall, 1987), and it is now evident that experienced judges can reliably rate these emotions.

It is important to emphasize that the use of the emotion and personality language does not mean that we are using a subjective, imprecise terminology. All important terms in psychology are about inferred states, including such common terms as learning, memory, conditioning, displacement, pair bonds, and ritualization. An extensive, nonverbal communication system is evident in chimpanzees: they bow, kiss, hold hands, touch and pat each other, embrace, tickle one another with their fingers, bite, punch, kick, scratch each other, and pull out one another's hair. Not only do many of these movements look remarkably like many of the expressive postures and gestures of our own species, but the contexts likely to elicit the behaviors may be strikingly similar in chimpanzees and humans. In addition, "each call of the chimpanzee is fairly reliably associated with some specific emotion" (Van Lawick-Goodall, 1973). The point is that terms like gregarious, timid, depressed, and aggressive are fundamentally no more subjective or less useful than other terms currently used in psychology or ethology.

An Example of Abnormal Behavior in a Chimpanzee

An interesting clinical observation resulted from this study (Buirski and Plutchik, 1991). Among the sample of chimps that were observed was one female, named Passion, whose ratings suggested considerable variation from the average of other females. For example, Passion was judged to be considerably more aggressive than the other females, more depressed, and more distrustful. She was also rated as less timid and less controlled. The overall impression of Passion was that of an isolated, aggressive individual who would be considered in human terms to be severely disturbed.

One may consider this image of Passion in the light of her past history and subsequent behavior. Passion's daughter Pom was born in 1965, and from the beginning Passion was observed to display extraordinarily inefficient and indifferent maternal behavior. In all respects, Passion was a somewhat unnatural mother. Whereas other chimp mothers were protective of their infants, Passion seemed dissatisfied and neglectful. It appeared that Pom had to fight continually for her own survival. Passion was not a nurturant mother and did not facilitate her daughter's suckling, often ignoring Pom's whimpers completely. If Pom happened to be suckling when Passion wanted to travel, she typically moved off without waiting for her daughter to finish. Passion showed a similarly callous attitude toward Pom when her daughter was learning to ride and later walk. Pom would often be seen frantically trying to catch up with Passion, who had suddenly gotten up and walked away. Later on, rather than being able to separate from her mother to wander off a distance in play or exploration, as would be age-appropriate behavior, Pom would sit or play very close to Passion. For months on end, Pom could not play freely with other infants without holding tightly to her mother's hand. Pom seemed to fear being abandoned by Passion.

A year or so after these ratings were made, Passion, in collaboration with her daughter Pom, was observed to steal three tiny chimpanzee infants from their mothers and to then kill and eat them. Passion and Pom worked as a team in attacking the mothers of their victims. Passion, heavier and stronger, grappled with the mother while Pom pulled at the baby. Once they had possession of the babies, they directed no further aggression towards the victims' mothers. Passion together with Pom were the only chimpanzees ever observed to show predatory interest in infant chimps. Over a 4-year period, these two were believed to be responsible for the disappearance and deaths of as many as seven other chimpanzee infants. After Passion died, Pom was never seen to engage in these kinds of behaviors again. The observations of Passion and Pom's infanticidal and cannibalistic behavior is unique and bizarre, not only in chimpanzee literature but in all primate literature.

This description illustrates the fact that emotional states or traits can be reliably related in animals as well as in humans, and they can be related to other classes of meaningful behavior.

Measuring Aggression in Rats

As stated earlier in this chapter, in order to measure something, one must have some idea of the concept to be measured. In trying to measure aggressive behavior in animals, one must have some ideas of what aggression is. Ethologists who observe animals in natural settings have provided many insights into this issue. For example, Moyer (1983) has described seven types of situations that usually elicit aggression in animals. The resulting types of aggression are called predatory, intermale, fear-induced, territorial, irritable, maternal, and instrumental. Brain (1981) proposed an alternate scheme that lists five types of aggression: self-defensive, parental, predatory attack, reproduction termination, and social conflict. Eibesfeldt (1979), another ethologist, suggested that aggression be defined as "all behavior patterns that lead to the spacing out of conspecifics (i.e., members of the same species) . . . or to the domination of one individual over another."

Based on these ideas, aggression has been measured in a variety of ways. Examples are the following (based on the review by Benton, 1989).

1. The latency to start fighting
2. The total time spent fighting
3. A single rating of aggression on a scale
4. The percentage of animals that fight
5. The number of bouts of fighting

However, Benton makes the point that aggressive encounters are so complex that single measures are bound to be inadequate. Figure 5.2 shows some of the aggressive and submissive postures seen in fighting rats.

Figure 5.2	Offensive Postures in the Rat

(a) The alpha rat displays sideways offensive posture; the submissive animal is boxing.
(b) The full aggressive and full submissive postures.

A   B

Source: Benton, 1989.

Table 5.7 reveals the variety of specific acts or behaviors seen when two male mice are placed together. Complex mathematical procedures are needed to describe the underlying patterns in this description of aggressive encounters. Benton (1989) concludes, "It is unreasonable to assume that a single measure will adequately reflect the multiple factors that will inevitably influence the behavior of an animal in a particular situation . . . aggression is not a unitary phenomenon and measures obtained in . . . the same situations, may not reflect common biological substrates. It follows that findings should be generalized only with great caution."

▌Measuring Emotions Through the Products of Behavior

Another approach to measuring emotions depends not on the observation of behavior, but rather on studying the effects or products of behavior. For example, if we see a child throwing a stone through a school window and shattering it, we might make an inference that the child is angry about something. But what if we see only the broken window? Can we also make a reasonable guess that someone who was angry broke it?

Many situations that occur in everyday life are like that. For example, we may read a book and conclude that the author was depressed, or see a modern painting that suggests strong feelings of anger or anguish in the artist, as was probably the case when Picasso painted the Guernica picture based on the bombing of a Spanish town. Such judgments may be wrong, of course; yet clinical psychologists make such judgments all the time.

Table 5.7	Postures Observed in a Dyadic Encounter of Male Mice

Posture	Comments
Offensive	
Aggressive groom	Vigorous grooming of immobilized opponent
Biting attack	Bites standard opponent
Chase	Pursues standard opponent
Circle	Cycles of approaching and leaving with no intervening activity
Fight	Intense biting and kicking of opponent
Lunge	An "intention movement" for biting standard opponent
Sideways offensive	Attention to opponent, eyes slitted, and ears flattened; orientation toward opponent with at least one forepaw on the substrate
Tail rattle	Tail vibrated against substrate
Upright offensive	Upright or vertical position, ears flattened, eyes slitted; head horizontal and extended toward opponent
Defensive	
Crouch	All paws on substrate, body hunched; generally immobile with slight scanning movements of the head
Flag/evade	Avoids standard opponent
Flee	Runs from standard opponent
Freeze	Immobile in any position except crouch
Kick	Fends off other mouse with hindpaws or forepaws
Sideways defensive	Lateral orientation to opponent, head up, eyes open and ears extended; at least one forepaw on the substrate
Upright defensive	Forepaws off the gound, head up, eyes open, and ears extended; sometimes regarded as a submissive response
Social	
Approach	Moves towards standard opponent
Attempted mount	Palpation of opponents' sides with forepaws, pelvic thrusting
Attend	Directs head toward standard opponent
Body sniff	Sniffs standard opponent's body
Crawl under	Tunnels under standard opponent
Follow	Moves after standard opponent
Genital sniff	Sniffs perianal region of standard opponent

Posture	Comments
Groom	Grooms standard opponent
Head groom	Grooms head of standard opponent
Head sniff	Sniffs head of standard opponent
Leave	Ambulates away from standard opponent
Nose to nose	
Stretched attention	Orientating to opponent at a distance—an extreme version of attend
Walk round	Locomotion around opponent at close quarters
Nonsocial	
Abbreviated dig	Forepaws kick sawdust backward
Back rear	One or both forepaws on opponent's back without nose or whisker contact
Dig	Substrate displaced backward; forepaws and hindpaws used in alternation
Explore	Ambulation around cage with sniffing
Jump	
Push dig	Forepaws push sawdust forward
Scan	Scanning movements of head while standing; attention not on opponent
Scratch	Scratches self, often with hind paw, cf. a dog
Self groom	Auto grooming

Source: Benton, 1989.

They infer something about a client's emotions on the basis of the fantasy behavior of the client. These are the so-called projective tests.

A well known example of this is the Rorschach inkblot test, in which an individual is presented with a series of symmetrical inkblots and asked to describe what he or she sees in each one. Depending on the images presented and the number of responses obtained, a clinical psychologist makes inferences about the client's anger, anxiety, hatred, and mental status. Similarly, the Thematic Appreciation Test, or TAT, requests an individual to make up a series of stories on the basis of cards depicting various scenes involving people.

Figure 5.3 illustrates this idea. The picture is an etching made in the last century and shows a seated man surrounded by many children. A

Figure 5.3	An Illustration of an Ambiguous Picture About Which Stories Can Be Created to Reveal Emotional States

Source: K. Grob, 1879.

woman stands at the door in the background with her arms around the shoulders of two small children. What kind of story would you create about this scene?

When shown to one student, she said, "This is a clinic and the man in the center is the doctor in charge. The doctor is a very kind man, and very permissive. He is trying to make the new child brought by the young man, comfortable. The woman at the door is bringing her two children." Another student said, "This is a man that everyone looks up to—like a doctor. The mother in the corner with her two children really needs help. She is frightened."

In these brief descriptions, one student emphasizes the permissive quality of the key figure, while the other student describes him as having high social status. The first student ignores the emotions of the woman, while the second emphasizes her frightened appearance. From such stories as these, one may gain limited insight into the emotions of the viewer.

One of the most widely used projective measures of emotions is the Figure Drawing Test. In this test, the client is simply asked to draw a male figure and a female figure. Depending on such things as details included on the figures, their location on the page, and the style of the drawing, clinicians make many inferences about the emotions and psychological adjustment of the client.

Figure Drawings as Measures of Emotion

A study that compared figure drawings in normal and abnormal geriatric and nongeriatric groups (Plutchik, et al., 1978) illustrates that such drawings can measure emotion. In this investigation, 72 normal adults, 48 adult psychiatric inpatients, 30 senior citizens living in the community, and 33 elderly inpatients in a mental hospital produced figure drawings. The drawings were coded and then each was rated without knowledge of the group to which it belonged. Investigators rated 12 emotional indicators that had been previously identified. These indicators included such things as shading on the face or body, gross asymmetry of the limbs, strongly slanted figures, crossed eyes, teeth shown, and big hands. From these drawings, experienced clinicians were to make blind ratings on such emotions as aggression, depression, anxiety, emotional conflict and impulsivity. The use of several independent judges revealed that these ratings could be made reliably. Figure 5.4 shows examples of the drawings.

The results showed that various measures of dysfunction increased with age. The figures were smaller, and ratings of such problems as emotional conflict and depression increased. It was also found that adult psychiatric patients tended to draw small figures lacking in sexual differentiation and with signs of emotional conflict and depression. The differences between adult patients and adult normals were similar to the differences between adult normals and elderly persons of any status. When the figure drawings obtained from normal elderly were compared with psychiatric patients (elderly or adult), very few differences were found.

These findings indicate that clinicians could easily confuse the figure drawings of a normal elderly person with those of a psychiatric patient. Norms based upon figure drawings of children do not apply to the elderly, and clinicians should use considerable caution when using figure drawings as a measure of psychopathology in elderly persons. The study cited is important not only in revealing these facts, but in showing that emotions may reliably be rated from figure drawings, thus providing another indirect measurement for emotions.

Figure 5.4	Figure Drawings

These drawings were drawn by (a) normal adult, (b) psychiatric adult patient, (c) normal elderly, (d) psychiatric elderly patient. The figures are not presented in their original true proportions.

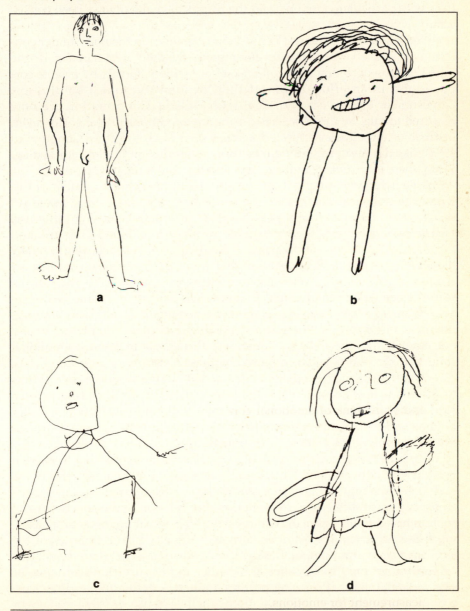

a

b

c

d

Source: Plutchik, Conte, Weiner, and Teresi, 1978.

▌ Physiological Measures of Emotions

Ever since William James claimed that an emotional feeling was basically a perception of internal bodily changes, there has been much interest in the measurement of autonomic changes as measures of emotion. Most of this research, however, has dealt with generalized stress or arousal rather than with particular emotions, and the results have not always been consistent.

One result of this interest in autonomic changes in the body under conditions of stress has been the development of the field of *lie detection*. By the mid-1980s, lie detection tests were used very widely, mostly by private corporations, in an effort to detect theft or identify honest employees. Government employees who deal with classified information are now required to take lie detector tests during investigations of leaks. However, because of the criticisms leveled against such tests, the U. S. Congress in 1988 passed a law prohibiting most nongovernmental lie detector testing. What, then, is the nature of the claims and the counterclaims?

A lie detector is simply a polygraph used to measure a number of different physiological changes in a person while he or she is being asked *yes* or *no* questions related to a possible theft or other crime. Typically, the measures obtained are breathing pattern, pulse rate, blood pressure, and the electrical resistance of the palm of the hand, which is believed to reflect the level of sweating. It is assumed that when a person tells a lie, this act will be associated with some degree of stress as compared to parts of the record when no lie is told. If this assumption is true, there should be noticeable changes in the physiological indices when the lie is told. This assumption does not mean that there is an unambiguous connection between any one emotion and the recorded autonomic changes, only that any emotional state related to stress will be reflected by these measures of arousal.

Over the years, investigators have carried out many studies in an effort to determine how accurate the lie detector polygraph is. The results of such studies suggest that a trained administrator will detect deception at better than a chance level, but far from perfectly. Therefore, most state courts do not accept polygraph evidence in criminal cases.

Table 5.8 lists the many kinds of physiological measures that have been used in studies of emotion. They represent most of the organ systems of the body, and although hundreds of studies have been carried out using such measures, great differences exist, not only in relation to the conclusions of such investigations, but also with regard to the actual methods of measuring those variables. For example, although the electrical properties of the skin have been examined in literally thousands of studies, there is still disagreement on such basic issues as whether to measure skin resistance or skin potential, what types of electrodes are best, whether to use direct current or alternating current stimulation, whether to use constant voltage or

Table 5.8	Physiological Measures Most Often Used in Studies of Emotion

1. Electrical phenomena of the skin (skin resistance or conductance, and skin potentials)

2. Blood pressure (systolic and diastolic pressures)

3. Electrocardiogram and heart rate

4. Respiration rate, depth, and pattern

5. Skin temperature

6. Pupillary response

7. Salivary secretion

8. Skin sweating

9. Analysis of blood, saliva, and urine (e.g., blood sugar, hormones, metabolites)

10. Gastrointestinal motility (contractions of stomach wall)

11. Metabolic rate (oxygen consumption)

12. Muscle tension (muscle potentials)

13. Tremor (of striated muscles)

14. Eye blink and eye movement

15. Electroencephalograph (electrical activity of the brain)

16. PET scans (measures metabolic activity in the brain)

constant current, and whether to use electrode paste and skin-rubbing techniques. Such issues apply to all the measurement procedures to some degree. No one knows to what extent inconsistent reports reflect variations in instrument techniques.

Another problem frequently noted with regard to the use of physiological measures is that there seems to be considerable independence in the modes of reaction of the different organ systems. This phenomenon results in little or no correlation between different measures of autonomic reactivity. It means that multiple measures of physiological activity must be used in order not to miss physiological reactions when they occur, and also to avoid overgeneralizing from single measures. No single measure can serve as an accurate index of general arousal.

Problems connected with identifying physiological correlates of emotion relate not only to the measuring instruments, but to other factors as well. First of all, such research requires an independent measure of emotion, which must be based either on self-report or behavioral observations (or both). Unfortunately, many studies have simply assumed that changes in skin resistance or heart rate necessarily mean that an emotion has occurred, without some independent assessment of the emotion. Second, since most research situations in which subjects are evaluated are complex, it is likely that complex, or mixed, emotional states are aroused. The problem then becomes one of relating some pattern of physiological changes to some pattern of mixed emotion; an extremely difficult problem. Third, present technology is capable of recording many covert and subtle responses of which a subject is totally unaware. No one knows whether the lack of awareness is a universal biological fact or whether it reflects the operation of defenses, repressions, and the like. In such cases, it is especially difficult to relate the physiological index to an emotional state. A fourth problem is that each physiological system has several different functions within the body. For example, the sweating system and the cardiovascular systems act not only in relation to emotions, but they regulate temperature as well. The result is that different environmental conditions, and different fatigue and hunger conditions, will influence the pattern of physiological changes that occur in response to an emotion-producing stimulus. They will therefore obscure the nature of the physiological response. Finally, it has been demonstrated that different emotional states (e.g., fear and anger, pleasure and pain) have some physiological changes in common. The result of all these problems is that it is very difficult to establish clear-cut relations between emotional states and physiological responses. There is no way that we can read a skin resistance meter or a cardiotachometer and say: "This person is experiencing an emotion, and that emotion is fear." The emotional life is richer, more subtle, and more varied than are physiological changes. No one-to-one correspondence between self-reports of emotions and physiology has yet been established.

One example of an alternative approach is a study by Morton (1986) that measured regional brain activity in rats or mice during emotional behavior. In this investigation, a form of sugar used by the brain during metabolism (2-deoxyglucose) was injected into an animal's blood with some radioactive tracer in it. During a 30-minute period while the rat is engaged in some form of emotional behavior, the radio-labeled glucose is deposited in active brain sites. After the animal is sacrificed, researchers use

X-ray film to detect the brain structures where increased or decreased metabolic activity occurred during the emotional behavior, in contrast to control animals.

In this investigation, Morton studied three emotional situations: fighting induced by introducing an intruder male into the colony cage; fear induced by the experimenter approaching the animal in a confined area; and copulatory behavior. Eighty-six brain loci were analyzed for each of 52 animals in the study.

The results showed significant increases in glucose uptake in the fearful rats in the prefrontal cortex and in the corpus callosum, and significant decreases in parts of the hippocampus and amygdala. In the attacking animals there was an increase in lateral hypothalamic glucose uptake and a decrease in septal metabolism. The copulating animals showed large increases in metabolic activity in the globus pallidus of the forebrain and in the cerebellar cortex. Almost all the changes that were found were in limbic or limbic-associated brain structures. The value of this method for studying emotions in animals is that it allows examination of the functioning of the brain uninfluenced by drugs, electrodes, or lesions. This method is also similar to the procedure called *positron emission tomography* (or PET scans), which can be used with humans. Through the use of similar methods in humans and animals, it may be possible to reveal emotional continuities across phylogenetic levels.

Summary ■

Because emotions are complex states of the organism involving feelings, behavior, impulses, physiological changes and efforts at control, the measurement of emotions is also a complex process. Investigators have developed many approaches to measuring emotions. These approaches include adjective checklists, structured and unstructured questionnaires, behavioral rating techniques, observations of the products of behavior through the use of projective techniques, and physiological indices. No one method is necessarily better than any other, and all have sources of bias connected with them. Some, such as behavior ratings, are obviously more useful with psychiatric patients, children, and animals. Others, such as projective methods, are useful in getting at emotions that are hidden or repressed, and that even the respondent may not be aware of. Physiological measures of autonomic functions require appropriate equipment, and may measure general arousal better than specific emotional states.

In addition to the need for multiple measures of emotions, there is a need for a theoretical framework that provides a rationale for the measurement technique to be used. The idea that theory should guide and determine measurement methods is well established in the physical sciences. It should also be the basis for measurement in psychology.

Facial Expression and Emotions

The face is the mirror of the mind,
and eyes without speaking confess
the secrets of the heart
—St. Jerome

▌Goals of This Chapter

The previous chapter was concerned with the complex problem of how to measure emotions. We saw there that a great variety of methods have been developed for measuring the complex state called emotions. These methods include self-reports of feelings, ratings of behavior, and measures of internal bodily states, particularly of the autonomic system and the brain.

One of these methods of assessment has been considered to be so important that it has captured the attention of many psychologists, as well as researchers in other disciplines. This method is the study of facial expressions, and it already had a venerable history by the time Charles Darwin began to study the role of facial expressions in animals and humans. His observations were also the basis for the theory of emotion that he proposed. Studies of facial expressions have continued to intrigue researchers and have led to new theories of emotion.

In this chapter and the following one, we will examine the methods used to study facial expressions in human adults and will discover what kinds of conclusions have been reached. We will trace these methods from the early work of the French physiologist who studied expression by using electrical stimulation of particular muscles, to the contemporary studies of recognition of emotions by nonliterate people living in isolated regions of the world.

Over the years, attempts have been made to determine if judges can agree on the emotions expressed in posed pictures of the face, unposed pictures, and pictures of parts of the face. Evidence has begun to accumulate on the cross-cultural meanings of facial expressions. Other evidence to be described on the meaning of facial expressions comes from studies of children who are born blind and deaf. This chapter concludes by pointing out that facial expressions are part of a general nonverbal system that includes gestures, posture, voice quality, and other expressions, all of which act to communicate information. The following chapter deals with the implications of this idea as well as with the neurophysiology of facial expression.

Important Questions Addressed In This Chapter

- What are the facial muscles that determine the expression of emotions?
- What are some reasons for the inconsistencies in judgments of emotion from posed pictures of facial expressions?
- Which part of the face best reveals emotions?
- What was wrong with Landis's early study of facial expression that seemed to demonstrate no connection between expressions and verbal reports of feelings?
- What evidence exists that certain facial expressions are universally recognized?
- How does the study of masks contribute to our understanding of emotional expressions?
- What does the study of emotional expressions in blind and deaf children reveal about emotions?
- What kinds of nonverbal behaviors communicate emotions?
- What do gestures reveal about emotions?

■   ■   ■   ■   ■   ■   ■   ■

▌Studies of Facial Musculature

By the time Darwin wrote his book on emotional expression in 1872, a number of other scientists had already studied the expressions of the face. In 1844, a British physiologist named Charles Bell had written a book on emotions and had concluded that facial expressions were connected with changes in respiration. For example, during screaming, loud laughter, sneezing, and vomiting, the orbicular (eyelid) muscles of the eye contract strongly, thus forming part of the expression associated with these actions. In all such cases, the muscles of the chest and abdomen strongly contract, as do the muscles around the eyes at the same time. Darwin suspected that the eyelid contractions had some protective role.

| Figure 6.1 | "Terror Mixed With Pain, Torture" |

Source: G.B. Duchenne de Boulogne, 1990/1862.

Another early investigator of facial expression was the French physiologist Duchenne, who published a book that attempted to show the role of particular muscles in producing facial expressions. He used small electric currents to produce contractions of various muscles of the face and then took pictures of the resulting expression. Figure 6.1 is a picture illustrating the method Duchenne used to produce an expression that he called, "Terror mixed with pain, torture..." Figure 6.2 is a copy of a photograph produced by Duchenne using electrical stimulation of facial muscles. When Darwin showed this picture to 23 adults, most said that it expressed horror or agony, while some said that it looked like anger.

Some of the muscles that are involved in facial expressions are shown in Figure 6.3. In Duchenne's photograph, the muscles mostly involved are

---

| Figure 6.2 | An Expression Produced by Electrical Stimulation of Facial Muscles |

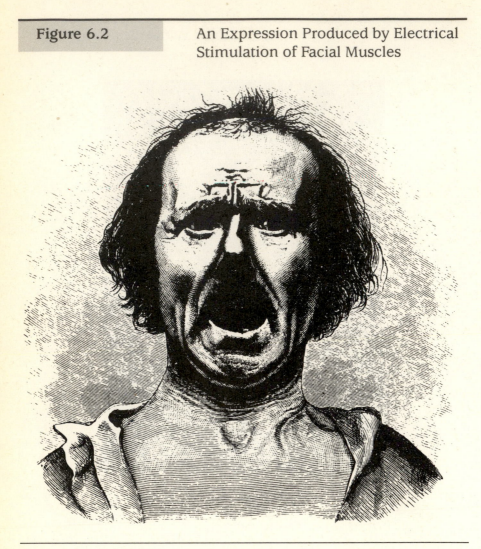

Source: C. Darwin, 1965/1872.

the corrugator (frown) muscles, the frontal (forehead) muscles, the orbicular (eyelid) muscles, and the platysma (neck) muscles.

Although differences of opinion exist among anatomists on the precise description of all the muscles of the face, there is reasonable agreement on the functional units of facial expression. From this point of view, Ekman and Friesen (1976) have tried to identify those facial muscles or groups of muscles that produce visible changes in particular parts of the face, such as the eyebrows or nose, that human observers can reliably distinguish. Table 6.1 presents their list of facial actions and the muscle or muscles

Figure 6.3	Some Muscles Involved in Facial Expressions

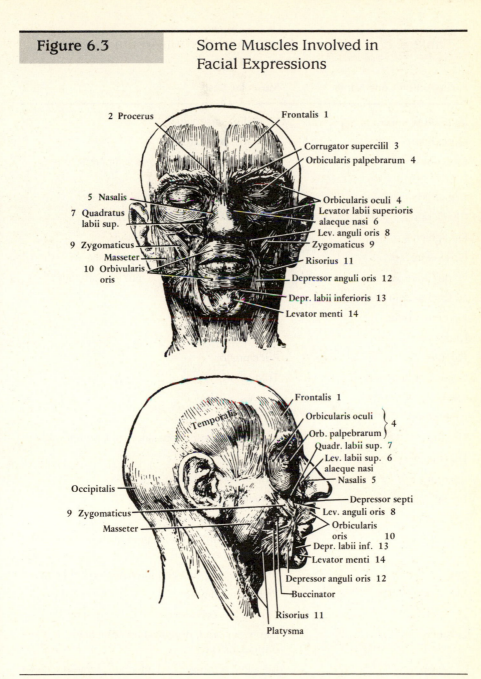

2 Procerus
Frontalis 1
Corrugator supercilil 3
Orbicularis palpebrarum 4
Orbicularis oculi 4
Levator labii superioris alaeque nasi 6
Lev. anguli oris 8
Zygomaticus 9
Risorius 11
Depressor anguli oris 12
Depr. labii inferioris 13
Levator menti 14
5 Nasalis
7 Quadratus labii sup.
9 Zygomaticus
Masseter
10 Orbivularis oris

Frontalis 1
Orbicularis oculi
Orb. palpebrarum } 4
Quadr. labii sup. 7
Lev. labii sup. 6 alaeque nasi
Nasalis 5
Depressor septi
Lev. anguli oris 8
Orbicularis oris 10
Depr. labii inf. 13
Levator menti 14
Depressor anguli oris 12
Buccinator
Temporalis
Occipitalis
9 Zygomaticus
Masseter
Risorius 11
Platysma

Source: T.V. Moore, 1948.

that produce those actions. This work is based on the prior efforts of a Swedish psychologist named Carl-Herman Hjortsio (1970). He carried out

Table 6.1	Single Action Units in the Facial Action Code
Facial Action Code Name	**Muscular Basis**
Inner brow raiser	Frontalis, pars medialis
Outer brow raiser	Frontalis, pars lateralis
Brow lowerer	Depressor glabella, depressor supercilli, corrugator
Upper lid raiser	Levator palpebrae superioris
Cheek raiser	Orbicularis oculi, pars palebralis
Lid tightener	Orbicularis oculi, pars palebralis
Nose wrinkler	Levator labii superioris, aleque nasi
Upper lid raiser	Levator labii superioris, caput infraorbitalis
Nasolabial fold deepener	Zygomatic minor
Lip corner puller	Zygomatic major
Cheek puffer	Caninus
Dimpler	Buccinnator
Lip corner depressor	Triangularis
Lower lip depressor	Depressor labii
Chin raiser	Mentalis
Lip puckerer	Incisivii labii superioris, incisive labii inferioris
Lip stretcher	Risorius
Lip funneler	Orbicularis oris
Lip tightener	Orbicularis oris
Lip pressor	Orbicularis oris
Lips part	Depressor labii, or relaxation of mentalis or orbicularis oris
Jaw drop	Masetter, temporal and internal pterygoid relaxed
Mouth stretch	Pterygoids, digastric
Lip suck	Orbicularis oris
Lips part	Depressor labii, or relaxation of mentalis or orbicularis oris
Jaw drop	Masetter, temporal and internal pterygoid relaxed
Mouth stretch	Pterygoids, digastric
Lip suck	Orbicularis oris

Source: P. Ekman and W. V. Friesen, 1976.

detailed studies of the facial muscles that are associated with different expressions. Figure 6.4, for example, presents a schematic presentation of sad, mournful expressions. According to Hjortsjo, these expressions depend upon the cooperative action of the following facial muscles: the glabella depressor, the eyebrow depressor, the sphincter muscle of the eye, the upper lip and the nasal wing levator, the incisive muscles of the upper lip and the lower lip, and the sphincter muscles of the mouth. Generally, every facial expression involves the cooperative action of a large number of individual muscles.

Darwin's interest in facial expressions stimulated a number of psychologists early in the twentieth century to begin the systematic study of facial expressions in humans. One of the questions they were interested in was whether college students could correctly judge emotional expressions from

Figure 6.4	Schematic Presentation of Expressions of Sadness and Grief

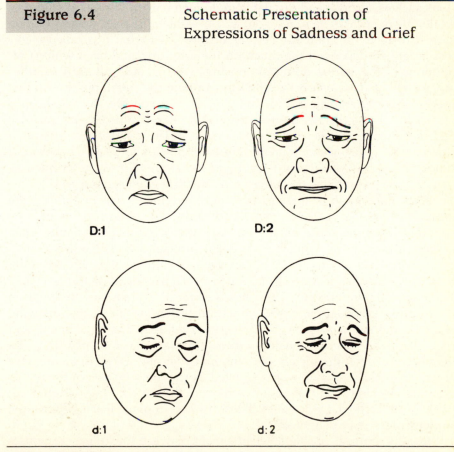

D:1   D:2

d:1   d:2

Source: Hjortsjo, 1970.

posed photographs. They were also interested in the relative importance of different parts of the face in influencing such judgments. What did they learn from these studies?

▌ Studies of Photographs of Facial Expressions

The Judgment of Posed Facial Expressions

The early studies of the judgment of posed facial expressions involved posed photographs or drawn portraits. These were presented one at a time to college students, who were asked to label each picture with an emotion word or phrase. Widely used for such studies was a set of posed photographs of an actress who provided her own labels as to what she had meant to convey with each expression. Her labels were defined as the correct response for each picture (Feleky, 1914).

The results of this and similar studies were ambiguous. Some expressions such as surprise and disgust were judged correctly by most students, while others such as hate, religion, and breathless interest were not often judged correctly. It gradually became obvious that what was called a correct judgment depended too much on the arbitrary (and even whimsical) opinions of the actress doing the posing (who is, after all, only another judge). This led Woodworth (1938) to examine the overlapping of terms used to describe a given pose, with the result that considerable consistency was found. For example, the fear pose was often confused with surprise and suffering but never with contempt or love. The disgust pose was often confused with anger and contempt, but never with surprise. Therefore, if synonyms of the correct word for the posed expression were accepted as correct, it turned out that the judges were in fairly good agreement.

A second way to increase agreement of judgments was by limiting the number of responses each judge could make. The need for this became apparent when the posed picture for hate was called mental pain by some judges, disgusted dread by others, and self-sufficiency by still others.

The increase in consistency of judgments resulting from a limited set of response words is illustrated in the study by Tomkins and McCarter (1964). These investigators prepared 69 photos of facial expressions designed, in their opinion, to exemplify either a neutral feeling or one of the following eight emotions: interest, joy, surprise, distress, fear, shame, disgust, and rage. Tomkins's theory considers these emotions basic or primary. The judges were given the pictures in random order and asked to identify the emotions expressed using words selected from nine brief lists of terms. For example, the judge could choose a word from the cluster: afraid, frightened, panicky, or terrified. Or he could choose a word from the list: joyful, happy, smiling, pleased, or delighted.

Results showed considerable agreement between the judges' responses and the intended posed emotions. It was found that joy and shame were almost always judged correctly, while the accuracy of judgments of surprise and interest was only moderate. Certain overlappings or confusions were also found. Surprise and interest were often confused. So too were fear and surprise, anger and disgust, and shame and distress. These confusions suggest an implicit similarity structure of emotion expressions. Schlosberg (1941), using the date reported by Feleky, concluded that the overlap of judgments about facial expressions of emotion leads to a circular scale rather than a linear one.

Despite the relatively good agreement that Tomkins and McCarter found among judges, they suggested a number of reasons the judgments were not unanimous. First, they pointed out that the actors who posed for the pictures did not always express the pattern the investigators wished. These actors also had unique lines or expressions on their own faces that influenced the final pose to some degree. Second, and perhaps more important, is the fact that an emotional response is an event that occurs over time. "The smile is a set of widening mouths. The eye blink in surprise or startle is a set of narrowing of the eyelids. The sneer of contempt is a set of liftings of the upper lip. The cry is a set of rhythmic sobs." Any still photograph is a very limited sample of this complex, temporal pattern. Third, the naming of affects is often ambiguous because each individual has a different personal history connected with the learning of the emotion language. Finally, many facial expressions are mixtures or blends of two or more primary emotions. If a judge is asked to select only one name for a facial expression, it is bound to be inadequate to some degree.

Judgments of Parts of the Face

A number of investigators have tried to discover which areas or features of the face offer the best clues for judging each emotional expression. Some have reported that the upper part of the face is more important for correct judgments of emotion, others have claimed that the mouth is more important, while the consensus seems to be that different emotions are judged from different parts of the face (Coleman, 1949).

In an effort to avoid some of the problems of posed facial expressions, Hill (1955) had two subjects pose their faces into most of the theoretically possible partial expressions the face could assume, without any reference to emotions per se. For example, the forehead can assume the three expressions of being raised, of frowning, and of frowning and being raised simultaneously. The eyes can assume expressions in which they are slightly, moderately, or widely open, and in which they are looking ahead, up, down, or to the side. The mouth can have various expressions relating to circular or elliptical shapes and to crescent or inverted crescent shapes.

Photographs were taken of all these expressions and the resulting slides prepared in such a way as to present only the desired part of the face, such as the forehead, the eyes, or the mouth. By this method, investigators obtained 25 partial facial expressions for each subject. These slides were shown to a group of 50 students who were asked to judge which emotion each partial expression represented. However, their responses were limited to the eight emotions of surprise, fear, sadness, disgust, expectancy, acceptance, anger, or joy.

The results showed the frequency with which different partial expressions were associated with each emotion label. Certain expressions were almost consistently attributed to certain emotions. For example, almost everyone agreed that the "mouth slightly open, corners drawn down" depicted disgust, and that "eyes half closed looking ahead" depicted sadness. The terms *fear, acceptance,* and *expectancy* were less consistently applied to the various partial expressions. The data did allow a tentative synthesis of each basic emotion from these elements. Thus, anger seemed to be defined by "tightly pursed lips," "forehead frowning," and "eyes slitted, looking ahead"; expectancy was defined by "eyes wide open, looking to the side," and "pursed lips."

Hill, also obtained evidence of overlap. He discovered that when the eyes were looking to the side, the expression was called anger about as often as it was called disgust. Pursed lips were often called surprise as well as expectancy, and a slightly open mouth was often called both fear and anger. Conversely, when an expression was called anger as a first choice, it was frequently called disgust as a second choice. If called joy as a first choice, acceptance was the most frequent second choice. If expectancy was the first choice, then fear was the most likely second choice.

In a related type of study, Boucher and Ekman (1975) identified a set of posed facial expressions that college students agreed on quite well (70% agreement) as representing the six emotions of disgust, fear, sadness, happiness, anger, and surprise. The pictures were then cut apart to yield three partial facial pictures: a brow-forehead picture, an eyes-eyelid picture, and a cheeks-mouth picture. Each partial photograph was rated on the degree to which it expressed one or another of the six emotions cited above.

Results showed that the facial area that most accurately reflected the total expression varied from emotion to emotion. It appears that there is no one area of the face that best reveals all emotions, but the value of the different facial areas in distinguishing emotions depends on the emotion being judged.

Unposed or Natural Expressions

Probably the best known study of unposed or natural expressions was carried out by Landis in 1924. He asked college students to allow themselves to be subjected to various conditions, mostly unpleasant, while he took motion pictures of their facial expressions. They were asked, for example, to look at pictures of people with ugly skin diseases, to accept a strong electric shock, and to cut off the head of a live rat with a knife. To facilitate later analysis of his pictures, Landis marked the major muscle outlines of each subject's face in black charcoal.

When he analyzed his film records, he found little evidence of any clear-cut relations between the subjects' reported feelings in a situation and patterns of facial expression. He concluded that "there is no expression typically associated with any verbal reports," and this statement has often been repeated in psychology textbooks as proof that facial expressions and emotions are not linked in any meaningful way.

This study can be criticized on a number of grounds. For one thing, many of these students, standing in front of a camera with black marks on their faces, showed a sheepish grin through most of the situations. There is thus a strong likelihood that all emotions generated in this context were mixed emotions, containing such elements as embarrassment, disgust, and surprise, and therefore no simple connection between *one* emotion and expression could be established. Second, in 1934 Davis reanalyzed the Landis data and showed that smiling occurred in cases of reported pain in 7% of the observations, whereas smiling occurred in 60% of the emotional responses reported as sexual. A particular muscle group of the face was found to be involved in 3% of reported cases of sexual feelings and in 50% of cases of reported pain. In addition, the facial expressions seen when looking at pornographic pictures were quite recognizably different from those seen when the subjects were listening to music. Davis concluded that there were definite tendencies for certain muscles to be involved in one emotion and not in another.

It should be evident by now that it is very difficult to study facial expressions in humans through the use of still photographs of facial expressions. Many problems exist: Still photographs are poor samples of the variety of changes that actually occur over time during emotions; they reveal little or nothing about the situation an individual is in, a fact that is part of the way people usually judge the likelihood of an emotion being present; it is difficult to establish a standard to determine what emotion is being expressed. Further, judges typically use a wide variety of words to describe what they see in a photograph. If every word is taken to mean a different emotion, agreement among judges is poor. If, however, the words are grouped in terms of similarity of meaning, agreement among judges is relatively good. Finally, it is evident that the language of emotions contains hundreds of possible words to describe emotions while the number of different facial expressions is relatively limited. Asking judges to label facial expressions with whatever terms come to mind is therefore likely to produce many inconsistencies. If broad categories are used, agreement is greater.

Another factor that influences the degree of agreement of judges is the intensity of the facial expression. Mild expressions are more likely to produce differences in judgment than extreme ones. This tendency is illustrated by Figure 6.5, which shows drawings of a number of extreme facial

Figure 6.5   Extreme Facial Expressions

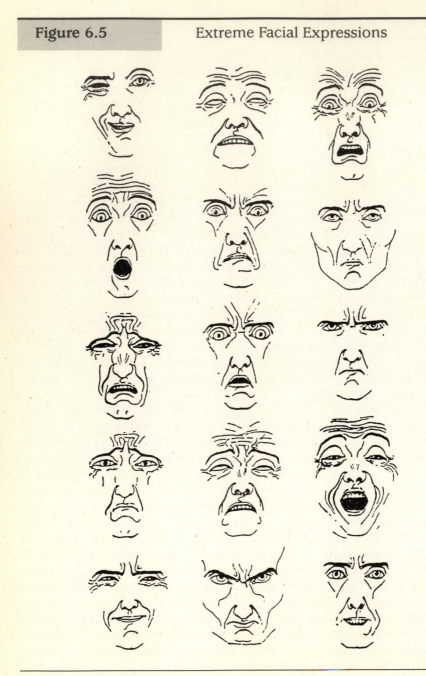

Source: D. Morris, 1977.

expressions. Most of these expressions are easier to identify than more neutral, less intense ones.

■ The Search for Universal Facial Expressions

Are facial expressions of emotion learned like the words of a language or are they innate? Darwin believed that some facial expressions in humans are unlearned, just as many expressions in chimpanzees and other primates are unlearned. The evidence he presented for this point of view included the following: (1) Some facial expressions appear in similar form in lower animals, particularly primates; (2) some facial expressions are seen in infants and young children in the same form as seen in adults; (3) some facial expressions are shown in identical ways by those born blind as in those who are normally sighted; and (4) some facial expressions appear in similar form in widely distinct races and groups of humans.

Based on these kinds of observations, Darwin concluded that facial expressions act as signals or as forms of communication between individuals. He believed that facial expressions reveal something about the likelihood of action. There is usually some probability that making an angry face will be followed by angry words, threats, or physical attacks. If one individual can judge the probable behavior of another individual, or accurately estimate his or her intentions, this fact can be very useful. It will allow the second person to adjust his or her behavior, and possibly affect the outcome of the interaction. Such communications and adaptations may even influence the chances of individual survival.

In recent years, many studies have been reported that deal with these issues. Of particular interest has been the question of the universality of facial expressions of emotion.

Judgments of Facial Expressions in New Guinea and Elsewhere

In 1969, Ekman, Sorenson, and Friesen published a cross-cultural study concerned with recognition of facial expressions. Out of 3,000 photographs, these investigators selected 30 that, in their judgment, showed only pure expressions of single emotions. These 30 photographs represented six emotions that Tomkins and others have proposed as primary or basic: happiness, surprise, fear, anger, disgust, and sadness. The photographs were of male and female Caucasians, adults and children, actors, and mental patients. The pictures were shown to college students in the United States, Brazil, and Japan and to adult volunteers in New Guinea and in Borneo. The six emotion words were translated into each appropriate language, and the judge was requested to pick a word from each group of six in order to name the facial expression.

The results showed high agreement by the students in the United States, Brazil, and Japan, with percentage agreement ranging from the 60s to the high 90s. Izard (1971) has reported similar results for seven other literate cultures. Relatively less agreement was found for the two preliterate societies. Happiness was judged consistently (92%) in Borneo and in New Guinea, but the percentage agreement for anger (using medians) was around 56%, for sadness about 55%, for fear 46%, for surprise 38%, and for disgust 31%. All these results are better than chance judgments, but it is evident that the preliterate groups do not judge the facial expressions in quite the same way as do the westernized groups. Ekman and his colleagues conclude that their "findings support Darwin's suggestion that facial expressions of emotion are similar among humans, regardless of culture, because of their evolutionary origins." This conclusion is undoubtedly an overgeneralization in view of the various limitations of the study. For example, the study used only 30 pictures; the number of judges was only 15 judges in Borneo and 14 in one of the New Guinea groups; the study used only six affects; and the results showed less agreement among the preliterate groups than the literate ones. In addition, one could argue that people even in the preliterate societies have been influenced by western-made motion pictures.

To deal with this last criticism, Ekman and Friesen (1971) provided a detailed report of a study carried out with members of the Fore linguistic cultural group of Southeastern New Guinea. Until 1960, these people were an isolated "Stone Age" culture with little or no contact with westerners. The judges used in the study were selected because they had seen no movies, neither spoke nor understood English or pidgin, had not lived in any government towns, and had never worked for a Caucasian. These criteria were met by 180 adults and 130 children.

Because of literacy and other problems that the judges had, the judgment task was simplified. The judge was read an uncomplicated story and then shown three pictures simultaneously. He or she was to select the picture in which the person's face showed the emotion described in the story. Some other members of the Fore tribe served as research assistants and recruited subjects, read and translated the stories, and were discouraged from prompting.

Using this technique, researchers found extremely high agreement among both adults and children for almost all emotion expressions. For adults, the median agreement for the happiness picture was 92%; for the anger picture, 87%; for the sadness picture, 81%; for the disgust picture, 83%; for the surprise picture, 68%; and for the fear picture, 64%. In this sample, fear and surprise expressions were often not clearly separated.

As a follow-up of this study, Ekman and Friesen briefly mention that they obtained pictures of posed emotional expressions from these same New Guineans and showed them to American college students. These students correctly judged the intended emotions in most cases. As a result of these studies, Ekman and Friesen conclude that "particular facial expressions are universally associated with particular emotions." However, they do emphasize that cultural factors and learning will influence emotional expression in three ways: by creating differences in the conditions that elicit emotion, by the consequences of an emotion, and by the rules that regulate when to show or not show an expression.

Another study has been reported using a methodology somewhat similar to that Ekman and his associates developed. Boucher (1973) had five male American subjects pose six emotions each. The photographs were judged by an American group of college students who agreed that each photograph depicted only one emotion. These photos were shown to 31 adult Temuan judges from Selangor in Southeast Asia, and to 30 Malay males from the Kuala Lumpur area. The judges were shown each picture and were asked which of the six emotion terms best described the emotion the man in the picture depicted.

The correlation coefficient between the Temuan and American judges was +.71, between the Malay and American judges +.55, and between the Malay and Temuan judges +.63. Happy faces were most often judged correctly, with median agreements of 93%. The agreement for the other emotions was disgust (80%); surprise (72%); sadness (69%); and fear (56%). Boucher concluded that "American facial affective behavior can be identified accurately, by both Temuan and Malay peoples" and that this finding further supports the idea of certain facial expressions being universal. He added the interpretation that "all people share the same neurophysiological elements corresponding to fear, for example, but they can learn what to be afraid of, and they can learn how and when to manage their fear behavior when the emotion is experienced" (Boucher, 1974).

Other Cross-Cultural Studies

Another way to examine cross-cultural similarities in facial expression is to videotape subjects' facial expressions, without their knowledge, while they watch both neutral films and stress-inducing films of body mutilation. Ekman obtained such videotapes on 25 Japanese college students and 25 American students. Using the Facial Affect Scoring System (shown in Table 6.1) to identify the facial muscles and expressions resulting from the stress, he found that the frequency with which American and Japanese students showed anger, fear, disgust, surprise, sadness, and happiness was quite similar. The correlation was +.88. However, when a fellow countryman entered the room, the facial behaviors of the two groups of students was quite different. The Japanese students tended to show polite smiles, while the Americans replayed the expressions they had originally had. These observations imply that different display rules may operate in different cultures.

In a recent cross-cultural study, Ekman and Friesen (1986) created three variants on the expression of contempt: (1) tightening and slightly raising the corner of the lip unilaterally; (2) the same expression bilaterally; and (3) raising the entire lip slightly, without tightening or raising the lip corners. Photographs of these expressions, as well as those for six other emotions, were shown to students in 10 countries: Estonia, Greece, Hong Kong, Italy, Japan, Scotland, Turkey, the United States, West Germany, and West Sumatra.

Results showed high agreement (between 73 and 90%) for the six emotion expressions of happy, surprise, sad, fear, disgust, and anger. There was equally high agreement on the first variant (unilateral lip corner raising) of contempt, but not for the others. The authors concluded that the unilateral contempt expression appears to be recognized by most subjects in each culture studied, and should therefore be added to the list of basic emotions.

Recognition of facial expressions, however, is only one aspect of emotions. Others concern the regulation and control of emotions, the evaluation of situations that elicit emotions, and the verbal and nonverbal reactions to such situations.

Cross-Cultural Questionnaire Studies

A study by Matsumoto, Kudoh, and others (1988) asked a sample of Japanese and American college students to describe various reactions to the emotions of joy, fear, anger, sadness, disgust, shame and guilt. Each subject was asked to recall and describe a situation in detail, in which they had felt each of these emotions. They were then asked such questions as the following: How long did they feel the emotion? How intense was the feeling? Was the event pleasant or unpleasant? Did they try to hide or control the feeling? How did they cope with it? How did it change their relationships with the people involved?

One of the findings reported was that the emotions of sadness, shame, and guilt were subject to much more self-control than the other emotions, with joy being associated with the least control. Although there were some differences in how students from the two cultures responded to these questions, the differences were relatively small. At the same time, reaction to the various emotions showed large differences.

Walbott and Scherer (1989) carried out an extension of this type of study using detailed questionnaires administered to 2,500 subjects in 30 different countries. The subjects were asked about the nature of the situations that elicit emotions, their cognitive evaluations, physiological symptoms, verbal and nonverbal reactions, and control attempts. The emotions studied were joy, sadness, fear, anger, disgust, shame and guilt.

As one might expect, the results are extensive, but a few illustrations follow. In terms of physiological symptoms that are reported, sadness tends to be associated with a lump in the throat, crying, withdrawal, and silence. Fear tends to be associated with a change in breathing, feeling cold, faster heart beat, tense muscles, perspiration, and silence. Joy is associated with feeling warm, faster heart beat, smiling, moving toward someone, and lengthy utterances. In terms of the types of situations that elicit emotions, injustice tends to produce anger; interactions with strangers and unknown, novel situations tend to produce fear; loss of relationships and death tend to produce sadness; and achievement and close relationships tend to produce joy. The authors of the study emphasize the value of this questionnaire approach for the study of emotion. It has demonstrated fairly specific triggers for different emotions, as well as differential reactions and symptom patterns. The fact that they have found a considerable amount of generality in these observations in 30 countries worldwide suggests the likelihood of some degree of universality to the reactions associated with some emotions.

Studies of Anthropological Artifacts

Several studies in recent years have indirectly examined the issue of cross-cultural similarities in emotional expressions. For example, Aronoff, Barclay, and Stevenson (1988) were interested in the ways that different cultures show threat through facial expressions as revealed by their art work. In order to study this problem, the investigators began by asking American college students to imagine themselves in a preliterate society and then to draw a picture of a mask they would wear to frighten their victims into surrender. From these drawings, coders compiled a list of commonly drawn elements that included horns or a pointed head, disheveled hair, pointed ears, diagonal eyebrows, vertical lines between eyebrows, eyes oriented diagonally, triangular eyes, a pointed chin, a pointed beard, and so forth.

Investigators then obtained pictures of masks from ethnographic sources representing *threatening* and *nonthreatening* wooden masks as constructed in 18 different subcultures. These pictures were then coded for the number of threatening signs appearing on each mask. The total number of threatening signs was considered to be an index of the amount of threat present in each mask. The results showed that all but one of the threat characteristics (pointed chin) significantly discriminated between the threatening and nonthreatening masks. The authors concluded that the basic underlying feature that most of the signs had in common was the geometrical pattern of diagonality and angularity (i.e., the use of diagonal and triangular forms).

As a follow-up of this conclusion, researchers selected 10 features from the list of threat characteristics and then presented them as abstract patterns to another group of college students who were asked to rate their emotional reactions to the pattern. The ratings involved semantic differential scales measuring *evaluation* (e.g., bad-good, dangerous-safe, cruel-kind, unfriendly-friendly), *potency* (e.g., weak-strong, feminine-masculine, cowardly-brave), and *activity* (e.g., passive-active, inert-energetic, calm-excitable). Examples of the patterns used are shown in Figure 6.6. The students who evaluated the patterns found the diagonal and angular displays significantly more potent, active, and negative than the comparison figures. The authors suggest that certain geometric patterns act cross culturally as displays that signal threat or danger, although they do not propose an underlying reason for this generalization.

Figure 6.6   Examples of Display Patterns

The more threatening stimulus of a pair is presented on the left.

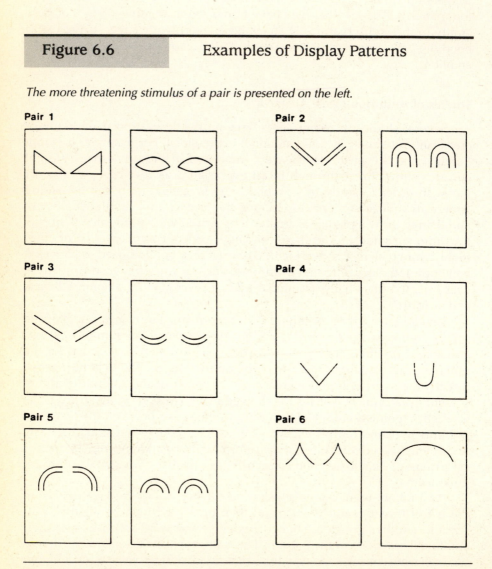

Source: J. Aronoff, A. M. Barclay and L. A. Stevenson, 1988.

Anthropological Studies of Facial Expression

A German ethologist named Eibl-Eibesfeldt (1990) has used anthropological analyses extensively. He has been studying emotional displays in various preliterate cultures around the world and has reported many parallels in the patterns of emotional expression revealed in their art and sculpture. He reports that the facial expressions of threat, fear, and submission are universally found. Staring at an opponent, for example, is a widely used expression to intimidate. Lowering and tilting the head together with pouting and gaze avoidance are submissive signals. Showing clenched teeth by pulling down the corners of the mouth is widely seen as a display of anger both in some primates and in humans. This finding is illustrated in Figure 6.7.

Figure 6.7	Display of Anger

(a) A mandrill bares imposing canines in this characteristic mouth position.
(b) A kubuki player simulates anger.

a   b

Source: Eibl-Eibesfeldt, 1971.

Because dangers and threats are universal, we find avoidance, flight, and defensive responses in all animals, including humans. The need for protection from strangers and enemies is manifested in many ways. For example, apotropaic figurines (also called scaredevils) are found all over the world. These sculptures show stare threats, teeth threats, phallic displays, female genital displays (mocking), and anal threats in an exaggerated manner. In Gothic churches all over Europe there are stone sculptures commonly called grotesques. Many of them appear as frozen expressions of threat intended to scare away or appease evil spirits or demons. An example of such faces is shown in Figure 6.8, along with a similar sculpture

Figure 6.8	Grostesque Sculpture

(a) 12th Century Johanni Church, Schwäbisch Gmünd, Germany. The threatening face shows often a "biting" expression with a widely open mouth and exposed teeth. (b) A Japanese amulet devil's mask in the form of a typical scare-face, with exaggerated teeth. (c) Corbel figure from the gothic church of Nôtre Dame in L'Epine, France. The gesture of pulling the mouth apart with both hands is common in grotesque sculpture and mimics furor. (All drawn from photographs by I. Eibl-Eibesfeldt). (d) An Eastern example before a temple in Ubud, Bali. (Drawn from a photograph by C. Sütterlin).

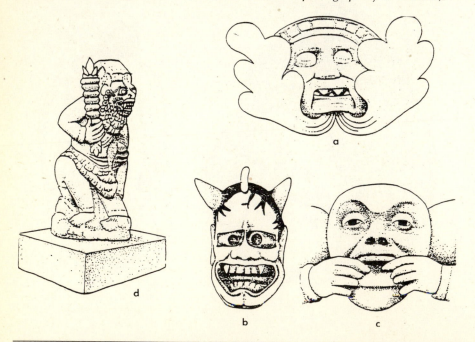

a

d

b

c

Source: I. Eibl-Eibesfeldt and C. Sutterlin, 1990.

standing before a temple in Bali. Sticking out the tongue, another facial display often seen in old churches, is shown in Figure 6.9. Eibl-Eibesfeldt believes it to be a universal expression derived from spitting and disgust. Rozin and Fallon (1987) have also cited evidence that tongue protrusion is seen in disgust in all cultures that have been studied. It is also seen in various primate species (Smith, Chase, and Lieblich, 1974). The widespread appearance of these facial displays around the world and in higher primates suggests that human beings have some common patterns of expression related to basic protective and defensive experiences. Does this pattern mean that emotional displays are innate or genetically determined? How consistent is such a conclusion with the obvious fact that human beings can control the expression of their emotions to varying degrees? Is it possible to disentangle the complex issue of the connection between innate emotional expressions and the influence of learning?

Figure 6.9	A Universal Expression of Disgust

This figure is found at the entrance to the Piacenza Cathedral, Italy. The extended tongue is widespread in avertive figures in all cultures and derived as expression from a ritualized aggressive behavior of spitting and disgust (Drawn from a photograph by C. Sütterlin).

Source: P. F. Brain et al. (Eds.), 1990.

▮ Emotional Expressions in Children Born Blind

Darwin was the first to bring to our attention the importance of observing children who were blind from birth as evidence concerning the innateness of facial expressions of emotion. In his 1872 book, Darwin stated that children born blind blush from shame and display emotions in the same way as do those with normal eyesight.

Almost no one attempted to follow up these observations until the third decade of the present century. In 1932, Goodenough reported her observations of a 10-year-old girl who had been born blind and deaf and who had had almost no training. This child showed typical signs of surprise on her face when something unexpected occurred; she whimpered and looked sad at the loss of an object; she frowned when she was frustrated; and she laughed and smiled when given pleasant things. She showed resentment by pouting of the lips, and when she was happy, she often danced.

These kinds of observations were replicated by Thompson (1941). Photographs were taken of 26 blind children, aged 7 weeks to 13 years, in natural emotional states. Similar photographs were taken of a matched control group of seeing children. It was found that facial activities of laughing, crying, and smiling were comparable at all ages in both groups. During mild punishment, children in both groups showed a pouting expression, as well as the downturned mouth characteristic of sadness. Judges accurately judged the facial expressions of both the blind and seeing children in about 70 percent of the photographs.

In a second study of this type (Fulcher, 1942), 118 normal boys and girls, 4 to 15 years of age and of normal intelligence, were asked to look happy, sad, angry, or frightened. Researchers compared their facial expressions with those of 50 congenitally blind boys and girls of approximately the same age and intelligence who were asked to do the same task. Both the seeing and the blind children showed distinct patterns of facial expression for each of the different emotions. In addition, the blind and seeing children showed quite similar patterns.

Another study of children born blind and deaf was reported by Eibl-Eibesfeldt (1973). Motion pictures were taken of six children, all deaf and blind from birth. Two of the children had extensive brain damage, two had moderate brain damage, and two had slight or no brain damage. All showed retarded development to varying degrees and all showed some stereotyped behaviors such as teeth grinding, head or body swaying, and kicking.

Despite the fact that these children could neither see nor hear the world around them and were also greatly impaired in cognitive capacity, they showed many normal emotional reactions. Eibl-Eibesfeldt writes:

Smiling was observed in all the deaf-and-blind-born studied so far. It occurred spontaneously during play, and in Sabine when she sat by herself in the sun patting her face with the palms of her hands. Smiling could be released by patting, mild tickling, and engaging in social play. The smiling started with an upward movement of the corners of the mouth. At higher intensities the lips opened wide in front, exposing the teeth in the way sighted people do; the eye slits were narrowed, and finally the head was raised and tilted back.

In addition to smiling, the children all showed laughter, generally during rough social play such as wrestling as well as during tickling. The children cried when hurt or when left in an unfamiliar environment. In such cases the corners of the mouth usually turned down and opened, the eyelids pressed together, and tears were shed. Sometimes the eyebrows were raised, furrowing the brow at the same time that frown lines appeared between the eyes. Occasionally, angry crying was observed when someone persistently offered a child a disliked object. The children also spontaneously embraced, caressed, and kissed other people on some occasions. Despite their deafness, these children often uttered many mono- and bisyllabic sounds. Table 6.2 lists the many types of emotional expressive behaviors these children showed in appropriate contexts.

This study of deaf-and-blind-born children and the earlier cited studies of blind children indicate that these children all show emotional expres-

Table 6.2	Expressive Behavior Patterns Observed in Children Born Deaf and Blind

1. Smiling	13. Biting of own hands and lips
2. Laughing	14. Jerking back of the head
3. Crying in distress	15. Strong exhaling
4. Crying in anger	16. Contact seeking by embracing movements
5. Frowning	
6. Pouting	17. Contact seeking by reaching out
7. Surprise reactions	18. Signaling of the hand with the palm facing out
8. Headshaking as a gesture of refusal	
9. Turning around and walking away	19. Caressing
10. Clenching teeth	20. Nibbling
11. Clenching fists	21. Rubbing the forehead against a person
12. Stamping feet	

Source: Eibel-Eibesfeldt, 1973.

sions very similar to the expressions shown by normal children. This phenomenon occurs without imitation or other kinds of direct information about how one is supposed to behave. These observations strongly support the position that many emotional expressions are unlearned and reflect basic neuromuscular, genetically determined programs. Such a view does not assume that all facial expressions are innate, since some expressions may be learned like the words of a language (for example, winking at someone to express approval, or wrinkling the nose to express disdain). The belief that certain emotional expressions are innate also does not mean that such expressions cannot be modified, suppressed, or inhibited. It is an empirical research problem to determine which expressions are innate and the extent to which experience can modify such patterns. In addition, it should be emphasized that many emotional expressions are not facial expressions, but bodily expressions, a point we shall now consider.

■ Facial Expressions as an Aspect of Nonverbal Behavior

Everyone knows that parts of the body other than the face also express emotions. The erection of body hairs, the flushing of the skin, the raising of the shoulders, and restless pacing all can reveal something about emotional states. People often say one thing but imply another by tone of voice or gesture. It is evident that nonverbal behaviors are intimately related to emotions.The range of nonverbal communicative behaviors is quite large. Examples of nonverbal events that can communicate affect states follow:

> facial expressions
> eye movements and gaze direction
> gestures
> posture
> voice qualities such as pitch and inflection
> speech hesitations
> nonlanguage sounds such as laughing, yawning, and grunting
> use of social space
> touching
> odors and sniffing

To illustrate this point, what emotions do you believe the following common expressions imply?

> "Tied up in knots"
> "In a cold sweat"
> "Made my skin crawl"
> "Butterflies in my stomach"
> "Goose pimples"
> "Frozen to the spot"
> "Pain in the neck"

"Blew my top"
"Lump in my throat"
"Gave me the chills"

Most of these expressions are easily recognized as being associated with fear, anger, disgust, or sadness.

Body odors also convey emotional messages, although we seldom talk about them. The intensity of our concerns about odors, however, is reflected in the billions of dollars we spend every year on soaps, deodorants, perfumes, and mouthwashes. Some odors are obvious and simply reflect poor personal cleanliness. Others are more subtle, or even not recognized, and yet have an influence upon our emotions. Such subtle odors, called *pheromones,* have been detected and measured in both humans and lower animals. The typical sniffing behavior that takes place among most animals functions to identify sexual and emotional signals. They enable animals to recognize mates, give alarms, mark territory, and indicate sexual receptivity.

In humans there are two types of sweat glands: eccrine glands and apocrine glands. The eccrine glands are the true sweat glands and occur over most of the body. They produce a relatively odorless secretion whose evaporation aids the body to lose heat and regulate salt balance. The apocrine glands are found in both men and women and are located in only a few places in the body: on the eyelids, in the armpits, on the nipples and areolae, and in the genital and anal areas. They secrete a slightly oilier substance than the eccrine glands, as well as pheromones. Although most people cannot consciously detect the pheromones, they are still influenced by them. In one study, one group of married women were given a perfume containing a pheromone derived from secretions of musk deer. A control group of women were given an identically smelling perfume, but without the pheromone. All the women applied the perfume before going to bed at night. Questionnaires completed by both husbands and wives, after a trial period, revealed that overall sexual activity markedly increased in about one quarter of the women who had received the perfumes containing the pheromones (Marsh, 1988).

Vocal Expression of Emotion

Compared to studies of facial expression, the vocal mode of affect expression has been relatively neglected. This condition is probably related to the fact that measuring vocal characteristics requires special electronic methods, and their results are not always easy to interpret.

Studies of animals have led to some tentative conclusions concerning the relations between vocal sounds and emotions. As summarized by Scherer (1989), in states of relaxation and play, one tends to find repeated short sounds with relatively low frequencies (e.g. purring). Defense calls tend to be short, high-amplitude sounds with a broad frequency spectrum (e.g., shrieking). Submission calls are usually long high frequency sounds with repeated frequency shifts.

On the basis of studies of calls made by squirrel monkeys, Jurgens (1979) describes warning sounds as short, loud sounds, with a rapid decrease in energy from high to low frequencies. He is in agreement with Morton (1977) that "birds and mammals tend to use relatively low frequency sounds when hostile, and higher-frequency, more pure tone like sounds when frightened, appeasing, or approaching in a friendly manner."

Human speech makes use of vocal sounds, but it represents a complex mixture of both linguistic patterns (that is, the codes we call words), and nonlinguistic elements that refer to such things as loudness, pitch, variability, breathiness, and nasality. The problem of separating these two components of human speech is an extremely difficult one. However, although words of a language are obviously learned, the specific vocal quality is probably largely determined by genetic factors. Speech patterns seem to be as characteristic of a person as are fingerprints, a fact well known to the police of all nations.

Research in this area has two major traditions; one is concerned with the process of encoding emotions in speech (that is, identifying aspects of speech that reflect emotions), and the other is concerned with decoding (that is, the ability of judges to recognize emotion in speech). Data on encoding reveals some differences between emotions (as least as generated by actors who are role playing), but the overlap is great. For example, in a summary of this literature Scherer (1989) reports that the emotion of joy is characterized by high pitch, large variability in pitch, loud sound, and fast tempo. Anger is described by a high pitch, wide frequency range, large variability, loud sound, and fast tempo. Fear is similar to anger. Grief has a low pitch, narrow range, soft sounds, and slow tempo. The overlap, especially among joy, anger, and fear, is evident and this may be due, in part, to a lack of knowing what best to measure.

With regard to the ability of humans to decode the emotions in human speech, a review of 30 studies has revealed an average accuracy of about 60% in contrast to chance agreement of 12%. This agreement is about the same degree found when making judgments from photographs (Scherer, 1989).

▌Gestures as Communications

In an effort to find out what certain common gestures mean, Morris, Colett, and others (1979) identified 20 gestures and showed pictures of them to 1,200 people at various locations in England and Europe. The judges were asked to indicate what each gesture meant. Some of the gestures involve the face and others involve only the hand. Illustrations of the gestures used are shown in Figure 6.10; the most common meanings given to each gesture are listed in Table 6.3.

Figure 6.10   Twenty Gestures Studied

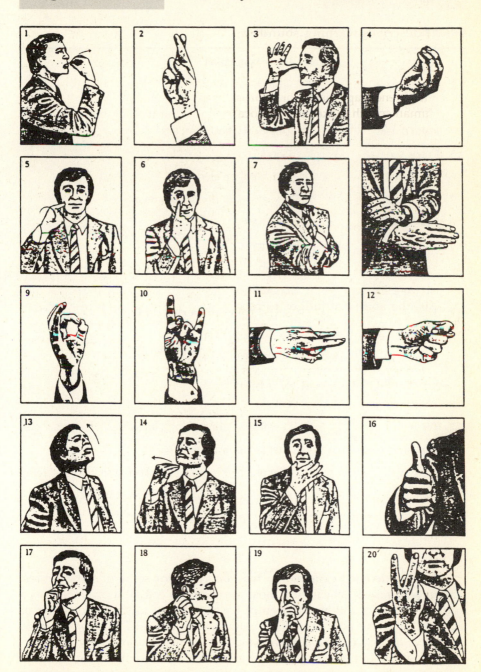

Source: D. Morris et al., 1979.

Table 6.3	The Meanings of Gestures

Gestures	Meanings
1. Fingertips kiss	Praise, salutation
2. Fingers cross	Protection
3. Nose thumb	Mockery
4. Hand purse	Question, good, fear, lots
5. Cheek screw	Good
6. Eyelid pull	I am alert, be alert
7. Forearm jerk	Sexual insult, sexual comment
8. Flat-hand flick	Go away
9. The ring	OK, good
10. Vertical horn	Cuckold
11. Horizontal horn	Cuckold
12. The fig	Sexual comment, sexual insult
13. The head toss	Negative, beckon
14. Chin flick	Disinterest, negative
15. Cheek stroke	Thin & ill, attractive
16. Thumb up	OK
17. Teeth flick	"I will give you nothing", anger (defiance), revenge
18. The ear touch	Effeminate, warning
19. Nose tap	Complicity (It's a secret, or keep it secret.), be alert
20. Palm back V-sign	Victory, two, sexual insult, sign in WWII

Source: D. Morris et al , 1979.

A more detailed explanation may be given for some of the gestures. The *fingers cross* is believed by most to mean protection. It originated as a sign of the cross and as an attempt by the devout to gain protection or ward off evil. We now say, "Keep your fingers crossed" to hope for luck. *Thumbing the nose* is almost universally seen as insult or mockery. It apparently originated in medieval Europe as a jester's way of insulting his audience. It implies that someone has a bad smell while at the same time the face often takes on an expression of disgust. Widely recognized as a sexual insult, the *forearm jerk* appears to be a phallic gesture implying insertion by a large penis. Because men usually use it against each other, therefore it suggests anal threat. In primates, dominant males make phallic threats against subordinate males, usually by mounting and making some pelvic thrusts without anal insertion. The forearm jerk is an enlarged version of the old middle finger jerk (known by the Romans as the obscene finger). In Malta, the gesture is so obscene, one can be arrested for using it in a public place. The fig is an ancient symbol meaning a sexual comment or insult, or as a protection. The ancient Greeks carried amulets of female genitals (in the shape of a fig) as a way to avert evil. Such amulets are still seen today. Another meaning of the fig is as a reference to a woman being sexy and available, usually made as a comment from one man to another. It has also been interpreted as a symbol of copulation.

What may we conclude about nonverbal gestures and emotions? It appears that gestures are a kind of visual slang with some gestures having an ancient origin and others (such as V for victory) having a quite recent origin. They express emotions just as words do, but they are not spontaneous or unlearned. They often have somewhat different interpretations in different places and when used, they tend to emphasize the spoken word. Gestures are more common and acceptable in the lower social classes and in children or younger people. Men use them more often than women. Most people have no idea of the historical sources of the gestures they use. And most important in the present context, gestures express strong emotions, usually of anger, disgust, mockery, disinterest, wariness, fear, praise, and acceptance. Most of these things may be said of facial expressions as well.

Summary ■

Anatomic studies of the face have identified the muscles that determine facial expressions, and several psychologists have developed coding schemes for scoring the muscles active in any given expression. Over the past century, psychologists have carried out many studies to try to determine how well the face reveals emotions. One method requires judgments of emotions from posed facial expressions. There are many problems with this method and the results of its use have been far from unanimous. Judgments of emotions from parts of the face have shown some consistency, although it appears that no one area of the face best reveals all emotions. Studies of unposed *natural* expressions have also shown limited consistency of judgment, partly because of many methodological problems.
In an effort to determine whether facial expressions of emotion are innate, investigators have conducted several cross-cultural studies in widely distinct races and groups of humans. Results have revealed that most adults, regardless of culture and education, are generally able to recognize

the facial expressions of happiness, surprise, fear, anger, disgust, sadness, and contempt. Different cultures vary in the controls or *display rules* they use to inhibit the expression of particular emotions. In addition, cross-cultural questionnaire studies of the cognitive triggers of emotion have revealed a great deal of consistency in reported elicitors of emotions. Anthropological investigators have shown how we see certain expressions of emotion consistently in many different artifacts such as masks, sculptures, and art. All these findings support the idea that certain emotional expressions are universal.

We find further evidence in observations of children born blind and/or deaf. Such children generally show the same patterns of emotional expressions that normally sighted or hearing children do in response to eliciting conditions.

Clearly, facial expressions are only one of kind of nonverbal behavior that may reveal emotions. Others are postures, gestures, sounds, and odors. These various patterns may be seen in both humans and lower animals and are recognized as methods by which individuals communicate information.

Neurophysiology and Theories of Facial Expression

*He that has eyes to see and ears to hear
may convince himself that no mortal
can keep a secret. If his lips are silent, he
chatters with his fingertips, betrayal
oozes out of him at every pore.*
—Sigmund Freud

▌Goals of This Chapter

This chapter continues the discussion of the meaning of facial expressions. It begins with a review of the neurophysiology underling facial muscle action. It summarizes some of the major things we know about facial expressions of emotion, and then proceeds to describe several theories that attempt to explain emotional expressions. So-called peripheral theories are summarized as represented by the theories of Tomkins, Izard, and Zajonc. Such theories assume that feedback from facial expressions influences emotional feelings. Central theories assume that facial expressions reflect inner feeling states. Still another type of theory assumes that facial expressions are communications that attempt to influence a social encounter, regardless of inner feelings.

The chapter then considers the evolutionary origins of facial displays using a major study of baboons as a basis for many illustrations. Other examples are based on studies of African monkeys called *guenons*. The chapter concludes with some ethological thinking about the evolution of facial expressions.

Important Questions Addressed In This Chapter

- What do neurological studies of patients with paralysis of half of the face reveal about emotional expressions?
- What kinds of drugs can produce laughter?
- What is meant by a *peripheral theory* of facial expression?
- What is meant by a *central theory* of facial expression?
- How does the concept of facial expressions as social communications differ from the two types of theories mentioned above?
- What is meant by a *functional theory* of facial expressions?
- From what biological activities did facial expressions probably evolve?

■   ■   ■   ■   ■   ■   ■   ■

The Neurophysiology of Facial Expression

It is important to emphasize that the face is capable of providing information of many kinds about an individual. The size, shape, and color of the features provide information about the beauty, race, and age of an individual. The gradual accumulation of wrinkles and pouches provides more detailed information about age and health. Rapid changes in the face are usually produced by muscles and to some degree by alterations of blood flow and skin temperature. These latter changes are what are usually considered when studying emotions. To understand them and their functions requires some knowledge of the underlying physiology and neurology of the face. Rinn (1984) has reviewed this topic, and the following description is based on his account.

Facial muscles are evolutionary offshoots of the respiratory muscles of fish. In humans, some of the nerve connections to the facial muscles are from the autonomic system, and, for this reason, some anatomists classify the face muscles as viscera. Some of the major face muscles are involved primarily in chewing and eating, while others are involved in speech and lip articulation. One of the results of these functions is that the oral region is moved in almost any direction by many small muscles. In contrast, fewer muscles move the brows, which can move only up, down, or in a vertical furrow. Unilateral movements of the lips, for example, are easy, but difficult in the upper face (brow) because of differences in the ways that muscles are connected to nerves (Feyereisen,1986).

Two major nerve pathways innervate the facial muscles, the fifth (trigeminal) and seventh (facial) nerves. The muscles innervated by the trigeminal nerve control chewing movements. In contrast, the muscles innervated by the facial nerve do not move any skeletal structures. Instead, they are specialized for communication.

The transneuronal tracts for each side of the face are independent of each other, which means that a nerve injury may conceivably affect only one side of the face. The pattern of innervation also shows considerable individual variation. In the brain, the motor area that controls lower facial movements (that is, around the mouth) is much larger than the part of the motor area controlling upper facial movements.

Of great interest is the fact that there are two motor pathways from the brain that influence facial movements. One is through the pyramidal tract while the other is through the phylogenetically older extra-pyramidal tract. These differences have important clinical implications. For example, a lesion or injury of the cortical motor area on one side may produce a paralysis of half of the face (hemiparalysis) for voluntary movement. However, the same patient may show a normal bilateral smile to an amusing joke. In contrast, a patient with a lesion of the extra-pyramidal motor system as in Parkinson's disease may retain the ability to move the facial muscles to verbal commands, but loses all spontaneous emotional movements. Separation of voluntary from involuntary function is also seen in cases of multiple sclerosis and some cases of stroke. Many patients with this condition (pseudobulber palsy) often find themselves laughing or crying with slight or no provocation. Once the response starts these patients are unable to inhibit it.

> These episodes are generally indistinguishable from normal laughing and weeping. The face muscles contract into convincing smiles or crying faces, the face reddens, tears flow. The respiratory and vocal responses are also at least grossly identical to emotional responses. The only obvious difference is that these patients report no emotional experience during these bouts, or may even report the presence of an emotion incompatible with the expression (e.g., anger or pain while laughing). . . . It appears that the involuntary expressions stem from an inability to involuntarily inhibit those motor release phenomena through normal cortical influences (Rinn, 1984).

Some kinds of laughter are a manifestation of epilepsy. The laughter is inappropriate to the situation and inconsistent with any reported feelings, and may be associated with other epileptic symptoms such as falling or spasms. Patients may not recall the laughing fit, and will deny any feeling of amusement (Moody, 1979).

Drug use may also produce laughter that is unrelated to any precipitating situation. Nitrous oxide (laughing gas) was used for its laughter-inducing capacities long before it was used as an anesthetic agent. Marijuana users often show hilarious laughter during their highs. Manganese miners and persons who assembled dry-cell batteries would often develop laughing spells. In all these instances, the laughter was a symptom of acute drug intoxication or poisoning.

From the point of view of evolution, in simple organisms, simple reflex neural circuits handle survival issues related to feeding, mating, fight, and flight. Stimulation of the hypothalamus produces coordinated threat displays in cats (Flynn, 1966) and in rhesus monkeys (Plutchik, McFarland, and Robinson, 1966). During the course of evolution, the simple circuits are not eliminated as more complex systems evolve. For example, dogs and cats without a cortical motor system can still walk, eat, fight, and show sexual activity. A comparable lesion in humans would produce massive paralysis. Some primitive responses that are organized neurally at the level of the brain stem and hypothalamus would remain. These include coughing, sneezing, swallowing, gagging, laughing, and crying. Most of these reactions cannot be performed voluntarily except as an approximation, and most can be only partially inhibited.

It has been observed that infants can produce almost all the discrete facial movements that adults produce, but the capacity to inhibit these expressions does not appear until middle childhood, when frontal lobe development is complete. Infants born with no cortex still show facial expressions of crying and disgust, implying that the integration of these expressions occurs at subcortical levels. Cortical control is a relatively late evolutionary development, but as a result of the learning of display rules, the cortex influences the degree and form of expression of facial movements. Rinn concludes: "The cortical (i.e., pyramidal) motor system frequently competes with the more primitive systems for control of overt behavior. More commonly, however, they work together, each contributing certain elements to the final response. Thus any given behavior is the product of both cortical and subcortical influences, although these influences are not always equally strong." It thus appears that facial expressions of emotion are complex expressions of the interaction of both the involuntary and voluntary systems of the brain.

▍Theories of Facial Expressions of Emotions

Theories are designed to explain facts. Good theories explain more facts than poor ones, and they stimulate research as well. What are some of the facts that need explaining in relation to facial expressions of emotion? Here is a partial list.

1.   Most people are strongly influenced by, and interested in, the face. They keep pictures of other people's faces on their desks, in albums, and on the walls. The faces of great individuals are often photographed and enlarged to gigantic proportions. Our preoccupation with mirrors suggests that we constantly examine our own face, as well.

2.   Our faces express some emotions clearly, but not all emotions. We believe that we can easily read expressions of anger, fear, surprise, sadness, joy, and disgust from the face, but many emotions are harder to judge from the face, such as guilt, envy, jealousy, and boredom. To say judging is difficult, however, does not mean that it cannot be done.

3.   In laboratory studies, the ability of judges correctly to read, or decode, emotions from photographs is relatively poor. The rate of "correct" judgments increases if the judges are given a restricted list of emotion words to use, and if synonyms and near-synonyms are grouped as correct answers.

4.   The use of photographs of posed or spontaneous expressions is probably not an ideal way to study emotions, in view of the fact that emotional expressions have a beginning, a time course, and an ending. Still photos miss much of the complexity of facial expressions.

5.   Infants show many of the same facial expressions as do adults, apparently without the benefit of learning. Children born blind and deaf also show what appear to be typical emotional expressions on the face. This suggests that genetically determined brain mechanisms organize the expression of at least some emotions.

6.   Electrical stimulation of certain subcortical neurons or pathways produces typical emotional expressions in animals, supporting the notion of specialized brain centers for organizing emotional expressions.

7.   Observations of humans with various kinds of brain or nerve damage reveal that a person can show strong emotional expressions (such as laughing or crying) and report not being either happy or sad. Individuals with other types of nerve lesions (e.g., hemiparalysis) cannot voluntarily show typical emotional expressions, yet amusing or sad events may trigger normal patterns of expression.

8.   Young children begin the process of learning how to hide some of their emotional expressions and many adults are very adept at this (e.g., poker face). Adults are also quite capable of voluntarily creating any expression they wish regardless of how they may feel at the moment. They may smile when they are sad, and appear friendly even when angry.

9.   Most investigators assume that an emotion is a feeling that an individual can report. This assumption ignores the fact that many people have difficulty finding words for their feelings, that they may sometimes repress or distort their feelings, or that people may sometimes deceive others about their true feelings. These facts make it difficult to interpret simple correlations between reported feelings and overt expressions, no matter how accurately the expressions may be measured.

10.   Emotional expressions seldom, if ever, occur in isolation. Ambivalence and conflict are the rule in human and animal social relationships. Therefore, facial expressions will generally reflect mixtures or blends of emotions, and mixtures of cortical and subcortical influences.

11.   Considerable evidence exists that a small number of facial expressions, fear, anger, disgust, sadness, and enjoyment, are judged consistently in a wide range of cultures, including those having little or no contact with western societies.

12.   According to Ekman (1993), emotions can occur without any characteristic facial expressions. In addition, some emotions have no distinctive expressions at all.

Given these reasonably well-established facts, what kinds of theories have been developed to help understand them?

Darwin's Principles

As stated in Chapter Two, Darwin suggested three hypotheses to help account for expressive behavior. The first principle (of functional value) was that some expressions are of value in gratifying desires. If, for example, showing the teeth with the mouth open acts to intimidate others, or reduce threats, it has survival value and is likely to be maintained. The second principle (of antithesis) states that if certain feelings lead to useful expressions, then opposite feelings will lead to movements of an opposite appearance. Thus, smiling brings the lips up in a U-shape while sadness brings the lips down in an inverted U. This movement makes sense, since signals between individuals should be easy to recognize and to discriminate. Signals that are easy to detect, easy to discriminate, and easy to remember should represent important characteristics for development during the course of evolution (Guilford and Dawkins, 1991). Darwin's third principle (of direct action of the nervous system) stated that strong excitation of the nervous system affects various systems of the body resulting in such expressions as blushing, pallor, sweating, and trembling.

Darwin's central notion was that facial (and other bodily) expressions were forms of communication designed to influence important life events such as mating, dominance, and access to food. Since Darwin was concerned largely with animals lower than man, he had little to say about subjective feelings.

Peripheral Theories of Facial Expression

Stemming from the theories of William James, a number of contemporary theories have developed the implications of his ideas in relation to facial expressions. These theories are called peripheral theories because they assume that the muscles in the face generate sensory feedback that is evaluated to produce emotional feelings. These muscular responses are organized at subcortical centers where specific programs for each distinct emotion are assumed to be stored.

One of the prominent members of this group of theorists is Tomkins (1980), who assumes that there are eight basic emotions (or affects, as he prefers to call them). The positive ones are interest, surprise, and joy. The negative ones are anguish (or sadness), fear, shame, disgust, and rage. Tomkins assumes that differences in the appearance of different emotions depends on variations in the number of neural firings in the brain per unit of time. If neural firings suddenly increase, an individual will startle or become afraid. If the neural firing reaches a high constant level, the individual will respond with anger or distress. If the neural firing suddenly decreases, the individual may feel joy. These ideas are highly speculative, and no evidence yet exists to support them.

Tomkins later changed his mind about the role of facial muscles in providing emotional information to the brain. Instead, he proposed that the skin of the face plays a more important role than the muscles in influencing feeling. He believes that changes in the skin associated with movements and with changes in blood flow provide the basis for feelings of anger, sadness, fear, and so forth. Unfortunately, only anecdotal evidence exists for this hypothesis.

Another contributor to these ideas about the role of facial feedback is Izard (1990). He assumes that there are 11 basic emotions. In addition to the eight cited above, Izard adds contempt, shyness, and guilt. He believes that there are separate, innately programmed neural mechanisms for each of the fundamental emotions. These are present in infants and are revealed through distinctive facial expressions. "The ontogenesis and morphology of the facial expressions of the fundamental emotions are largely functions of maturation and innate biological 'givens.' They play a significant part in the infants' earliest human interaction, forming the basis for the development of the attachment bond." The intensity of an individual's emotions, however, can be modified by voluntary control of facial movements. Some research that supports this idea suggests that intensifying or inhibiting facial expressions in pain can increase or decrease both the self-report of pain and the physiological reaction to it. The theories of Tomkins and Izard assume that facial actions (through feedback from muscles or skin) play a major role in generating feelings of emotion. The chicken-and-egg problem remains, however: Why does the facial pattern occur in the first place?

Another theory consistent with this general approach has been recently proposed by Zajonc, Murphy, and Inglehart (1989). This theory assumes that muscle movements of the face regulate blood flow to the brain and thereby affect the temperature of the brain. Variations in brain temperature are believed to influence feeling states. Limited evidence on this point was found when cool air introduced directly into the nasal cavity was experienced as pleasurable, whereas warm air similarly introduced was experienced as unpleasant. Zajonc et al (1982) concluded that changes in the vascular system of the face tend to generate emotional feelings. They therefore believe that emotional expression and temperature regulation of the brain are closely related.

As developed thus far, the theory has something to say only about pleasant versus unpleasant feeling states, but has nothing to say about specific emotions, such as why anger feels different from fear or grief, for example. Basically, the theory is simply another way of saying that feedback from facial expressions (or the consequences of facial expressions) can influence emotional feelings.

Central Theories of Facial Expressions

Most people assume that facial expressions reflect inner emotional states; that is, we cry or look sad when we are grieving and we smile when we feel pleased. From this point of view, facial expressions are a *readout* of inner feeling states.

However, in various studies in which attempts are made to correlate facial ratings of emotion with self-reported emotional states, the correlations are often low. In addition, facial expressions of disgust as measured by Ekman's Facial Action Coding System correlated with a number of different self-reported emotions including anger, sadness, fear, and pain, as well as disgust (Ekman, Friesen, and Ancoli, 1980).

Another problem with this central view of facial expressions is that many people (including subjects for these kinds of studies) often show little or no facial expressions, even though they report feeling emotions. This observation has usually been explained by assuming that each person is socialized to use certain *display rules* about what emotions to show and under what conditions. For example, we often assume that girls are taught to display feelings of sadness easily, as well as joy, whereas boys are taught not to cry or show fear. We see support for this idea in the study cited earlier indicating that Japanese and American students show similar expressions (to an unseen observer) while watching a distressing film, but different expressions when asked to talk about the film in public. However, there is little empirical data on the nature of display rules and their effects on people.

Another problem with this central theory of facial expressions is that there are large numbers of emotions, as well as mixtures of emotions, for which no discrete pattern is known. How does one express on the face whether one is jealous, vengeful, kind, sarcastic, or curious? Many people also deliberately prevent their face from revealing any emotions if it is to their benefit to do so. And many people will deliberately show an emotional expression they do not feel in order to accomplish some goal, such as hiding their anger when criticized or looking friendly despite a wish for revenge. These observations suggest that there may be, and often is, a discrepancy between an inner emotional feeling and its outward expression on the face.

An interesting study illustrates both the controlled nature of the facial response and its impact on other people. In this study, subjects were asked to deliver electric shocks to another subject (actually a confederate of the experimenter). Some victims were told to smile during the shock experience while others were told to look angry. The results revealed that victims who showed anger received less shock, whereas smiling victims were given increasing levels of shock (Savitsky, Izard, Kotsch, and Christy, 1974). These findings suggest that people can deliberately choose, if they wish, to show certain expressions on their faces in order to elicit sympathy and support, or in order to create fear or anger. This implies that facial expressions are forms of communication that we use to satisfy our needs, wishes, and motives.

A Functional Theory of Facial Expressions

Instead of thinking of facial expressions as a reflection of an inner state of emotion, or as a generator of emotional feelings, various authors (beginning with Darwin) have suggested that facial expressions are simply forms of communication. From this point of view, facial expressions reflect intentions or attempts to influence or regulate a social encounter, regardless of inner feelings.

In observations of infants, it is evident that they cry when they are hungry, tired, or in pain, and they smile when a mother or another caregiver arrives. Fridlund (1988) suggests that cries and smiles function to make sure that the mother is attentive and will probably carry out actions useful to the infant's survival. From an evolutionary viewpoint, selection pressures exist on children to capture the attention of their parents, particularly in settings in which there may be multiple children all competing for parental attention. This view does not assume that the infant's facial expression directly reflects an inner emotional state; it does assume that the facial display acts as a signal of a need to maintain the mother-infant relationship.

Camras's (1977) study illustrates facial expressions as communications in young children. She placed two children at a time in a conflict situation involving the question of who gets to play with a small animal, and observed how they tried to resolve it. It appeared that those children who showed an aggressive facial display (lowered brows, lips thrust forward, prolonged stare, and face thrust forward) were more likely to obtain the desired object than children who showed an unaggressive face.

Smiles are often seen when adults greet one another, but do they reflect feelings of pleasure or happiness, or do they have some other communicative functions? In a study of feedback from listeners during two-person interactions, Brunner (1979) concluded that smiles acted in a way equivalent to such communications as "yes," or "uh-huh," or nodding of the head. Smiles are a way of telling a speaker that you are listening, or that you understand what is being said, or that you agree with what is being said. The smile acts to maintain a relationship between a speaker and a listener without necessarily reflecting any emotional state at all.

This view of facial displays interprets them in functional terms. They may or may not express inner feeling states, but they do function independently to influence an interaction between two or more people. When no one is around and individuals are subjected to emotion-inducing situations, facial display behavior is seldom seen. For example, subjects were asked to pose facial responses to pleasant, neutral, or unpleasant odors.

These could be readily recognized by observers. However, when the subjects smelled the odors in private, few facial responses were seen, despite the large differences in the rated degree of pleasantness of the odors (Gilbert, Fridlund, and Sabini, 1987).

Using a similar functional viewpoint, the cry-face is a signal that one needs or wishes help. The threat-face indicates that one is ready to fight, or that one has the ability to fight (or as some biologists say, that one has *resource-holding potential*). This view of facial expression does not imply that emotions do not exist, or that the face does not show emotions at times. Rather, it assumes that in most situations, people and animals use facial displays to try to influence others so they may get what they want. Some theorists have called this process *deception*, but it does not imply some kind of evil-doing. Deception, as a form of protection, is found widely throughout the plant and animal kingdom. Camouflage markings are forms of deception, as are eye-spots on the wings of butterflies. These are natural, survival-related adaptations. Presumably, the same is true for human facial displays.

▌Evolutionary Origins of Facial Displays

An ethologist, Strum (1988), who has long studied baboons in natural environments in Africa, has commented on the functional value of facial expressions. She writes:

> All animals need to communicate with one another. Solitary creatures who reproduce sexually need only to be able to communicate about mating. Creatures who care for their offspring need to be able to exchange information about themselves and their children. Animals who live in social groups, temporarily or permanently, need to be able to communicate on a much more sophisticated level. . . . As a result signals were borrowed from one context—sexual behavior, for example—and used in another—parenting or social communication—with a shift in meaning to extend the dialogue.

Baboons

As a result of closely observing several groups of baboons for a period of 15 years, Strum developed considerable insight into their social interactions. The following summary is based on her book, *Almost Human: A Journey into the World of Baboons.*

When a sexually receptive female *presents* her bottom for a male to inspect, this is a communication about sexual intentions. However, presenting can also be an invitation from an adult female to an infant to approach, or it can be a greeting asking permission to approach. When two males show a slight variation on the presenting position, and at the same time grunt, narrow their eyes, and smack their lips together, they convey friend-ly intentions but also some nervousness. Presenting can also be a request for grooming. *Embraces* can be a type of greeting, usually between an adult and an older infant. When two adults embrace, it usually occurs after an upsetting incident in the troop.

Aggressive displays can vary greatly in intensity. At low intensity, rais-ing the eyebrows reveals white eyelids. As aggression increases, an open-mouth threat (with canines showing) is added to the eyelid signal as well as some erection of body hair. At more intense levels, animals add sounds and ground slapping. Submissive displays often occur in response to aggressive threats. In such cases the animal makes short staccato grunts, an open-mouth fear-face that looks somewhat like a grin, and crouches low.

Play behavior is accompanied by a special facial display called a play-face that signals that the ensuing behavior is not serious. Figure 7.1 shows two juvenile baboons biting at each other, but showing the play-face at the same time.

Of great importance is the fact that most social interactions among the baboons are confused and ambivalent. Males will often first exchange friendly greetings, then threats, and then friendly greetings again. Strum concludes that these various displays communicate emotions and imply

| Figure 7.1 | Two Juvenile Baboons Biting and Showing the Play-Face |

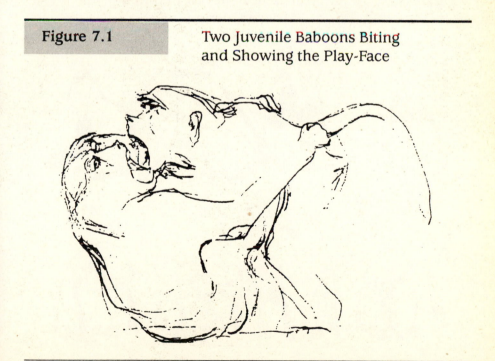

Source: S. C. Strum, 1988.

such statements as, "I am angry," "I am content," "I am ambivalent," or "I am not aggressive."

Guenons

In another interesting book about primates, a great deal of information was obtained about a group of African guenons, which include the patas monkeys and the hamadras baboons, macaques, colobines, and mangabeys, among others. These monkeys live mainly in forest areas or tall grass and communicate largely by vocalizations. They have at least three types of calls: alarm calls, cohesion calls, and spacing calls. In addition, their faces and bodies show bright colors, such as a blue face, white belly fur, and red sexual swelling, all of which provide instant information from one individual to another about sex, rank, and age. Each group of guenons also shows threat behavior in quite consistent ways, as Figure 7.2 illustrates.

In this species, the underside and inner linings of arms and eyes are pure white, while cheeks and brows are also very pale. Adult males respond to a monkey puppet with stereotyped threat behavior. The threat

Figure 7.2	Threat Behavior in the African Guenon

Source: A. Gautier-Hion et al., eds., 1988.

response goes from a "cut-off" phase where the animal is hunched over and is apparently avoiding interaction, to an "advertising" phase in which various body parts are exposed while the posture is changed. The third phase is one of threat (hard stare and lunge) plus vocalization followed by another cut-off. During the cut-off, the dullest areas of the animal are exposed to view. These examples illustrate the role of facial and other displays in regulating the course of social interaction.

▮ Evolutionary Origins of Various Displays

Ethologists have long been interested in the origins of these various displays. It is usually assumed that displays developed from patterns of behavior that originally possessed no communication value. These patterns include regulation of body temperature, intention movements (that is, initial movements of attack or retreat), and protective reactions. Protective reactions include eye closure, arrested respiration, repeated tongue protrusions, and lateral shaking of the head.

In a review of the origin of calls and facial expressions in primates, Andrew (1962) came to the conclusion that primate calls and facial expressions probably originated from protective reflexes evoked by unpleasant or startling stimuli. For example, if a noxious fluid is placed in the mouth, a primate usually shakes the head from side to side, draws back mouth corners and lips, and repeatedly protrudes the tongue. The eyebrows tend to be lowered and the eyes close. Finally, a throat reflex closes the glottis or mouth of the windpipe to prevent the noxious material from being ingested.

Another expression frequently seen in primates is the grimace. In this display, the corners of the mouth and lips retract to expose the teeth. This expression is frequently observed in animals who are the target of an attack or threat, or in response to a close approach by another animal. In one study of baboons, a subordinate animal gave 97% of the grimaces to a dominant one (Redican, 1982). Ethologists believe that the function of the grimace is appeasement. Supporting this idea is that in most circumstances potential or actual attack terminates as a consequence of the display.

Scientists believe that the grimace evolved from high-frequency vocalizations such as screeching or screaming heard in fear-inducing situations. This vocalization evolved into a silent scream. Hence, the assumption is that the emotional state typically associated with the grimace is fear.

Another aspect of a fear-related display is gaze aversion. Avoiding visual contact is a means of avoiding social interaction. Primatologists consider gaze aversion to reflect less intense fearfulness than does the grimace.

In threat, the mouth was originally opened with no lip retraction. Baboons and lemurs raise the upper lip before an attack in an expression that looks like a snarl. Facial snarls are also seen in apes such as the chimpanzee. Ear flattening is observed in threats against equals and often in connection with overt attacks. The effect of ear flattening is to raise the eyebrows, seen in baboons as a rapid threat signal.

Both the apes and humans frown in threat. This appears as a lowering of the eyebrows, and through the action of the corrugater muscles as a vertical line in the skin between the eyes. The eyes remain wide open. This kind of frown is believed to have originated from the intense scrutiny of a nearby object. Throughout the primates, a steady gaze is one of the features of confident threat.

Andrew emphasizes the close connection between the production of sounds (calls) in different situations and the evolution of facial expressions. "Changes in facial expressions come to alter the quality of calls, so that calls carry more specific information." He concludes that a variety of types of environmental situations in different primates elicit the various facial expression components, and that therefore no perfect correlation is possible between any particular facial component and any single emotional state. Figure 7.3 shows a variety of chimpanzee facial expressions. They highlight the fact that different species have different ways to communicate the same underlying emotional states.

Facial expressions are essential to the welfare of animals that live in groups. Through facial expressions, vocalizations, and other displays, animals avoid or approach one another, determine the timing of reproductive activities, and in general, regulate social interactions.

Summary ■

The literature reviewed in this and the previous chapter indicates that facial expressions in humans are imperfect communicators of emotional states. Emotions and facial expressions are only partially related and the connections between the two classes of events are subject to many disrupting influences. Evidence exists to support the idea that certain facial expressions can be seen in many different cultures in fairly similar forms; this phenomenon implies that there is a genetic basis for some facial expressions of emotion. However, it is also likely that certain facial expressions (such as winking or sticking out the tongue) may be learned like the words of a language. Generally, learning helps determine the stimuli to which facial expressions are made, as well as the mixtures of facial expressions. Probably most expressions are based on genetically determined brain programs; the overt appearance of an expression depends on the presence of particular stimuli and their interpretation, which in turn depend on social learning. Certain patterns of reaction (or displays) apparently are elicited by significant stimuli in the life of an individual. But in many situations, facial expressions are muted, hidden, or deceptive, and are largely controlled by the wishes or needs of the individual, including needs for power, acceptance, love, and intimidation. This viewpoint interprets facial expres-

| Figure 7.3 | Some Facial Expressions of Chimpanzees |

The expressions range from anger to playfulness.

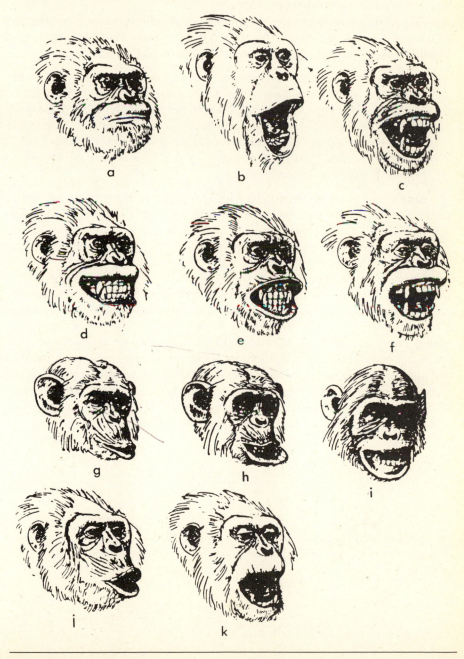

Source: Chevalier-Skolnikoff, 1973.

sions as compromises between innate tendencies to react in protective ways to dangerous situations, and desires to accomplish one's aims indirectly with the help of camouflage. Facial expressions are only one aspect of general social signals that include various types of vocalizations as well as other types of nonverbal behavior.

A question that is frequently raised is whether animal displays are associated with subjective feelings of emotion. The primatologist Chevalier-Skolnikoff (1973) answers this question in the following way:

> It is not possible to know what an animal is thinking. However, through the examination of behavioral sequences and interpretation of how the behavior functions, primatologists are fairly confident that the interpretation of the emotional nature of facial behavior in nonhuman primates is correct . . . because of these primates' close evolutionary relationship and biological similarity to man. Such interpretations are supported by similarities in the forms and activities of the brains of human and nonhuman primates.

Studies of patients with neurological injuries that produce partial paralysis of facial muscles have shown that integrated laughing and weeping can still occur. The interpretation of such findings is that facial expressions of emotion are complex expressions of the interaction of both the involuntary and voluntary systems of the brain.

Three general types of theories of facial expression are described. Peripheral theories assume that the muscles and skin of the face generate sensory feedback that is then evaluated to produce emotional feelings. Central theories assume that facial expressions reflect inner emotional states. Functional theories assume that facial expressions are forms of communication that attempt to influence a social encounter, regardless of inner feelings. Evidence for each of these viewpoints exists, although the functional theory is more general and has been shown to apply to lower primates as well as to humans. Ethologists have offered a number of speculations on the evolutionary origins of expressions of emotion.

Emotional Development

*I used to think in terms of the evil emotions
of fear and anger as opposed to the good
emotion of love, but considering that all of
these can lay claim to having had survival
value over the evolutionary eras, none can
properly be considered to be entirely evil.*

—Harry Harlow

▌ Goals of This Chapter

The study of emotion in infants and young children creates many conceptual problems. If emotions are considered to be inner feelings or experiences, it is obviously no more possible to discover such inner feelings in an infant than in a chimpanzee. If an emotion is something other than a feeling, just what is it? If we choose to attribute emotions to infants, on what basis do we make such inferences? How many emotions do infants start with and how do they develop? Although there are no simple answers to these questions, they should surely be addressed. Therefore, in this chapter we consider the many behavior patterns infants exhibit, the criteria we use in making judgments about infant emotions, the functions of emotions in infants, the nature of infant attachments, facial expressions in infants and what they mean, and how young children learn emotion concepts.

Important Questions Addressed In This Chapter

- How many types of behavior patterns may be found in neonates?
- At what age do patterns of anger expression appear in infants?

- What is meant by an infant ethogram?
- What kind of evidence can one use to make inferences about emotions in lower animals?
- What is the function of emotional behavior in infants?
- How similar are infant reactions to separation and adult reactions to bereavement?
- What evidence is there that certain behaviors of infants produce strong reactions in mothers?
- What is the difference between the endogenous and the exogenous smile?
- What is meant by attachment theory?
- When do children begin to use emotion words correctly?

■   ■   ■   ■   ■   ■   ■   ■

▌Behavior Patterns in Infants

It is obvious that inferences about emotions in infants must be based on evidence other than verbal reports. Most discussions of this issue rely on an infant's facial expressions or vocal output such as crying, and relatively little attention has been paid to other responses or behavior. However, from an evolutionary point of view, it is likely that too much attention has been paid to the face. In most lower animals, although relatively few facial expressions communicate information, many other display behaviors reflect emotional states. For example, lower animals use the displays that involve various parts of the body in special ways in the following contexts: greeting, recognition, courtship, mating, dominance, submission, warning, alarm, defense, challenge, distress, defeat, victory, feeding, and food-begging. Ethologists think of these kinds of displays as signals that function to communicate important information from one animal to another. In most cases, these display reactions appear without prior learning or experience and apparently are genetically programmed. Many of these displays are found in young organisms as well as mature ones.

From an ethological point of view, it would be expected that some of these display behaviors should be found in humans, at least in rudimentary form. For example, the cry of the newborn human infant is remarkably like the cry of the newborn chimpanzee and newborn gorilla (Lieberman, 1975), and the grasp reflex is found in human newborns just as in monkeys. Therefore, if we are to understand the nature of emotions in infants, it should be useful to consider the many different expressive behaviors of which infants are capable.

Expressive Behavior in Infants

Charles Darwin was probably the first to attempt systematically to investigate emotions in infants. In his autobiography, Darwin wrote, "My first child was born on December 17, 1839, and I at once commenced to make notes on the first dawn of the various expressions which he exhibited, for I felt convinced, even at this early period, that the most complex and fine shades of expression must all have had a gradual and natural origin" (Darwin, 1887). In his book, *The Expression of the Emotions in Man and Animals* (1872), Darwin described some of the observations he made on his own infants and those of others. For example, he noticed that infants will utter screams when in hunger, pain, or discomfort and that the facial expression will be the same in all of these situations. When screaming, the eyes are closed, the skin around them wrinkled, and the forehead is contracted in a frown. The mouth is widely open, with the lips retracted in such a way as to create a squarish form, with the teeth or gums exposed. Darwin also reported that tears are not associated with crying until the second to fourth month of life, and that sobbing is observed only in humans and never in lower primates. He also suggested, without further elaboration, that the character of crying associated with pain is different from the crying associated with grief. Some of the pictures he took of his children are shown in Figure 8.1.

Despite these intriguing beginnings of a comparative psychology of infant development, relatively little attention was paid to the problem until well into the twentieth century, when Watson, the founder of behaviorism, provided a major contribution. Watson was influenced both by Darwin and by Freud. In his book, *Psychology from the Standpoint of a Behaviorist*, he pointed out that humans are innately endowed with various adaptive life-conserving propensities that influence food intake, waste elimination, and procreation. "These purely vegetative functions serve [humans] as they serve animals lower than man and are possibly just as 'perfect' " (Watson, 1929). He went on to write:

> Man at birth and at varying periods thereafter is supplied with a series of protective attack and defense mechanism, which while not nearly so perfect as in animals, nevertheless form a substantial repertoire of acts. They need supplementation by habit before being of direct utility to the individual in his struggle for food, against enemies, etc. These are the protective and defense reactions—the unlearned part activities at first predominate. . . . The principal role of all unlearned activity, neglecting the vegetative and procreative . . . is to initiate the process of learning.

Watson performed with infants a series of experiments designed to identify the reactions that various stimuli elicited. He tried the following kinds of stimuli:

Figure 8.1   Facial Expressions of Weeping and Sadness in Infants and Young Children

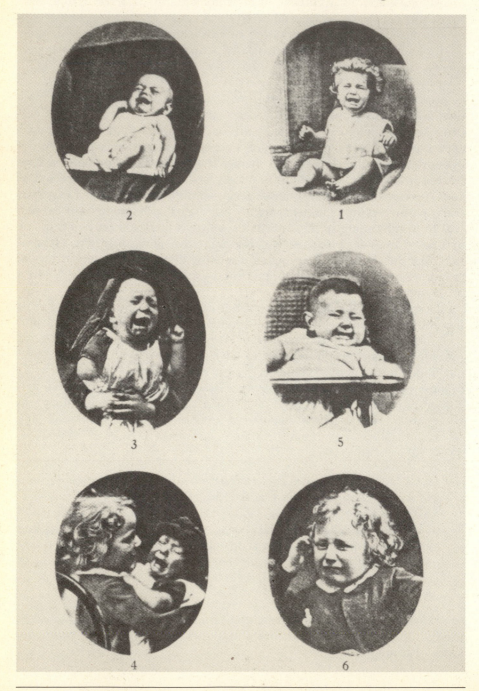

Source: C. Darwin, 1965/1872.

sudden dropping of the infant
loud sounds
slight shaking when the infant was falling asleep
holding the infant's arms at side
holding the infant's head to prevent movement
tickling
shaking
gentle rocking
patting
stroking an erogenous zone
odors such as oil of peppermint, asafoetida, butyric acid, and ammonia
light pinching of nose or inner surface of knee

Watson noticed that within hours after birth, the infant showed a variety of spontaneous behaviors as well as reactions to stimuli. These included sucking, sneezing, hiccoughing, yawning, crying, erection of the penis, defecation, urination, turning of the head, raising the head, various hand, arm and leg movements, and various reflexes such as the cling, Moro, and plantar reflexes. (These reflexes are described later in this chapter.)

After observing many infants exposed to the stimuli listed above, Watson concluded that they showed three major patterns of reaction that could be called X, Y, and Z. He then indicated that other common psychological terms might label these patterns, but proposed these with great hesitation: fear, rage, and love. Parenthetically, Watson stated that his use of the word *love* was approximately the same as Freud's use of the word *sex* (Watson, 1919).

Watson then reported that the fear (X) response was produced by sudden dropping of an infant, by loud sounds, and by shaking the infant as he or she was just falling asleep. Hampering the infant's movements produced the rage (Y) response. Stroking or manipulation of an erogenous zone of the infant produced the love (Z) response. Watson gave relatively little information on the exact forms of these responses. He also assumed that individual differences were largely a result of differences in the type of environment to which an individual was exposed.

Although Watson's observations were interesting, his stimuli were not standardized, and many psychologists began to examine infants and young children systematically in an effort to confirm or disprove these ideas. Let us examine one such recent study concerned with the development of anger expressions in infancy (Stenberg and Campos, 1990).

Anger in Infancy

Anger is an important and probably universal experience in human life, but relatively little research has been directed toward describing its earliest manifestations and tracing its development over time. In the study by Stenberg and Campos, restraint of the infant's arms, the stimulus condition, was applied to 48 infants, whom they divided into 4 equal groups of ages 1, 4, and 7 months. The investigators measured facial and vocal expressions, flushing, and crying. Independent raters sampled several 3-second episodes taken before, during, and after the restraint and coded the facial expressions by means of a coding system developed by Izard (1979) called MAX (Maximally Discriminative Facial Movement Coding System). The MAX system has already identified the facial component expressions believed to be associated with anger in adults; the present study attempted to determine the extent to which the infants' facial expressions during restraint matched the "standard" expression.

The results indicated that the infants did not show the anger expression spontaneously before the arms were restrained. However, both 4 and 7-month-old infants clearly showed the anger pattern following restraint, while the 1-month-olds never did. Flushing of the face was observed in 92% of the babies following restraint. None of the babies except one shed any tears during restraint. Also of interest is the fact that the anger facial displays in 4-month-old infants appeared to be directed toward the immediate source of the frustration, while by 7 months, the expressions seemed to be directed toward the mother, who was sitting nearby. It thus appears that the capacity to exhibit the organized expression of anger develops in infants sometime between the first and fourth months of life.

▌The Varieties of Infant Behaviors

Infants are capable of a great variety of facial expressions. Ekman and Friesen (1976) have also developed a facial action code that defines 24 rather specific facial expressions. Oster and Ekman (1978) claim that we can see virtually all the facial action code movements in both premature and full term newborns. Extensive video recordings have been made of infants' facial expressions during the first few months of life. Researchers have attempted to establish the meaning of different facial expressions on the basis of two types of criteria: evidence of patterning based on the simultaneous occurrence of independent muscle actions, and the timing of particular facial movements in relation to stimulus events. Oster and Ekman (1978) report, for example, that the earliest smiles are produced by the action of a single muscle, but smiles become increasingly complex, in terms of muscle action unit involvements, as they become more related to social interactions.

Brazelton (1976) has also described the range of behaviors of which newborns are capable. His Neonatal Assessment Scale lists 26 behavioral and 20 reflex activities of the human neonate in interaction with an adult. These include the following.

1. turning head in direction of human voice
2. responding to a female vocal pitch over a male voice
3. humanoid sounds preferred to pure tones
4. using the eyes to follow a picture
5. responding to milk smells rather than sugar water

It is now known that newborn infants have a surprising ability to process sensory information. Infants show the pupillary reflex; visual pursuit behavior; sustained fixation; color sensitivity; tracking objects with coordinated movements of the head and eyes; visual accommodation; the ability to discriminate visual patterns; differential attention and preferences for some patterns over others; sensitivity to pitch, intensity, and duration of sounds; head and eye movements to locate a source of sound; and a preference for human speech over other types of sound.

Many other researchers have mentioned the behavioral characteristics of infants. For example, infants show automatic walking movements, eyes-closed smiling, and spontaneous erections. They are able to imitate mouth and tongue movements, some vocalizations and hand movements, and often synchronize hand or arm movements with vocalizations or facial grimaces (Trevarthen, 1977). Trevarthen also claims that when a mother shows a lack of response or an inappropriate response, 8-week-old infants show expressions of confusion, distress, or withdrawal. Spitz (1957) has pointed out that infants show rooting behavior (a head-turning response to touching the cheek called an oral orientation reflex), as well as head nodding. Kinsey, Pomeroy, and Martin (1948) have described evidence of orgasm in infants. Andrew (1972) has drawn our attention to patterns of behavior found in the young of lower animals (as well as in the mature animal). He mentions respiratory reflexes that cause dilation of the nostrils and contribute in some degree to facial expressions. He describes thermoregulatory responses such as sweating, panting, and flushing, which act to cool the body, and the total body response of immobility. He also mentions secretions (odors) and excretions (defecation), which play an important role in social displays.

This section, dealing with the concept of infant display behaviors, has revealed the presence of many different behaviors, expressions, or patterns. It thus appears that human infants show diverse patterns of behavior in the first year of life. Most such patterns have not been studied extensively and only a few of them have been considered as measures of emotion. However, it is certainly possible to consider infant behaviors somewhat the way ethologists examine animal behaviors. They do this by creating an ethogram.

An Infant Ethogram

The newborn infant is not simply a blank screen upon which experience writes. Within the first hours and weeks after birth, many organized behavior patterns may be identified either as reactions to stimulations or as spontaneous events. For example, a number of reflexes can be elicited in most human infants at birth, but they usually disappear after three or four months. These include the rooting reflex (turning the mouth toward a tactile stimulus), the Babinski, or plantar, reflex (spreading of the toes when the sole of the foot is scratched), and the grasp reflex (clinging to an object with the hands). A loud noise will elicit a Moro reflex (extension of the limbs and arching of the back) in most infants during their first four months. After that they show a startle response to any loud noise.

Although one can observe many behaviors in infants, few investigators have attempted to catalog them in any systematic way. However, Young and Decarie (1977) have compiled what might be called an *ethogram* of human infant behaviors. The term ethogram is taken from the vocabulary of the ethologists, and describes an exhaustive list of behaviors observable in a given species of animal under naturalistic conditions.

Young and Decarie decided to establish a list of facial expressions and vocalizations that might be broadly considered as related to emotional expressions. This criterion meant that observers had to judge the behavior as social, affective, or communicative in nature. Such behaviors as sneezing or coughing were not included.

The ethogram was established by first observing six infants in six different situations (e.g., approach of a stranger with the mother present, departure of mother, physical restraint, and so forth). They videotaped these infants and their reactions, and drew up a preliminary catalog of behaviors. They then applied the catalog to 30 other infants and further refined it. It was finally applied to another group of 40 infants, approximately 8 to 12 months of age.

The result was a catalog of 42 facial expressions and 10 vocalizations. Based on the situations connected with each expression, an inference was made of the hedonic tone; that is, the pleasant or unpleasant quality presumable associated with the expression. This rating resulted in 16 positive expressions, 15 negative ones, and 21 neutral, ambivalent, or undifferentiated ones. These expressions, as labeled by Young and Decarie, are presented in Table 8.1. They are assumed to be "basic" expressions of interpersonal communication that combine in numerous ways to produce all the complex emotional expressions observed in infants and older children. For example, the kidney-mouth or square-mouth faces were often accompanied by wails (or soft wails) and tended to be evoked in situations in which the mother frustrated the child. However, it should be emphasized that a behavior expression does not occur at a single moment in time but occurs in

Table 8.1	An Ethogram of Facial and Vocal Behaviors in 8- to 12-Month-Old Infants

INFERRED HEDONIC TONE

Positive	Negative	Ambiguous
Close-mouth smile	Tremble	Yawn
Coy smile	Tight-lip face	Wide-eyed stare
O-mouth smile	Square-mouth face	Tongue out
Open-mouth smile	Kidney-mouth face	Blink
Shy smile	Clenched-teeth face	Brow-raise stare
Semismile	Pout	Lip roll
Slight open-mouth smile	Sad face	Sigh
Positive face	Negative face	Sober frown
Brighten	Grimace	Sober stare
Sparkle	Frown	Surprise face
Play face	Fear face	Perplexed face
Babble	Disgust face	Shy face
Coo	Harsh wail	Detached face
Laugh	Soft wail	Frozen face
Squeal	Wail	Attentive face
Positive vocalization		Ambivalent face
		Ambivalent smile
		Undifferentiated face
		Normal face
		Ambivalent vocalization
		Undifferentiated vocalization

Source: G. Young and T. G. Decarie, 1977.

sequences and combinations of units over varying periods of time. In other words, a sequence starts and later stops, and somehow most observers recognize the beginning and end of each sequence.

Inferring Emotion in Infants

Although the descriptions given above demonstrate that infants are capable of a wide variety of behaviors, it is not evident that babies have subjective feelings anything like those in adults. At best we can only guess or make inferences about inner states in infants. However, if we accept the definition of emotion proposed by the ethologist Marler (1977), it is reasonable to infer emotional states in young babies. Marler proposes that inferences about emotional states are based on the fact that they are generalized, that they affect many patterns of behavior, that autonomic arousal is often involved, that there seems to be a sense of urgency when they appear, that they have a momentum that makes rapid stops difficult, that they seem to involve the involuntary muscles mostly, that they are not easily trained, that approach or avoidance behavior is often associated with them, and that they are usually directed toward other individuals in the environment.

It is important to emphasize that in the absence of one or more of these characteristics, a judgment of the presence of an emotion may still be made. An example of the role of inference in judging emotions in infants may be illustrated in regard to the smile. Certain smiles are not triggered by social events, are not conditionable, and are related to rapid eye movement (or REM) states of drowsiness. A certain stage of sleep is associated with eye movements, which can be seen through the closed eyelids. This sleep stage, called REM sleep, is found in adults, infants, and many animals. Other smiles are clearly responses to the caretaker, appear to be anticipatory reactions, and appear at times of high alertness. The latter smiles are inferred to be emotional, the former are not.

A parallel problem exists with regard to inferring emotions in monkeys. Seyforth and his colleagues (1980) had noticed that vervet monkeys seemed to show appropriate emotional reactions to alarm calls that other monkeys emitted. For example, so-called leopard alarms were associated with other monkeys running into trees; eagle alarms were associated with monkeys looking up; and snake alarms with monkeys looking down. These alarm signals were tape-recorded and played back to the vervets in the absence of actual predators, with comparable results. In addition, researchers found that age, sex, context, and various acoustic properties had little effect on the animals' reactions. Thus, the convergence of various kinds of evidence led to the conclusion that an emotional signal of a specific kind had been emitted.

The judgment of social attachment in infants is also based on a variety of observations. Freedman (1974) states that social attachment is inferred on the basis of the following kinds of data: the attempt to maintain physical proximity; the appearance of mutual watching; mutual smiling; mutual cooing; mutual laughter and play; and signs of protection of the young. It thus appears that the inference of attachment is based on an evaluation and interpretation of specific behaviors engaged in by the mother and infant.

The judgment of fear in an infant is usually based on observations of gaze aversion and crying when a stranger approaches. But these reactions may also be evoked by placing the child on a glass table several feel above the floor. This setting is called a *visual cliff* and although it is not dangerous for the child, it does evoke crying and aversive reactions. Inferences about emotions should rely on as many sources of information as possible. Of particular importance is a description of the stimuli that precede the emotional expression, the detailed appearance of the response itself, and the kind of effects the expression appears to have on other organisms in the immediate environment. Figure 8.2 shows the reaction of a 7-week-old infant to the experimenter wearing a plastic mask. Infants stare, frown, and stop smiling. Some begin to cry, as shown in the figure. The inference made is that the mask is aversive.

Haskins's (1979) study of kitten vocalization illustrates this approach to defining emotion. Kittens were exposed to cold stimuli, restraint, and isolation at various times during their first 6 weeks of life. The results showed

---

Figure 8.2   A 7-Week-Old Infant's Reaction to the Investigator Wearing a Plastic Mask

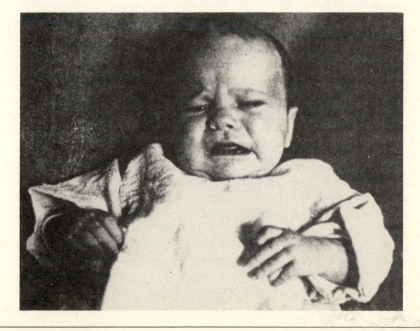

Source: P. Wolff, 1987.

that the kittens cried more during restraint than during either cold exposure or isolation. The entrance of the mother into the litter box also increased the frequency of crying, as did shifts in position of the mother during nursing. Crying decreased when kittens congregated in huddles. The crying of the kittens also influenced the mother to come into the litter and to make nursing possible. Sound spectograph analysis revealed that the peak fundamental frequency of the crying was significantly greater during the cold stress than during either isolation or restraint. These results imply that vocalizations carry information about the stimulus conditions to which kittens are exposed and have an effect on the caretaker that is related to the probability of survival of the young. They also imply that we make judgments about probable emotional states by considering the stimuli that seemed to trigger the response as well as the effect the response had on the mother cat.

Another illustration of a similar approach was reported by Scoville and Gottlieb (1980). They recorded the vocalizations that Peking ducklings made from several hours before they hatched to 48 hours after hatching. Vocalizations were recorded in a variety of situations, such as in the presence of other ducklings, during exposure to maternal calls, and during social isolation. Sound spectograph analysis revealed two acoustically distinct types of sound patterns: contentment calls, which have short note durations, fast repetition rates, and low pitch, and are elicited by the presence of peers and/or maternal calls; and distress calls, which have longer note durations, slower repetition rates, and higher pitch, and are emitted during social isolation. The second category of sounds appears to attract attention of the hen to any duckling that has become separated from the brood. Such attraction serves to maintain group cohesion and to increase the chances of survival of the ducklings.

In a similar type of investigation, Scott (1980) recorded distress vocalizations in puppies and tried to identify variables that would either increase or decrease them. Food, novel objects, and tranquilizers had no effect, although an antidepressant (Imipramine) reduced distress vocalizations in certain breeds of dogs. Morphine also reduced these vocalizations as did exposure to a warm (29° C) incubator. The most effective reducer of these vocalizations was social interaction with other puppies or adult dogs. These and other observations led to the conclusion that these vocalizations are, in fact, emotional signals of distress that function to increase the probability of social contact with other animals.

There is one further point in regard to inferring emotions from indirect evidence. One important reason that emotional states are sometimes very difficult to define in a simple, clear-cut way is that emotions are often mixed states, and reflect the interaction of opposite tendencies. Hinde (1966) has given many examples from the animal literature of the concept that overt displays often reflect combined impulses of approach and avoidance, attack and flight, or sex and aggression. Van Hooff (1973) has identified 5 display systems in the chimpanzee that he calls play, aggression, submission, affinity, and excitement systems. He concludes that all facial expressions seen in the chimpanzee are a result of the conflict of two or more of these motivational systems. Harlow and Harlow (1972) point out that the separation that occurs between a young rhesus monkey and its mother is produced through a mixture of maternal punishment and infant curiosity. And Sroufe (1979) concludes that infant behavior is a vectorial resultant of opposing forces such as wariness and curiosity, security in the familiar, and attraction to the unfamiliar. For all the reasons given, emotions in infants (and adults as well) are complex hypothetical states whose existence and properties can be determined only by a series of inferences. Ekman and Oster (1979) make a similar point when they write, "Since there is no single, infallible way to determine a person's true emotional state, it is unfortunate that so few investigators have followed the approach of using multiple convergent measures to gain a more reliable indication of the emotion experienced."

▌The Function of Emotional Behavior in Infants

From an evolutionary point of view, the newborn organism is most vulnerable to the dangers of the environment. This reality is the basic reason behind the various signals, displays, communication patterns, and behaviors found in immature organisms and that are present at or shortly after birth. These various behaviors have effects that increase the chances of survival in the newborn. And since the problems of survival exist from the moment of birth, certain mechanisms must exist both in the child and in the mother or caretaker to help ensure survival. If young organisms had to wait until the infant learned how to attract its mother's attention and support, and if the mother had to learn how to provide it, the chances of species survival would be small. Communication patterns have to work the first time they are used. From this viewpoint, emotions may be thought of, in part, as communication signals emitted by the infant that help increase the chances of survival. Emotions are not disruptive, maladaptive states, but act rather to stabilize the internal state of the organism. Emotions are autonomic behavioral patterns that act to maintain homeostasis rather than to disrupt it. They represent transitory adjustment reactions that function to return the organism to a stable, effective relationship with its immediate environment when that relationship is disrupted. Emotions help the individual maintain a steady state in the face of environmental fluctuations.

The ethologist Andrew (1974) has pointed out that the emergency reactions we tend to label as emotions are associated with exertion in general, rather than being restricted to attack or fleeing. Many of these reactions precede behavioral exertion and therefore may become important in communication of an organism's intentions. To that extent, they become part of the complex chain of events called an emotion. Examples of reflex, anticipatory reactions are vasodilation in skeletal muscles to increase their blood supply, blood pressure increases due to cardiac acceleration, and vasoconstriction in the skin and intestines. "This pattern occurs as a first response to a new stimulus in a previously quiet organism. The function of this pattern is to prepare for a sustained or violent muscle action."

Andrew (1974) suggests that the generalized mammalian response to noxious stimulation is characterized by mouth corner withdrawal, lip retraction, and eye closure. Other behaviors often found as part of the protective response pattern are tongue protrusion and lateral shaking of head and body. Vocalizations imply that the organism is uncomfortable, lost, wants something, or is likely to flee. These patterns are found in young organisms as well as mature ones.

The idea that emotional behaviors in infants have functions has also been elaborated by Bowlby, an English psychiatrist (1969). He suggests that at least four systems work together to control the infant's behavior. One is called the *attachment system*, whose function is to maintain proximity, closeness, or contact between the infant and the caretaker. The second system he calls the *fear/wariness system*, whose function is to help the infant escape or avoid potential dangers. The third is the *exploratory system*, which motivates the infant to play or interact with others and with parts of the environment. And the fourth is the *affiliation system* that prompts acquisition of social skills and connections with a person other than the key attachment figure. It is evident that all these systems (patterns of behavior) play a role in gaining support and nourishment, and avoiding dangers. They therefore function to increase the chances of survival. Bowlby believes that these four systems interact and function without the infant being cognitively aware of them (in the adult sense). As the child's intellectual capacities develop, the child may become more aware of the operation of these systems and more able to exercise conscious control over them.

To illustrate some of these ideas, we may examine the work of Hofer (1984), a research psychiatrist who has studied bereavement in young organisms. Table 8.2 shows the typical pattern of acute and chronic signs of bereavement or grief reactions in human adults to the loss of a close family attachment. In the acute stage there is often great agitation, crying, aimless activity, or near total passivity and feelings of muscular weakness. In the chronic stage of bereavement that may last weeks or months, there is often social withdrawal, decreased concentration, restlessness, anxiety, decreased appetite, sleep disturbances, and depressed mood.

Of considerable interest is the fact that the infant reacts with much the same pattern to separation from the mother. In infants, the acute stage has been called the phase of *protest*, which may last minutes to hours. Agitation, vocalization, searching behavior or passivity, and increased heart rate characterize this stage. If the separation continues, the infant enters the chronic or *despair* phase, which may last for hours or days. In this phase the infant

Table 8.2	Typical Pattern of Acute Signs of Bereavement

BEAREAVEMENT REACTIONS IN HUMAN ADUTS	INFANT REACTIONS TO SEPARATION
Acute Reactions	**Acute Reactions**
Agitation	Agitation
Crying	Vocalizations
Aimless activity	Searching activities
Preoccupation with image of deceased	Increased heart rate
Tears	Increased cortisol
Sighing	Increased catecholamines
Muscular weakness	Decreased social interaction and play
Social withdrawal	Mouthing
Decreased attention	Rocking
Restlessness	Variable food intake
Anxiety	Variable responses to stimulation
Variable food intake	Facial expression of sadness
Facial expressions of sadness	Decreased body temperature
Depressed mood	Decreased oxygen consumption
Decreased body weight	Decreased cardiac rate
Sleep disturbance	Decreased growth hormone
Muscular weakness	Decreased T-cell activity
Endocrine changes	
Immunologic changes	

Source: M. Hofer, 1984.

shows decreased social interaction, rocking behavior, changed responsiveness to outside stimuli, decreased food intake, and sleep disruptions, among other signs.

These changes described as protest and despair phases have been interpreted as strategies that have evolved because they have survival value. The agitation and vocalization of the initial phase increases the chances that the mother will return to the infant and find it. The decreased behaviors of the second phase may help the infant hide from predators, or strangers who may be a source of danger to the child. The various physiological changes are believed to be adaptations that reduce risk under these stressful circumstances.

The Mutual Interaction of Parents and Infants

The previous section has introduced the idea that many patterns of behavior in infants function to avert or decrease dangers and to increase support, protection and nourishment. These patterns of behavior are what we call emotions even though we cannot say much about the mental states of the infant. These behavior patterns act as signals that the infant sends to its caretaker, and these signals are in essence attempts to change the behavior of the caretaker. The interesting thing about these signals is that they work, as many studies carried out in recent years demonstrate.

For example, Bowlby (1969) has proposed that the attachment that a mother develops for her infant depends to a considerable degree on the crying, smiling, clinging, and sucking behavior of the infant. In an effort to test this hypothesis, Moss and Robson (1968) interviewed 54 mothers and also observed the interaction of these mothers with their infants in their homes. The extent to which the mothers showed care-giving behavior and physical contact was rated.

Moss and Robson found that maternal behavior occurred following 77% of the situations where the baby cried or fussed. At the age of one month, crying of the baby tended to produce the following behavior in the mother: attend, hold the infant close, burp the infant; talk to the infant; imitate his or her vocalizations; engage in mutual visual regard with the infant; and rock the infant. At the age of three months, fussing and crying of the female infants tended to initiate talking, imitative vocalization, and mutual visual regard in the mothers. Crying of male infants was more likely to initiate close physical contact. These findings may be interpreted as indicating that "an infant's expressive behavior certainly affects others by modifying their behavior toward the infant. The functional value of expressive displays (available immediately after birth) is, in fact, to modify others' behavior in such a way that the infant's probability of survival is increased" (Saarni, 1978).

Frodi and her colleagues reported two studies that strikingly reveal the impact of the infant on its caretakers. In one investigation (Frodi, et al., 1978), a group of mothers and fathers of newborn infants looked at videotape presentations of an infant. Some of the parents were shown a crying baby and others were shown a smiling baby. The parents were asked to rate their moods on seeing the infants, and at the same time the parents' blood pressure and skin conductance were recorded.

The results showed that parents who viewed the crying baby reported feeling more annoyed, irritated, distressed, disturbed, indifferent, and at the same time less attentive and less happy than the parents who viewed the smiling infant. These results were obtained for both mothers and fathers, although the mothers' ratings tended to be more extreme. When viewing the crying infant, the parents' diastolic blood pressures rose significantly, but no blood pressure changes occurred during the observation of the smiling child. Skin conductance increased while the subjects were viewing the crying infant, but it was unaffected when they saw a smiling infant.

The authors concluded that crying and smiling infants elicit different emotional and physiological reactions from parents. They suggest that parents perceive crying as aversive and have a strong desire to terminate this aversive signal from an infant. A smiling infant produces pleasant feelings with little or no arousal. However, both crying and smiling tend to elicit feelings from the parents that incline them to move close to the infant, in one case to stop the crying, and in the other to prolong the smiling.

The second study (Frodi et al., 1978) was concerned with determining whether premature babies elicited different emotional and physiological reactions from parents than did full term infants. A group of parents viewed videotapes of a normal full-term infant and another group saw videotapes of a premature infant. Sound tracks were dubbed into the videotape so that sometimes the normal infant appeared to emit the actual cry of the premature infant, and sometimes it emitted its own cry. Similarly, the premature infant sometimes appeared to emit a full term baby's cry and sometimes its own cry. Researchers recorded self-reported moods and physiological reactions to these cries.

The results showed that when an infant is crying, regardless of whether it is full term or premature, parents report feeling more irritated, annoyed, disturbed, distressed, frightened, alert, and sympathetic, and less happy, than when it is quiet. Autonomic arousal in the parents also increased while the infant was crying. It was also discovered that the cry of the premature infant was significantly more irritating and had a significantly greater autonomic arousal effect than did the cry of the full term infant. The investigators raise the possibility that the greater aversiveness of the premature infant's cry (and perhaps appearance) may sometimes create a condition in ill-prepared or troubled mothers that could increase risk of child abuse. These two studies by Frodi and her associates thus strongly support the concept that infants have a powerful effect on the emotional states of their parents.

That parents have strong effects on the emotional behavior of their infants has also been experimentally demonstrated. Campos and his colleagues (1983) received permission from mothers to allow their 10-month-old infants to explore a "visual cliff," essentially a large piece of glass mounted across two tables with a space between. On one side there is a checkered pattern just under the surface of the glass. In the space between the tables there is a similar checkered pattern placed anywhere from a few

---

Figure 8.3	A Baby Exploring a "Visual Cliff"

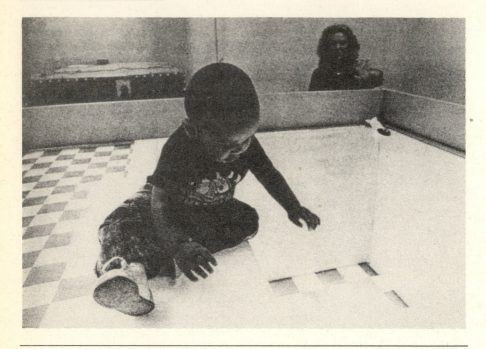

Source: J. Campos, 1983.

inches to 4 feet below the glass. Investigators found that when the apparent drop-off is about 12 inches, about half the infants will avoid crossing and half will cross in order to reach their mothers on the other side of the table.

In the Campos study, the infant was placed at one end of the table while the mother was placed at the other end with an attractive toy. In one condition, the mother was instructed to smile at her child, while in another she was told to show a fearful expression. The results demonstrated that if the child looked at his or her mother's face, almost all crossed the visual cliff when she was smiling. In contrast, if the mother showed a fearful expression, not one infant crossed the visual cliff. The study thus indicates that facial expressions of the mother had a powerful effect on the exploratory behavior of her infant.

Brazelton (1983), a child psychiatrist, provides many descriptions of the subtle interactions that take place between a mother and her infant. He cites many reports that when an infant clings tightly to the mother and presses his or her face into the crook of the mother's neck, she feels a tightening sensation in her breasts, followed by a "let-down" reflex of milk.

Careful observations of a few minutes of apparently pleasant mother-infant interaction demonstrate how the smiles and vocalizations of the mother tend to produce the same kind of reactions in the infant. Further, the smiling and vocalizing of the infant increases the same behaviors in the mother. If the mother is asked to sit in front of her seated infant and maintain an expressionless face with no touching or other interaction, the infant shows a strong reaction; the baby shows repeated attempts to elicit a response from the mother, and, when unsuccessful, eventually withdraws attention. Brazelton observes this reaction in babies as young as 1 to 4 months. He concludes that normal mother-infant interactions function as a goal-oriented, reciprocal system in which infants play a major, active role, constantly modifying their expressions and actions in response to the feedback their mothers provide.

What Kinds of Infant Faces Are Attractive?

Another way of looking at the issue of infant effects on caretakers is in terms of ethological concepts. From that point of view, certain infant behaviors act as releasers of caretaking behavior in human adults. In an effort to test one aspect of this hypothesis, Sternglanz, Gray, and Murakami (1977) asked college students to rate the attractiveness of drawings of an infant's face. Different dimensions of the face such as eye placement and forehead, eye, chin, and iris size were systematically varied. Examples of the facial expressions used are shown in Figure 8.4 on the next page.

Results showed some sex differences in ratings, but that experience with children had no relation to ratings. In general, intermediate levels of any given variable were more preferred than extremes. Using the maximum ratings for each dimension, investigators derived a composite drawing of the most attractive infant face, shown in Figure 8.5. This face fits the image of an infant that artists have frequently drawn: high forehead and large eyes in a rounded face. Whether the attractiveness measure correlates with actual behavior toward an infant remains to be determined by future research.

Facial Expressions in Infants

Given the importance of facial expressions in infants, many studies have addressed this issue. Ekman and Oster (1979) reviewed the evidence on facial expressions in human infants and arrived at the following conclusions:

1. The facial musculature is fully formed and functional at birth.
2. Distinctive facial expressions resembling certain adult expressions are present in early infancy. Expressions of crying, smiling, disgust, and startle are observable in the first days of life.

Figure 8.4	Examples of Facial Expressions Used to Study the Attractiveness of an Infant's Face

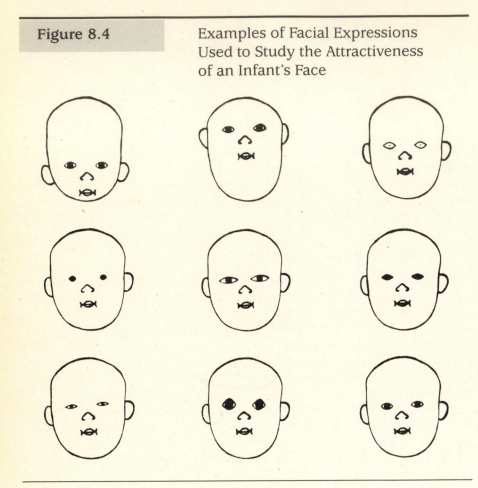

Source: S. H. Sternglanz, J.L. Gray, and M. Murakami, 1977.

3. Three- to 4-month-old infants show differential facial responses to exaggerated facial responses of caretakers.
4. Imitation of certain facial expressions of caretakers (mouth opening and tongue protrusion) has been shown by 2- to 3-week-old infants.
5. Preschool children know what the most common facial expressions look like, what they mean, and what kinds of situations typically elicit them.
6. Facial expressions play a role in social communication.

These generalizations illustrate the important point that facial expressions suggestive of emotions are present at birth and continue to appear long before any language exists. It has been found that the human infant begins to show fragments of facial expressions in the last trimester of preg-

Figure 8.5

Composite Drawing of the "Ideal" Infant Face

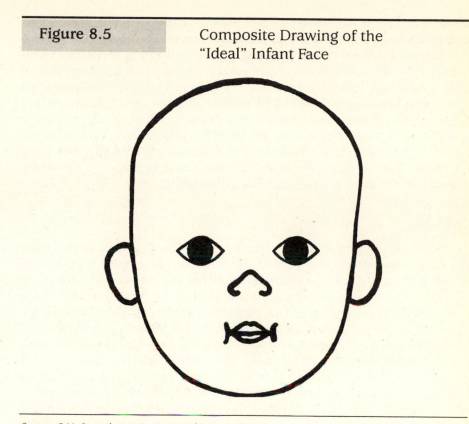

Source: S.H. Sternglanz, J.L. Gray, and M. Murakami.

nancy. In the newborn, smiling may occur as part of one of the sleep states (rapid eye movement or REM sleep), and in the next two months, it may occur in response to a wide range of stimulus conditions. Smiling may occur in a 3-month-old while the infant is learning a task even when no one is present. After about 6 weeks, smiles appear in response to the sight of the human face and may also be triggered by rocking the baby or by ringing a bell.

The ethologists have paid the most attention to displays or expressive behavior as signals of emotion, generally without reference to inferred subjective states. From their point of view, facial expressions are only one kind of display system that includes such varied communications as warning signals, threat signals, food signals, and territory signals, among others. These displays may be vocal, visual, postural, or olfactory (e.g., production of odors through scent glands or urine). In lower vertebrates, expressive emotional behavior tends to be whole body displays. At higher phylogenetic levels, displays are more discrete and, at the same time, the parts of the display are less highly correlated with each other. Also found at higher levels is less all-or-none behavior and more gradation of signals. Such gradations allow greater flexibility in the expression of meanings.

There is no doubt that facial expressions play a role in social communication. This rule is true for all infant emotional expressions. Infants do not simply emit signals that have emotional meaning. The signals are part of an interaction between the infant and its caretaker. Parents help shape and organize the expressions of infants by influencing their timing, intensity, and threshold. According to Trevarthen (1977), infants show various movements of their head, trunk, or limbs that are closely synchronized to facial expressions or vocalizations of the mother. There is thus a rudimentary grammar of the sequence of interactions (Plutchik, 1983).

The Smile

More detailed information concerning the development of the smile illustrates some of the above points. Data on the development of smiling shows that during the first few weeks, infants will occasionally turn their lips into a smile without any identifiable stimulus being present. Such smiles, without the presence of eliciting external stimuli, are called endogenous smiles. Investigators discovered that such smiles occurred during states of rapid eye movements (or REM states), which are normal concomitants of both sleep and drowsiness in infants. The frequency of such endogenous smiles was about 1 smile for every 2 minutes of REM time in infants aged about 8 months postconception. At 9 months postconception (i.e., at birth for a normal term baby), the rate of endogenous smiles is about 1 for each 8 minutes of REM time. For the next few weeks after birth, the rate of endogenous smiles is about 1 for each 13 minutes of REM time. Endogenous smiling rapidly decreases by the third or fourth month of life and is rarely seen after the sixth month.

In contrast to the endogenous smile is the exogenous smile, which is a smile in response to external stimulation. It is not present at birth but begins to appear around the first or the second month as a reaction to various stimuli. Mild nonspecific stimulation, such as ringing a bell or rocking the infant, may trigger a smile. Sometimes the infant shows repetitive smiling to the stimulus, as often as 1 or 2 per minute for as long as 10 minutes.

From the age of 6 or 8 weeks on, smiling is best elicited by the sight of a human face, and after 3 or 4 months the mother's face is the most potent elicitor of smiling. Thus, the endogenous smile and exogenous smile are inversely related; as the first disappears, the other becomes more firmly established.

The onset of the social smile is dependent to some degree on the nature of the caretaking to which the infant is exposed. For example, Gewirz (1965) studied the development of the smile in 4 different settings in Israel. He found that infants raised in families and in the stimulating environment of the kibbutz showed social smiling earlier and more persistently than did infants raised in institutional and day nursery settings.

That the initiation of the exogenous smile is under genetic and maturational control is indicated by Fraiberg's (1971) work on children who are blind from birth. These infants show the same pattern of smiling in response to multiple stimuli, and the development of smiling has essentially the same time course. The major difference is that social (exogenous) smiling became increasingly responsive to the mother's voice and touch instead of her face.

Since social smiling appears with greater frequency after the age of 3 or 4 months, the mother's behavior can increasingly influence it. Studies have shown that social smiling can be influenced by operant conditioning procedures (i.e., by giving the child rewards for smiling) after this period. Although these studies clearly demonstrate that mothers can reinforce the responses of babies, there have been few studies of the reinforcing effects of the babies' smiles on mothers. General observations reveal that an infant's smiles increase a mother's attachment to the infant and also tend to increase (attract) new kinds of social stimulation.

▌Attachment Theory

The theory of attachment behavior is largely the work of one man, John Bowlby, although many investigators have contributed to it. Bowlby was a British child psychiatrist whose experiences during World War II led him to an interest in studying prolonged mother-child separations and deprivation of maternal care. His observations suggested that the deprived infant or young child went through a stage of distressed *protest*, followed by stages of *despair* and *detachment* if the separation continued for more than a week.

Bowlby found parallels to these patterns of reaction in the ethological literature. Many birds and mammals show comparable kinds of reactions under similar conditions of separation from mothers. Bowlby concluded that attachment behavior was biologically rooted and the possible basis for long-term affectional bonds. He believed that attachment behavior, that is, the maintenance of close contact with a mother or caretaker, had evolved through natural selection because it increased the chances of survival of an infant through protection by its mother.

Attachment theory assumes that the infant is equipped at birth with a set of species-characteristic behaviors that increase the likelihood of proximity to its mother. Examples of such behaviors are crying, smiling, and grasping, which act as signals, plus such things as a large head, large eyes, soft skin, and other characteristics that appear to attract adults. One of Bowlby's collaborators, Mary Ainsworth, described 13 behaviors that she considered examples of attachment-inducing behaviors: crying, smiling, vocalizing, visual-motor orientation, crying when the attachment figure leaves, following, scrambling, burying face in lap, exploring from a secure base, clinging, lifting arms in greeting, clapping hands in greeting, and moving toward the mother (Lamb, Thompson et al., 1985). These behaviors act to attach the infant to its mother, which in turn leads to protection and increased chances of survival.

Separation of the infant from its mother is a dangerous situation for the child and such separation activates all the mechanisms and behaviors the child has available, the most obvious of which is crying. Subsequent studies found that parents who responded promptly and consistently to infant crying had infants who by the end of the first year cried relatively little. It appears that prompt and close bodily contact does not spoil babies or make them fussy (Ainsworth and Bowlby, 1991).

Harlow's Extension of Bowlby's Ideas

Harry Harlow was a psychologist who carried on research in his University of Wisconsin laboratory for many years. He studied the effects on infant monkeys of separating them from their mothers for varying periods of time. Generally, the effects were devastating. Despite adequate food, cleanliness, and environment, the monkeys became severely dysfunctional, rocking back and forth in a corner, sucking or biting their fingers or skin, screeching or crying, walking on their hind legs while clasping their own body, or curling into a ball. When they were allowed to join other monkeys, their behavior was one of panic, and they were unable to engage in normal social interactions.

In studying such animals, Harlow and his associates began to learn a great deal about the antidote to such disturbed behavior, which he called *contact comfort,* or *love.* He discovered that young monkeys raised without their mothers showed strong attachments to cloth pads used to cover the cage floor. Given the choice of going to a crude wooden model of a mother that supplied milk versus a model with no milk that had a terry cloth covering, all the monkeys chose the latter. It appeared that contact comfort was more important than food in these young animals.

These findings were inconsistent with the old idea that hunger, thirst, and sex are the primary drives, while love and affection are secondary drives learned by association or conditioning. From this old point of view, the mother is loved because she is a secondary reinforcing agent who provides food. This did not seem to be the case in Harlow's study. In addition, the presence of the terry cloth mother (but not the wooden mother) provided a secure base from which the infant could explore any strange or novel situation, as Figure 8.6 illustrates.

Harlow also demonstrated other kinds of attachments besides that between mother and child. His experiments showed that social attachments between female pairs of rhesus monkeys, housed in pairs during their second year of life, outlasted 2 years of separation. When the animals

| Figure 8.6 | Contact Comfort |

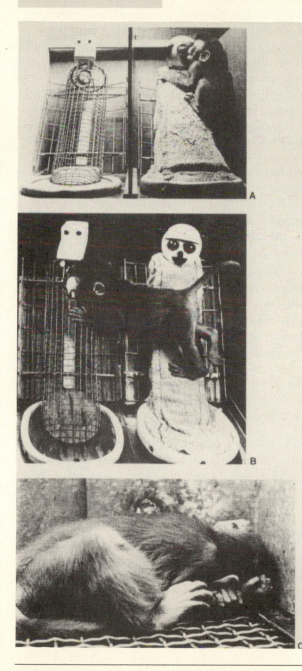

(A) A monkey clings to its terry cloth surrogate mother. (B) A monkey stays in contact with the terry cloth mother even as it nurses from the wire mother. (C) Typical posture of a monkey raised in isolation.

Source: C. B. Wortman and E.F. Loftus, 1985.

were reunited, no female showed aggression against her previous cage-
mate, although she did show aggressive behavior toward unfamiliar
females. The reunited pairs generally showed high levels of embracing,
grooming, and proximity behavior (Harlow and Mears, 1983).

One of Harlow's special concerns was with the identification of factors
that reduce or ameliorate fear or aggression in animals (and presumably in
humans as well). His research demonstrated, consistent with the observations of Bowlby, that complete or partial isolation of infants creates serious
disturbances in their solitary behavior as well as in their social interactions.
Harlow and his associates then tried to create various procedures that
might undo the damage created by isolation. Here are his words:

> One year after another we devised experiments testing different methods of reha-
> bilitation to undo the damage of asocial rearing and to create animals whole in
> personality as well as in physical health. We first placed them with peers, hoping
> that the power of peer play would work wonders, but the isolates did not know
> how to play. We tried surrogate mothers—unheated, heated, and rocking.
> Acceptance of contact was achieved, but nothing more.

> We had no notable success until we were able to take fear out of the picture. This
> we achieved with the aid of junior therapists. The three-month-old therapists were
> just one-half the age of the isolates, young enough to still seek gentle contact with
> other monkeys. The therapists were so gentle that they did not present any threat
> to the fearful six-month isolates. At three months of age, the little rhesus monkeys
> were just learning to play, and they led the isolates along with them, little by lit-
> tle. It took approximately five months for virtually complete reversal of the behav-
> ioral deficits to occur, a year of one-to-one therapy to develop play and social
> interaction along with social roles and rules. And eventually, maturation pro-
> duced realistic sex (Harlow and Mears, 1983).

Harlow believes that social play is a key element in undoing the dam-
aging effects of isolation. Play has survival value and prepares the individual for entry into the adult world of social roles and rules.

▌When Do Children Learn Emotion Concepts?

Much of the previous discussion has dealt with the development and
recognition of various emotional expressions in infants and young children.
There is, however, another side to the issue. When and how do young children learn to correctly use the emotion language appropriate to their culture? There must be some reasonable congruity in children's use of emotion
words, or communications with peers and parents would be confused and
confusing. In recent years a number of investigations have examined this
issue.

Research on children's use of emotion words depends obviously on the child being old enough to use words. Thus, most such research has been done with the children from about ages 2 or 3 years to adolescence. In some of these studies, the investigator simply asks mothers for their recollections of when their children first used such emotion words as *happy, sad, mad,* and *scared.* In a variant of this kind of study, mothers are asked to keep a diary and to record instances of use of emotion words as well as the contexts. Another approach presents young children with pictures of facial expressions and asks them to identify the emotion seen. Still another method for investigation of this problem is based upon filmed interactions of children fighting, crying, kicking, and receiving gifts. The subjects are interviewed and asked how the various participants feel. Generally, these studies reveal that the child's ability to make some correct inferences about emotions in pictures or in others begins at about the age of 2 or 2 1/2 years. At that time about half the children can identify *happy* faces from photographs and some can identify *sad* or *mad* faces. By the age of 4 years, all children understand *happy.* By 5 years, most children can identify *surprised* and *scared* from pictures, and *sad* pictures by age 7. If children are presented with short descriptions of events that might lead a child to feel a particular emotion, 4-year-olds could usually identify happiness, sadness, anger, disgust, and surprise (Camras and Allison, 1985). When children aged 2 to 5 years were required to make forced-choice judgments between various pairs of facial expressions on photographs, they often confused *mad* with *scared.* When the facial expressions were color movies of actors creating each expression over a 5-second period, most 4-year-olds discriminated all five faces (*happy, sad, mad, surprised,* and *scared*) (Smiley and Huttenlocher, 1989).

It is also of interest that 6th- and 7th-grade children identified as depressed were aware not only of the sadness they felt, but also their simultaneous feelings of anger. Eight of 10 depressed children volunteered that depression was a combination of sadness and anger. They were thus aware of the fact that emotions (such as sadness and anger) may blend and interact to produce special qualities that have labels of their own (such as depression).These findings indicate that by the age of 3 or 4, young children can recognize a number of basic emotions in others, and that the complex vocabulary of emotion is gradually added much later. By the age of 10, children recognize that emotions can be mixed, and most children can draw pictures expressive of the basic emotions, as Figure 8.7 illustrates.

Do Children Understand the Causes of Emotions?

A number of studies have been carried out with adults in an effort to determine how consistent they are in judging the causes of different emotions. For example, loss experiences are generally believed to be the origin

Figure 8.7	A Child's Drawing of Five Primary Emotions

Joy   Anger

Fear   Disgust   Sadness

Source: R. Plutchik, 1990.

of feelings of sadness, while frustrations of various kinds are generally believed to trigger feelings of anger.

The question to be considered in the present section is how children think about the causes of their emotions. In a major study of this question, Harter and Whitesell (1989) obtained open-ended descriptions from children ages 4 through 11 on the causes of 4 of the basic emotions: happy, sad, mad, and scared. They compared the responses of the children to those of adults asked the same questions in a study by Shaver, Schwartz, et al. (1987).

For happiness or joy, Shaver and others identified four major categories of causes in adults: getting what you want; being accepted, belonging, receiving affection or love; experiencing highly pleasurable sensations; and achieving a task. In the study of children, 70% indicated that the cause of happiness was getting something they wanted, while the other three causes were mentioned infrequently. No age trends were noticed for most of these categories, although happiness resulting from task achievement increased from 2% among young children to 18% among the 9- to 11-year-olds.

With regard to anger, adults describe several major causes: physical or psychological pain; loss of power, status, or respect; insult; and things not working out as expected. In children, 62% of the responses corresponded to physical or psychological pain (e.g., being hit, yelled at, or having feelings hurt), while most of the rest corresponded to things not working out as expected. These causes were described even in young children and did not change very much with age.

In adults, 5 classes of events triggered the emotion of sadness: loss of a valued relationship; an undesirable outcome; feeling rejected or disapproved by others; feeling helpless; and feeling empathy with the sadness of others. The first 4 of these categories could be identified in the responses of children, but sadness resulting from empathy with the distress of others could not. Some of the categories show a marked change with increasing age. Sadness resulting from feelings of rejection decreased from 62% in the youngest children to 17% in the oldest. Loss of a valued relationship was a cause of sadness in 14% of the younger children and in 47% of the older ones.

Adults describe the emotion of fear as having three major causes: threat of harm or death; being in an unfamiliar situation; and threat of social rejection. In children, a threat of harm or being in an unfamiliar situation causes most fears. Developmental trends were noticed. Threat of harm as a cause of fear decreased from 73% of the 3- to 5-year-old children to 40% of the 9- to 11-year-olds. Fear of unfamiliar situations increased from 25% in the young children to 49% in the older ones. "Young children made numerous references to their fear of mythical or fairy tale figures, e.g., monsters, dragons, and ghosts. The increase with age for the category of unfamiliar or novel situations seemed due to the wider range of potentially fearful novel situations in which older children may find themselves, as exemplified by responses involving walking home at night, being in a dark alley, going to junior high school, or being in a scary movie without your parents" (Harter and Whitesell, 1989).

All these observations imply that the causes of four basic emotions described by children, when considered in terms of major categories, are pretty much the same as the causes of these same emotions reported by adults. What changes with age are the specific, age-appropriate stimuli (e.g., being gobbled up by monsters vs. being in an automobile accident) that cause or trigger emotional reactions. Somehow, young children by the age of 3 or 4 years have a fairly accurate sense of the social situations that generate at least a few basic emotions.

This research dealt with only four emotions and therefore has nothing to say about whether the same conclusions hold true for many other emotions such as surprise, disgust, jealousy, pride, and curiosity. On the basis of the research reported in an earlier chapter on the understanding of emotion words, it is likely that the comprehension of these emotion concepts develops relatively late (adolescence or later), and even then only to a limited degree. If we consider most emotions to be mixtures or blends of a small number of basic ones, it is easier to understand why the comprehension of their causes develops late and remains somewhat obscure. The blending of emotions depends on the simultaneous occurrence of many and varied experiences, and the subjective components become fuzzier and more difficult to specify. Despite these problems, it is hoped that future research will help tackle these difficult problems.

Summary ■

The study of emotions in infants creates a difficult conceptual problem if emotions are defined as inner feelings. What kind of evidence should we use to infer the existence of emotional states in nonverbal babies? These same issues exist with regard to the judgment of emotions in animals.

The kinds of evidence psychologists use in inferring emotions in infants relate to the similarity between infants and adults on two general characteristics: similarity of eliciting conditions and similarity of effects. Other specific criteria are that certain generalized reactions affect many aspects of behavior and physiology simultaneously; that they are usually elicited by important (survival-related) events in the child's life; that they appear to have a sense of urgency; that they have a momentum that makes rapid stops difficult; that approach or avoidance behavior is often associated with them; and that they are usually directed towards other individuals in the environment. These criteria can be used to infer emotions in animals as well.

Studies of human infants and infant animals have led to the conclusion that emotional expressions, including both behavior and sounds, are forms of communication that function to have certain effects on other individuals. For example, emotional signals indicate the need for nourishment or protection, and they signal distress of any sort. Such signals increase the probability of social contact with a mother. Since both situations and individuals are complex systems, most emotional signals tend to be mixed signals reflecting two or more emotional systems such as fear and anger. Emotional signals are thus in the service of motives and needs, or, put more generally, in the service of survival.

The concept of infant attachment as an expression of emotions has attracted the attention of many researchers, and some of the important ideas related to this domain are presented. When infants are separated from their mothers, patterns of reaction called *protest* and *despair* occur. These strategies have evolved presumably because they have survival value. They tend to stimulate nurturant behavior in the mother, or aversive behavior to crying. When mother-infant separation continues for a long time (as in studies of monkeys), the effects on the infant are extremely disturbing, and interfere with later social and sexual behavior.

Since it is evident that children learn to use the language of emotions as they grow, studies have been directed toward assessing the sequence of changes that typically occur. Very young children use only a few emotion words, such as happy, sad, and scared. As they mature, their emotion vocabulary increases, and their understanding of the elicitors of emotion increases: It is possible to identify prototype elicitors for particular emotions, as well as typical types of reactions. Problems of specification arise, however, because older children and especially adults have to learn to recognize and describe the mixed emotions or blends that characterize emotional development.

Emotions and Evolution

*Ethology . . . emphasizes the essential
unity of living things and the similarity,
in much that is fundamental, between
animals and men.*
—William H. Thorpe

▋ Goals of This Chapter

Previous chapters have provided evidence that emotions function to provide information from one individual to another. Such information may influence the behavior of the interacting individuals so that the well-being or survival of the individual expressing the emotion may be enhanced. A simple way of expressing this idea is that emotions are adaptive.

The concept of adaptation is a central notion in evolutionary thinking. The concept relates both to the behavior of individuals attempting to deal with the daily problems of the animate and inanimate worlds, and also to the idea of species changes over generations, in response to changing environments. This chapter will therefore provide a brief introduction to some ideas related to evolution and will suggest how they may be connected to our ideas about emotions.

From a broad evolutionary point of view, the concept of emotions should apply to lower animals as well as to humans. The idea of continuity of physical structures and biological functioning is central to evolutionary thinking and implies, as Darwin and many ethologists believe, that emotions can be recognized in all animals. Such a belief indicates the need to conceptualize emotions in such a way as to enable us to recognize emotions at all phylogenetic levels.

This chapter will therefore begin with a brief overview of evolutionary ideas and then discuss the issue of how one can identify mental states in animals. The important work of Hebb will be described, followed by a discussion of different ways that we use to infer the existence of emotions in animals. The following chapter will then provide more detailed examples of how animals communicate emotional states.

Important Questions Addressed In This Chapter

- What is meant by *natural selection?*
- What are the basic functional requirements that must be met if organisms are to survive?
- What are the two meanings of the word *adaptation?*
- On what evidence does one attribute mental states to animals?
- What has been learned about the use of language by chimpanzees?
- Do animals show evidence of self-awareness?

Darwin was the first to recognize that the concept of evolution should apply not only to the development of physical structures but to the evolution of mind and emotions as well. In his book The Expression of the Emotions in Man and Animals, published in 1872, he gave many illustrations of parallel ways that different animals express emotions. He felt that such observations would provide a basis for generalizations about the origins of various types of expressive behavior, since in contrast to humans, animals are not likely to base expressions upon social conventions.

The expansion of research has confirmed Darwin's conception of the basic unity of living systems. There seems to be little question that basic processes exist in common at all levels of biologic development. In order to fully understand emotions, it is necessary to recognize their evolutionary origins as well as their origins in individual development. This chapter will therefore briefly describe the concept of evolution and how it helps throw light on our own understanding of emotions.

■ ■ ■ ■ ■ ■ ■ ■

▌The Nature of Evolution

Evolution has often been described as the most general and important idea in biology. Darwin's concept of natural selection implies that most features of each existing species have survival value; this is as true of an animal's behavior, including its emotional behavior, as it is of its bodily structures. Behavior, like all features of an animal, is a product of evolution. In light of these facts, let us examine some of the important ideas of the theory of evolution.

A cornerstone of the theory is the concept of natural selection. Darwin recognized that the capacity of any given plant or animal population to reproduce was far greater than was needed to keep a constant population size. Many more animals are born than achieve sexual maturity. This meant that, in the long run, the animals that did survive were better equipped, in some way, to live in their environment. A further implication was that the surviving members of the population would leave offspring that were also likely to be better adapted to their environment. If this process of differential fertility continued over a sufficient number of generations, then major changes could take place in the characteristics of the surviving population.

A simple but interesting example of this process is seen in the development of a black moth in certain areas of England. A gray moth is found over wide areas of the countryside. A black version of this moth has appeared in this century in certain factory areas where there is so much soot in the air that many chimneys and rooftops, and even trees, become blackened by it. Gray moths stand out as easy targets in these areas and are preyed upon by birds. Over the course of generations, the moths less likely to be eaten by predators were those moths that showed a darker gray color as examples of naturally occurring variability in color. The light gray moths produced fewer and fewer offspring, whereas the dark gray moths produced relatively more offspring. In time, there were only black moths and no gray ones. In this case, the cause of differential fertility of one part of the population relative to another is predation, but other causes may also affect fertility.

This illustration of natural selection highlights several ideas. Although natural selection affects individuals, it is the population that changes over a period of time. In other words, selective fertility changes the relative distributions of various kinds of genes (or genotypes) in the population. Such changes usually affect the phenotype or overt appearance of a trait. Evolution refers to changes in gene frequencies that occur over the course of generations within interbreeding populations.

A second important idea is the notion of adaptation. The changes that took place in the color of the moth population had the effect of decreasing predation. It made the moths less likely to be killed off and thus increased their "fitness" to the environment. The concept of adaptation thus refers to the fitness of a trait or characteristic of a population for a particular environment. If the environment changes, the trait may no longer be adaptive. Other examples of adaptations are the color and stereoscopic vision primates developed for forest living, the keen olfactory sensitivities of certain animals, and the constant (warm-blooded) body temperatures of mammals that allow them to be relatively independent of environmental changes of temperature.

Variables That Affect Genotypes

In the example of the British moth, the frequency of the genes that determine color were affected by predation from other animals. Thus, *selective predation* is one kind of variable that affects gene frequencies in a population.

Another kind of variable affecting the genotype is *sexual selection*, illustrated most clearly in the effects of animal and plant breeding. Through selective breeding, it is possible to produce roses of almost any color, cows that yield large quantities of milk, and dogs with certain desirable behavioral traits. Selective breeding has produced the large working dogs such as the collie, the ferocious war dogs such as the mastiff, and the babyish toy dogs such as the Pekingese.

A third source of variation in gene frequencies is *mutation.* For reasons that are not fully understood, spontaneous changes occasionally occur in the genes. Such mutations are random and their effects are usually lethal since no complex structure benefits from random interference. Those mutations that do allow for survival often change the gene frequency for a certain characteristic. An example of such an effect is the change in eye color of the common fruit fly, due to mutations produced by X rays.

A fourth source of changes in gene frequencies is called *genetic drift.* This type is simply the result of small groups of individuals being isolated for long periods from the larger population of which they are a part. Any small differences in gene frequencies between the isolated group and its parent population will tend to become magnified over generations as a result of continued inbreeding, and will eventually lead to different genotypes. The fact that human groups were small throughout most of human history, coupled with the fact that social rules differ from group to group, has acted to widen the genetic gaps among populations. Recent reports from geneticists suggest that all the Native Americans from the Eskimos in the north to the Algonquins of the east to the Incas and other groups of South America were all descended from a small band of pioneers who crossed the Bering Sea from Asia to Alaska about 20 to 30,000 years ago.

The four types of factors affecting natural selection, as illustrated by predation, sexual selection, mutation, and genetic drift, all influence gene frequencies in a population. Over the course of generations, these changes in genotypes are what constitute evolution. Although evolution implies adaptation or increased fitness, the degree of fitness is related specifically to a given environment. As the environment changes, the degree of fitness changes.

These concepts apply to humans as well as to lower animals. "The human species, *Homo sapiens,* is an outcome of the same natural processes that have produced all other species of organizations during the history of life on the earth. Man is related to varying degrees to all other organisms, living and extinct" (Simpson, 1972).

The Evolutionary Record and Biological Continuities

Living creatures appeared in the oceans about three billion years ago in the form of tiny bacteria. Large bacteria appeared about one billion years ago, and small multicellular organisms appeared about 600 million years ago. Fishes appeared in the oceans about 350 million years ago, and reptiles evolved on land about 300 million years ago. The mammals began as tiny nocturnal creatures about 180 million years ago and evolved into the many species we see today. Evidence for humanlike primates is about 2 million years old.

One of the major reasons life was confined to the seas for the first three billion years of this planet is that cells can escape the lethal effects of ultraviolet radiation by staying under water. Only very gradually did oxygen develop in the atmosphere, permitting the gradual development of an ozone layer. Protection against lethal radiation developed in a variety of ways: for example, by encasing the embryo in a shell, or by internal development of embryos, or by plants sending their germinative roots underground. In addition to local or periodic changes in environmental conditions, the major environmental event was the gradual change on the earth from an atmosphere without oxygen to one with it. This change led to a large increase in the size of cells (eukaryotes) and to a change in their system of metabolism. "As oxidative metabolism came on line, there was sufficient chemical energy available for bacteria to explore the possibilities of directed cell movement. A set of genes evolved to generate flagella and twirl them such that they moved the whole cell toward attractive compounds and away from repellents. In this way metabolism became coupled to adaptive behavior" (Loomis, 1988).

Because no environment is optimum for growth indefinitely, there is a strong selective advantage to moving around. The large eukaryotes became predators that engulfed the smaller bacteria. They evolved nuclei, internal membranes to encase their chromosomes, and special intracellular proteins, all adaptations found in many current living cells. In fact, "all eukaryotic organisms, from algae to trees to elephants, appear to have descended from a single protoeukaryotic cell" (Loomis, 1988). Evidence for this conclusion comes from work in molecular biology. A related idea is that various systems developed millions of years ago worked so well they have never been improved upon. For example, mammalian sperm now use the same flagellum for locomotion that evolved 600 million years ago to keep algae cells near the surface of water. Similarly, the amino acid sequences for both X and B tubulin (the bases of the microtubules that form flagella) are more than 70% similar in yeast, algae, sea urchins, chickens, rats, pigs, and humans. Certain peptide hormones such as insulin and ACTH are virtually identical in yeast cells and human beings. The gene order on the sex chromosome of mice (the X chromosome) is almost identical with that on the human X chromosome. The development of sexual

| Table 9.1 | The Geological and Evolutionary Record |

Geologic Periods	Number of Years Ago	Appearance of Animals (examples)
CENOZOIC ERA		
Recent	10,000	Homo sapien
Pleistocene	2 million	Human (Australopithecus)
Pliocene	11 million	Prehuman primate
Miocene	25 million	Prehuman primate
Oligocene	40 million	Elephant, ape, whale
Eocene	60 million	Octopus, mastodon, monkey
Paleocene	70 million	Horse, toothless bird
MESOZOIC ERA		
Cretaceous	135 million	Snake, turtle, bird
Jurassic	180 million	Lobster, frog, lizard, flying reptile
Triassic	225 million	Shrimp, bony fish, crocodile
PALEOZOIC ERA		
Permian	270 million	Spider, dinosaur
Pennsylvanian	300 million	Snail, insect, lamprey
Mississippian	350 million	Shark, scorpion
Devonian	400 million	Starfish, clam
Silurian	440 million	Jellyfish, coral
Ordovician	500 million	Cystoid, graptolite
Cambrian	600 million	Sponge, worm, trilobite
PRECAMBRIAN		
Eukaryotes	1 billion	Large bacteria
Protoeukaryotes	3 billion	Small bacteria

dimorphism (specialization of males for sperm production and females for egg production) is also extremely widespread. The advantage of this system is that the variability of genetic potentials increases the chances of the individual to successfully deal with changing or catastrophic environments.

Similarities in evolutionary patterns are also found through studies of development. For example, the similarity of developmental patterns in limb bones is evidence that amphibians, reptiles, and mammals all evolved from a common stock of lobe-fin fish. More than 100 years ago scientists noted that there are remarkable similarities in the structures that appeared in the early stages of embryogenesis in mammals, amphibians, birds, reptiles, and fish. A small number of developmental genes can radically change the behavior of cells and change an amoeba into a multicelled organism. Loomis (1988) estimates that fewer than 1,400 developmental genes may have been sufficient for the evolution of simple cells into fish, and fewer than 2,500 developmental genes may be sufficient for the embryogenesis of humans. "The important evolutionary differences between a guppy and a primate probably lie in only a few hundred genes" (Loomis, 1988).

These various observations from evolutionary and molecular biology emphasize the points that Darwin first made: that evolutionary continuities of structure, function, and development imply continuities of behavioral adaptations and mental life.

General Evolutionary Adaptations

The process of achieving fitness of a population to a given environment has also led to certain types of adaptations that are quite general and have the effect of making the organism less vulnerable to changes in the environment. For example, the development of genetic mechanisms that produce a constant body temperature (homeothermy) enabled animals to adapt to a wide range of environments. The evolution of lungs made the land environment available to vertebrates.

However, there are even more general adaptations than these. Certain complex chemical molecules evolved to form amino acids. These in turn formed long, chainlike molecules of deoxyribonucleic acid, or DNA, which is the basis of the genes, the reproductive units of all living things. Although evolution has produced many new groups of plants and animals, it has not changed the basic reproductive mechanism of amino acids, DNA, and genes. In other words, evolution does not change whatever works well. Evolution is thus basically "ultraconservative" (Wilson, 1975).

This idea also applies to the behavior of organisms. All organisms, in order to survive and maintain their populations, must find food, avoid injury, and reproduce their kind. This condition is as true of lower animals as it is of higher ones. The nature of the environment creates certain functional requirements for all organisms if they are to survive. Any organism must take in nourishment and eliminate waste products. It must distinguish between prey and predator and between a potential mate and a potential enemy. It must explore its environment and orient its sense organs appropriately as it takes in information about the beneficial and harmful aspects of its immediate world. And in organisms that are relatively helpless at birth and for a while thereafter, there must be ways of indicating the need for care and nurturance. The specific behaviors by which these functions are carried out vary widely throughout the animal kingdom, but the basic prototype functions remain invariant.

A key problem all organisms face is dealing with danger (with threats to survival), but only a limited number of modes of reacting are available. With respect to stimuli arising from within the organism, survival is favored by expulsion or by isolation. With respect to stimuli referring to a source of danger arising from the outer environment, survival is favored by flight, submission, attack, and vocalization, in the order of apparent phylogenetic development.

Scott (1958) has also elaborated on this theme. He suggested that only a few classes of adaptive behavior are found in most species and phylogenetic levels. He describes them in the following terms: ingestive behavior, shelter-seeking behavior, agonistic (fight or flight) behavior, sexual behavior, care-giving behavior, care-soliciting behavior, eliminative behavior, allelomimetic (imitative) behavior, and investigative behavior. These general classes of adaptive behavior clearly apply to the higher animals, but some of the categories are not relevant to the lower ones. For example, reptiles typically lay eggs but show no parental behavior toward the newborn organisms.

Still another example of behavioral adaptations that have similar functions at various phylogenetic levels is given by Wilson (1975), a leading sociobiologist. He writes:

> As my own studies have advanced, I have been increasingly impressed with the functional similarities between invertebrate and vertebrate societies and less so with the structural differences that seem, at first glance, to constitute such an immense gulf between them. Consider for a moment termites and monkeys. Both are formed into cooperative groups that occupy territories. The group members communicate hunger, alarm, hostility, caste status or rank and reproductive status among themselves by means of something on the order of 10 to 100 nonsyntactical signals. Individuals are intensely aware of the distinction between groupmates and nonmembers. Kinship plays an important role in group structure and probably served as a chief generative force of sociability in the first place. In both kinds of society there is a well-marked division of labor, although in the insect society there is a much stronger reproductive component. The details of organization have been evolved by an evolutionary process of unknown precision, during which some measure of added fitness was given to individuals with cooperative tendencies—at least toward relatives. The fruits of cooperativeness depend upon

the particular conditions of the environment and are available to only a minority of animal species during the course of their evolution.

Genetics and Learning

These observations by biologists of similar classes of adaptive behavior identifiable at various phylogenetic levels suggest the following conclusions: During the course of evolution, two general types of adaptation have appeared and can be seen in the most primitive organisms as well as in the most advanced. These types of adaptation are what might be called innate responses and learning. Even simple protozoa and metazoa show innate (genetically programmed) reactions to certain types of stimulation. The types of stimulation include food objects, gradients of chemical substances in solution, toxic substances, electromagnetic radiation (light), and vibrations at certain frequencies. The reactions to these stimuli are primarily movements toward or away from the stimulus.

The capacity to learn from experience has also evolved. This capacity to benefit from experience is as much a product of evolution as any other species characteristic. Genetic programming determines the limits and nature of the modifications that each individual can undergo as a result of life experiences. For example, shortly after hatching from the egg, ducks will learn to follow any moving object they see. This process is called imprinting, and although it normally occurs in relation to the mother, the response may become attached to humans or other animals if the mother is absent. However, the timing of the response is under the strict control of the genetic structure of the duck. If young ducks are isolated for a few days and are then presented with an appropriate stimulus (even their own mother), they will not learn to follow. In other words, the amount an animal can learn, the complexity of the stimuli they can discriminate, and the complexity of the responses they can make are largely limited by genetic restraints; only the context is determined by experience.

Another way in which learning relates to evolution has been discussed in detail by Breland and Breland (1966), who have used operant techniques with thousand of animals representing over 60 species. The Brelands point out that the vast majority of the species of the earth use only limited kinds of learning in their interactions with the environment. Most organisms enter the world prepared to cope with it through the use of certain fixed sequences of behavior that particular species-specific stimuli, or *releasers*, activate. Moths find mates by responding to certain types of odors, most birds have fixed styles of nest building, and fighting behavior is often triggered by particular colors or movements of an animal.

Not all behaviors are equally conditionable. For example, although it may take a pigeon days or weeks to learn to pull a string, a chicken can learn this task in a matter of minutes, probably because the chicken normally eats by pulling worms from the ground, whereas pigeons normally peck at food. It is virtually impossible to get a chicken to vocalize for food reinforcement, whereas other birds can easily be trained to do this (Breland and Breland, 1966). Similarly, efforts to train chimpanzees to use a vocal language have all failed (Hayes, 1951; Kellogg & Kellogg, 1967). The Brelands suggest that the degree to which behavior patterns are rigid and relatively unchangeable depends upon the phylogenetic level to which an animal belongs. It also depends on the size of the environmental niche of the animal. Animals that occupy only a small segment of the environment, such as rabbits do, show relatively more fixed behavior sequences than animals such as the raccoon that occupy a broader environmental niche. As one illustration of a factor that influences the size of an environmental niche, note that animals that eat both meat and plant foods tend to have a wider niche than those that eat plant foods alone.

The Concept of Fitness

In the biological context there are two different meanings of the word *fitness*. One of these meanings has already been discussed in relation to the idea of fitness to the environment. Such fitness is a species characteristic and reflects the process of genetic changes over the course of generations. The second meaning refers to the ability of individuals to adjust body systems to changes of the environment. Under conditions of stress, changes in heart rate, blood pressure, glucose secretion, hormonal secretions, sweating, and a variety of other activities all prepare the body for action during emergency conditions.

It is important, however, to emphasize that the process of adaptation to stress or emergency conditions does not end with internal changes in biological systems. Those changes function to prepare the individual to act, and it is the integral action of the entire organism that completes the process of adaptation. Cannon was right when he said that internal changes in the body prepare the organism for flight or fight behavior. Although Darwin had relatively little to say about internal biological processes, he correctly focused his attention on adaptive behaviors of individual animals in response to particular environmental events. And although Freud did not consider internal physiological events, or animal behavior, he correctly looked for the adaptational meaning of all human behaviors.

The point is that all organisms show certain classes of adaptive behaviors in response to certain special events that occur in their environment. These adaptive behaviors are clearly evident in simple form in the lowest animals on the phylogenetic scale. They are also evident in more complex or derivative form in higher animals and in humans. It is reasonable to consider these general classes of adaptive behaviors as the precursors or prototypes of what are called emotions in higher animals.

▍An Evolutionary Definition of Emotions

From an evolutionary point of view, one can conceptualize emotions as certain types of adaptive behaviors that can be identified in lower animals as well as in humans. These adaptive patterns have evolved to deal with basic survival issues in all organisms, such as dealing with prey and predator, potential mate and stranger, nourishing objects and toxins. Such patterns involve approach or avoidance reactions, fight and flight reactions, attachment and loss reactions, and riddance or ejection reactions. The evolutionary perspective suggests that these patterns are the prototypes of what we call emotions in higher animals and in humans. These interactional patterns of adaptation may be thought of as the prototypes of fear and anger, acceptance and disgust, and joy and sadness. The subjective feelings that we usually identify as emotions are a relatively late evolutionary development and should not be used as the only or major criterion of the presence of an emotional state. Emotions are complex, interactional adaptations and must therefore have a variety of expressive forms, each of which can be used to infer properties of the underlying state. Even though the details of the adaptive processes vary among different animals, species, and phyla, depending on the nature of the environment and genetics, the *function* of each pattern of adaptation has remained unchanged throughout all phylogenetic levels. From the evolutionary point of view emotions are patterns of adaptation that increase the chances of individual and genetic survival.

▍How To Study Emotions in Animals

The observations made so far in this chapter indicate the need to identify systematic ways to infer emotions in animals. The problem in some ways is similar to that involved in inferring the existence of any subjective feeling state. The reason the two problems are not identical is that an emotion is a more general reaction, of which feeling states may be one aspect.

The belief in animal feelings is widespread. The Society for the Prevention of Cruelty to Animals is based on the idea that animals can feel pain and can suffer. The contemporary flourishing of animal rights groups is a reflection of the same widespread belief. However, if animals can feel pain and suffering, there is no reason to assume they cannot feel other states as well: anger, fear, affection, pleasure, and disgust. Yet, if one can justify the probable experience of pain in an animal, one can also justify the probable experience of fear as well. It is important to emphasize that the argument that animals can feel some emotional states does not mean that they can feel all states. Let us now consider several different descriptions of how one can infer emotions in animals.

Donald Hebb on Emotions in Chimpanzees

In an early paper Hebb wrote in 1946, he discussed the problem of inferring emotions in chimpanzees. The paper appeared after Hebb had worked for several years at the Yerkes Laboratory for primate studies in Florida, and it described some of his conclusions concerning the problem of how to recognize emotions in animals and in humans.

At the time Hebb worked at the Yerkes Laboratory, it contained 30 adolescent and adult chimpanzees, almost all of whom had been under daily observation for periods of 6 to 19 years. Staff members kept detailed diary records for each animal, particularly at times when emotional states were ascribed to the animals. There was thus detailed and intimate knowledge of each animal over most of its life span.

With all this information available, Hebb and his colleagues had no reluctance at all in inferring the existence of emotions in these animals. He wrote in 1972:

> The dog is definitely capable of jealousy and occasionally, in some dogs, there are signs of sulking. In the chimpanzee, however, we have the full picture of human anger in its three main forms: anger, sulking and the temper tantrum. The peculiar feature of sulking is refusing to accept what one tried to get in the first place. The peculiar feature of the temper tantrum is the inclusion of apparent attempts at self-injury, the child holding its breath, pulling his hair, banging himself against the wall—and watching meanwhile to see what effect this is having on the adult who is denying him what he wants. There is a purposive element that is also clear in the year-old chimpanzee infant who takes surreptitious looks at his mother in between his attacks of choking to death or pounding his head on the floor.

Hebb goes on to point out that not only are such basic emotions as anger, fear, and curiosity seen quite clearly in chimpanzees, but so too is altruistic behavior. Although many philosophers have argued that humans and animals are basically selfish, governed only by "those twin masters, pleasure and pain," there is increasing evidence that altruistic behavior is widely found in the animal kingdom. Altruism may be defined as purposive behavior that functions to help another person or animal even at the risk of one's own danger or death. A number of documented cases show that a dolphin, a mammal with a brain larger than a human's, will help other dolphins who are in trouble (for example, caught in a net). Two cases are known where a dolphin helped a human swimmer to reach safety. Adult baboons will deliberately place themselves between their harem, consisting of adult females and younger animals, and a predator such as a lion. Chimpanzees and gorillas observed in the wild have given help to youngsters in trouble even though it meant going into the dangerous area of the human observer (Hebb, 1972). Hebb concludes that these many instances of altruistic behavior reflect an inferred emotional state, and that the capacity for this state is largely a product of evolution rather than learning.

Hebb developed many important ideas as a result of his experiences with the chimpanzees at the Yerkes Laboratory. For example, he emphasized that the names given to emotional behavior are seldom based on the immediate behavior alone; they are based on a knowledge of the animal over an extended period of time. The same behavior might be labeled fear, nervousness, or shyness, depending upon a number of factors. In each case, the immediate behavior is some form of avoidance, but in the case of fear it is strong, clearly related to an identifiable stimulus and not a common occurrence in that particular animal. Nervousness refers to a long-term characteristic of the animal and is usually recognized by a low startle threshold. Shyness implies that the animal tends to avoid strangers generally. Without knowing something about the stimulus, the details of the behavior, and the animal's typical past behavior, an accurate inference is difficult. In addition, it is evident that the same emotion word, such as *shyness*, can refer *both* to a temporary state and to a long-term condition akin to a personality trait.

Although a knowledge of the stimulus is helpful when making an inference about an emotional state in someone else, it is not always, or even often, known. Sometimes a lack of a stimulus (such as a lack of attention) produces an emotional reaction. Sometimes, the stimulus is so slight or minimal ("she gets mad over nothing at all") that the observer cannot identify it. More importantly, it implies that there are few, if any, invariable connections between a stimulus and a response. The emotional response is primarily a function of the *meaning* or interpretation one gives to a situation or some aspect of it.

Given the fact that an inference is made of an emotional state in an animal, is there any way of verifying the judgment? Hebb states that the validity of the label is its practical ability to predict the animal's behavior. In other words, if an animal is called shy, caretakers know what to expect of it in the future. If an animal is called angry or hostile, the caretakers will know enough to be cautious in its presence.

Useful as these labels can be, staff members more often than not refused to utilize them in situations where the cues were ambiguous. This condition implies that observers use some kind of implicit weighting of cues in order to arrive at a probability estimate of the presence of an emotional state.

Another important idea Hebb presented concerns the significance of subliminal or minimal levels of excitation as factors in the development of emotions. He illustrates this with the following examples (Hebb, 1946):

In an experiment on avoidance a mounted snake was carried in the experimenter's hands up to the part of the enclosure where Shorty [a chimpanzee] sat. He moved calmly away to another part of the enclosure with no hint of excitement; but when the snake was again brought near him in his new position, he sprang up with hair erect and screaming, and hurled a large piece of timber at the experimenter with excellent aim. The same kind of summation effect is often seen in discrimination training, where a single failure may have no apparent effect but repeated failures lead to sulking, temper tantrums or destructive attacks on the apparatus. In such instances existence of a subliminal excitation is purely a matter of inference . . .

Individual signs of the development of frustration responses are quite varied. They include the animal's scratching himself, ducking his head, . . . restlessness, moaning, whimpering, and erection of hair . . . knowledge of the species has considerable importance in the interpretation of the associated behavior of emotional excitation.

One implication of this concept of summation of sublimal excitation is the idea that low levels of emotional arousal are inherently vague and relatively undifferentiated. Thus, even a human observer may have difficulty labeling his or her own emotional state when it is aroused only to low degree. This idea is probably the basis for some of the variability found in studies of self-attribution of emotions under mild conditions of stress in college students (Schachter & Singer, 1962). It may also help account for the fact that false autonomic feedback can often induce students to label their states as emotions, even when objective indices of arousal show minimal levels (Valins, 1966).

Identifying Mental States in Animals

Arnold (1960) has pointed out that ascribing emotion to animals is no different in essence than ascribing memory or imagination to animals. She argues that the presence of a similar sensory apparatus in both humans and animals implies that animals have sensory experiences. Similarly, the fact that animals, like humans, can learn implies that they remember earlier situations and have expectations about the future.

In a review of parallels in thinking (representational processes) in apes and humans, Masod (1976) concludes that:

Apes have good memories, they remember selectively, they anticipate the consequences of their own actions (or to a lesser extent, the actions of others), and they give every indication of perceiving their surroundings as structured and constrained . . . .

It is possible to show parallel sensory experiences in humans and animals in the following way: Using forced-choice or matching tasks with certain stimulus patterns, investigators can behaviorally test animal or human subjects. They need no verbal responses for such testing. The investigators can measure the effect of these stimulus patterns on the brain by recording the standard EEG (electroencephalograph) and using computer averaging of visually evoked cortical potentials. Humans with clinical conditions such as cataracts or astigmatism can be compared with animals to which experimental visual deprivations have been produced.

Based on these ideas, Millodot and Riggs (1970) used the evoked-cortical potential to measure visual acuity. They found that the strength of the electric potentials obtained from the scalp decreased as vision was decreased through the use of artificial distorting lenses. At the same time, the subject received lower and lower scores on a standard chart test for visual acuity. The authors conclude that they "have a completely objective test that can be used for fitting corrective lenses to the eyes of nonverbal subjects such as babies, animals and clinical patients" (Riggs, 1976). Researchers have used similar methods to determine the relative sensitivity to color of pigeons and to determine the absolute sensitivity to colors of a 2-month-old baby (Riggs, 1976). It is thus possible to measure inner, private events without recourse to formal language. There are several additional ways that this can be done.

Judging Emotions on the Basis of Choice Behavior

For many years, P.T. Young has been concerned with the concept of choice behavior and its implications for a theory of hedonic states. The word *hedonic* simply means pleasure, and Young has tried to reintroduce the concept of pleasure as a meaningful subjective state definable by overt experimental operations.

In order to carry out this aim, Young distinguished between the intensity of stimulation and the quality of stimulation. For example, in studies of taste, rats chose to drink from salt solutions of low concentration and tended to avoid salt solutions as the concentration of salt became greater. When sucrose (sweet) solutions were mixed with quinine (bitter) solutions, the rate of ingestion was found to be an algebraic sum of the positive (sweet) and negative (bitter) values of the solution. Similarly, humans more frequently rate low-intensity tones as pleasing than loud tones. They also more frequently rate sounds of low pitch as pleasant than sounds of high pitch.

These observations and many more examples that Young cites all imply that a simple one-dimensional activation concept is inadequate. Behavior is not just strong or weak, present or absent. Behavior has a directional aspect, implying a movement toward or away from certain objects or conditions. This idea of bidirectionality of behavior, of both positive and negative forms of activation, is what Young meant by the concept of *affective arousal* (Young, 1967). Affective arousal recognizes the reality of attraction and repulsion. For example, foul odors, bitter tastes, or painful burns are not simply at low levels of attractiveness on a unipolar scale of attraction; they are repulsive. Pleasantness is not simply a decrease in pain, but it has a distinctive quality of its own.

Pleasure and pain represent internal states in both humans and animals. Choices tell us that positive or negative feelings are involved, but they do not tell us directly which of any possible positive or negative emotional states are present. For example, the emotional states of affection and curiosity may both lead to approach reactions rather than withdrawals, but these two emotions are quite different from each other. Thus, although choice behavior is a method of communication of inner states, it does not have high precision and additional types of evidence must supplement it in order to tell us exactly which emotions are involved.

Judging Emotions on the Basis of Peer-Group Behavior

Another important way to identify emotional reactions in an animal (as well as a human) is by observing the behavior of other animals toward the identified one. There are a number of illustrations of this idea. In his book *The Year of the Gorilla* (1964), ethologist George Schaller described a female gorilla who usually sounded an alarm call when she saw him. However, instead of the call producing appropriate and typical protective responses from other gorillas in the band, the other animals ignored her. Schaller concluded that what appeared to him as a typical alarm call was interpreted differently by the other gorillas. They apparently recognized that the female was either not afraid, despite the call, or not in danger.

Delgado gives several illustrations of this same idea. He points out that the behavior of one monkey in a colony will produce emotional reactions from other animals. If the other monkeys provoke submissiveness or retaliation, it indicates that threat has occurred. Which of these two reactions occurs depends upon the relative positions of the animals within the dominance hierarchy; higher-dominance animals will retaliate, whereas lower-dominance animals will usually become submissive. We can thus identify the nature of the initial emotional stimulus by carefully observing the ensuing behavior of the other animals in the troop (Delgado, 1966).

Delgado gives another example of this point in relation to the effects of electrical stimulation of the brain in monkeys and cats. An electrode was placed in the rhinal fissure at the tip of the temporal lobe in a rhesus monkey. Electrical stimulation of this point produced opening of the mouth, rotation of the head, and scratching of the face, a pattern that to a human observer looked aggressive. However, this evoked behavior had no effect on the social behavior of the other members of the monkey colony. In contrast, electrical stimulation of the central gray area of the brain produced behavior that caused the other animals to withdraw, grimace, and show submissive behaviors (Delgado, 1964). We can thus reasonably infer that stimulation of the central gray area produced aggressive behavior, whereas stimulation of the rhinal fissure did not, even though there were some superficial similarities in the two patterns of behavior.

Similarly, stimulation of the lateral hypothalamus in the cat produces well-organized attack behavior against other cats. If they retaliate, a full-fledged fight breaks out. Stimulating the anterior hypothalamus produces an aggressive display, which may induce another cat to attack in return. Despite its apparently aggressive display, however, the stimulated cat lowers its head, flattens its ears, withdraws, and does not retaliate. This behavior implies that the apparent aggressive display does not truly reflect a state of aggression. The behavior of other animals of the same species provides a basis for judging the existence and type of emotion present in a given, identified animal. This condition therefore represents still another kind of evidence to be used, when available, to infer the presence of emotions in an animal.

These illustrations imply that the study of aggressive and submissive displays is a way of studying emotion regardless of how certain we may or may not be of whether the animal feels anger or fear. Because emotions are complex phenomena, investigators study, assess, and interpret different aspects without necessarily assuming that there is only one "golden standard" for defining emotion. As demonstrated in Chapter 2, subjective states are not even clearly measurable in human adults.

Can Apes Develop Language with Which to Express Their Emotions?

During the past 20 years or so, a number of attempts have been made to teach humanlike communication to the great apes. When attempts to teach spoken words were unsuccessful, various researchers beginning with Gardner and Gardner (1974, 1978, 1984) tried to teach chimpanzees American Sign Language, (ASL). Their first chimpanzee trainee, called Washoe, acquired her signs in two ways: first, by imitating her tutors, and second, by having her hands shaped by her trainers. As a 5-year-old, Washoe could appropriately use 132 signs and respond to several hundred more when they were directed toward her. Washoe's signs were comprehensible to observers who could not see what her referents were.

The Gardners report that Washoe signed the word "quiet" to herself when going to a forbidden part of the yard and signed herself "hurry" while running to her potty. After tasting a radish, she signed "cry hurt food." When her trainer refused some of her requests, she signed "dirty Roger." The sign for dirty was used for feces.

Somewhat similar experiences have been reported with other chimpanzees, with organutans, and with gorillas (Tuttle, 1986). As an interesting example, several trainers raised an infant gorilla named Koko in an ASL environment. By the time Koko was 5 1/2-years-old, she had mastered 246 ASL signs. Her trainers, Patterson and Linden (1981), stated that Koko sometimes combined signs into novel statements of from 2 to 11 signs, and that she used ASL to talk to herself, lie, argue, threaten, express her desires, and insult offenders.

These reports of primate language have not been without critics. For example, Terrace (1979) also trained a chimpanzee to learn 125 ASL signs, but concluded that many of them were prompted by the teacher's prior signs. His belief is that apes can label objects with arbitrary signs and remember the symbols, but it is not clear as to exactly what they know.

Despite these controversies, there is some evidence for emotional communication in apes. Premack (1976) suggests that one kind of evidence for emotional communication is the existence of behavior considered to reflect intentionality. He cites anecdotes to show that a female chimp was capable of devious behavior (a female desirous of touching another's infant looked away from the infant to distract the mother and then touched the baby) and that another showed cooperative behavior (she spontaneously invented the behavior of offering food pellets in exchange for sips of coffee from the caretakers).

Researchers then set up a formal experiment to determine whether a chimp would intentionally give or withhold information about the presence of food under a container. In one part of the experiment, if a chimpanzee gave an uninformed trainer information about the location of the hidden food (by pointing, glancing, or grunting), it received the food. In the second part of the experiment, a "bad" trainer takes the food for himself when informed of the correct location. The problem is: Will the chimp withhold information (or "lie") in the second situation?

Three of the four animals tested did not show any evidence of deception. The fourth chimpanzee pointed to the correct food container for the "good" trainer. After a few trials with the "bad" trainer, she stopped pointing and began throwing objects at him. Finally, when this had no effect on his behavior, she simply ignored him.

In order for one to infer an emotion in this chimpanzee, several conditions must exist. For one thing, something is known about the average or typical behavior of the animal. Second, something is known about the nature of the situation, which in this case deprives the animal of food objects that the animal is willing to work for. Third, the animal engages in goal-directed behavior of a particular kind that has a probable outcome (she throws objects at the trainer and can thereby injure him).

In an abstract sense, these elements are needed for inferences about emotions: baseline behavior; a situation that affects an important motive; and goal-directed behavior of a specific type. This last point is important because we implicitly accept the idea that only certain classes of goal-directed behaviors are emotional. If the chimpanzee had simply turned around and gone to sleep, we would not have interpreted it as emotional behavior.

Menzel's (1971) study of primate communication illustrates these ideas. He kept a group of chimpanzees in a house near a large field. One at a time, he would show an animal a hidden pile of food and then return the animal to the group. Generally, the guiding ape would lead its companions to the food. If it was a dominant animal, it would walk toward the hidden food, and most of the others would follow. If it was a subordinate animal, it would tug at the other apes' hands and fur. If they paid no attention to the guide, he might throw himself onto the floor and show what looked like a temper tantrum.

In another experiment Menzel carried out, he hid a frightening object such as a rubber snake and showed its location to one chimpanzee. In this situation, the other apes also followed the guide, but with erected fur and a more tentative approach. They proceeded to unearth the reptile with sticks. It appears that the other animals were able to interpret the bodily cues and sounds of the guide and to exhibit appropriate emotional behavior, (Figure 9.1).

▌The Problems of Self-Awareness of Emotional States

Let us assume that the preceding arguments are sufficient to justify the idea that emotions occur in lower animals as well as in humans, despite the lack of a verbal repertoire in animals. This premise now suggests the question: "What about self-awareness in animals? Do animals know that they have emotions?"

Figure 9.1	Communication Among Chimpanzees

A young chimpanzee cautiously uncovers a hidden rubber snake that had previously been shown to her companion at the far right, who has led the other chimpanzees to this site and conveyed to them that a frightening object is found here.

Source: E. W. Menzel, 1971.

First of all, we need to make a distinction between having an experience and being aware of that experience, just as we may distinguish between behaving and being aware of the behavior. Human beings show many behaviors that they are usually not aware of, such as frowning, breathing, swallowing, and personal mannerisms such as scratching their heads. They may also show various automatic reactions, such as eye blinks, knee jerks, or pupillary contractions, of which they also are unaware.

But what about emotions? Do animals know they are having an emotion when they show emotional behavior? Griffin (1976), a zoologist, takes up the issue of animal awareness. His argument is that research on social communication in bees, orientation and navigation in animals, and language acquisition in chimpanzees suggests the possibility that "conversations" take place between members of a given species and that animals have mental experiences and communicate with conscious intent.

Unfortunately there is little existing evidence, other than anecdotal, for intentionality in animals, and there is even less evidence for their self-consciousness. One ingenious set of investigations, however, does provide some information about the issue. Gallup (1977) presented chimpanzees with a full-length mirror so that they could see their own reflection, under the assumption that self-awareness is based upon self-recognition. Within a few days the behavior changed from the kind that would normally be directed toward another animal to the kind that was clearly self-directed (e.g., grooming parts of the body that could not be seen, picking food from their teeth, or making faces at the mirror). When researchers placed red paint on the faces of the chimpanzees, they showed greatly increased attention to the area. This behavior was not true for control animals who had had no previous exposure to the mirror.

Investigators have replicated this phenomenon of self-recognition (and, by implication, self-awareness) in orangutans as well as chimpanzees, but every attempt to replicate the phenomenon in lower primates—spider monkeys, capuchins, mandrill and hamadryas baboons, and gibbons—has failed. These results, while apparently demonstrating self-awareness in some of the apes, seriously questions Griffin's thesis that self-awareness may be found at all evolutionary levels.

The possibility that self-consciousness of emotional states may not exist at phylogenetic levels below the great apes does not imply that emotions cannot exist at these phylogenetic levels. As we have already seen in earlier discussions in this chapter, the evidence used to infer emotional states in animals involves such things as knowledge of an organism's typical behavior and the presence of certain classes of goal-directed behavior. Given these kinds of cues, we can make inferences about emotional states without considering the issue of self-awareness as such. In other words, the question of self-awareness in animals is an interesting one, but it is essentially irrelevant to the broader one of how we recognize emotions in animals.

Summary ∎

This chapter examines the evolutionary perspective on the nature of emotions. Such a perspective implies that emotions are complex adaptive patterns of reaction that have effects on the individuals or conditions that elicited the reaction in the first place. The function of these reactions is to increase the chances of survival of the interacting organisms.

In order to understand this idea more fully, a brief overview of evolutionary theory was presented. One key idea is that all organisms have certain common survival problems to deal with: for example, finding prey and avoiding predators, mating, and rejecting toxic substances. The evolutionary perspective suggests that these basic issues require certain types of adaptive reactions that are common to almost all organisms. One assumes such adaptive patterns to be the prototypes of emotions as seen in human beings. They are complex states involving adaptive changes in behavior, physiology, and subjective states.

If one accepts these premises, then the problem arises of how to make meaningful inferences about subjective states in animals. This problem is no different in essence from the issue of how to make inferences about subjective states in humans. Previous chapters have revealed how variable and invalid verbal reports of subjective states can be. Therefore, investigators need to develop more general methods for assessing the complex, adaptive processes called emotions in both animals and humans.

The chapter reviews a number of suggested types of evidence. These include a knowledge of an animal's typical behavior; observation of the pattern of reaction to stimuli; responses of conspecifics to the behavior; and observations of levels of arousal. Other types of evidence include forced-choice testing procedures and the use of a type of EEG recording called evoked-cortical potentials. Limited evidence exists on the acquisition of nonverbal sign language by chimpanzees and gorillas that hints at the possibility that such animals may express some information about subjective emotional states. Finally, studies of self-awareness have revealed evidence of self-awareness in chimpanzees and orangutans, but not in lower monkey groups. One may interpret such evidence to mean that the subjective aspect of emotions is a relatively late evolutionary development, and therefore only one indicator among many of an emotional state.

Emotional Communication in Animals

*We respond to gestures with an extreme
alertness and, one might almost say, in
accordance with an elaborate and
secret code that is written nowhere,
known by none, and understood by all.*
—Edward Sapir

▌Goals of This Chapter

The earlier chapter, "Facial Expression and Emotion," focused primarily on humans. However, it is obvious that some animals also show facial expressions and that all animals can vary their behavior, posture, displays (e.g., erection of hair or fur), odors, and sounds under various conditions. The previous chapter, "Emotions and Evolution," has tried to indicate that one can interpret different types of complex adaptive behavior patterns as aspects of emotions. Also, such emotional patterns convey information from one individual to another. The present chapter examines the issue of emotions as communications in more detail.

It begins by describing the many types of behavioral displays animals show and the type of emotional systems believed to be reflected by each. Further examples include sound displays of monkeys, chimpanzees, and gorillas, and what emotions ethologists believe they express. To illustrate the methods used to arrive at the communication functions of emotional displays, examples are given of the behavior of gulls, the songs of birds, the use of scent by tigers, aggressive behavior in elephants, and sound patterns in monkeys.

241

Of great interest is the fact that display behaviors in animals often express simultaneously two or more emotions. Several examples include the interaction of aggressive and submissive impulses in birds, threat and fear interactions in cats and dogs, and approach-avoidance conflicts in gulls.

Observers often make the point that animals in natural settings show displays that seem to exaggerate their size or strength, in terms of facial hair or manes as threat displays. Finally, there is discussion of possible evolutionary bases for some of the communications that have been described.

Important Questions Addressed In This Chapter

- How many types of emotional displays do animals show?
- Through what modalities are these displays expressed?
- How do ethologists determine the nature of the emotional communications various displays express?
- What are some functions of courtship displays?
- How do ethologists recognize that mixed-emotional impulses are often seen in animals?
- What is meant by the idea that displays can act as deceptions?
- What are some evolutionary origins of display behaviors?

■   ■   ■   ■   ■   ■   ■   ■

▐ Display Behavior in Animals as Communications

All animals produce display signals of various sorts. Such signals include postural changes, color changes, odor secretions, sounds, light production, electrical fields, and facial expressions. These displays generally communicate information from one animal to another, information that can be used as a guide for action.

According to ethologists, one may label the various displays in terms of the emotional or motivational state that is most clearly evident. From this point of view, the following list describes the specific types of interactions associated with each display.

1. Greeting or recognition displays
2. Courtship displays
3. Mating displays
4. Dominance displays
5. Submissive displays
6. Warning displays
7. Alarm displays
8. Defense displays
9. Challenge displays
10. Distress displays
11. Defeat displays
12. Victory displays
13. Feeding displays
14. Food-begging displays

From the list, it is evident that displays function to communicate information from one animal to another. This observation may be illustrated in many ways.

Rowell's (1962) study of sounds that rhesus monkeys make indicates that at least eight separate sounds can be distinguished and related to various types of emotional interactions:

A dominant animal makes a *roar* when threatening one of lower rank. A less confident animal makes *pant-threats* toward another, but it appears to try to gain the support of the rest of the group in the threatened attack. An animal that is slightly alarmed produces a *growl* sound, while a *shrill bark* is the typical alarm call of rhesus monkeys to imminent danger. A *screech* occurs when a lower ranking animal threatens a higher ranking one, and a monkey makes a *scream* while being bitten. A monkey who has been defeated in a fight often makes *squeaks*.

These are not the only kinds of sounds that rhesus monkeys make. According to Prince (1975), they show different varieties of an alarm call for different kinds of predators. In addition, lip smacking appears to act as a kind of appeasement signal in that it often precedes grooming and also acts to calm nervous infants.

Chimpanzees are acknowledged to be among the noisiest of apes. On the basis of an electronic analysis of chimpanzees' sounds, Marler and Tenaza (1977) concluded that they could identify about 13 fairly distinct sounds under natural field conditions, although they also found some degree of gradation.

Pant-hoots are the most frequent sound, and males most often utter them. These sounds occur spontaneously while the chimpanzees feed, meet with other chimpanzees, eat mammalian prey, and when a group divides into smaller foraging parties. Chimpanzees seem to listen to distant pant-hoots and then answer them (Tuttle, 1986).

Young chimpanzees often throw noisy tantrums when their mothers wean them. Observers have seen adults, particularly deposed dominant males, exhibit tantrums. During grooming, both sexes show quiet panting. Youngsters who have been tickled produce sounds suggestive of human laughter.

The sound called a *pant-grunt* has been used to assess the relative status of individuals, since subordinate chimpanzees pant-grunt as they move closer to dominant animals. Both males and females emit *wraaa* calls in response to human intruders and predators. In a group of chimpanzees that Jane Goodall studied on the Gombe preserve in Tanzania, she frequently heard wraaa calls following the death of an adult male who fell from a tree.

Fossey (1972) carried out studies of sound patterns in gorillas. She described 16 vocalizations and many situations associated with them. The older dominant males, generally referred to as silverbacks, sometimes utter low growls when an animal approaches, with the result that the latter usually retreats. Mildly alarmed adults emit staccato barks, most frequently when a human observer moves suddenly into view. When an adult is startled by close contact with a dangerous animal such as a buffalo, he may emit a loud alarm bark that has been described as a wraa sound, pitched somewhere between a roar and a scream. Following wraas, groups usually move away from the source of the disturbance. A sound that tended to induce group members to cluster together was the *hoot-bark*. When gorillas heard this sound, many would climb a tree and look around. The ethologist Marler (1976) believes that there are marked similarities in the sound patterns and eliciting circumstances in gorillas and chimpanzees.

▌ How Ethologists Identify the Communication Functions of Emotional Displays

Ethologists make most observations of display behaviors of animals under more-or-less natural settings. The conditions cannot generally be manipulated, nor is it possible to know in advance whether a predator is about to appear, whether an infant is about to be weaned or whether two adults are about to engage in a contest or battle. Therefore, investigators require considerable patience and long hours of observation. Despite the necessity of relying on somewhat unpredictable events, they have obtained much insight into patterns of animal behaviors, the conditions that tend to trigger such behaviors, and the usual consequences of the behaviors. Some examples will be given of how researchers conduct these kinds of studies in order to reveal connections between emotional states and overt behavior.

The Sounds of Attack in Gulls

Attack behavior in birds acts to chase away predators or intruders into nesting areas. Attacks are usually preceded and accompanied by visual and/or vocal displays. In one species of bird called the little gull, found in the Netherlands, attack behavior directed toward intruders into nesting territory is typically associated with two distinct vocalizations, which have been transcribed as *eeyit* and *whet*. The problems that ethologists examine concern the distinctions between these calls in terms of their relations to attack motivation and impact on the intruder (Piersma and Veen, 1988).

Using sound spectragraph equipment in a natural setting, researchers found that these two sounds were always given by the gull performing the attack rather than by the bird being attacked. On most occasions, the nest intruder reacted to these calls with avoidance behavior. When a stuffed adult gull model was placed near the breeding bird's nest, the eeyit sound occurred mostly when the birds circled above the model and when they dived at the model. However, when the retreat of the nest intruder (movement away by the model) did not folow the eeyit call, the nesting bird always attacked the intruder. If the model was moved away, the nesting bird never attacked it. The investigators therefore concluded that the signal eeyit is a warning; that is, it is a consistent indicator of the sender's motivation to attack. The whet sound typically accompanied the moment of attack.

The Functions of Bird Songs

The recent literature on ethology is filled with studies on the survival implications of particular patterns of behavior as well as on the communication content of expressions. For example, researchers studied the function of song in a Florida population of Scott's seaside sparrows by temporarily muting male birds in the field. This procedure left the birds songless for about 2 weeks before recovery. During this time, the songless birds did not acquire mates, or lost previously acquired mates. Their territories either shrank or were lost, although they established new territories after voice recovery. The muted birds also experienced more close-range aggressive behavior than controls (McDonald, 1989). It thus appears that bird song in this species influences both reproductive behavior and aggressive interactions.

Many studies have identified the functions of bird songs. In a review of the literature, Bright (1984) described 16 bird calls of the chaffinch and the adaptive meaning of each call, shown in Table 10.1. In this table the phonetic sound is given, followed by a brief description of various aspects of the sound or some conditions under which it occurs. The last column lists the adaptive significance of each sound in terms of its survival function. It is evident that several different sounds may all be alarm calls (for example, "Tew," "Seee," and "Whit"), while several other sounds may all be courtship calls (for example, "Tzit," "Tchirp," and "Seep"). Sometimes, slight variations in the quality of the sound lead to different behaviors, which is one of the reasons for apparent inconsistencies in the interpretations.

Let us consider one last illustration of an attempt to identify the communication functions of bird sounds (Rothstein, Yokel, and Fleischer, 1988). Cowbirds in California produce three separate vocalizations: songs stationary birds (PS) give, usually perched on branches, wires, or the ground; a single syllable call (SS) the cowbird gives while flying; and a multisyllabic tone called a *flight whistle*, also given while the bird is flying. Investigators recorded these sounds in the field and later played them back under various conditions. They discovered that cowbirds used the perched song (PS) over short distances to express aggression between males, but males also used it in an effort to attract females.

The flight whistle and the single syllable call are long distance calls that usually increase the likelihood that a female cowbird will come to where

Table 10.1	The Call Vocabulary of the Chaffinch	
Call	**Remarks**	**Adaptive Significance**
Tsup or Tupe	A short penetrating call. Low pitch with single higher harmonic. Associated with flight or preparation for flight.	Flight call
Chink or Spink	Clear ringing call in two parts. Helps separated birds to meet again.	Social call
Cheenk	More shrill than social call. Used as escape call and during courtship by newly paired males.	Escape call
Zzzzzz or Zh-zh-zh	Low buzz uttered during attack and fighting in a few captive males.	Aggressive Call
Tew	Most frequent of three alarms. Common in young birds and more rarely adults of both sexes.	Alarm call
Seee	Extreme alarm in breeding male. Pure tone rising and falling and difficult for predator to locate precisely.	Alarm call
Huit or Whit	Commonly at rate of 30 per minute. Male chaffinches in spring. Moderate danger.	Alarm call
Tseee	Squeak given by birds hurt fighting.	Injury call
Kseep, Tsit, Tzit	Short and high-pitched in bursts of three simultaneous descending notes. Male gives it courting female at pair formation in early part of season.	Courtship call
Tchirp or Chirri	Coarse chirp. Replaces pair formation call during courtship later in season.	Courtship call
Seep	The only extra call of female during breeding season. Short and high-pitched but composed of only two notes.	Courtship call
Cheep	Soft note of nestlings.	Begging call

Call	Remarks	Adaptive Significance
Chirrup	Loud and penetrating call of fledglings.	Begging call
Huit/Seee, Huit/Chink	Occasional intermediates between alarm and social calls of mature birds.	Intermediates
Chrrp and variants or low-pitched rattles grouped together in various ways	Chirps and warbles of birds in first summer.	Sub-song
Tchip-tchip-tchip-Cherry-erry-erry-Tchip-Tcheweeoo	Trills and a terminal flourish lasting some two to three seconds. January or February to June, and September and October.	Song

Source: M. Bright, 1984.

the male is. Males give flight whistles usually immediately before copulation and they may influence the females' copulatory posture. Flight whistles and single syllable calls are also given when a potential predator approaches males, and may thus also serve as alarm calls. Because of the multiple functions of certain calls, it is evident that context and other sources of information must influence the type of behaviors observers actually see.

How Tigers Communicate by Scent

Thirty-three free-ranging tigers were studied over a four-year period in the Royal Chitwan National Park in Nepal. Each animal wore a radio collar and could also be identified visually. Since tigers live within fairly clear-cut boundaries within which they hunt and mate, a group of investigators was interested in identifying both the methods of marking boundaries and the functions of the boundaries (Smith, McDougal, and Miqualle, 1989).

In order to learn the answers to these questions, investigators recorded five types of marking behavior: spraying of urine on trees; scraping feces and urine and anal gland secretions on rocks and sand; flattening of vegetation; claw marks on trees; and rubbing sprayed trees with their cheeks. Urine spraying of trees was found to be the most frequent territory marker, and the scent was detectable by humans for as long as three weeks after spraying. Males generally marked their boundaries more frequently during the periods when females were in estrus. Consistent with this observation is the fact that most aggressive encounters between male tigers occurred when they were in the vicinity of a female in estrus. Although tigers marked along a network of trails used for travel through their territories, marking was generally more intense at potential contact points between adjoining territories. It thus appears that these various forms of marking behavior are communications between one tiger and another that both establish and maintain territorial boundaries as well as express claims on females in reproductive status.

Communicating Aggressive Intent in Elephants

Male African elephants over the age of 25 years show periods of sexual activity and other periods of inactivity. During the sexually active period, there are shorter times during which the male is in a heightened state of aggression, a period called *musth*. During the periods of musth, males are more successful in obtaining matings.

In a study carried out in Amboseli National Park in Kenya, Poole (1980) made observations on a population of 670 elephants, all of whom were known individually. The aim of her research was to determine the extent to which elephants are able to estimate aggressive intent in each other.

Poole observed a series of aggressive (agonistic) encounters between pairs of male elephants. Each encounter began with a threat (such as ear waving, chasing, or tusking) by the dominant animal and was concluded when the subordinate animal began to retreat. Poole found that generally, when neither of the elephants was in musth, the larger of the two animals was dominant. However, when one elephant of the interacting pair was in musth and the other was not, in most cases the animal in musth was dominant regardless of size. In the relatively few cases where two musth males challenged each other, serious fights resulted with several deaths and serious injuries. All fights ended with the dominant animal chasing the subordinate one.

What do these findings mean? The ability of small musth males to dominate larger nonmusth males indicates that the musth males are signaling their aggressive intent, and that the other animals somehow recognize their aggressive fighting abilities. Since the fighting ability of males in the herd changes frequently due to the presence or absence of musth, all elephants must be able to continually reassess their relative abilities in each contest or encounter. Thus, communication of aggressive intent and potential must occur during everyday encounters among elephants.

Alarm Calls in Vervet Monkeys

Ethologists have published many studies that have identified rather specific communication functions of most signals or displays. For example, Seyfarth, Cheney, and Marler (1980b) have shown that vervet monkey alarm calls function to designate different classes of external danger related to specific types of predators: Animals on the ground respond to leopard alarms by running into trees, to eagle alarms by looking up, and to snake alarms by looking down.

Table 10.2 describes the typical stimuli that tend to produce various types of alarm calls in vervet monkeys (Marler, 1977). Not only does the

Table 10.2	Vervet Monkey Alarm Calls			
Typical Stimulus	Typical Response of Troop Members	Tropical Call	Adult Males	Adult and Young Females
Minor mammal predator near	Become alert, look to predator	Uh!	yes	yes
Sudden involvement of minor predator	Look to predator, sometimes flee	Nyow!	yes	yes
Man or venomous snake —but the chutter is structurally different for man and snake	Approach snake and escort at safe distance	Chutter	yes (rare)	yes
Initial sighting of eagle	Flee from treetops and open areas into thickets	Rraup	no	yes
Initially and after sighting major predator (leopard, lion, eagle)	Attention and then flight to appropriate cover	Threat Alarm-Bark	yes	no
After initial sighting of major predator (leopard, eagle)	Flee from thickets and open areas to branches and canopy	Chirp	no	yes

Source: P. Marler, 1977.

appearance of various predators produce specific alarm signals, but also characteristic and different reactions by the members of the troop.

In a series of field trials, investigators played back recorded alarm calls to vervet monkeys of different ages. They found that infants were able to distinguish between general classes of predators (for example, between a terrestrial mammal and a flying bird), but that adults could distinguish among predators and other mammals, or eagles and other birds (Seyfarth, Cheney, & Marler, 1980a). These observations provide strong support for the idea that the ability to react appropriately to such calls is a genetically determined characteristic. Although experience may influence the degree of specificity, the initial appearance of such abilities does not appear to depend on learning.

Morton (1977) has explored the proposition that emotional calls or vocalizations in different species might have some evolutionary continuity. He examined the sounds of a large number of birds and mammals in a variety of settings and found that regardless of size, voice, or environment, each animal has a common vocal pattern: An animal interpreted as angry makes a low, harsh growl, and a fearful animal makes a high-pitched sound. Animals that are neither angry nor fearful, but active and involved, emit a grunt or barklike sound. Morton found various combinations of these sounds; for example, a screech contains components of both anger and fear.

Morton's (1977) theory is that these basic sound patterns are indicators of inner impulses in response to outer stimuli and that they serve to communicate messages that have implications for successful adaptation. Larger animals are generally more capable of making low-pitched, harsher, and louder sounds than smaller animals. The use of such low-pitched growls represents an evolutionary adaptation by which a small animal may imitate a larger animal. This is a pseudo-largeness principle analogous to the expansion of body size through feathers, fur, arching, or air pouches in order to provide a threatening appearance. Such displays often prevent actual combat.

Similarly, young animals inherently make higher pitched sounds than do older ones, generally because their vocal apparatus is not as large as that of an adult. An adult animal that intends to express submission or fear will whine or squeak out high-pitched sounds in mimicry of a younger, more vulnerable creature.

After investigating vocalizations of the Japanese monkey (*Macaca fuscata*), Green (1975) concluded that there were a large number of parallels between human vocalizations and the vocalizations of this monkey.

> Humans also employ cries, shrieks, screams, screeches, and a variety of other sounds. These sounds are not only acoustically homologous with those described here for the Japanese monkey, but they are also used in analogous situations by primates with similar inferred internal states. Roars are used by enraged people, cries by babies abandoned or otherwise distressed, screeches in tantrums of youngsters, and whines as they reach the comfort of a mother's embrace.

These various studies have been carried out in natural settings with the researcher's minimal interference of the spontaneous interactions of the animals. However, it is possible to demonstrate through laboratory studies how expressions can communicate information and can be used as a guide for action.

How Monkeys Can Read Faces

A study by Miller, Caul, and Mirsky (1967) illustrates this point. They trained three rhesus monkeys to press a key in order to avoid an electric shock each time a certain light went on. With this conditioned avoidance response well established, they introduced the following procedure. One monkey was arbitrarily selected as the *sender* and another was the *receiver*. The receiver monkey could see only the face of the sender monkey on closed-circuit television while the sender was exposed to the signal light that indicated an electric shock was coming. The receiver monkey could avoid getting a shock if he pressed a key within 6 seconds after the stimulus came on. In order to do this, the receiver monkey had to recognize a change in the facial expression of the sender monkey when the signal light appeared.

During the initial testing of individual monkeys, each one made a correct response (pressed the key within 6 seconds after the signal light came on) in approximately 95% of the trials. When the new procedure was introduced, the percentage of correct avoidance responses of the receiver monkey watching the sender was 77%, a figure based on all possible pairs, since each monkey had a turn being the sender as well as the receiver. This result clearly indicated that these rhesus monkeys were able to use the expressions on the faces of other monkeys as appropriate cues to influence their own behavior. This finding supports the view proposed by Darwin that facial expressions are communication signals between social animals.

Further important findings resulted from this experiment. The investigators tested three additional monkeys who had been separated from their mothers at birth and maintained in totally isolated closed cages for the first year of their lives. When tested by themselves, these animals learned to avoid the shock by pressing on the key just as well as did the normal monkeys. However, when they were placed in receiver roles, their behavior was markedly inferior to that of the normal monkeys.

In other words, when an *isolate* monkey was the sender of facial cues and a normal monkey was the receiver, the percentage of correct avoidance responses was 62%, or slightly less than with two normal monkeys. This finding indicated that the isolate monkey was sending more-or-less familiar facial expression cues to the normal receiver monkey. However, when either an isolate monkey or a normal monkey was the sender and an isolate monkey was the receiver, the percentage of avoidance responses was around only 8%. These results imply that monkeys who were socially isolated during the first year of their life tend to show fairly normal facial expressions, but they are greatly deficient in recognizing the facial expressions of other monkeys. This variance emphasizes that the expression of emotions and the recognition of emotions are two different processes and are affected by different variables. Only a small beginning has been made thus far in identifying the factors that influence both the expression and recognition of emotions.

Breeding and Courtship Displays

Researchers have extensively discussed the various types of display signals in relation to the process of breeding or mating. Bastock (1967), for example, has pointed out that displays serve multiple functions in connection with courtship.

1.   Since many animals breed only during a limited time of the year, courtship displays bring animals together at the appropriate times. Such displays include bird songs, scent dissemination, and light signals (as by fireflies).

2.   Many animals breed only in special locations, and give displays only in such locations. These signals are called luring, nest-site, or spawning displays. Such location displays function to assure a nearby food supply for the young.

3.   Since successful mating depends on a synchrony of certain physiological processes in males and females, courtship displays sometimes initiate processes concerned with the release of ova and sperm. Courtship displays also create a mating mood designed to overcome aggressive or fearful barriers between the male and female.

4.   Another function of displays is to prevent attempts at cross-mating. In many animals, courtship consists largely of identity checks between male and female; fertilization occurs only after females have identified males of their own species.

5.   Courtship displays often include elements of threat. Threat signals function to keep other males at a distance, and at the same time they appear to attract ripe females.

6.   Some courtship displays help position the females for easier coitus or lure them to a more secluded area.

It is worth adding that courtship displays are found at almost all phylogenetic levels. They have been identified in fishes, birds, arthropods (e.g., fruit fly, spider, crab), mammals, and all primates. Odors are also extensively used as forms of signals. In some animals, the organs of smell are so sensitive that both species and individual identification are possible. Odors used to attract the opposite sex are called pheromones, and most species, including insects, use them widely. They have been found to produce alarm reactions, sexual attraction, grooming, exchanging of food, and identification of members of one's own family, caste, or species.

▌Conflicts Among Emotional Displays

Variations in body postures are also widely used as signals. Figure 10.1 shows four distinctive postures in the zebra finch *(Peophila guttata)*. Posture (a) is an *aggressive* posture associated both with threat and with pecking behavior. Posture (b) shows a fearful vertical posture; the more vertical the posture, the greater the probability of flight. Posture (c) is seen both in a bird at rest and in a frightened bird that cannot escape. Posture (d) is the courtship posture seen just prior to mounting (Bastock, 1967; Morris, 1954). An important point that we will return to later is that intermediate postures are possible. Such intermediate postures reflect the existence of conflicts between impulses—for example, conflict between the impulse to attack and to flee or conflict between the impulse to mount and withdraw.

This idea of postures reflecting conflicts is more clearly seen in Figure 10.2. Observations of cats in a variety of situations led Leyhausen (1956), cited in Hinde (1966), to conclude that postural changes expressed the interaction of *both* fear and aggression. When fear was low, cats expressed aggressiveness in one way; however, when fear was high, they expressed aggressiveness by the highly arched back and uplifted tail.

Researchers have reported this same idea in regard to dogs (Lorenz, 1952). Figure 10.3 shows expressions that reflect variations in the intensity of threat a dog shows. A graded series of changes exist that reflect increasing likelihood of submissive behavior. These tendencies may simultaneously exist to varying degrees, so that any given facial expression is a transitory resultant of the interaction or conflict of two opposing tendencies.

In black-headed gulls, the conflict between courting and fighting involves the interaction of impulses to attack and impulses to withdraw. In the *oblique* and *aggressive upright* displays shown in Figure 10.4, impulses to attack predominate, but the intensity of motivation is higher with the oblique display. In the *forward* and *anxiety upright* displays, the predominant impulse favors withdrawal. When the impulse to attack is balanced by an equally strong impulse to withdraw, the gull shows the *choking* display. These observations further support the idea that each expression or display that an animal shows is most likely a result of the interaction of two or more conflicting impulses.

Displays as Deceptions

Actual fights between animals tend to be relatively rare. Fights are too dangerous for both parties; even the victor may suffer injury and thus have a lessened chance of survival. Therefore, the most successful way for male animals to achieve dominant status and/or access to females is through intimidations and threats.

Figure 10.1 Distinctive Postures in
the Zebra Finch

(a) The "aggressive" horizontal posture associated with threat and with pecking behavior. (b) The "frightened" sleeked vertical posture. (c) The "submissive" fluffed posture. (d) The courtship posture.

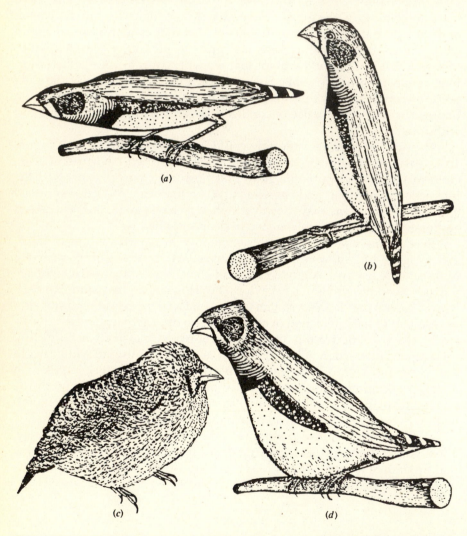

Source: D. J. Morris, 1954.

Figure 10.2	"Aggressive" (Threat) and "Fear" Expressions in the Cat

"Aggressive" postures increase in degree from left to right and "fear" postures increase in degree from the top down. Almost any observed expression is a combination of both aggression and fear in varying degrees.

Source: P. Leyhausen, 1956.

Figure 10.3	"Aggressive" and "Fear" Expressions in the Dog

"Aggressive" expressions increase from left to right and "fear" expressions, indicating readiness to flee, increase from the top down. Different facial expressions in the dog result from the combination of different intensities of fighting and flight intentions.

Source: K. Lorenz, 1952.

Figure 10.4	Approach-Avoidance Conflict

The displays of the black-headed gull used in courtship and fighting are thought to involve degrees of attack and withdrawal. In the "oblique" and the "aggressive upright" displays, aggression predominates. In the "forward" and "anxiety upright" displays, the balance favors withdrawal. The "choking" display seems to represent a balance of attack and withdrawal elements, with very strong motivation.

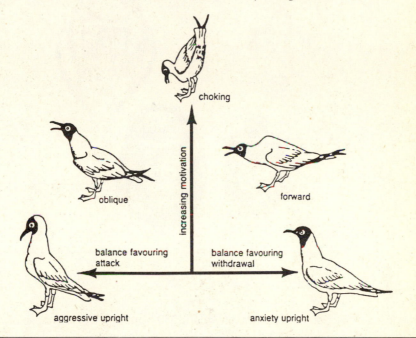

Source: J. A. Gray, 1988.

Observations of animals in natural settings indicate that certain features of an animal tend to exaggerate an animal's capabilities or camouflage an animal's weaknesses. For example, male animals with the largest antlers, fangs, or tusks tend to be victors in encounters with the males of the same species. To exaggerate apparent size, many animals have evolved face ruffs or beards (or manes), illustrated in Figure 10.5.

It is interesting that beards or ruffs appear only on adult males. This characteristic is apparently because the most serious confrontations over rank occur among sexually mature males, and the beards represent an aspect of a more general threat display.

Social Action Sequential Behavior Analysis in Chimpanzees

In 1973, van Hooff reported the results of an intensive investigation of behavior patterns in 25 chimpanzees, in an effort to identify the emotional

Figure 10.5	The Evolution of Menace

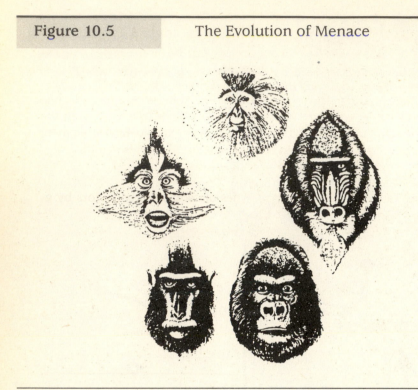

Source: R. D. Guthrie, 1973.

meaning of various behaviors. He spent 200 hours observing these animals and recording sequences of social behavioral elements, each of which was delimited by nonactivity or nonsocial activity of at least 10 seconds, or by a change of social partner. Based upon these observations he listed more than 60 behavior elements, including clinging, grooming, silent pout, crouch-presenting, gnaw, mount, hit, avoid, and vertical head nod. Among these elements is the following list of vocalizations.

1. Bared-teeth scream
2. Pant scream
3. Bared-teeth yelp
4. Pout whimper
5. Pout moan
6. Shrill bark
7. Bared-teeth bark
8. Rising hoot
9. Waow barks
10. Grunt or grunt bark
11. Rapid oh-oh series
12. Pant

Each of these vocalizations usually occurs in a special context and an identifiable facial expression and/or a certain posture frequently accompanies it. For example, panting often accompanies mouth-to-mouth contact and embracing. It is important to emphasize that although investigators have suggested discrete labels for different vocalizations, Marler (1965,

1969) has shown that such labels are only convenient abstractions, since chimpanzee vocal signals are continuously graded over various intervals. Among the behavioral elements are several different facial expressions, including relaxed open-mouth display, silent bared-teeth display, silent pout-face, lip-smacking face, and horizontal head shake.

In order to determine the functional meaning of these various displays and behavioral elements, van Hooff determined the number of times each behavior element preceded or followed every other behavior element. For example, grooming succeeded certain behavior elements significantly more often than it preceded them. The data suggest that behavior elements tend to occur in certain sequences.

Van Hoof analyzed the frequencies of sequential behaviors by grouping them into categories such that any one behavior is correlated more strongly with the behaviors of its own category than with behaviors in any other category. The results of this analysis suggested 5 basic behavioral categories. Table 10.3 lists the categories along with the behavior elements

---

Table 10.3	Cluster Analysis of Chimpanzee Behaviors

Group I: The Affinitive System

Examples: Touch, cling, hold out hand, smooth approach, silent pout, groom, embrace, pant, mount

Group II: The Play System

Examples: Relaxed open mouth, grasp, poke, gnaw wrestle, gnaw, pull limb, gymnastics, hand wrestle

Group III: The Aggressive System

Examples: Trample, tug, brusque rush, bite, grunt-bark, sway-walk, hit, stamp, shrill bark

Group IV: The Submissive System

Examples: Flight, crouch, avoid, bared-teeth scream, bared-teeth yelps, parry, shrink-flinch, hesitant approach

Group V: The Excitement System

Examples: Squat-bobbing, rapid *ohoh*, rising hoot, upsway

Source: J. A. R. A. M. van Hooff, 1973.

Figure 10.6   Facial and Vocal Displays
in the Chimpanzee

The range of facial and vocal displays in the chimpanzee have different probabilities of being associated with the "affinitive" and "submissive" behavioral systems.

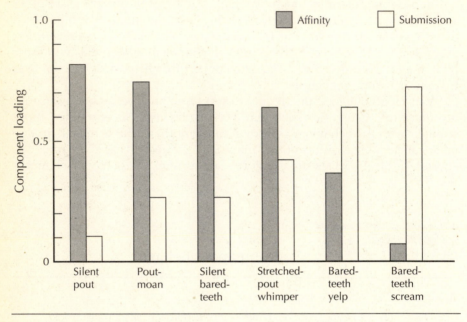

Source: J. A. R. A. M. van Hooff, 1973.

---

that most clearly define them. It is evident that the basic systems are defined in terms of different kinds of behavioral elements. They include facial displays, vocalizations, postures, and movements. These observations support the conclusion that facial expressions are one kind of display subsystem that participates with a variety of other displays to communicate information from one social animal to another.

Van Hooff makes one other important point. Facial expressions are represented in the different behavioral systems with different probabilities of occurrence. Figure 10.6 shows this concept graphically, for example, in that a silent pout has a high probability of being part of the affinity system, and a low probability of being part of the submission system. In contrast, the bared-teeth scream has a high probability of being part of the submission system and a low probability of being part of the affinity system. Other expressions have varying probabilities of being found in these two systems. These observations further imply that facial expressions are not unique and clearly discrete from one another. Rather, they overlap and show transitional states that continue to reflect the conflicted underlying motivational states of the animal. Facial expressions show gradations, as do vocalizations, and they reflect the emotional systems that are interacting at any given time.

▌Origins of Display Behaviors

Several biologists have speculated that emotions originate in primitive reflexes that have evolved to provide protection from extremes of heat and cold (Stanley-Jones, 1966). In support of this argument, Stanley-Jones points out that adrenaline secretion acts to protect the individual from overheating and that hypothalamic mechanisms control temperature regulation just as they control many emotional expressions and outputs. This whole thermoregulatory mechanism is available to the infant within a few hours after birth.

From this point of view, Stanley-Jones (1966) argues that emotions are not disruptive, maladaptive states, but rather act to stabilize the internal state of the organism. Emotions are thus autonomic and behavioral patterns that act to maintain a stable body temperature rather than to disrupt it. Zajonc, Murphy, & Inglehart (1989) have suggested a related idea on the role of heat and cold in eliciting emotions.

Andrew (1974) has elaborated on the view that Stanley-Jones (1970) presented. He points out that emergency reactions are associated with exertion in general, rather than being restricted to attack or fleeing. Many of these reactions precede behavioral exertion and therefore may become important in communicating an organism's intentions. To that extent, they become part of the complex chain of events called an emotion. Examples of reflex, anticipatory reactions are dilation of the blood vessels in skeletal muscles to increase their blood supply, blood pressure increases due to cardiac acceleration, and constriction of the blood vessels in the skin and intestines. This pattern of changes in blood flow occurs as a first response to a new stimulus in a previously quiet organism. The function of this pattern is to prepare for a sustained or violent muscle action.

Andrew suggests that all such reflexes maintain a balance between total inhibition, or immobility, and extreme motor action. These reflexes may be thermoregulatory (sweating, panting, flushing), respiratory (rapid breathing or dilation of nostrils), and postural (crouching, huddling, or arching). He concludes that the generalized mammalian response to noxious stimulation is characterized by ear withdrawal and flattening, mouth corner withdrawal and lip retraction, and eye closure. Other behaviors often found as part of the protective response pattern are tongue protrusion and lateral shaking of head and body. Observers often see these kinds of protective responses as part of greeting displays that "are most predictably evoked in primates by sudden mutual perception, particularly if the eyes meet . . . Vocalizations reflect such states as that the organism is uncomfortable, or lost, or wants something, or is likely to flee, or that it has perceived a novel stimulus" (Andrew, 1974). We find these patterns in young organisms as well as mature ones.

Summary ■

The various cited examples concerning emotional display behaviors, calls and signals that animals show suggest some important conclusions. First, displays generally are related to important events in the life of each animal: events such as threats, attacks, alarms, courtship, mating, social contact, isolation or separation, greetings, appeasement, dominance, submission and play. Of particular importance is the relation of the display to sex and social rank. Second, it is evident that these displays communicate information from one animal to another, and, even if the amount of information is limited, the displays have some impact on the animals' survival prospects. Third, most displays appear to be species characteristics present even in young animals that lack much opportunity for learning. Most animals immediately recognize these species-typical displays and react appropriately, suggesting that there is a genetic basis for many of the signals. Fourth, the various communication signals often occur in combination with one another. Animals can express impulses to attack at the same time they express impulses to withdraw; they can express impulses to mate at the same time as impulses to dominate. These conflicting impulses produce expressions that reflect the conflicts. Fifth, display behaviors express impulses of various kinds. However, one must use indirect evidence to decipher the meaning of the observed expressions. It is not always easy to interpret the survival implications of a particular display or to know exactly what impulses are involved.

Last and most important in the present context, these illustrations and our conclusions reveal some important things about emotions. Display behaviors tell us something about emotions but they are not emotions. Emotions are the inferences we make about impulses to actions, internal states, and triggering stimuli. Emotions are about the important events in an animal's life related to issues of survival. They generally occur in special circumstances, are fairly transient, involve brief but intense arousal, and act to help the animal return to a more *normal* unaroused state; that is, the state that existed before the triggering stimulus occurred. From this point of view, the whole complex pattern of inner and outer activity acts to deal with emergencies and tries to restore the homeostatic balance within an organism. *Emotions may thus be conceptualized as homeostatic devices (patterns of inner and outer action) that are designed to maintain a relatively steady ("normal") state in the face of environmental emergencies. Emotions represent transitory adjustment reactions that function to return the organism to a stable, effective relationship with its immediate environment when that relationship is disrupted.*

Chapter

11

Emotions and
the Brain

*All plants and the most primitve animals get
along well enough without nervous systems,
for the distinctive nervous functions, that is,
irritability, conductivity, and integration, are
essential properties of all protoplasm.*
—C. Judson Herrick

Goals of This Chapter

Most investigators concerned with the study of emotion agree that emotion is a concept that includes a number of aspects: a cognitive appraisal of situations; a set of physiological changes of great diversity; a series of overt expressions or display behaviors; a motivational component reflecting an intention or readiness to act; and a subjective feeling state. Although it is recognized that changes occurring in an individual are often widespread, research on physiological aspects of emotion are often limited to a few autonomic changes such as increases in heart rate, blood pressure, or skin conductance.

However, over the years, investigators have developed an extensive literature that is concerned with the nervous system and the role that it plays in emotion. In order to understand this literature, one needs some familiarity with the structure and function of the nervous system in general, and with the biochemical systems that act as neurotransmitters. In addition, since much of this research is carried out on lower organisms, we need a sense of the extent to which the nervous systems of lower and higher animals are related. And, last but not least, we need to approach this research literature with a critical mind, particularly in view of the problem of how we are to define the concept of emotion in a lower animal. Although most people accept the idea that chimpanzees, cats, and dogs probably have emotions, are they ready to apply the idea to other experimental animals on which such research has been done, creatures such as birds, reptiles, fish, and insects.?

This chapter will deal with each of these issues. It will begin with a description of the simplest organisms in existence and then trace the development of the nervous system as we ascend the evolutionary scale. A description will follow of basic brain structures and systems believed to be involved in emotions. The following chapter will present an account of the major theories of how the brain is involved in emotions.

Important Questions Addressed In This Chapter

- What are the major types of adaptive behaviors present in all organisms?
- In what form does the nervous system appear in primitive animals?
- What are the five major subdivisions of the mammalian brain?
- Why is the amygdala called the sensory gateway to the emotions?
- What is the Kluver-Bucy syndrome?
- What are the major structures of the limbic system?
- What is meant by the *triune brain?*
- What do studies of epilepsy reveal about emotions?

In an earlier chapter, we looked at some of the similarities in expressions of emotions in humans and lower animals. We saw how animals express alarm, aggression, courtship, threats, affiliation, and play. We saw how the biologist John Paul Scott (1980) has recognized a few major classes of adaptive behavior found in almost all species. He calls these adaptations ingestive behavior (eating), shelter-seeking behavior, agonistic (fight or flight) behavior, sexual behavior, care-soliciting behavior (from a young animal towards its mother), care-giving behavior (from adults toward young organisms), eliminative behavior (getting rid of waste products or inner toxins), allelomimetic (imitative) behavior, and exploratory (including play) behavior. His point is that most organisms engage in these types of activities even though they do them in different ways. A cat cares for its kittens in a different way than a bird cares for its young, but the act of caring is the same in both. Similarly, although a shark's attack is different from an attack of a pit bull, both can be recognized as agonistic behavior.

To summarize: In order to survive and maintain their populations, all organisms must find food, avoid injury, and reproduce their kind. This cycle is as true of lower animals as it is of higher ones. The nature of the environment creates certain functional requirements for all organisms if they are to survive. Any organism must take in nourishment and eliminate waste products. It must distinguish between prey and predator and between a potential mate and a potential enemy. It must explore its environment and orient its sense organs appropriately as it takes in information about the beneficial and harmful aspects of its immediate world. And organisms that are relatively helpless at birth and for a while thereafter must have ways of indicating the need for care and nurturance. Although the specific behaviors by which organisms carry out these functions vary widely throughout the animal kingdom, the basic prototype functions remain invariant (Plutchik, 1980). But the logic of these parallels should not stop at monkeys, cats, or ants. Several recent papers by molecular biologists have implied that we should expand our view of adaptive processes to encompass even single-celled organisms.

■　■　■　■　■　■　■　■

■ Animals Without Nervous Systems: Is the Concept of Emotion Relevant?

For their first three billion years on earth, living creatures were no larger than a single cell—the prokaryotes (protozoa or small bacteria), which lived without the use of oxygen. About a billion years ago, larger bacteria called eukaryotes evolved. They still exist today and prey on the prokaryotes as well as each other. "These single-celled eukaryotes can display remarkable complexity of function: some have features as specialized and diverse as sensory bristles, mouth parts, muscle-like contractile bundles or stinging darts" (Kabnick and Peattie, 1991).

A biologist, Nicola Ricci (1990), has recently pointed out that every protozoa is a functional unit, "a complete self-sufficient organism, and is exposed to risks in its daily life like any other individual being." Single-celled organisms carry out a whole series of vitally important activities, including feeding, reproduction, sexually related behavior, avoidance of danger, search for safety, colonization of new habitats, and predatory behavior. Dr. Ricci concludes: "Protozoon behavior . . . is the complex and variable adaptive response of protozoa to the problem of reconciling their necessities and activities with varied and constantly changing external conditions, by means of which response the organism equilibrates its relationship with the environment."

A molecular biologist, Dr. Ursula Goodenough (1991), has been studying the immune system for many years. She points out that a common metaphor used to describe infectious disease is *warfare;* bacteria or viruses launch an attack and the immune system puts up a defense. Many pathogens do not take on the human body directly, but use deceptive techniques to get at their targets and survive. For example, some bacteria *camouflage* themselves so that the immune system does not recognize them as foreign (this is true for the HIV virus, which is one of the reasons it is so difficult to deal with). Another strategy of pathogens is *mimicry*, by which it resembles a known substance and thus gets past the defenses (as in rabies). Goodenough adds, "The key discrimination made by the detection apparatus of the immune system is between self and nonself. The body continually asks, in effect, 'Does this molecule belong to me, or is it part of an invading organism?' If a molecule is recognized as self, it is spared; if it is perceived as nonself, destructive mechanisms are set in motion to kill the cell with which it is associated" (1991).

These ideas suggest that organisms without nervous systems can still engage in relatively complex behaviors that are *functionally* similar to the complex behaviors we see in animals with nervous systems. And if we think of aggression and defense as emotions, then even very simple organisms can be said to show aggression and defense. If emotions are thought of as applying to all living things, then we can consider them to be functional adaptations for dealing with life problems and emergencies. This view ignores the issue of subjective reports or feelings that are available only from normal human adults. The extent to which such feelings are available to lower organisms is a question that may never have a satisfactory answer. This functional way of thinking about emotions, however, allows us to examine the possible relations between brain mechanisms at any phylogenetic level and emotions (broadly defined in functional terms).

Following the same line of thinking, the neurophysiologist Paul MacLean (1986) has pointed out that any organism of a complex, highly evolved type mimics what have been fundamental processes of individual cells over evolutionary times. These processes refer to internal signals of need for food to maintain metabolism, the presence of catabolites (waste products of metabolism) that need to be expelled, and the presence of stimuli outside their organism that needs to be avoided or approached.

Finally on this issue, we should consider the ideas of John Bonner, a biologist writing about some fundamental ideas in biology (1962). He points out that the cells of all animals and plants (with the exception of bacteria) from the smallest amoeba to the largest whale are constructed roughly the same way. They all have a nucleus containing the chromosomes that hold the genes, which are the basis of inheritance. This nucleus is surrounded by cytoplasm containing various particles. There are at least three functions: the cell takes in fuel (food) and converts the energy of the fuel to cell movement; the cell reproduces, or duplicates parts of itself; and the cell is responsive to environmental stimuli including other cells. This third function is also called the property of irritability, which is a property of all cells even without an elaborated nervous system.

Bacteria are smaller than cells and have a simpler internal structure. Despite this, bacteria have evolved many different ways to obtain energy. Besides using carbohydrates, fats, and proteins, like most cells, some species of bacteria derive energy from photosynthesis, and some from the oxidation of sulfur, iron, or methane gas. Bacteria have two kinds of sexual mechanisms, one of which involves the union of "male" and "female" cells and the mixing of their genetic material.

Why did single-celled organisms become multicellular? The probable answer is that larger organisms can develop new methods for taking in food, new methods of movement, and may enter new environments not easily available to smaller ones. But an increase in size creates problems as well, such as how to establish support to facilitate movement. One experiment in size expansion led to the development of plants, the other to the development of animals, both invertebrates and vertebrates. This process took over a billion years to occur. In both plant and animal evolution, the problems of adaptation were similar. In both cases, they were faced with the problem of preventing loss of water from cells, with the problem of support, and with the problem of reproduction independent of water. Plants solved these problems by becoming immobile, sun-catching energy converters, while animals became mobile and obtained energy through preying on other animals, or by converting the energy of plants.

As animals increased in size, the need increased for a mobile animal to obtain information about its close and far environments. This need led to the development of both sensory and motor systems with a corresponding need to integrate and coordinate their activities. Thus was born a nervous system that provided a specialization of the inherent property of irritability that all cells possess, along with an increase in the speed and complexity of integration.

The Evolution of the Brain

Studies of evolution indicate that the single-celled protozoa gave rise to three lines: the sponges, the jellyfish, and the flatworms. From these simple combinations of cells eventually arose worms, arthropods (insects, spiders), mollusks (snails, clams, squid), and then echinoderms (starfish) and finally the chordates (bilaterally symmetrical animals with spinal cords). Primitive examples of chordates are the jawless fish (hagfish and lamprey eels). Vertebrates that evolved later are sharks, amphibia (frogs and salamanders), reptiles, birds, and mammals, as Figure 11.1 illustrates.

If we consider the nervous system of a very primitive animal, the jellyfish, it appears that there is no brain center, but simply a continuous web of nerves called a nerve net. If one touches the animal at one point, nerve impulses will pass around the animal like a wave. The nerve net serves two functions. It is sensitive to external stimuli, and it coordinates the muscular activity of the animal that allows integrated, goal-directed movements of approach or avoidance.

In bilaterally symmetrical animals, several important changes took place in the nervous system in the course of evolution. At the head end of the animal where the mouth is and where a visual system began to devel-

Figure 11.1   Animal Evolution and the Conquest of Land and Air

The succession of vertebrates is on the left, and similar environmental adaptations have been achieved independently by various invertebrate groups, as shown on the right.

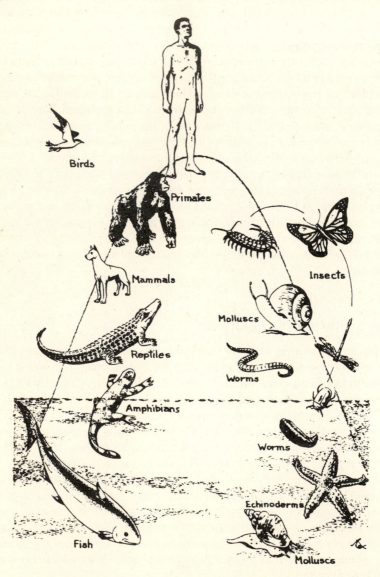

Source: J. T. Bonner, 1962.

op, there was an increase in the relative size of the neurons. This process is called cephalization, and it presumably increases the capacity of the organism to make coordinated movements in response to sensory inputs.

In vertebrates, the nervous system is made up of the spinal cord and brain, and peripheral nerves that extend from the central nervous axis to all parts of the body. A vertebrate animal is basically a series of segments (fundamentally like an earthworm) though this plan is not externally obvious. However, the spinal column remains segmented, and each segment has a pair of spinal nerves connecting sense organs and muscles. Simple coordinations are possible by this means. For example, in humans the knee-jerk reflex illustrates this condition, as does pupillary contraction in response to light. Such reflexes also partly regulate visceral organs. Sweating, evacuation of bladder and bowel, local vasoconstriction, and vasodilatation in response to cutaneous cold and warmth are examples.

Because this form of integration is not adequate for the organism as a whole, a number of other neural structures were formed at the head end of the animal. One was an expansion of the spinal cord to integrate breathing reflexes. Another was the development of the *reticular formation*, which exerts facilitating and inhibiting effects on nerve impulses received from all levels. Anatomically, reticular substance appears unspecialized and consists of a maze of interconnected nerve fibers, with cell bodies evenly distributed within it. However, modern neuroscience research has begun to identify a good deal of neurochemical and functional specialization, so that it is more accurate to consider the reticular formation as made up of multiple systems.

When mudfishes emerged from the water to become amphibians, fins were transformed into legs, and quadrupedal locomotion required more complicated coordination than swimming. This change from water to land began about 300 million years ago and led to the development of a basic brain pattern that has remained similar from reptiles to humans. This plan is shown in Figure 11.2 (on page 271), which represents a dorsal (top) view of an amphibian brain.

The key structures are the medulla, the midbrain, the thalamus, and the cerebral cortex. These structures have a hollow center or core called ventricles, through which flows cerebrospinal fluid. The spaces inside the two cerebral hemispheres are called lateral ventricles, the space in the thalamus and hypothalamus is called the third ventricle, while the space inside the medulla is called the fourth ventricle, which in turn is continuous with the spinal canal. In higher vertebrates the relative sizes and positions of these structures vary greatly, but the underlying plan remains the same.

For vertebrate brains, five general subdivisions have been identified. These are listed in Table 11.1.

In Figure 11.3, a drawing of the primate brain shows the location of these major structures. To provide a sense of the changes that have taken place in the brain during evolution, Figure 11.4 shows photographs of

Table 11.1	General Subdivision of the Brain

General Division	Major Structures Included
Myelencephalon	Medulla
Metencephalon	Pons Cerebellum
Mesencephalon	Midbrain
Diencephalon	Hypothalamus Pituitary gland Optic tracts Subthalamus Thalamus
Telencephalon	Cerebral hemispheres Basal ganglia Olfactory bulb and tracts

Source: R. F. Thompson, 1962.

cross-sections (cut front to back) of the brains of seven animals: the rat, dog, sheep, cow, monkey, human, and dolphin. It is evident that the brain gets larger, and the outermost layer, the cortex, becomes increasingly fissured or convoluted. The brain of a human being weighs about 48 ounces or about 1,360 grams. In contrast, the brain of a kangaroo, which is of equal body weight to a human, weighs only 2 ounces. Similarly, the cortex or outer layer of brain tissue of a human is about four times the area of that of a chimpanzee.

▌An Overview of the Major Brain Structures

As Figure 11.5 (on page 275) shows, the brain stem is an enlarged continuation of the spinal cord. It contains many groups of nerve cells or nuclei as well as nerve fiber tracts, which include the medulla, pons, and midbrain. The *medulla* contains all the ascending and descending nerve tracts that connect the brain and spinal cord. It also contains nuclei that influence respiration, heart rate, gastrointestinal motility, eye and facial movement, balance, and tongue movement.

The *pons* is a further continuation of the brain stem and contains ascending and descending fibers as well as nerve nuclei for cranial nerves concerned with chewing movement and salivation. The pons also contains generators for producing rapid eye movements during sleep.

The *midbrain* is the most anterior (frontal) extension of the brain stem that still shows the tube-like structure of the spinal cord. The dorsal (tectum or roof) part of the midbrain contains major relay nuclei for the auditory and visual systems in humans. Some information processing takes place there as well. The relay nuclei are called inferior (meaning below) and superior (meaning above) colliculi. Other nuclei found in the midbrain control eye movement. The relative size of these various nuclei is generally related to the behavioral importance of the sensory and/or motor modality involved. Thus, bats, which rely heavily on auditory information, have enlarged inferior colliculi.

It is important to emphasize that these brain stem structures are surprisingly uniform from fish to man, and they manage quite well to coordinate a lower animal's behavior. For example, if one removes all brain tissue above the midbrain in a cat, it can still walk to some degree; it can purr, eat

Figure 11.2	Dorsal View of an Amphibian Brain

The roof of the cerebral hemisphere and thalamus has been removed on the right side to open the lateral and third ventricles.

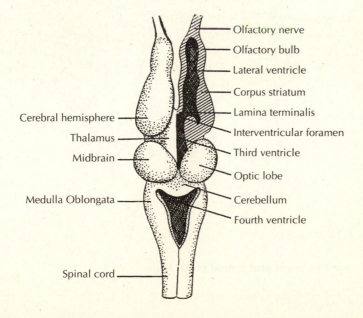

Olfactory nerve
Olfactory bulb
Lateral ventricle
Corpus striatum
Lamina terminalis
Interventricular foramen
Third ventricle
Optic lobe
Cerebellum
Fourth ventricle

Cerebral hemisphere
Thalamus
Midbrain
Medulla Oblongata
Spinal cord

Source: C. J. Herrick, 1956.

Figure 11.3   Divisions of the Primate Brain

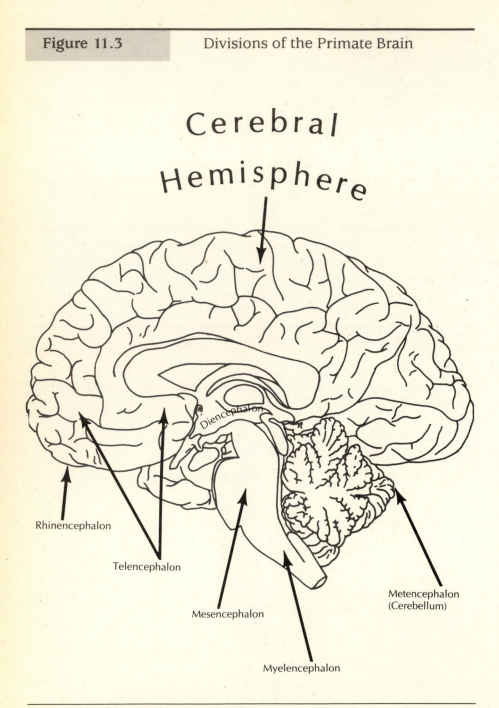

Source: M. W. Woerdeman, 1960.

| Figure 11.4 | Cross Sections of the Brains of Seven Mammals |

Rat

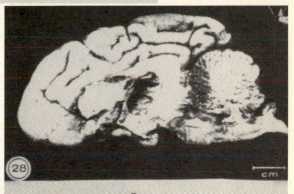

Dog

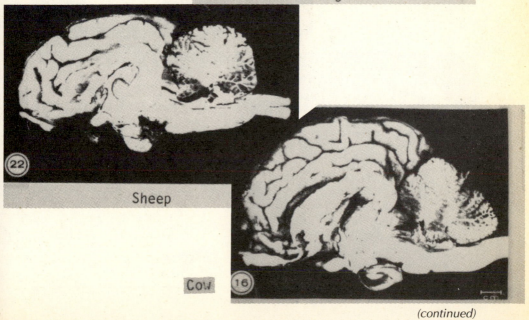

Sheep

Cow

(continued)

Monkey

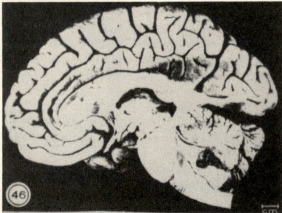

Man

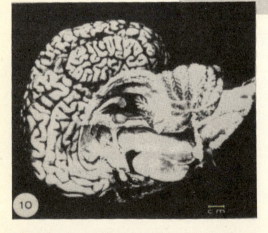

Dolphin

Source: W. L. McFarland, P. J. Morgane, & M. S. Jacobs, 1969.

Figure 11.5	Central Nervous System

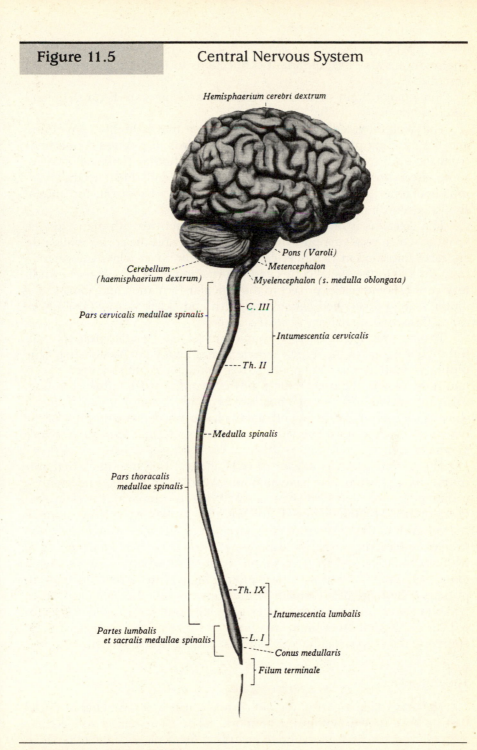

Hemisphaerium cerebri dextrum

Pons (Varoli)
Metencephalon
Myelencephalon (s. medulla oblongata)

Cerebellum
(haemisphaerium dextrum)

Pars cervicalis medullae spinalis

C. III

Intumescentia cervicalis

Th. II

Medulla spinalis

Pars thoracalis
medullae spinalis

Th. IX

Intumescentia lumbalis

Partes lumbalis
et sacralis medullae spinalis

L. I

Conus medullaris

Filum terminale

Source: M. W. Woerdeman, 1960.

if food is placed in the mouth, sleep, and show signs of emotional behavior. The midbrain also has important connections to the limbic system to be described shortly.

Some major brain structures in humans are shown in Figure 11.6 and described below.

The *cerebellum*, a relatively large structure that is highly convoluted and lies over the pons, is well developed in birds. It receives connections from the auditory and visual systems, the vestibular (balance) system, some visceral organs, and the cerebral cortex. It sends fibers to the thalamus and other parts of the brain stem. If removed in a cat, the animal shows uncoordinated movements.

The *thalamus* is an extremely complex structure with many nuclei, some of which receive inputs from sense organs and the cortex while others relay information to higher centers of the brain. It relays information from the eye to the visual cortex and information from the ear to the auditory cortex. Some nuclei project to the reticular formation and some to the limbic system (described below). Gellhorn and Loofbourrow (1963) have called this structure the *gateway to the neocortex*.

The *hypothalamus* refers to a group of nuclei that lie adjacent to the ventral (bottom) part of the third ventricle. It has neural connections with the pituitary gland and has an important role in regulating the secretion of certain hormones in the body. Nuclei in the hypothalamus influence eating, drinking, sexual behavior, temperature regulation, and emotional expressions of certain types. The hypothalamus has connections with parts of the old cortex (such as the amygdala and hippocampus) and with the olfactory system as well.

The *cerebral cortex* is a layer of cells about 2 to 3 mm thick that surrounds the cerebrum. Fish have no cerebral cortex, amphibians have only a rudimentary one, and birds have a small one. In humans, it is estimated that 9 of the 12 billion neurons in the brain are in the cortex. Nerve impulses from each of the senses project to specific parts of the cortex. In addition to sensory-receiving areas, there are motor areas that control movements of the body muscles, and an "association" cortex that is believed to be related to the elaboration of sensory information in higher intellectual functions. In primates, the large development of the cortex is called new or neocortex, while in lower vertebrates the cortex is usually referred to as allocortex or old cortex. Several other brain structures and systems play a major role in emotions: the amygdala, the hypocampus, and the limbic system.

The Amygdala

The amygdala, a part of the old cortex, consists of a number of nuclei that lie buried deep within the temporal lobe. It has neural connections with many other parts of the brain including the neocortex, the hypothalamus, the septal area (an area near the hypothalamus in the midline or

Figure 11.6	Major Structures of the Human Brain

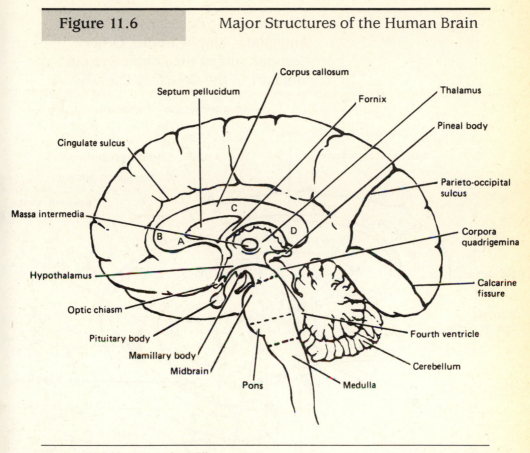

Source: N. Gluhbegovic and T. Williams, 1980.

medial plane), the thalamus, the hippocampus, the olfactory system, and the reticular formation. Different inputs from most of the sensory systems of the cortex arrive at the amygdala. Figure 11.7 shows some of these.

Injury to the human amygdala through trauma or disease has been known to produce psychomotor epilepsy. Such epileptic seizures are brief periods of confusion with no subsequent memory for the period of the seizure. Electrical stimulation of the amygdala produces an array of autonomic reactions including respiratory, cardiovascular, gastrointestinal, uterine, and pupillary changes. Interestingly, this structure too has been called the *sensory gateway to the emotions* (Aggleton and Mishkin, 1986). Figure 11.8 shows an outline drawing of the human brain indicating the approximate location of the amygdala and other structures.

More than 50 years ago physiologists did a study in which they removed both temporal lobes in monkeys (including the amygdala) and

| Figure 11.7 | The Anatomic Relationships of Amygdala, Hippocampus, Other Components of the Limbic System, and Part of the Olfactory Pathway |

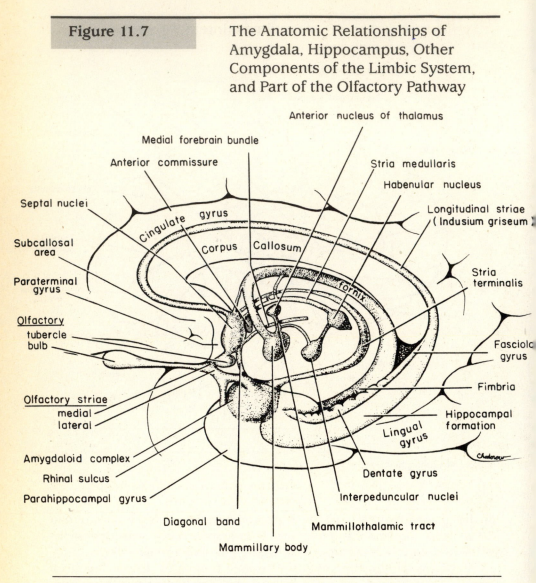

Source: M. B. Carpenter and J. Sutin, 1985.

discovered a wide variety of effects. Wild animals became emotionally unresponsive to visual, auditory, tactile, and taste stimuli, and would eat feces and meat. Although they were not blind, the animals did not seem to recognize objects, and placed all kinds of food and nonfood objects in their mouths. There was a decrease in their social activity and an increase in their sexual activity. They even attempted copulation with members of other species. The amygdalectomized animals decreased their social rank

Figure 11.8   Approximate Internal Locations
of the Basal Ganglia Within the
Cerebral Hemisphere

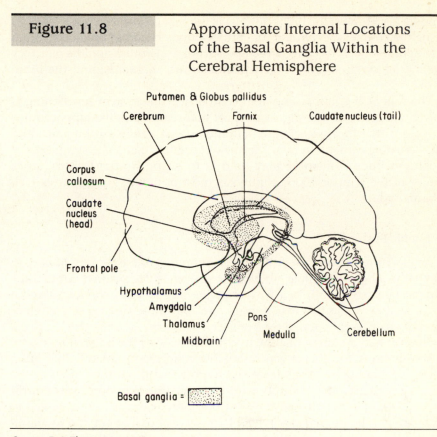

Source: R. J. Thompson, 1962.

and became increasingly withdrawn. This pattern of changes has come to be known as the Kluver-Bucy syndrome after the physiologists who first identified it. In an analysis of this phenomenon, Aggleton and Mishkin (1986) interpret amygdalectomy as a way to disconnect cortical sensory systems from diencephalic nuclei that regulate emotional reactions.

The Kluver-Bucy syndrome has occasionally been reported in humans. After a 19-year-old man with epilepsy underwent bilateral removal of the anteriortemporal lobes, he was unable to recognize close relatives, and showed increased sexual appetite and activity. At the same time, he revealed a severe memory deficit as well as a lack of emotional responsiveness (Clarke and Brown, 1990).

The Hippocampus

In primates, the hippocampus consists of a large group of nuclei lying along the floor of the third ventricle deep within the temporal lobe. In primitive vertebrates, the hippocampus is the first cerebral cortex to appear. During the course of evolution the hippocampus becomes enfolded within the temporal lobe. It receives nerve fibers from the septum and the olfactory system, and sends fibers to the hypothalamus, thalamus, and the brain stem.

The role of the hippocampus in central nervous system functioning is not well understood. Investigators report that removal of the hippocampus produces difficulties with immediate memory functions in humans, and makes learning difficult in rats. They also recognize that some symptoms of the Kluver-Bucy syndrome may be due to hippocampal lesions, since removal of the temporal lobe eliminates most of the hippocampus as well as the amygdala.

The Limbic System

In 1937, the neurologist J. W. Papez proposed the existence of certain brain pathways that mediate emotional experience. He pointed out that the word *emotion* refers both to a way of acting (emotional expression) and a way of feeling (subjective experience), and that these two aspects of emotion involve different parts of the brain.

Cannon had assumed that the hypothalamus was the integrating center for the emotions, but that it was intimately connected to many other brain structures. Neural impulses from the hypothalamus to the cortex of the brain were assumed to be the origin of emotional experience; neural impulses from the hypothalamus to various motor centers were assumed to be the basis for emotional expression. Papez's proposal attempted to identify some of the other brain structures involved in these processes.

He pointed out that nerve impulses that come from the receptor organs of the body—the eyes, ears, skin, and muscles—all go first to various parts of the thalamus. At this point, the impulses break up into three major pathways. One pathway goes to various structures of the forebrain (such as the corpus striatum) and coordinates the *stream of movement*. A second pathway goes to lateral parts of the cerebral cortex and handles the *stream of thought*. The third pathway goes through the hypothalamus to the mammillary body to the medial wall of the cerebral hemisphere and handles the *stream of feeling*. Papez based these ideas on fact and partly on speculation. He then went on to describe other brain structures that are probably tied into the circuits for the stream of feeling.

Of particular interest to him was the hippocampus. This structure, located deep inside the temporal lobes of the brain, was believed to be an integrating center for olfactory (smell) impressions. Papez pointed out, however, that lesions of the hippocampus are often associated with rabies, a disease that produces intense rage and convulsive symptoms. He therefore hypothesized that the hippocampus is involved both in emotional expressions and in subjective experience.

In addition to the hippocampus, Papez cited evidence to suggest that several other brain structures are involved in the various phases of emotional behavior and consciousness. These other structures are the hypothalamus, the anterior thalamic nuclei, the gyrus cinguli, the hippocampus, and their interconnections. Although researchers have usually considered these structures to serve olfactory functions alone, the evidence for this belief is weak. The evidence for Papez's proposal was not overwhelming, but the proposal itself stimulated a good deal of interest among neurologists on the problem of brain structures underlying emotional experience. During the next several decades, a number of investigators experimentally examined Papez's hypotheses and have greatly expanded knowledge of brain anatomy as it relates to emotions.

▌Paul MacLean and the Triune Brain

One prominent investigator who has devoted much research to understanding the role of the limbic system is Paul MacLean, a neurophysiologist. He has spent much of his career at the National Institute of Mental Health studying the neurology and behavior of the squirrel monkey. MacLean points out that the course of evolution has, in a sense, juxtaposed three different types of brains into one, and despite differences in structure, they must function together. The oldest type of brain is basically reptilian; the second is inherited from lower mammals; and the third is a late development in terms of evolution, found most highly developed in the primates. The earlier type of brain is basically an olfactory brain or rhinencephalon. In lower animals, many brain structures are connected with the activity of smell, which, from an adaptive point of view, plays an important role in food gathering, courtship, mating, and warning of predators. Brain centers for correlating smell, taste, oral, and visceral sensations have a relatively large development in primitive animals, but in the course of evolution a new cortex, or neocortex, develops that exerts more and more control over adaptive behavior. MacLean suggests that the rhinencephalon continues to exercise a large degree of control over visceral activity, even in higher primates, and should be called a *visceral brain*.

Structures that MacLean calls the visceral brain include the hippocampal gyrus (a part of the temporal lobe), the mammillary body (a small structure found at the back of the hypothalamus), the anterior thalamic nucleus, and the cingulate gyrus (found on the medial surface of the cerebrum). The fornix is a large bundle of fibers connecting the hippocampus to the mammillary body. Additional structures that MacLean considers to be part of the visceral brain are the amygdala and hippocampus (both found within the temporal lobes), and the septum (found near a juncture of the thalamus and the frontal lobes). Some pathways that are part of the visceral brain are the fornix, the medial forebrain bundle, the stria terminalis, and the stria medullaris.

Although these structures are prominent in animals that rely greatly on a sense of smell , some of these structures such as the hippocampus and the cingulate gyrus reach a high level of development in humans (and an even higher level in whales and dolphins), for whom the sense of smell is of relatively limited importance. It therefore seems likely that the rhinencephalon has functions other than olfaction. MacLean proposes that it is largely involved in the control of visceral and emotional activities.

In a later paper, MacLean (1963) pointed out that what he called a visceral brain in 1949 is now more often called the *limbic brain* or *limbic lobe.* A series of investigations have tried systematically to determine the functional characteristics of limbic structures. For example, a number of studies have shown that bilateral injuries or lesions of the temporal lobes (which eliminate the normal functions of the amygdala and the hippocampus, among other structures) tend to make wild and dangerous animals passive, tractable, and hypersexed (the Kluver-Bucy syndrome).

Other studies have concerned the effects of electrical stimulation of small areas of the brain. Such experiments have found, for example, that stimulation of the amygdala produces patterns of behavior related to eating or swallowing, or behaviors related to searching or fighting. Electrical stimulation of the hippocampus, or of the septum to which it is connected, frequently produce penile erection and grooming reactions. It thus appears evident that these limbic system structures are involved in the integration of oral behaviors, sexual behaviors, and agonistic (fight or flight) behaviors—in other words, emotional behaviors.

MacLean points out that his research has repeatedly shown that very small changes in the location of the stimulating electrode tip often produces very marked changes in emotional behaviors. For example, at one point in the brain, stimulation may produce penile erection. One millimeter away, it may produce rage-like reactions or vocalizations that suggest fear. He thinks the proximity of brain structures associated with such diverse emotional behaviors possibly explains the frequently noted interest of humans in horror movies, scary experiences, and aggressive encounters. He further speculates that the spread of neural impulses to adjacent structures may account for some of the mixed emotions people report.

One of the most interesting aspects of MacLean's discussion of the brain and emotions is his attempt to relate his concepts about the visceral brain to the more "natural" behavior of animals. For example, in squirrel monkeys, penile erection is used as a form of display; that is, it is a social signal to other monkeys. As Figure 11.9 illustrates, the squirrel monkey displays his penis both in courtship and in dominance situations. The thighs are spread and the erect penis is thrust almost up into the face of the other animal. If a male receiving a display does not remain submissive during this time, the other male may attack him. Observations have shown that who displays to whom correlates directly with dominance rank in the group.

Figure 11.9	Social Signals in Male Monkeys

In the communal situation the male squirrel monkey may display penile erection in the act of courtship, or, as illustrated, it may display to another male as a means of exerting and establishing dominance. In each case the display is performed with the thighs spread and the erect penis thrust almost into the face of the other animal.

Source: D. W. Ploog and P. D. MacLean, 1963

MacLean interprets this close connection between courtship and dominance as a direct reflection of the structure of the brain. He speculates about other types of emotional relations that reflect brain structure and then concludes that emotional expressions are adaptive and serve the goals of the species and the individual. In his own words: "Emotional feelings guide our behavior with respect to the two basic life principles of self-preservation and the preservation of the species" (MacLean, 1963).

In his elaboration of these ideas, MacLean suggests that the reptilian brain is quite capable of carrying out complex forms of social and emotional behavior. Among examples, he lists establishing a territory, ritualistic displays in defense of territory, intraspecies fighting, hunting, formation of social groups, courtship displays, and mating. It is important to emphasize that in naturalistic situations with animals, the establishment of a territory is an essential prelude to mating and breeding. Thus, it is understandable that territory, defense, fighting, courtship, and mating are closely interrelated. It is also worth noting that most display behaviors in animals are innate; for example, a squirrel monkey raised in isolation will display to other monkeys when first placed in proximity to them.

MacLean's laboratory studies on squirrel monkeys have revealed some of the major limbic pathways. For example, electrical stimulation of the amygdala and parts of the hippocampus elicits biting, mouthing, and eating activities. Electrical stimulation of the septum and cingulate gyrus elicits penile erection. And in areas in and around parts of the hypothalamus, it elicited oral, genital, or aggressive behavior. MacLean interprets this evidence to indicate that the same neural mechanisms may be involved in combat, whether as a prelude to eating or mating. A third limbic pathway does not involve the olfactory system, but sends nerve fibers from the hypothalamus to the cingulate gyrus, and then to the neocortex. Stimulation along this pathway elicits penile erection. The concerns of the limbic system, overall, thus seem to be the regulation of feeding, fornication, fighting, and fleeing.

Investigators used the method of evoked potentials for further research on limbic structures. Researchers placed tiny microelectrodes into small groups of neurons and recorded any electrical signal. MacLean found that stimulation of all sensory systems—olfaction, vision, hearing, touch, pressure, and taste—elicited electrical signals in individual cells of different parts of the limbic system. For example, visual stimulation elicited evoked responses in the hippocampus.

MacLean also suggests (1984) that three main forms of behavior characterize the evolutionary transition from reptiles to mammals: nursing in conjunction with maternal care; vocal communication for maintaining maternal-offspring contact; and play. The separation call (or isolation call) of young mammals (e.g., dogs, monkeys, babies) probably functions to maintain contact with the mother and with other members of a social group. MacLean's research indicated that thalamic-septal-cingulate connections play a major role in all three of these behavior patterns. Also of interest is that the cingulate cortex has a high concentration of opiate receptors and that morphine intake (which blocks their action at certain dose levels) eliminates the separation call. Researchers have also found that naloxone, a substance that acts as an antagonist of morphine, reinstates the separation call. Lesions of the cingulate area tend to reduce opiate craving in humans.

MacLean (1986) has described one other set of data that throws light on the functioning of certain limbic structures in humans. Psychomotor epilepsy (also called temporal lobe epilepsy and complex, partial seizures) in humans is known to result from abnormal electrical discharges in certain limbic structures that head injury or diseases usually trigger. For unknown reasons, many such abnormal foci arise in the hippocampus and spread to other parts of the limbic system. Depending on the particular areas activated, a person with epilepsy will experience a number of strange sensations (the *aura*) at the beginning of an epileptic attack. Examples of these sensations include feelings of nausea, choking, hunger, thirst, a need to urinate, distorted sounds, hallucinations, disturbances in one's sense of reality, and disturbances of emotion. Epileptic patients may further report feelings of elation, anger, or sadness.

In an effort to evaluate this kind of information, MacLean reviewed the many reports in the world literature that describe the subjective feelings associated with psychomotor epilepsy. He was interested in identifying the kinds of subjective emotional feelings patients reported. His review led him to conclude that patients reported about six emotions during their auras. One was fear. For example, a 23-year-old medical student stated that he invariably had an aura consisting of a peculiar sensation in the upper part of his abdomen, and an intense feeling of fear. A 42-year-old newspaper editor described his aura as "a feeling of impending disaster. It's a horrible sensation" (MacLean, 1986). Several neurosurgeons have reported that electrical stimulation of parts of the hippocampus or amygdala in conscious patients during brain surgery for removal of part of the temporal lobe elicited feelings of fear.

Researchers report anger, too, as part of the epileptic aura in as many as 17% of the cases. MacLean saw one patient so guilt-ridden by his unpredictable attacks on other people that he attempted to commit suicide. Another reported that during his aura, "I just get an electrical feeling, and it goes all the way through me; it starts in my head and then it makes me do things I don't want to do—I get mad." Patients also have reported feelings of disgust and depression.

Not all feelings connected with the aura are unpleasant; many reports are of pleasurable, pleasant, joyful, or even ecstatic feelings, as well. One epileptic women said, "My fingertips began to vibrate thrillingly, and then the sensation passed to my head, giving me the most ecstatic physical pleasure."

These various reports concerning psychomotor epilepsy patients strongly suggest that some parts of the limbic system are involved in the generation of emotional states. In these studies, evidence exists of abnormal electrical activity in various limbic structures, based on EEG recordings, CAT scans, or surgical records. As these electrical changes spontaneously recur from time to time, the various emotional feelings associated with the epileptic aura also occur. The fact that fear and rage experiences are more common than other types may be related to the fact that medial temporal structures (involving the amygdala and hippocampus) are more susceptible to injury and disease than those in other lobes.

MacLean's reports of a connection between psychomotor epilepsy and emotional feelings have been largely confirmed by Ervin and Martin (1986). They reviewed the work of neurosurgeons and neurologists concerned with electrical stimulation of various brain points in conscious patients following brain surgery for relief of epilepsy. These observations revealed that stimulation of the cortex of the brain never elicits emotional responses, whereas stimulation of limbic structures often does. For example, when one patient was stimulated at a ventral amygdaloid site, she cursed, struck out, and smashed a heavy panel with her fist. A few seconds later she apologized for her act and could not imagine what had motivated her to do it.

The records of 2,000 cases of epilepsy revealed that patients reported a number of emotions in association with the aura preceding the epileptic attack. These emotions included feelings of anger, fear, pleasure, sadness, disgust, acceptance, anticipation, and surprise. A 28-year-old woman who had a friendly personality, with no evidence of maladjustment, illustrates one reaction. Her epileptic attack would begin with a shivering feeling in the abdomen, a general feeling of weakness, and a feeling of sadness, accompanied by some fearfulness. She had no associated motor or sensory changes and no hallucinations. The attacks last for about 3 minutes. Electroencephalographic evidence indicated some electrical abnormality in the posterior (back) parts of both temporal lobes. All these observations support the idea that limbic structures have an important role in the processing of information and the experience of emotions.

Summary ∎

This chapter has provided a brief overview of brain evolution from the lowest organisms to humans. It has pointed out that all living organisms need to deal with certain basic adaptive challenges that relate to prey and predator, exploring and mating. One may argue that these fundamental patterns of behavioral adaptations are the functional prototypes of emotions as we usually observe them in humans.

This chapter reviews the development of the nervous system from amphibia to humans. It includes brief definitions of the major brain structures and descriptions of their interrelations. Particular attention is given to the amygdala and the hippocampus, which many neuroscientists have considered to be important parts of the organizing systems for emotions. They are part of the larger limbic system, which is believed to mediate emotional expression as well as emotional experience.

A detailed exposition is provided of the work of Paul MacLean, who has developed the concept of a *triune brain,* that is, the notion that the human brain consists of the elements of a primitive reptilian brain, an early mammalian brain, and a primate brain. Electrical stimulation studies, lesion studies, and electroencephalographic studies have begun to reveal the roles that the components of each of these brain systems play in determining emotional behavior and experience. Electrical stimulation of the brain of conscious human patients has been shown to produce, depending on the location of the electrodes, reports of fear, anxiety, anger, rage, disgust, surprise, and joy or pleasure. It is evident that activity of the brain plays a major role in emotion.

Theories of Brain Function in Emotion

The world of man is made possible by the great advance in human brain structure and function, which allows an enormous increment in the complexity of man's cognitive and affective functioning.
—Alden Wessman and David Ricks

Goals of This Chapter

During the past few decades neuroscientists have been making large increases in our understanding of how the brain works. These contributions reflect the collaboration of many disciplines that include neurophysiology, physiological psychology, ethology, and biochemistry. We have learned a great deal about the many systems in the brain and their interactions. As a result, a number of theorists have presented hypotheses of how the brain contributes to emotional behavior and experience.

The present chapter will review the ideas of some important contributors to theories of the brain and emotions. Included will be the ideas of Robert Heath, a neurophysiologist who has provided important insights on the pleasure and aversive systems in humans, Karl Pribram, a neurologist who has provided specific information about neural programs in emotion, Jose Delgado, a neurophysiologist who has studied offensive and defensive patterns in various animals, James Henry a neurophysiologist who has emphasized the role of biochemical systems in the brain as mediators of emotions, Jaak Panksepp, a physiological psychologist who has identified at least four emotive circuits in the brain, Detlev Ploog, a neuroethologist who has contributed important new insights on the brain systems involved in the vocal expression of emotions, and Joseph LeDoux, a physiological psychologist who has identified some of the neural pathways underlying emotions. It should be emphasized that these theories generally have a lot to say about emotions in addition to the identification of brain structures and circuits connected with them. Most theories also address issues of adaptation, cognitions, the role of autonomic changes, neurotransmitters, and subjective experience.

Important Questions Addressed In This Chapter

- What have researchers found when conscious human patients allow electrical stimulation of parts of their brains?
- What is meant by a pleasure system in the brain?
- What does Delgado mean by an *emotion atlas of the brain*?
- What is meant by the concept of the *fragmental organization of behavior*?
- How do hormonal changes in the body help prepare an individual for emotional behavior?
- What does Panksepp mean by his concept of an *emotional command circuit in the brain*?
- What evidence is there that vocal calls expressing emotions in monkeys are innate?
- What are LeDoux's views about the role of consciousness in emotions?

■   ■   ■   ■   ■   ■   ■   ■   ■

▌Robert Heath and the Neural Substrate for Emotion

Since the mid-1940s, Robert Heath has carried out detailed studies of brain physiology and biochemistry in patients and in animals. This research has led to an expanded view of the neural bases of emotion.

The evidence that Heath uses to justify his ideas is of diverse types. Electrical stimulation at neocortical locations in patients has little or no effect on emotions. Lobotomies generally did not change the emotional behavior of schizophrenic patients. In contrast, ablation of subcortical sites often produces profound disturbances of memory as well as of emotional behavior. Electrical stimulation of subcortical centers in patients who were able to report their thoughts and feelings demonstrated that scientists could elicit pleasurable feelings by stimulating septal areas and unpleasant feelings by stimulating parts of the hippocampus. Using evoked potentials to map the interrelated anatomic network led Heath to identify the following areas as involved in emotional expressions.

1. septal region, hippocampi, and amygdala
2. subcortical sensory relay nuclei for audition (medial geniculates), vision (lateral geniculates), somatosensation (posterior ventral lateral thalamus), and vestibular proprioception (fastigial nucleus of the cerebellum)
3. sites involved in facial expression and eye movement (superior colliculus, third nerve nuclei, inferior olive in the pons)
4. midbrain nuclei that have been found to contain large amounts of the major neurotransmitters of the brain. Dopamine is found in the substantia nigra, norepinephrine in the locus coereleus, and serotonin in the raphe nuclei.

These and other observations led Heath to conclude that the conventional limbic system was only a small part of the system involved in emotional behavior. All major parts of the brain—hindbrain, midbrain, and forebrain—participate in emotional states. This condition makes sense in view of the fact that emotions generally involve widespread bodily changes of the skeletal muscles (such as postural changes or facial expression) as well as the autonomic system, and changes also in perception and appraisal. Of special interest is the fact that Heath discovered pleasure-inducing sites that act functionally to inhibit activity at aversive sites.

The Pleasure System

In an effort to learn about the functions of subcortical systems in humans, in the early 1950s, Heath studied 106 intractably ill patients who were willing to allow the implantation of tiny electrodes into deep parts of their brain. In some cases the electrodes were left for a few days, and in others for as long as 8 years. In some cases, he also implanted very fine tubes or cannulas used to introduce chemicals into the brain.

Heath found that when patients reported pleasurable feelings, neural changes consistently occurred in recordings from the septal region, deep cerebellum, and dorsal lateral amygdala. When he administered addictive-type drugs such as marijuana and cocaine through the cannulas, patients most often reported pleasurable feelings when the septal area was stimulated.

After Olds and Milner demonstrated in 1954 that rats would repetitively self-stimulate certain areas of their brains with small electric currents, Heath tried this technique with some of his patients. He found that patients would repeatedly stimulate sites in the pleasure system, but particularly the rostral septal area. Introduction of acetylcholine, a neurotransmitter, into septal areas also produced pleasant feelings and in one patient, it induced orgasms. At the same time, activity in the hippocampus, an aversive system, was inhibited. This reciprocal relation worked for physical pain as well as unpleasant feelings. The result was that Heath was able greatly to reduce the pain of metastatic cancer by electrically stimulating the pleasure system. He could similarly reduce epileptic seizure activity by septal stimulation.

The Aversive System

While using the deep electrodes to record electrical changes in various brain structures, Heath interviewed patients. When the patients reported unpleasant feelings or memories, he noted electrical changes from such nuclei as the hippocampus, the cortical medial amygdala, and the cingulate gyrus. When he administered electrical stimulation to these sites, the most common responses were feelings of fear, anger, and sometimes violent behavior. Three patients, who periodically became violent and psychotic, showed abnormal electrical activity in the hippocampus and at sites in the amygdala.

Electrical stimulation of the hippocampus and the dorsal lateral amygdala tended to induce seizures in experimental animals and patients. Electrical and chemical stimulation (acetylcholine) of the septal region consistently reduced the incidence of seizures in epileptic patients and also reduced abnormal electrical activity in the hippocampus. Heath concludes that there is an inverse relationship between the pleasure system (represented primarily by the septal region) and the aversive system (represented primarily by the hippocampus).

Heath further concludes that the earlier concept of a limbic system as the basis for emotions is too limited. Almost all parts of the brain play a role in determining the expression of emotions, in behavior, and in verbalizations reflecting inner feelings. Most important is the concept of pleasure and aversion systems interacting in reciprocal ways. However, not all neurophysiologists are convinced that all these observations are valid, and a number of researchers have proposed other theories about the neural mechanisms underlying emotion. We will now review several of these theories.

▋Karl H. Pribram: Emotion as Neural Programs

Pribram, a neurologist, has little sympathy for a Jamesian view of emotion, the idea that neural feedback from the viscera to the brain determines feeling states. One of his major objections to this theory is that many of the circulating hormones that stress produces cannot pass the blood-brain barrier and reach the brain; another is that the biological effects of stress are often very brief, whereas moods can linger indefinitely. Pribram also objects to the Papez-MacLean theory, which emphasizes the role of the limbic system in emotion. His claim is that stimulation or destruction of limbic structures affects nonemotional functions such as memory; in addition, stimulation of nonlimbic areas such as parts of the frontal cortex can produce visceral changes.

Pribram's theory of emotion differs from others in a number of ways. First of all, rather than emphasizing visceral changes as a major source of input for feeling states, he emphasizes memory factors. He states that unexpected events, or incongruities between past experience and current input, produce an alerting reaction. This reaction sets in motion various brain processes that attempt to control the input to the sense organs.

Such control can occur in one or both of two ways, by *preparatory* processes or by *participatory* processes. Examples of preparatory processes are repression and perceptual defense in the sense that these reactions tend to ignore or repudiate those aspects of the situation that initiated an emotional state. Participatory processes tend to deal with incongruity or disequilibrium by readjusting the organism in some way. In other words, the experience becomes part of the memory system of the individual, and incongruity between stimulus and memory is then minimized. Such states as interest, admiration, and wonder are examples of participatory processes that have in common some kind of involvement in environmental events.

These ideas are based upon the notion that the stability of an individual depends on the existence of a set of neural programs based on both genetics and experience. Emotions occur when environmental events create incongruities, which in turn set the control mechanisms into action. He defines emotions as "the result of neural dispositions or attitudes that regulate input when action is temporarily interrupted" (Pribram, 1967). This view of emotion emphasizes the idea that an emotion is an internal neural event, not an expressive behavior. In fact, Pribram quite explicitly says that "emotion need not be expressed in behavior" (Pribram, 1970).

These ideas provided the basis for a series of empirical investigations that Pribram and his colleagues have reported. Many are concerned with neural centers that are involved in preparatory and participatory control of input.

The writings of Pribram, thoughtful as they are, suffer from a sense of vagueness when it comes to dealing with specific emotions. It is interesting to speculate that incongruities between stimulus inputs and "plans" activate neural processes called emotions. But how does this speculation help us understand fear or anger or joy? Nothing is said about such questions. The value of Pribram's work is that it directs our attention toward another way of looking at emotions and the brain.

▌Jose M. R. Delgado: Emotions and the Fragmental Organization of Behavior

Jose Delgado is a neurophysiologist who, through a long series of investigations, has contributed to our understanding of brain mechanisms in emotion. He has demonstrated, for example, that there are three types of brain structures in relation to emotions. In the first type, electrical brain stimulation produces no observable effects that can be considered emotional. Examples of such structures are the motor cortex, the pulvinar (a part of the thalamus), and the substantia nigra. When electrically stimulated, the second type of structure will produce behavioral manifestations of emotion but will not produce subjective experiences of emotion. An example of such a structure is the anterior part of the hypothalamus. The third type of structure will produce both emotional behavior and emotional experience when electrically stimulated, as researchers have demonstrated in the central gray area of the midbrain, in the posteroventral nucleus of the thalamus, in the tectal area of the thalamus, and in certain parts of the hippocampus (Delgado, 1960).

But Delgado has done far more than provide us with a kind of emotion atlas of the brain. In a 1966 publication he considered many of the important issues involved in a theory of emotion; the following remarks are based mostly on this monograph.

Whatever an emotion is, it is not simply a subjective feeling. Delgado emphasizes that one may express emotional states in so many different ways that no one single aspect (such as reported feelings) is the final or ultimate criterion of its existence. This condition implies that we can recognize emotions in lower animals as well as in humans; illustrations of the kinds of evidence he uses are: how animals behave with purposeful effects, such as the killing of another animal; the way other animals of the same type react (e.g., submissive behavior of monkeys toward an aggressive male); and the willingness of an animal to work in order to induce an emotion in itself, as we see in electrical self-stimulation studies. In addition to these kinds of indices, many expressive behaviors reflect emotions. Table 12.1 provides a list of cat behaviors that are related to offensive or defensive actions.

The variety of such behaviors leads Delgado to his theory of the *fragmental organization of behavior.* Each bit of behavior listed in the table is involved not only in emotional expressions but also in other types of activities. For example, licking may be part of eating, exploring, playing, and mothering. It is unlikely that the motor pattern of licking has a separate representation in the brain for each type of activity. A more plausible hypothesis is that one neural center organizes licking behavior, but nerve impulses from other parts of the brain activate this center, depending on the initiating stimulus (e.g., food, a novel object, a baby, and so forth). The result is that simple fragments of behavior (such as licking, hissing, or biting) may become part of different sequences of action and thus take on different functional meanings.

This idea implies that there is no single brain circuit for anger or pleasure but that there must be a group of structures that play a role in integrating the various behaviors that define each emotion. Consistent with this theory is the fact that electrical stimulation of different brain locations can produce the same emotion. For example, electrical stimulation of the lateral

Table 12.1	Offensive-Defensive Manifestations in the Cat		
Vocal Signs	**Expressive Signs**	**Autonomic Signs**	**Functional Behaviors**
Growling	Alerting	Pupil dilation	Circling
Hissing	Retracting ears	Salivation	Prowling
Spitting	Unsheathing claws	Piloerection	Stalking
Snorting	Arching back	Sweating	Pouncing
High-pitched screaming	Lashing tail	Urination	Striking with paws
	Showing teeth	Defecation	Biting
	Opening mouth	Respiratory increase	Chasing
	Snarling		Fighting
	Pawing floor		Cringing
			Hiding
			Escaping

Source: J. M. B. Delgado, 1966.

hypothalamus and midbrain central gray areas has produced aggressive attacks, but stimulation of the frontal lobes or occipital cortex never has.

Although it is important to identify brain centers involved in the integration of emotional behavior, it is also important to discuss the stimulus conditions that produce emotions. Delgado points out "that some emotional reactions depend on sensory inputs while others do not; that conscious interpretation is necessary for some types of emotions and not for others; that emotional stimuli may originate in the environment, in memory, or even within neuronal circuits activated by chemical or electrical triggers" (Delgado, 1966). Some emotion-producing stimuli are "natural" and have a similar impact on all members of the same (or even different) species. For example, unexpected loud noises and pain tend to produce fear, and events that satisfy basic drives lead to pleasure. Many stimuli are culture-specific, so that their meanings depend on general shared experiences and teachings that begin in early childhood. Frequently, stimuli that evoke emotions are personal and idiosyncratic and achieve their effect because of the accidents of individual sensitivities and personal histories.

Of particular interest is Delgado's work on the inhibition of behavior. Of central importance to the study of emotion, it is a necessary requirement of the organization of behavior into meaningful patterns. The appearance of a single act, such as striking an opponent with the right hand and not the left, implies a selection of one sequence of action and, simultaneously, the inhibition of all other sequences.

Using unanesthetized monkeys with implanted brain electrodes, Delgado has demonstrated several different types of inhibition of activity. In one type, he taught monkeys a certain response to get food. Electrical stimulation of the anterior commissure, pallidum, and putamen stopped the movement needed to get the food. As soon as the stimulation was turned off, the animals went to the food. A second type of inhibition appeared to be a form of sleep. Stimulation of the septum for five minutes or more produced dozing in most animals, which sometimes continued for a few minutes after the cessation of stimulation. A third type of inhibition was an "arrest" reaction. Stimulation of motor pathways under the motor area of the cortex produced a sudden stopping of all activity but with a maintenance of normal postural tension. In other cases, stimulation of the anterior cingulate gyrus and certain points of the reticular system stops all activity and is associated with a steady loss of muscular tone. The animal becomes limp, and external stimulation (such as electric shock) has no effect.

Delgado also describes several cases of humans who have been stimulated by electrodes implanted in their brains. This treatment is done with the permission of the patient, only in connection with attempts to treat epilepsy, Parkinson's disease, or intractable pain due to cancer. In these cases, researchers have shown that the electrical stimulation can produce reports of feelings of anxiety, anger, pleasure, and sadness, among others. These studies with humans strengthen the belief that patterns of emotion that brain stimulation induces in animals are very much like those that similar stimulation produces in humans. Delgado's work is a good example of an attempt to integrate both neurological data and psychological concepts.

▌James P. Henry: Neuroendocrine Patterns in Emotional Behavior

Most research and theorizing described thus far concerns the effects of electrical stimulation of brain structures and the effects of injury to or removal of parts of the brain. However, it is increasingly well known that biochemical factors play a major role in determining the reactions of the

Figure 12.1	Three Basic Emotions: Anger, Fear, and Depression

Anger and fear are associated with fight-flight aspects of the sympathetic adrenal medullary axis, respectively. Typical behavior and neuroendocrine patterns are presented in their respective boxes.

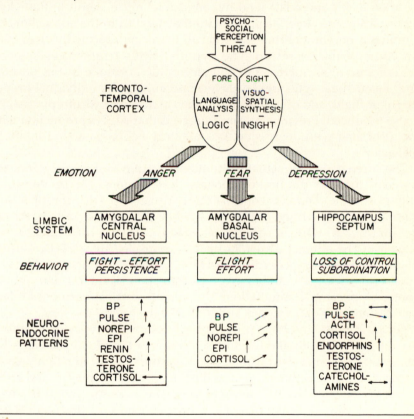

Source: J. P. Henry, 1986.

brain. James P. Henry (1986), a neurophysiologist and psychiatrist, has focused on this aspect of brain function in relation to emotions.

Figure 12.1 represents Henry's way of looking at three basic emotions: anger, fear, and depression. He believes that emotional reactions always begin with a perception of a situation, what others have called appraisal, or evaluation. One evaluates the situation in the fronto-temporal cortex in relation to both short term and long term memory, and then, depending on the nature of the evaluation (that is, to attack in anger, to flee in fear, or to submit with depression, for example), emotional circuits are activated. For anger, Henry believes that the central nucleus of the amygdala in the limbic system plays a major role; for fear, it is the basal nucleus of the amygdala, and for sadness, it is the hippocampus or septum. These circuits trigger both subjective feelings and/or overt behavior such as fighting, attack, biting, or running. To support these complex, widespread actions, the neuroendocrine system is also activated, producing changes in blood pressure, pulse, norepinephrine secretion, testosterone, and other substances. Activation of the amygdala (and hypothalamic) nuclei result in the release of epinephrine and norepinephrine into the blood from the adrenal medulla. In anger, norepinephrine excretion in the urine reportedly rises faster than epinephrine excretion. The hypothalamus triggers testosterone increases due to an increase in gonadotrophic hormone in the pituitary gland. Blood sugar (glucose) levels increase to help the individual prepare for fight or flight, and other hormones such as adrenocorticotropin (ACTH) are also produced. Previous research suggests that ACTH production tends to be associated with depression, loss of effort, submission, and inhibition of behavior.

The adrenal gland is actually a combination of two separate glands that have come together during evolutionary development. The inside portion of the gland, the medulla, controls the peripheral production of norepinephrine and epinephrine (adrenaline), while the outside portion, the cortex, mainly produces glucocorticoids, which influence sugar metabolism.The adrenal cortex, in turn, is controlled by ACTH release by the pituitary gland. According to Henry, the production of ACTH in response to a fearful stimulus involves activation of the pituitary system through hippocampal stimulation. The adrenal cortical hormones release glucose, increase blood volume, and influence the immune system.

Social interactions have powerful effects on the types of hormones released. For example, the level of serotonin in the blood increases in a monkey who becomes dominant in a social group. Defeat in a fight increases parasympathetic activity, slowing the heart, relaxing muscle, and reducing urinary output. Henry interprets these effects as meaning that defeat leads to inhibition of activity to save energy expenditure, and to deal with possible loss of blood and pain, thus increasing the chances of survival. Other studies have shown that those individuals who win a contest tend to show an increase in testosterone level in the blood. To illustrate the importance of these hormonal changes in emotion is the fact that, at least in birds, the release of specific hormones precedes almost every step in complex patterns to behavior from territory selection to nest building, to brooding, to feeding and raising the chicks (Hinde, 1982).

Henry made one final but important point. In his view, it is too limiting to talk of the role of any particular brain structure in emotion, as if it somehow functions in isolation. Instead, we need to think of particular structures as part of larger systems or axes. He emphasizes two such axes. One, the sympathetic-adrenal-medulary axis, includes the amygdala, the locus coeruleus, and the adrenal medulla. High levels of activation are associated with alertness and fight or flight behavior. Low levels are associated with relaxation and sleep.

Interacting with this axis is what Henry calls the hippocampal-pituitary-adrenal cortical axis, which includes the raphe nuclei, serotonin as a neurotransmitter, the hippocampus, and the hormones released from the adrenal cortex. Low activation of this system is associated with grooming, social attachment, and pleasant feelings, while high activation implies depression and loss of attachments. When these two systems interact at varying levels of activation, Henry hypothesizes that various biological problems may result, as Figure 12.2 shows. He assumes that high levels of

Figure 12.2	Contrasting Axes of Neuroendocrine Response

Vertical axis: The sympathetic-adrenal medullary system responds to activity of the locus coeruleus with increased plasma norepinephrine and blood pressure. There is an increase with fight-flight and a decrement with relaxation. Horizontal axis: Represents activity of the pituitary-adrenal cortical system. There is an increase in depresssion as during separation, with loss of attachments. With nurturant grooming, levels of cortico-sterone decrease.

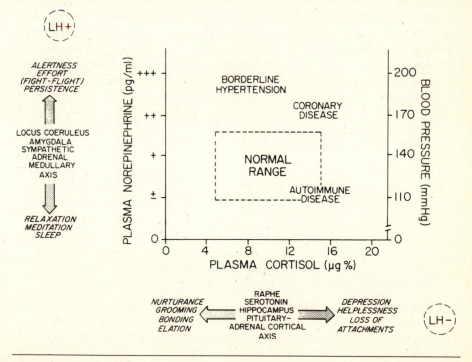

Source: J. P. Henry, 1986.

activation of these two systems may produce high cortisol levels and high norepinephrine levels in the blood, increased blood pressure, possible coronary disease, and possible autoimmune disease.

Although Henry bases these ideas upon research data, they are also speculative. The idea that emotional behaviors are based on a genetic, anatomic, biochemical *biogrammar* that hormones trigger is interesting and will undoubtedly continue to stimulate research.

■ Jaak Panksepp: Neural Control Systems for Emotions

Panksepp, a physiological psychologist, believes that emotions are complex psychophysiological-behavioral reactions of organisms to various kinds of stimuli. His investigations over a number of years have concerned the identification and study of emotional command circuits in the brain. He believes that research has identified at least four such emotive circuits, although the possibility exists of finding additional circuits in the future for such emotions as playfulness and joy (Panksepp, 1982; 1989).

Panksepp believes that certain types of stimuli or environmental events tend to produce emotional reactions. For example, restraint is one kind of event that triggers *rage* reactions; pain triggers *fear*; social losses trigger *panic*; and positive incentives such as social contact trigger *expectancy*. Panksepp cautions us not to misinterpret the use of these particular four terms, since we could use a variety of other related words just as well, such as hate and anger instead of rage, alarm and anxiety for fear, loneliness and grief for panic, and hope and curiosity for expectancy. He further assumes that certain general attributes define emotive command circuits, including the following.

1. The underlying circuits are genetically prewired and respond to major life-challenging circumstances (e.g., threat, pain, loss, and so on).
2. The circuits organize behavior by activating or inhibiting movement patterns and autonomic and hormonal changes that have been adaptive during the evolutionary history of the species (e.g., biting, flight, distress cries, and sniffing).
3. Emotive circuits can come under the control of neutral stimuli through conditioning.
4. Emotive circuits interact with brain mechanisms that influence appraisal, decision making, and consciousness (Panksepp, 1986).

Panksepp emphasizes that it is a mistake to view emotion primarily as a state of aroused autonomic reactivity. The evidence now available demonstrates that emotion is fundamentally associated with a number of well organized behavioral patterns related to survival such as attack, flight, and exploration, which autonomic changes support or reinforce.

Panksepp defines emotive command circuits as two-way avenues of communication that simultaneously recruit a number of brain structures and functions in response to life-challenging situations. They transmit information from sense organs, association cortex, and memory stores to limbic structures as well other parts of the nervous system. The final result of this complex interplay is the individual's integrated and appropriately adaptive behavior.

Although research data are far from unanimous on the exact nature of the emotive command circuits, data from animal and human studies suggest the following patterns.

1. Fear patterns are associated with activation of basolateral and central amygdala, central gray and ventro-lateral hypothalamus.
2. Anger patterns are associated with pathways in the corticomedial amygdala, central gray, and the medial hypothalamus.
3. Separation distress patterns are associated with activation of the dorsomedial thalamus and the bed nucleus of the stria terminalis, a band of nerve fibers that runs from the amygdala to the anterior hypothalamus.
4. Expectancy (curiosity-foraging) patterns are associated with activation of parts of the basal ganglia and orbito-frontal structures. These ideas are summarized in Table 12.2.

In this table, the major brain structures believed to be involved in each emotive command system represent only a partial list. It is obvious that cranial nerves must be involved in these circuits as well as spinal and autonomic reflexes of various kinds. For example, the trigeminal facial nerve is involved in the control of biting (rage), the occulomotor cranial nerves are involved in eye movements and foraging, and several cranial nerves are involved in the vocalizations of separation distress. Since emotions tend to be associated with characteristic sounds, each circuit may influence respiratory and vocal controls to generate the whines, screeches, screams, and coos identified with different emotions. Similarly, the circuits influence autonomic and skeletal muscle reactions that produce the changes in skin color, skin temperature, sweating, shivering, erection of hair, and cardiovascular responses characteristic of emotions. It is likely, given the evidence to date, that patterns of overt behavior are different for different emotions, but that autonomic changes are not. Panksepp believes that the autonomic changes that accompany emotions are supportive and congruent with the behavioral demands of the emotions (e.g., increased blood flow to muscles in anger).

These ideas that Panksepp developed represent another important approach to understanding the relations between emotions and the actions of the brain and nervous system. Future research will likely identify additional emotive command circuits, and will provide more precise localizations concerning the ones already known.

Table 12.2		Major Brain Structures Involved in Emotional Command Circuits	
System	**Related Emotion Terms**	**Environmental Triggers**	**Major Brain Structures Involved**
Fear	Anxiety Alarm	Pain or threat of destruction	Central gray, ventro-lateral hypothalamus, central amygdala nucleus, and lateral temporal lobe
Rage	Hate Anger	Restraint, irritation of body surface	Central gray, medial hypothalamus, and medial amygdala
Panic	Grief Separation Distress	Social loss	Dorsal mesencephalon, dorsomedial thalamus, bed nucleus of stria terminalis, ventral septal area, and anterior cingulate area
Expectancy	Hope	Incentives, e.g., food, social contact	Ventral tegmental area, lateral hypothalamus, basal forebrain, and frontal cortex

Source: Panksepp, 1986, 1989.

▌Detlev Ploog: Neuroethology and the Vocal Expression of Emotions

Detlev Ploog is a neurophysiologist and ethologist who has carried out his researches at the Max Planck Institute in Germany. He has been involved in a long term program concerned with identifying the neural mechanisms that underlie species-typical behavior. This approach is common in medicine where researchers attempt to find similarities and differences between lower animals and humans in such things as the organs of the body, the immune system, and the brain.

One example of Ploog's research deals with the neuroethology of social signaling, particularly vocal signaling. The following review is based on his analysis of this issue (Ploog, 1986).

From an evolutionary point of view, the ability to produce sounds has a long history. We see the rudimentary beginnings of a pharynx capable of sound production in lungfish. Further development occurs in amphibia (e.g., frogs) and in mammals in the differentiation in the laryngeal (vocal cord) musculature. In humans, movements of the tongue, lips, and soft palate produces verbal language with only minor involvement of the vocal cords. In contrast, both humans and animals produce nonverbal sounds almost exclusively with the vocal cords.

The neuroethological approach compares the vocal behavior of lower and higher animals and attempts to relate the differences to both life-style and brain systems. As a limited example, male frogs have about five calls: one is a mating call that attracts females, and another is a call that threatens other males. Both are species specific. In contrast, the squirrel monkey has a large number of calls with variants of each that serve as communication signals.

How can one learn about the role of the different vocal signals? One approach is to see how often one type of call follows another. This pattern gives some idea of the similarity of motivations associated with each call. Another approach is to implant tiny electrodes in the brain of the monkey and find sites from which different calls may be elicited. Researchers then give the animal an opportunity to turn the electrical current on or off by itself, thus providing an index of how aversive (unpleasant) or pleasant the inner state is for each call. Investigators assume that the lower the self-stimulation rate for a particular call, the greater the aversiveness of the inner state connected with that call.

Using these procedures, Ploog and his colleagues identified the properties of 15 types of calls in the squirrel monkey. They are grouped into five classes as follows:

1. **Warning Signals** include sounds described as "clucking," "yapping," and "alarm peeps."
2. **Protest Signals** include sounds described as "groaning," "cawing," and "shrieking." They vary from signs of slight uneasiness to intense threat.
3. **Challenging Signals** include sounds described as "purring," "growling," and "spitting."
4. **Desire for Social Contact Signals** include sounds described as "chirping," "isolation peeps," and "squealing." They act to draw another group member's attention to the caller.
5. **Companionship Signals** include sounds described as "twittering," "chattering," and "cackling." They seem to confirm social bonds or attachment.

A comparison of all the calls shows one feature in common. The more intense the expression of aggression, the greater the frequency range of the call. The fact that these species-typical calls relate to such emergency and survival-related events as warning, protest, challenge, aggression, social contact, and companionship implies that they are one kind of expression of emotion.

The Innateness of Calls

Several investigators directed studies toward the question of whether these squirrel monkey calls were innate or learned by social experience. In one study, infants were raised by mothers who were unable to make any sounds at all. Although deprived of vocal experience, the infants began to vocalize immediately after birth and they produced all types of adult calls. In another study, infant monkeys who were deafened on the fourth day of life produced vocal calls typical of the species. In a third study, researchers exposed infant monkeys raised without experience of species-typical vocalizations to tape recordings of alarm calls by adult monkeys. One call was an **alarm peep** for bird predators and the other was *yapping*, the alarm call for predators on the ground. The infant monkeys showed an immediate flight response to the mother in both cases. It thus appears that both the production of species-typical calls and the perception of such calls is innate.

A comparison of the vocal behavior of infant monkeys and human infants is instructive. During the first 3 months of life, both infants will vocalize whether or not they hear sounds or are themselves deaf. However, the deaf infant monkey will continue to express these limited vocal signals (what ethologists call fixed-action patterns) as they grow to maturity. The deaf infant will not learn to speak. These observations suggest that a different cerebral organization is involved in vocalizations of monkeys in contrast to humans.

The Cerebral Organization of Vocal Behavior

Electrical stimulation studies of the brain of the squirrel monkey have revealed a good deal about the brain mechanisms underlying species-specific vocal signals. Stimulation of the neocortex never elicits vocalizations in the squirrel monkey. When researchers stimulate various subcortical structures, they elicit species-typical expressions such as growls, shrieks, groans, and chirps. Investigators found locations in the hypothalamus, the thalamus, and the midbrain that produced vocalizations on stimulation. A section of the central gray area of the dorsal midbrain will yield vocalizations when stimulated in amphibians, reptiles, cats, dogs, and monkeys.

Ploog's research suggests a hierarchical system of organization for vocal expression in the brain. One level concerns the cranial nerves that determine movements of the larynx musculature and associated respiratory movements. The second level is represented by the central gray area of the midbrain, from which electrical stimulation can elicit a large number of normal calls. Destruction of this area causes mutism. The third level includes four different areas that mediate different motivational states such as threats, warnings, fear, and aggression, connected with vocalizations. These structures include the amygdala, the lateral hypothalamus, the dorsomedial hypothalamus, and the mediodorsal thalamus. The fourth level is represented by part of the cingulate gyrus, which is believed to exert a facilitating or inhibiting effect on activation of lower levels.

A comparison of monkeys and humans in vocal expression reveals that brain injury of certain neocortical areas in monkeys has little or no effects on their vocal behavior, although it may have marked effects on humans. Destruction of the anterior cingulate cortex in humans causes temporary mutism and a long term speech defect, but has no effect on monkeys' spontaneous vocalizations in a social situation. Injury to the mouth area of the motor cortex may paralyze the vocal cords in humans, and have no effects on a monkey's vocalizations. It appears that the voluntary control over vocal expression is a late evolutionary development. Only humans have gained direct cortical control over the voice.

Implications

Vocal behavior is clearly related to important survival issues in the life of an animal. It is used to express such things as warnings, threats, fear, aggression, social needs, and comfort, states that are clearly emotional. Thus, the study of vocal behavior is an aspect of the study of emotion.

From an evolutionary point of view, it is advantageous for an individual to communicate its likelihood of future action and for the receiver of the communication to understand it. In order for this to happen, there appears to be a gradual modification of a behavior pattern connected with a certain motivational state to make it more conspicuous. The ethologists call this change of behavior into a conspicuous signal *ritualization,* and the form of the ritualized behavior as a *fixed-action pattern.* Examples of fixed-action patterns are head nodding in lizards in competitive situations, and species-typical songs in birds, which act as territory markers and mate attractions. Although fixed-action patterns are genetically programmed and relatively constant in their expression, which pattern is carried out at a given time depends on the motivational state of the animal as well as on stimulus conditions. Ploog concludes, "Since social signals are expressions of emotions, we must concede that vertebrates—whether at a high or low evolutionary level—express emotions when they communicate via signals" (Ploog, 1986).

One final point. Electrical stimulation of the brain produces vocal expressions that observers cannot distinguish from natural, spontaneous species vocalizations. In contrast, it is not possible to evoke complex, nonvocal behavior such as running or grasping. This characteristic is presumably because vocalizing is a part of a larger class of motivated behavior, such as eating, attacking, or fleeing, in which fixed-action patterns are typical. Thus, the vocal expressions of animals express emotions and motivational states.

▋ Joseph E. LeDoux: Emotional Evaluation and Brain Systems

Joseph LeDoux is a physiological psychologist who has been interested in identifying the neural pathways that underlie emotions. However, he points out an ambiguity in the meaning of the word *emotion* as we customarily use it. Some researchers have studied emotion as reflected in *expressions*, some have been concerned with the *subjective experience* of emotions, while still others have been interested in the *evaluation* of sensory inputs to determine their significance to the individual. For each meaning of the word *emotion* there may be a different underlying neurophysiology.

In a chapter in the *Handbook of Physiology*, LeDoux (1988) has reviewed a great many of the studies concerned with the neurophysiology and neuroanatomy of emotions. He identifies the many inconsistencies in this literature, as well as the more replicable findings, and draws some conclusions about the relations between emotions and the brain. The following sections are based largely on this chapter.

For a long time, investigators accepted the idea that the limbic system is the basis for emotions, but recent research has raised questions about exactly what structures comprise the limbic system as well as what role they serve. After reviewing the literature, LeDoux suggests that the most acceptable way to describe the limbic system is in terms of certain forebrain areas: the hippocampus, the cingulate gyrus, the rhinal cortex (olfactory projection areas), the amygdala, and the orbitofrontal cortex. These areas and some of their connections are shown schematically in Figure 12.3.

Inputs from most senses go to relays in the thalamus and from there to primary receiving areas (which have been called koniocortex). The primary sensory receiving areas have projections to unimodal association areas of the cortex, which in turn have relays to a number of limbic structures. They also project to polymodal and supramodal association areas of the cortex, which have further relays to limbic structures. This schema applies to most of the senses; the olfactory system, however, does not have a thalamic relay, but goes directly to areas in the cortex as well as the amygdala. The amygdala receives afferent nerve impulses not only from the cortex and thalamus, but also from visceral pathways.

One of the complex issues about which little is known is the problem of how the emotional systems of the brain produce the movements of face, posture, and attack or retreat in an ongoing interaction between two individuals. Such adaptations clearly require intimate relations between sensory and motor systems mediated by evaluations of the nature of the interaction. In order for adaptive emotional behavior to occur, there must be some

| Figure 12.3 | Connections Between Sensory Cortex and Limbic Forebrain |

Sensory inputs are relayed through thalamus to primary receiving areas (koniocortices). Koniocortices project locally to unimodal association areas, which in turn project to areas in which sensory input converges (polymodal association zones) and to limbic forebrain. Polymodal cortex projects to complex (supramodal) association cortex and to limbic areas. Limbic areas also receive inputs from supramodal cortex and some limbic areas (rhinal cortices and hippocampus) qualify as supramodal cortex.

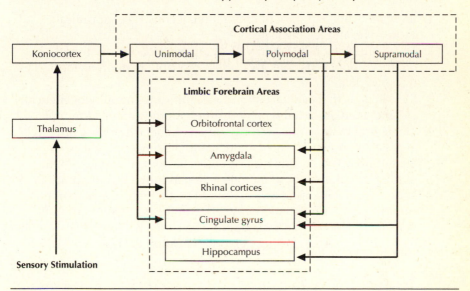

Source: J. LeDoux, 1988.

way in which stimulus inputs may be compared with stored information in the brain. This process of appraisal must be widespread throughout the animal kingdom, for without such a capacity, an organism could not survive (LeDoux, 1984).

Partly because of research on the Kluver-Bucy syndrome, it seems likely that appraisal processes are somewhat tied to the functioning of the amygdala as well as parts of the temporal lobe. The use of monkeys with split-brains and a destroyed amygdala on one side has demonstrated normal behavior when they view the world through the hemisphere with the intact amygdala. In contrast, the monkeys were tame and fearless to threatening stimuli when the only eye that was open was connected to the hemisphere with the destroyed amygdala. The amygdala contains receptors for hormones such as steroids, which also influence emotional states. Further evidence exists that the central gray region of the midbrain is also involved in the mediation of emotions.

One of LeDoux's major contributions is his demonstration that classical conditioning of fear, using auditory cues and shock, requires no cortical participation (at least in rats). It appears that a thalamic-amygdala linkage is sufficient. This phenomenon does not mean that emotions can occur without cognitions; only that we need to have a broader conception of cognition, since even without cortical participation, the brain needs to distinguish between an emotional event and a nonemotional event.

After reviewing these many anatomic and physiological studies, LeDoux comes to the following conclusions.

1. Emotion is not a unitary phenomenon. It consists of appraisal, expressive, and feeling aspects.
2. The evaluation of the emotional significance of sensory inputs occurs without conscious awareness probably in neurons located in the amygdala.
3. Mechanisms that evaluate stimulus significance are phylogenetically old and are distributed widely throughout the animal kingdom.
4. The neural mechanisms underlying emotional experience are phylogenetically recent. The are connected to the development of language and related cognitive processes. LeDoux also states, "One implication of these observations is that as humans, our ability to know ourselves consciously is limited by the patterns of anatomical connectivity. . . . Firsthand knowledge of the motivational conditions that underlie much of adaptive behavior will remain inaccessible to the conscious, feeling person" (LeDoux, 1984).

The Influence of Drugs on Emotions

Thus far we have considered the issue of brain and emotion in terms of studies of electrical and chemical stimulation of selected sites in the brain, in terms of self-stimulation studies, and in terms of the effects of lesions (either experimentally created in animals or as resulting from epilepsy or illness). Another line of research throws light on the role of the brain in emotion: the treatment with medications of individuals suffering from emotional disorders.

In the early 1950s, for the first time, physicians used new medications called neuroleptics for the treatment of schizophrenia. The treatments were remarkably effective for many patients and even those who had lived on the back wards of large state hospitals would often show rapid improvement. These findings started the major drug companies on intensive searches for other kinds of medications that would be helpful in treating various psychiatric disorders.

From a clinical point of view, there are several major emotional disorders (with many interactions and variants): depressive disorders, anxiety disorders, aggressive disorders, and pleasure disorders. The depressive disorders are characterized by symptoms such as feelings of sadness, loss of interest in usual activities, difficulties in sustaining attention, sleeping and eating too much or too little, and suicidal thoughts, gestures, or acts. Multiple fears, palpitations, shortness of breath, hot flashes or chills, and feelings of depersonalization (i.e., feelings of unreality or detachment) characterize the anxiety disorder. Such symptoms as loss of control of aggressive impulses, assaultive acts, destruction of property, cruelty, fighting, and impulsivity characterize the aggressive disorders. And symptoms such as anhedonia (loss of feelings of pleasure) or its opposite, mania, characterize the pleasure disorders. Such terms as inflated self-esteem, racing thoughts, increased sexual activity, decreased need for sleep, and distractibility define mania.

Over the years, clinicians have found a large number of drugs that are reasonably effective in dealing with each of these emotional disorders. A brief, oversimplified view of the biochemistry of nerve conduction in the brain will precede a description of these drugs.

Transmission of Nerve Impulses in the Central Nervous System

Nerve messages in the central nervous system are passed from neuron to neuron across junctions called synapses. Figure 12.4 shows examples of neurons schematically. As the electrical nerve impulse is transmitted along a nerve axon, various chemicals are simultaneously transmitted along the axon in very tiny tubes called microtubules. At the synapse, neurotransmitter chemicals are synthesized and stored in a presynaptic area before being released into the space between cells. The adjoining cells have postsynaptic receptors that the neurotransmitters activate to elicit an electrical signal sent down the dendrites to the cell body.

For a long time, researchers believed that only a few chemicals acted as neurotransmitters, but in recent years, they have identified a large number of new ones although they do not yet clearly understand their role in normal brain functioning.

The neurotransmitters that have been most studied are called dopamine, serotonin, norepinephrine, and acetylcholine. Neurons that use dopamine for neurotransmission are widely scattered throughout the central nervous system, usually as major projections from the medial forebrain bundle. Many studies have shown that brain sites from which high levels of self-stimulation may be obtained are typically areas of high concentration of dopamine cells. A deficiency of dopamine tends to produce tremors and muscular rigidity; an excess of dopamine may produce some of the symptoms of schizophrenia.

Serotonin neurons have their cell bodies in the upper pons and midbrain. They project to the limbic system, the basal ganglia, and the cerebral cortex. Low levels of serotonin in these structures are believed to have some relations to depression, anxiety, violence, and schizophrenia.

Figure 12.4	Schematic Examples of Neurons

(A) a "typical" neuron (spinal motor neuron). Dendrites conduct information to the cell body, and the axon conducts from the cell body to other nerve cells or muscle fibers (spinal motor neurons connect to muscle cells).(B–D) several common types of neurons. The cortical pyramidal neuron has both short dendrites and a long apical dendrite extending up through the cerebral cortex. The Golgi type II neuron has short dendritic processes. The bipolar sensory neuron has a specialized shape, with the "dendrite" and axon forming one continuous fiber from receptor to CNS.

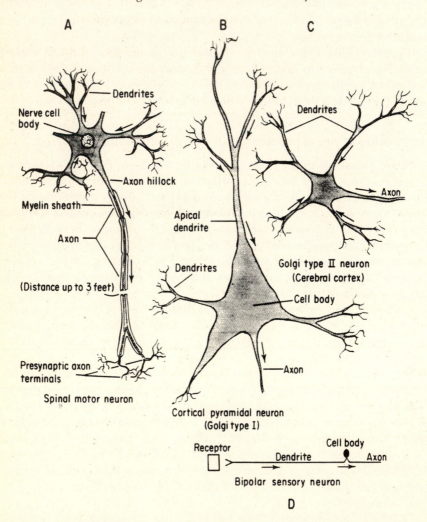

Source: R. J. Thompson, 1962.

Norepinephrine as a central nervous system neurotransmitter is found mainly in the locus ceruleus in the pons. The axons of these neurons have connections with the limbic system, the thalamus, and the cerebral cortex, and researchers believe them to have some regulatory effect on attention and emotion. A deficiency of norepinephrine may be associated with depression.

Acetylcholine is found in the reticular system, and its neurons project to the cortex, limbic system, and thalamus. Clinicians use acetylcholine drugs to treat the Parkinsonian (movement disorder) side effects of antipsychotic medication. Some researchers report excessive levels of acetylcholine production possibly to be related to depression.

Although researchers know a great deal about the biochemistry of these various neurotransmitters, their role in the genesis of emotional disorders is not well established. Pharmaceutical companies continue to develop new medications that influence neurotransmission (mainly through one or more of these four systems) in an effort to treat emotional disorders. Their efforts have been somewhat successful, since we now know various classes of medications that can reduce the extreme emotional changes we see in psychiatric patients. Table 12.3 summarizes the major drugs used to reduce extreme manifestation of emotions. These observations are consistent with the conclusions a variety of other research methods have yielded: that there exist sites, pathways, and systems in the brain that regulate and control the expression and experience of emotions.

Table 12.3	Classes of Medications That Reduce the Experience of Certain Emotions
Emotion	**Type of Medication**
1. Depression	Tricyclics, MAO Inhibitors
2. Anxiety	Benzodiazepams
3. Aggression	Serenics*
4. Mania	Lithium, Neuroleptics

*Serenics is the name given to a new class of medications that influence certain serotonergic receptors.

▌Some Implications of Knowledge of Brain Functionings

It is important to emphasize that an understanding of how the brain works and the development of theories about the brain are not academic exercises. Some important practical and clinical implications result from this knowledge. To illustrate this point, we may consider the implications of neurobiology for the understanding and treatment of addictions.

It has long been known that mild electrical stimulation of certain limited parts of the brain can be rewarding. Animals given control over the administration of the electrical signals will often self-stimulate themselves to exhaustion. Studies have shown that positive reinforcing effects are usually associated with stimulation of the medial forebrain bundle, a complex pathway connecting the forebrain and the midbrain. Further studies have revealed that reinforcing effects are related to increases in synaptic dopamine levels in the brain (Wise, 1988). Blocking of dopamine receptors will reduce or eliminate the reinforcing effects of cocaine and amphetamine.

Opiates such as heroine and morphine work by a similar mechanism. They activate all dopamine-containing cells of the ventral tegmental area and the substantia nigra (Mathews & German, 1984), and most drug effects can be blocked by dopamine antagonists. Opiates are known to have multiple effects. They can relieve the distress associated with pain, withdrawal symptoms (from any source), and isolation or loss of social attachments. Evidence shows that the mechanism of opiate physical dependence is different from the system of positive reinforcement associated with the medial forebrain bundle. In this case, morphine stimulation of the periventricular gray areas (either systemically or directly into the brain) will produce physical dependence that injections of opiate antagonists such as naloxone or naltrexone can block (Wise, 1988).

One implication of these findings is that many drugs of abuse probably activate the same neural systems. This inference is consistent with the belief shared by many rehabilitation programs that total abstinence from all drugs is a condition of treatment. The possibility also exists that nicotine, alcohol, and caffeine may stimulate the same systems so that such "recreational" drugs also should not be part of the addict's intake of substances.

A second implication of these studies of the brain is that drug treatment of addictions will be inadequate as long as it deals only with the withdrawal symptoms associated with avoidance of drugs of abuse. This is because a great deal of the craving for opiates and stimulants is associated with activation of the positive reward system of the medial forebrain bundle. Successful drug abuse treatment therefore requires approaches that have a twofold effect: reduction of withdrawal symptoms and reduction of craving.

Summary ∎

This chapter describes the work of seven theorists who have attempted to develop theories about emotions and brain function. The kind of evidence used to construct their theories varies from studies of human patients with implanted electrodes in the brain to studies of animals subjected to lesions of selected areas of the brain. Also included are investigations of biochemical changes in the neurotransmitters of the brain. Of course, in order to be able to relate such information to emotions, evidence also has to be available on the expressions of emotion, display behaviors, and/or reports of subjective experience.

These theories have helped us understand more about the role in emotions of the limbic system, as well as other brain circuits. Such structures as the amygdala, the hippocampus, the hypothalamus and their interrelations in connection with emotions have gained particular attention. But most theorists emphasize the point that overt action, facial expressions, and subjective experience must involve widespread systems and structures of the nervous system in order to enable integrated action to occur. Some have also emphasized the role of neurotransmitters and endocrine changes.

Most of the theories imply that the neural circuits underlying emotions are genetically prewired and primed to respond to important life-challenging circumstances. They utilize autonomic and hormonal changes to increase the organism's adaptive responses to emergency situations. Because emotional reactions such as fear can be conditioned to previously neutral stimuli, it is evident that emotion circuits must interact with those neural systems related to sensation, assessment, memory, decision-making, and consciousness. Knowledge of brain systems in emotion has many practical therapeutic implications, some of which are briefly described.

Love and Sadness in Everyday Life

> *Nature has placed mankind under the governance of two sovereign masters,* pain *and* pleasure. . . .*They govern us in all we do, in all we say, in all we think.*
>
> —Jeremy Bentham

▌ Goals of This Chapter

Two emotions that are a frequent part of everyday life and about which a great deal has been written are love and sadness. Not only are both a part of each person's life, they also represent opposites in that one is based on receiving, gaining, and attachment, while the other is based on loss of a valued attachment or on deprivation.

The present chapter begins with a review of ideas about love as reflected in Western culture from the time of the Bible to the present day. It reveals the many meanings of the word *love* as it has evolved over the centuries. In recent years, some degree of consensus exists on the idea that love is a complex mixed state with many elements, and even on what those elements may be. Love, too, has to be seen in the context of attachment theory.

The second part of this chapter concerns the nature of sadness and its offshoot, depression. Evidence indicates that depression is very common and that women report it more frequently than men. Theories of depression are described, as well as a number of approaches to the treatment of depression.

Important Questions Addressed In This Chapter

- What is meant by *courtly love?*
- How did the Puritans look upon love and marriage?
- What is the Freudian concept of love?
- How can one measure the components of love?
- What are the differences between eros and ludus as styles of love?
- How does attachment theory help us understand love?
- What are some differences between sadness and depression?
- What are some important causes of depression?
- How is cognitive-behavior therapy used to treat depression?
- How is psychodynamic therapy used to treat depression?

Love

Love has been a focus of human attention perhaps more than any other emotion. It is a favorite topic for novelists and poets, philosophers and clerics, and everyone else as well. We are all an eager audience in the desire to know and empathize with love.

The concept of heterosexual love was already part of Western thought more than 4,000 years ago, and it is often mentioned in the Old and New Testament. Of great interest is the fact that the word for love is used in a variety of contexts, so that it is evident that a number of different meanings were attached to it.

In the Old Testament, love is used to note passionate feeling between men and women, family affection as parent for child, and theological concerns as an expression of God's feelings about humans, the feelings of people for God, and the feelings of people for other people (as in "love your neighbor"). In most passages where the word occurs in the Bible, the words "to accept, adopt, or recognize" could probably be substituted for it. Other connotations of love are compassion, delight in, attachment, preference, and loyalty. In the Song of Songs, love designates sexual desire for a woman or man. In other places in the Bible, it means affection and esteem. Almost 4,000 years ago, the word *love* was used to describe the loyalty and friendship between independent and equal rulers, and between king and subjects.

With the early onset of Christianity, concepts of love began to change. Possibly because of the Roman emphasis on sensuality, the early Christians developed a strong counterreaction characterized by a preoccupation with asceticism and celibacy. "Virginity became exalted, marriage lost favor, polygamy was abolished, and sexual relations were condemned except for procreation" (Murstein, 1974). A practice called *syneisaktism* appeared, in which the sexes could live in the same household but with strict continence as "spiritual lovers." The attempt to repress sex led to a strong preoccupation with it and more was written about sex than about love.

By the twelfth century, a new phenomenon called "courtly love" appeared in Europe. Although there is controversy among historians about its origins, the forms it took are well known. Poets and musicians of that period described love as a burning passion that must be spontaneous; therefore, love within the confines of a contractual marriage was considered impossible and must be sought elsewhere.

A book written in the twelfth century listed rules to describe the qualities of courtly love. Here are some of them:

- A true lover does not desire to embrace in love anyone except his beloved.
- The easy attainment of love makes it of little value; difficulty of attainment makes it of great worth.
- When a lover catches sight of his beloved, his heart palpitates.
- A person who is truly in love eats and sleeps very little.
- A true lover is constantly possessed by the thought of his beloved.

These ideas, emphasized by the troubadours of southern France, were quickly eliminated by the Albigensian Crusade at the beginning of the thirteenth century. In their place new ideas extolled the difference between "pure" and "sensual" love. "To love women as sexual objects was wrong; to love the spark of God in them was good" (Murstein, 1974).

The Puritans' Ideas of Love

The Puritans in the colonial period in America considered love as sexual passion to be a threat to one's commitment to God. Love was not a prerequisite to marriage; marriage was based on the shared values of thrift, piety, and industriousness. The wife was expected to be submissive. The poor of that period carried out courtship by "bundling," which meant that unmarried couples could sleep in the same bed without undressing to get to know one another prior to marriage. Several methods prevented physical contact, including placing a wooden board in the middle of the bed, or restricting the young girls' clothing in various ways. After marriage adultery was a severely punished sin and adulterers were fined, whipped, and branded. Divorce was rare.

As American economic life changed more and more people moved from farms to cities. Women received the right to vote and other entitlements and social relations between men and women also changed. Both men and women became relatively emancipated from their parents and experienced the sense of free choice in love and marriage partners. With free choice came an increased emphasis on finding the right partner, based on ideas of romantic love.

Many people associated certain stereotyped ideas with romantic love, such as the idea that love occurs at first sight, that for each person there is only one true love, that romantic love is irrational and immature, and that women are more romantic than men. Cross-cultural surveys found Americans to be the most romantic on a *romanticism index,* and also holding the strongest wish to marry (Theodorson, 1965). In a series of other surveys in America, a majority of women reported their belief that men lose romantic interest in their wives after marriage and become more interested in sports and business than women. At the same time, more than half the women saw their own role as primarily *mother* rather than *wife.* In studies of lower-class marriages, women perceived their husbands as domineering, controlling, jealous, impulsive, and given to too much drinking, while men described their wives as temperamental, emotional, demanding, irritating, and irrational (Murstein, 1974).

The Impact of Freud

Early in the twentieth century, the writings of Freud and other psychoanalysts introduced many complexities into our ways of thinking about love. Psychoanalysts believe that unconscious drives based on infant and childhood experiences strongly influence humans. Sexuality is believed to begin at birth in the striving for pleasure, and then passes through various stages, oral, anal, and phallic, before reaching the final adult stage of sexuality. Humans can express the drive for pleasure in many different ways, but it always requires an object toward which it is directed. When the object is another person, we call the experience dependent or anaclitic love, but when the person him- or herself is taken as the object of the pleasure, we call the experience narcissism.

If a person has strong narcissistic drives, he or she tends to fall in love with someone who resembles him or her psychologically or in terms of past history. If a man is the dependent type, he may seek a love relation with a woman who will take care of him in a motherly way, while a dependent woman may seek a protective, father-like person. From the Freudian viewpoint, a happy love relation is one that has many infantile elements of which the individual in love is often not aware (Freud, 1949).

How Academic Psychologists Consider Love

For many years, academic psychologists largely ignored the subject of love, but beginning in the 1970s, a gradually increasing literature has attempted to conceptualize the nature of love. An early study concerned the difference between *loving* and *liking* (Rubin, 1973). On the basis of a review of novelists' and scientists' descriptions of friendship and love,

Rubin concluded that *love* implied idealization of another person, willingness to do things for that person, the desire for sharing, and sexual attraction, among other things. *Liking* of another person implied respect of the other, as well as a sharing of common interests. Rubin constructed a romantic love scale that included such items as "I will do almost anything for _____" and "If I could never be with _____ I would feel miserable." An example of a liking item is "I have great confidence in _____'s good judgment."

Using a somewhat similar methodology, Pam and his colleagues (1975) identified five major components of a love relationship: respect, congeniality, physical attraction, attachment, and altruism. A self-report questionnaire, The Love Scale, was developed in an effort to measure each of these components, as Table 13.1 shows.

Several groups of people completed The Love Scale about someone they believed they were in love with, or someone they were dating, and also in relation to a friend. Scores on the scales clearly differentiated the love relation from the other types of relations on four of the five scales, as well as on total score. Based on the findings, the most important aspects of a love relationship appear to be physical attraction and attachment. The two most important aspects of a dating relationship seem to be congeniality and physical attraction, and the two most important aspects of a friendship appear to be congeniality and respect. The results, however, indicate that there is no sharp line of demarcation between a love relationship and a dating relationship and it is likely that they blend into one another.

Sternberg (1986) has suggested another way of conceptualizing love relationships. He suggests that love always involves the components of intimacy, passion, and commitment in various combinations. A triangular model that helps us understand the differences among various types of love describes this idea. For example, according to the model, romantic love primarily involves intimacy and passion, while companionate love primarily involves intimacy and commitment. Sternberg also believes that each of these three components tends to follow a certain time course as a love relationship continues. Passion rises rapidly to a maximum and then gradually decreases. Both commitment and intimacy increase more slowly and then tend to remain stable. If these patterns change appreciably, the relationship is likely to be disrupted.

Lee (1973, 1988), a sociologist, developed still another approach to understanding love on the basis of detailed interviews with more than 100 adults. He concluded that there are three primary love styles, and a number of derivative, or mixed, love styles. The primary ones are labeled *eros* (love based on physical attraction), *ludus* (playful love), and *storge* (love as friendship), while the compounds are called *mania* (a blend of eros and ludus), *pragma* (a mixture of ludus and storge), and *agape* (a fusion of storge and eros). Some attempts have been made to measure these love styles (Hendrick and Hendrick, 1986).

Table 13.1	The Love Scale

Read each statement and decide how closely it describes your feelings toward your lover, or spouse. Score each from zero (if the staement is not at all true) to ten (if it is more true of your feelings for this person than for any other person you've known).

Respect

❑ You take his (her) suggestions seriously.

❑ You feel privileged to know him (her).

❑ You think he (she) copes well with his (her) own problems.

❑ He (she) has unusual competence or skills.

❑ He (she) has better judgment than the average person.

❑ He (she) is more intelligent than the average person.

❑ He (she) is more ethical than the average person.

❑ You respect him (her).

Attachment

❑ It is important to be noticed by him (her).

❑ It is important to be praised by him (her).

❑ You feel more secure when you are with him (her).

❑ You feel good when he (she) is sensitive to your moods and feelings.

❑ You would be jealous if he (she) became involved with someone else.

❑ He (she) is necessary for the fulfillment of your needs.

❑ You would suffer if you lost him (her).

Attraction

❑ You think he (she) is better looking than average.

❑ You like to show him (her) off.

❑ You spontaneously want to express affection toward him (her).

❑ He (she) is sexually attractive to you.

❑ You like being touched by him (her).

❑ You enjoy caressing him (her).

❑ You want to embrace him (her).

❑ You are sexually excited by him (her).

Congeniality

❑ You and he (she) get along well as a couple.

❑ You like sharing experiences with him (her).

❑ He (she) does not say or do things that embarrass you.

❑ He (she) can accept you as you really are.

❑ There are times when you seem to know what each wants without words.

❑ You are confident he (she) will stand by you through difficult times.

❑ You feel he (she) understands you.

❑ You and he (she) can work it out when you disagree.

Altruism

❑ You like giving gifts to him (her).

❑ You go out of your way to do things he (she) will enjoy.

❑ You enjoy taking care of him (her).

❑ You are willing to make sacrifices for him (her).

❑ You get very angry if someone hurts him (her).

❑ You suffer when he (she) suffers.

❑ You are willing to suffer to prevent him (her) from suffering.

❑ You would be willing to die for him (her).

Source: A. Pam, R. Plutchik, and H. R. Conte, 1975.

Love and Attachment Theory

Shaver and Hazan (1988) have recently proposed an approach to understanding love based on evolutionary biology. They point out that fundamentally love is an emotion whose characteristics are a result of the interaction of three behavioral systems: attachment, care-giving, and sexual mating. Using the work of Bowlby (1969,1979) as a basis, they suggest that falling in love is the establishment of an attachment bond, and that maintaining an attachment bond is a source of security. The establishment of a bond leads both to care soliciting and care giving, and, in adults, under the influence of hormonal and other elicitors, to sexual behavior as well. The complex of feelings associated with these states is believed to be what most adults experience as love.

It is also obvious that these three behavior systems may exist in isolation or interact in a variety of ways. The love of a parent for a child is a form of attachment and care-giving behavior without sex. This characteristic is also true of the relationships between friends. In professional settings, experts may provide medical or mental health care-giving services without either of the other two systems. In rape, the offender activates the sexual system without attachment or care-giving.

Shaver and Hazan point out the similarities between infant care-giver attachment and adult romantic love, as Table 13.2 shows.

Close proximity and contact define attachment behaviors in children. In adult lovers there is usually a preoccupation with touching, caressing, and kissing. In children, separation from the attachment figure causes intense distress, which also happens when adult lovers are unavoidably separated. Children wish to share discoveries and reactions with their attachment figures, while lovers typically have a strong need to give gifts to each other. Childhood attachments lead to baby talk and a special quality of mothering talk. Adult lovers also use baby talk and sometimes engage in childlike playfulness.

Shaver and Hazan conclude that this approach to understanding love within a broad evolutionary context offers a developmental perspective on the evolution of this complex state.

▌Sadness and Depression

The layperson often thinks of sadness and depression as more or less synonymous. Clinicians, however, recognize that the depressed person is not only sad; there are mixed feelings of pessimism and hopelessness, and possibly anger as well. Depression is thus a complex mixed emotion. A number of years ago Davitz (1969) asked college students to describe the ways they feel when they are depressed. The responses are described in Chapter 2.

Attachment	Romantic Love
Table 13.2	**Some Features of Attachment and Adult Romantic Love**
Attachment	**Romantic Love**
Attachment behaviors include maintenance of proximity and contact through holding, touching, caressing, kissing, rocking, smiling, and eye contact.	Adult romantic love is often expressed by holding, touching, caressing, kissing, rocking, smiling, and eye contact.
Separation from the attachment figure causes intense distress, and initiates vigorous, attention-getting efforts at reunion.	Separation from the lover that is unplanned causes intense distress, and initiates efforts to gain reunion.
If reunion is impossible, despair results.	If reunion is impossible, despair results.
Infants coo, sing, and talk baby talk, and the attachment figure talks in a special motherly way.	Adult lovers coo, sing, talk baby talk, and use affectionate baby-like names for each other.

Source: P. R. Shaver and C. Hazan, 1988.

The many descriptions of depression that Davitz gathered led to the conclusion that depression is a complex internal state having many elements. There are physical symptoms (*tired, sleepy*), negative feelings about oneself (*feel vulnerable*), impulses to action (*want to withdraw*), and physiological changes (*no appetite*). Any one class of descriptions is only a partial image of the total state we call an emotion. Not every student had all these feelings, but any one person might report a number of these elements.

If people describe depression in these terms, it is evident that such feelings can happen to anyone. However, if we consider depression from the point of view of psychiatrists, depression is a mental illness and must take certain characteristic forms in order to justify treatment with medication, psychotherapy, or hospitalization. In their manual (1987), the American Psychiatric Association defines a *major depression* in terms of such symptoms as feeling sad, losing interest in usual activities, gaining or losing weight, having trouble sleeping, and having trouble concentrating or making decisions.

Psychiatrists add some qualifications to these criteria of major depression. For one thing, a professional must determine that these feelings are not the result of an organic or medical condition about which the individual has just learned, nor should they be part of the normal reaction to the death of a loved one.

> *Illustration:* At the age of 16, Claire had become anorexic-bulimic. She went through periods of eating very little and losing weight, followed by binge eating associated with vomiting. Even though Claire did not report being depressed, the family pediatrician prescribed an antidepressant that seemed to help. Gradually, the anorexic-bulimic eating pattern disappeared and Claire went to college. In her fourth year at college, she began to feel increasingly depressed. She felt sad, hopeless, tired, had impaired appetite, and was unable to concentrate on her work. She consulted a psychiatrist who could not identify a specific precipitating incident for the current depression. Claire was given imipramine, an antidepressant, which was somewhat helpful in reducing the depression, but which had some unacceptable cardiovascular side effects. Another antidepressant greatly reduced the depression. At the same time, psychotherapy was also included as part of the treatment.

Not all depressions are major; other kinds are recognized. The two other most important mood disorders are called *dysthymia* and *bipolar disorder* (the latter is also called manic-depressive illness). The essential feature of dysthymia is a feeling of sadness along with certain associated symptoms, such as those listed for major depression, that last for at least 2 years. One may think of it as a chronic state of depression.

For some patients, a totally opposite mood called a manic state either precedes or follows the depressed state. Manic states sometimes confuse the inexperienced observer since they do not seem at first to interfere with a person's ability to function. For example, a manic person may feel very good about herself or himself, and able to handle any challenge. This person will often report feeling rested after only 3 hours of sleep. The manic talks a lot, his or her thoughts race, he or she is easily distracted. While in this state, the person is particularly concerned with doing pleasurable things such as buying wildly or engaging in indiscriminate sexual activity. Quite often, such manic individuals do not consider anything wrong with their behaviors, which often extremely upset spouses, parents, and other relatives.

Reactive versus Endogenous Depression

Clinicians usually recognize a spectrum of depression-related conditions. This spectrum ranges from feelings of sadness (feeling blue), to normal reactions of grief, to reactive depressions, and to endogenous depressions. Sadness reactions and normal grief reactions tend to be brief and are associated with sad thoughts and feelings. Reactive and endogenous depressions are generally prolonged, often lasting for many months or more, and they decrease an individual's ability to function normally. In addition to sad feelings and thoughts are often dysfunctional effects on sleep, appetite, and general activity; the risk of suicide is greatly increased, as well. The major difference between reactive and endogenous depressions is that a specific event such as the death of a family member, loss of a job, failure in school, or rejection by a lover usually triggers the former. In contrast, endogenous depressions occur out of the blue and usually have no association with a clear-cut triggering event.

▌The Epidemiology of Depression

Epidemiology refers to large scale studies of population groups in an effort to determine what factors seem to be associated with particular illnesses or mental conditions. Researchers attempt to identify risk factors, which are conditions that increase the likelihood of a person developing a particular disorder. For example, we know that risk factors for heart disease include such things as high blood pressure, high cholesterol levels, smoking, and a sedentary life style.

With regard to depression, a number of risk factors have also been identified.

Age

The onset of unipolar depressions usually occurs in young adults, but the highest prevalence of depression occurs in the midforties. Bipolar disorders tend to occur at a younger age, with a peak onset in the midtwenties; a third of all cases have an onset in adolescence. These disorders first appear at a younger age in women than in men. The average number of unipolar major depressions in a lifetime is four, although some individuals may have as many as 15 to 20. In the general population, bipolar episodes occur about 10 to 20% as frequently as unipolar depressions. However, for patients in whom they occur their frequency is higher, with a median lifetime frequency of about ten (Goodwin, 1985).

Sex

A great deal of research reveals that women are more likely than men to show unipolar depression. Studies reported during the past 30 years in various parts of the United States generally show that women have about twice the likelihood of unipolar depression compared to men. Similar studies in England, Scotland, and Israel report comparable findings (Nolen-Hoeksema, 1987). Efforts to explain these differences as artifacts due to variations in income, reporting biases, and types of symptoms reported fail to account for them. Biological explanations have focused on changes in women's hormonal levels and to sex-linked chromosomal effects. Studies in these areas have been inconsistent and do not provide a convincing explanation of sex differences in depression.

Nolen-Hoeksema (1987) base an explanation on the assumption that men react to their feelings of sadness and depression in a different way than do women. Men are believed to react to (or cope with) their moods by engaging in activities that tend to distract them from their moods, while women tend to be inactive and ruminate about the causes and implications of their depressed moods. Such rumination amplifies and prolongs a depressive episode, whereas distracting activity inhibits or reduces depressive moods. Active behavior increases the individual's chances for influencing the environment and obtaining positive reinforcers, and thereby decreases an existing mood state. Although some evidence supports this theory, more research is needed.

Other Demographic Factors

Various studies show that separated and divorced people have higher rates of depression than those people who are married and those who have never married. Depressive symptoms occur more frequently in lower socioeconomic classes than in those of higher classes. However, researchers report bipolar symptoms more frequently in people with higher social and educational achievements. Rates of depression in African Americans and whites do not differ, nor are there differences in depression among religious groups (Lobel and Hirschfeld, 1984).

▌Causes of Depression

The most obvious causes of depression are unpleasant and disruptive life events. These events include such things as death of a parent, spouse, or other member of one's family, loss of a job or promotion or other sign of devaluation, failure to accomplish important goals, and other personal losses such as separation or divorce. Studies show that depressed patients have had significantly more such loss experiences than other types of psychiatric patients, and that suicidal patients have significantly more loss experiences than other psychiatric patients, as well as greater degrees of depression (Plutchik, van Praag, and Conte, 1989).

Despite these findings, it is also obvious that not everyone who experiences a major loss develops a major depression. Most people are able to cope with such losses in a variety of ways, such as through finding social supports, redirecting one's energy, and improving shortcomings if they exist. The individuals who react to "bad" life events with depression are likely to be people who are *vulnerable;* such vulnerability may be related to experiences that occurred long before the bad event. Examples of vulnerability factors that seem to increase the impact of an unpleasant life event are unemployment, lack of a close relationship with a friend or partner, and childhood loss of a parent (Brown and Harris, 1978). Other vulnerability factors include a previous history of depression, suicide attempts, and poor performance at school. In addition, people who see themselves as defective, inadequate, worthless, and as failures, and who see the future as bad are more likely to react with overt depression to unpleasant life events than others. People who are quick to blame themselves when things do not go well, and who tend to evaluate events in extreme terms as good or bad also have the cognitive style of thinking that predisposes to depression (Beck, 1983).

It has gradually become evident that depressions occur in situations other than resulting from unpleasant life events. This discovery was made by accident. Many years ago, researchers discovered that patients with hypertension could be treated effectively with a drug called reserpine. In most patients it worked quite well in reducing blood pressure levels, but in about 15% of the patients a serious side effect occurred; they became severely depressed. This observation, along with others, led to an increasing volume of research on the biochemical mechanisms that underlie depression.

One hypothesis that has guided much of this research is that depression results from decreases in the availability of neurotransmitters in the brain, particularly serotonin and/or norepinephrine. Autopsy data have revealed low concentrations of serotonin and its metabolites in the brains of suicidal and/or depressed patients. These metabolites tend also to be present in lower-than-normal amounts in the cerebrospinal fluid of depressed patients. When a neurotransmitter has served its purpose, it is destroyed or rendered inactive in a variety of ways. One way is by conversion to an inactive substance called a neurotransmitter metabolite, which then appears in various fluids of the body: cerebrospinal fluid, blood, and urine, for example. Further support for the role of neurotransmitters in depression is the fact that most antidepressant drugs act by making serotonin or norepinephrine more available for neural transmission in the brain.

Depression and Physical Illness

Physicians have noticed that many illnesses are known to cause depression. For example, hypothyroidism, a disorder of low thyroid production, is frequently associated with clinical depression. Cushing's disease, a dysfunction of the adrenal glands, tends also to be associated with depression. This type of connection is also sometimes seen in individuals who have syphilis, multiple sclerosis, mononucleosis, pancreatic cancer, and ulcerative colitis. It is not always evident whether the disease causes the depression, or whether knowledge of the illness causes the depression, but sometimes these patterns are found even when the patient is unaware that he or she has any physical illness.

Physicians have also found that a number of medications tend to induce depressions in particularly sensitive individuals. As stated earlier, antihypertensive agents such as reserpine induce depression in 15% of patients. This tendency is also true of anti-Parkinson agents such as L-dopa and various hormones such as cortisol, estrogen, and progesterone. It thus appears that not only can unpleasant life events induce depression, but imbalances of neurotransmitters in the brain and changes in various hormones in the body can as well. One result of this latter fact is that depressions sometimes occur without a known or identifiable cause.

■ The Treatment of Depression

Given the heterogeneity of depressive syndromes, it is not surprising that clinicians have developed a large variety of treatment methods for the treatment of depression. Table 13.3 summarizes some of the therapeutic approaches that are being used. Since it provides a brief definition for each treatment modality, only two of the more frequently used methods will be described here in more detail.

Cognitive-Behavioral Therapy   This approach to treatment assumes that our emotions are a consequence of the ways that we think about ourselves and about the world. If for any reason we think of ourselves as insecure, dependent, helpless, and apathetic, and if we anticipate that the future will only bring more of the same, it is difficult not to be depressed. If, however, we feel competent, interested in things, and expectant of pleasant experiences in the future, it is hard to become depressed. Cognitive-behavioral therapy attempts to get the depressed person to change his or her thinking styles, to avoid unpleasant situations, to plan one's time more effectively, and to be more assertive about one's wishes. Therapists attempt to help patients decrease negative thoughts about themselves and their futures. They encourage responsibility, assertiveness, and an active lifestyle, and use homework assignments to help get patients involved in difficult tasks. Sometimes they teach social skills and new coping styles. A number of studies have revealed that these methods produce beneficial changes in depressed patients.

Psychodynamic Therapy   This treatment modality is based on Freudian psychoanalytic concepts and is widely used in private practice to treat depression as well as other conditions. This approach is based on the idea that a patient's current depression is influenced not only by a current loss, but also by certain types of early life experiences. These early life experiences may be related to a real or fantasied loss of a parent, they may be

Table 13.3	Overview of Treatment Approaches to Depression
Modality	**Definition**
Behavioral therapy	A form of psychotherapy that focuses on modifying faulty behavior rather than basic changes in the personality. Instead of probing the unconscious or exploring the patient's thoughts and feelings, behavior therapists seek to eliminate symptoms and to modify ineffective or maladaptive patterns by applying basic learning techniques and other methods. Brief treatment.
Relaxation training	Teaches techniques to help clients learn to relax, including biofeedback and guided imagery. Brief treatment.
Self-control therapy	Encourages depressed clients to attend to positive events, to set realistic self-expectations, to increase self-reinforcement and decrease self-punishment. Brief treatment.
Social skills training	Teaches clients communication and social interaction skills. Brief treatment.
Cognitive therapy	A psychotherapeutic approach based on the concept that emotional problems are the result of faulty ways of thinking and distorted attitudes toward oneself and others. The therapist takes the role of an active guide who helps the patient correct and revise perceptions and attitudes by citing evidence to the contrary or eliciting it from the patient himself or herself. The therapist uses cognitive and behavioral techniques to correct distortions of thinking associated with depression, that is, pessimism about oneself, the world, and the future. Brief treatment.
Interpersonal psychotherapy	A form of psychotherapy in which the therapist seeks to help the patient to identify and better understand interpersonal problems and conflicts and to develop more effective ways of relating to others. The therapist focuses on client's current interpersonal relationships. Helps clients learn more effective ways of relating to others and coping with conflicts in relationships. Brief, focused treatment.

(continued)

Modality	Definition
Psychodynamic psychotherapy	Any form or technique of psychotherapy that focuses on the underlying, often unconscious drives and experiences that determine behavior and adjustment. Usually long treatment.
Feminist therapy	A form of psychotherapy that views symptoms as reactions to cultural oppression rather than simply as intrapsychic phenomenon. It focuses on empowerment of the clients. Clients are helped to understand that depression stems, in part, from the cultural role of women in society. Typically open ended.
Marital and family therapy	Treatment of marital partners or parents and children. Wide range of treatment strategies, including insight-oriented and systems-oriented therapy, communication skills training, and reinforcement strategies. May be time limited or open ended.
Group therapy	Psychotherapy in a group setting. Typically led by a trained therapist. May be interpersonally oriented, behaviorally oriented, or insight oriented. Provides cohesiveness and support, sharing of feelings and experiences, feedback about interpersonal skills, and problem solving.
Support	Peer self-help and consciousness-raising groups. People provide support for each other in a setting that encourages sharing feelings and innovative problem solving. May be leader-led or leaderless. Typically open ended.
Pharmacotherapy	The use of pharmacological agents in the treatment of mental disorders in conjunction with psychotherapy.
Electroconvulsive treatment	The patient is prepared by administration of barbiturate anesthesia and injection of a chemical relaxant. An electric current is then applied for a fraction of a second through electrodes placed on the temples, which immediately produces a two stage seizure (tonic and clonic). The usual treatment is bilateral, but unilateral stimulation of a nondominant hemisphere has been introduced in order to shorten the period of memory loss that follows the treatment.

Source: E. McGrath, G. P. Keita, et al., 1990.

related to fears associated with the strong attachments children develop to one or another of their parents, and there may be constitutional or temperamental factors involved as well. Treatment requires uncovering these early fantasies and relating them to current issues in the patient's life, including his or her relationship to the therapist. This process usually takes a long time and is quite unstructured compared to the other methods. It should be emphasized that therapists often use medications in conjunction with these various psychological treatments. In a review of all 17 controlled studies of combined psychotherapy and pharmacology published between 1974 and 1984, Conte, Plutchik, Wild, and Karasu (1986) found that combined treatment produced a significantly better reduction in depression for outpatients with unipolar depression than did the placebo conditions. However, they also discovered that the combined treatment was only marginally superior to either psychotherapy alone, or pharmacotherapy alone. These effects varied depending on whether the patients had reactive or endogenous types of depression.

The Function of Sadness and Depression

From the point of view of several theories reviewed in previous chapters, emotions serve a function for the individual. What functions do sadness and depression have?

In order to infer the function of a particular emotion it is necessary to identify the events that generally trigger the emotion, and the events that generally follow the appearance of the emotion. In the case of sadness, the most common precipitating event is the loss of something important to the individual. This loss often results in characteristic facial expressions and vocalizations (such as crying or distress signals). Such distress signals typically produce a sympathetic response in adults who are exposed to them, a feeling often followed by some attempt at helpful actions. This sequence is probable and need not work exactly this way in every case. However, a helping response should occur often enough to have some long term beneficial effects on individuals who exhibit this kind of distress signal. Under these conditions, evolutionary forces will operate on the pattern of distress response to loss because it is a survival-related pattern. To summarize this point, the function of sadness signals seems to be to elicit helpful behaviors from other people. Depression may be considered to be an extreme and persistent distress signal that continually seeks to solicit help from others.

Summary ■

Two very different emotions that are quite common in everyday life are love and sadness. Both are the core of many works of literature and both have certain interesting relationships to one another. Love is frequently described in Western civilization and is a frequent theme in the Bible. Only in recent years has love been studied as an object of scientific investigation.

Current researches reveal that love can be considered as a complex state having a variety of components such as respect, attraction, and attachment. Other descriptions of love claim that it can be playful or a form of possessiveness. Attachment theory has attempted to understand love from an evolutionary point of view and has suggested that love results from an interaction of three biobehavioral systems: The attachment system, the caregiving system, and the mating system.

In contrast to love, which is associated with the experience of attachment, care-giving, and care-receiving, sadness is associated with the loss of an important attachment or bond. Sadness, or its more chronic state, depression, is also a complex condition with multiple elements and expressions. Clinicians recognize a spectrum of sadness-related conditions which vary from feeling blue, to transient grief reactions to the loss of a family member, to endogenous depressions which seem to appear from nowhere and which may last months or even years.

We know now that depression is much more likely to occur in women than men, although no generally accepted explanation has yet been found for this difference. Evidence also exists for biochemical variables that may affect the likelihood of depression, as well as genetic factors. Although psychiatrists ofter treat depression with the use of medications, psychological treatments include the use of cognitive-behavioral methods as well as psychoanalytic methods. Finally, it is evident that sadness and depression usually serve a function for the affected individual. These emotions tend to elicit helping behavior from other people.

Understanding Emotional Disorders

Life is filled with pain and suffering.
—Buddhist Principle

Goals of This Chapter

A book on emotions could not be considered complete without some discussion of what happens when our emotions do not function adequately: in other words, when an emotional disorder exists. This chapter, therefore, examines what clinicians mean when they write about emotional illness or emotional problems. In part, this means that some emotions are too extreme or persistent, or that some emotions are absent or too limited.

To illustrate these ideas, detailed descriptions are given of two emotions frequently seen as problems in clinical practice, namely fear/anxiety and anger, and its derivatives, suicide and violence. Included are descriptions of the epidemiology of anxiety disorders, the psychoanalytic and biological theories used to interpret and treat them, and a discussion of the adaptive function of fear and anxiety.

A parallel description is given of the subjective experience of anger and its correlates in the form of violence directed toward oneself or toward other people. Many variables influencing suicide risk are described as well as many of the overlapping variables influencing violence toward others.

Theories about the role of violent behavior are briefly reviewed. The chapter concludes with a discussion of the function of anger and aggression, and of methods for the control of anger and violence.

Important Questions Addressed In This Chapter

- What is meant by the term *emotional disorder?*
- What are the differences between fear and anxiety?
- What are the differences between social phobias and panic disorders?
- Do genetic factors play a role in vulnerability to anxiety?
- With the exception of medications, what is considered to be the best way to deal with phobias?
- What adaptive value does fear have?
- What are the most important variables that influence violence risk?
- How are suicide and violence toward others related?
- What adaptive functions do anger and violence have?
- By what methods can one control anger?

■   ■   ■   ■   ■   ■   ■   ■

▮ What Is an Emotional Disorder?

Defining an emotional disorder is not easy to do. Most clinicians agree that it is useful to classify mental or emotional illnesses. Such classifications can assist clinicians to make treatment decisions, and can make sure that different investigators doing research are dealing with the same conditions. Despite the evident usefulness of diagnostic categories, psychiatrists have had great difficulty deciding just how many emotional disorders there are. For example, in 1917, the classification system the American Psychiatric Association used included 59 mental illnesses. In 1952, when they made the first major revision of the diagnostic system, there were 106 illnesses. The 1987 revision of the *Diagnostic and Statistical Manual of Mental Disorders* lists 292 possible diagnoses. Are people becoming more mentally ill, or are psychiatrists making finer and finer distinctions?

Nicotine Dependence is included in the current manual, and psychiatrists are considering including *Minor Depression* in the next edition of the manual. The problem with casting such a wide net is that almost any departure from happy functioning is considered abnormal, and raises the questionable belief that experts should be called in to deal with all variations from some hypothetical norm. Therefore, instead of providing lists of emotional disorders, let us consider a few general observations and illustrations of how clinicians think about emotional disorders.

Lazarus (1991) describes psychopathology as involving three different classes of problems. One he calls *dysfunctional neuroses*, illustrated by obsessions, anxiety, phobias, and depression. A second he calls *existential problems*, characterized by vague feelings of unhappiness, boredom, and lack of meaning in life. The following case illustrates the second type of problem:

> *Illustration:* William R. visited a psychotherapist ostensibly because his marriage of 22 years was failing. He had lost interest in his wife and had started to date his secretary. His successful business seemed unimportant to him and he began to have fantasies of running off to a South Pacific island. Feeling bored and somewhat depressed, he could not see the point of spending the rest of his life in business and fantasized a different life style.

The third type of problem that Lazarus described is based on a lack of skill for handling such adaptational issues as bereavement, divorce, illness, and handicaps. An example of this type follows:

> *Illustration:* A relatively young man inherited his father's business after the father died suddenly of a heart attack. The son knew nothing about the business because he had begun training to go into one of the professions. He developed anxiety about making decisions and began to rely increasingly on his foreman, who in turn treated him like a "kid." The young man began to hate the foreman, but had to continue to rely on him because he knew the business so well. The result was great ambivalence and tension.

David Shapiro, a psychoanalyst, states that Freud's greatest achievement was the discovery of conflict between different parts of the self (1989). Patients may be caught up by *irresistible impulses* or the need to carry out a ritual against one's own will. They may have strong uncontrollable emotions that are strange to them, as the following case illustrates:

> *Illustration:* A freshman college student went to the counseling service because her "habits" were increasingly interfering with her schoolwork. She had become increasingly reluctant to touch things that other people had touched, such as door handles and coffee cups. She developed an intense desire to be clean, with the result that she took at least six or eight showers a day. If she did not follow these habits for any reason, she became very nervous and could not concentrate on her work.

Sometimes individuals experience conflicts between different emotions, such as having temper outbursts toward important persons in their lives versus the wish for close attachments; being humiliated and feeling furious with the need for revenge; wishing to be thought of as generous but recognizing one's greed or selfishness. An example of such inner conflicts is the following:

> *Illustration:* Mary was once sitting in a church and suddenly had the impulse to stand up and yell obscenities. She was shocked at her own feelings and left the church. Shortly after this event she began to fear going into a crowded place. When she went near a crowd, she would begin to feel faint and unsteady on her feet. She would become aware of her heart beating fast and she would often become nauseous. If she actually found herself in a crowd, she would develop a feeling of terror and an urge to run away.

There is one additional way in which emotions enter into our ideas about psychopathology. Almost everyone agrees that the concept of emotion applies not only to subjective feelings that human adults can describe in words. Because emotions are complex states with multiple elements, sometimes a disconnection occurs between different parts of this complex emotional chain of events. Thus, for example, it is possible to have a *free-floating anxiety* without an awareness of the source of the anxiety (that is, without an appropriate cognitive appraisal). It is possible to be depressed without knowing why one is depressed, or angry without an awareness of the source of anger. It is even possible to have the physical signs of a panic attack without any subjective feeling of fear or anxiety (Kushner and Beitman, 1990). Psychiatrists also report *masked anxiety* or *masked depression*, in which signs of anxiety or depression exist without the individual being aware of them. And *psychosomatic equivalents* are often reported in which a physical illness appears, presumably in place of, or in reaction to, strong emotions. The following is an example:

> *Illustration:* A patient was admitted to the hospital with complications of diabetes, chest pain, shortness of breath, and rapid breathing. The medical evaluation was negative, with no evidence of a heart or lung condition. The patient was referred to a psychiatrist who concluded that the patient was apparently experiencing repeated panic attacks that involved typical symptoms of panic, such as chest pains, palpitations, dizziness, cold flushes, sweating, and trembling. The patient, however, denied feeling either anxiety or depression, and insisted on a medical interpretation of his problem, that is, low blood sugar.

In summary, emotions are considered to be pathological under four conditions: when some emotions are extreme and persistent; when some emotions are absent or too limited; when strong emotions are in conflict; and when there are disconnections among such components of the emotion chain as cognitions, feeling, physiology, and behavior. It is important to emphasize that most clinicians believe that no sharp line separates normal from pathological emotional functioning (Brenner, 1982) and all the above points reflect the psychopathology of everyday life. The following sections describe two emotions most often found as aspects of emotional disorders, namely fear or anxiety and anger.

▮ Fear and Anxiety

Everyone knows what fear is. Anyone who has been in an accident or has been threatened by someone bigger or more powerful has probably felt fear. The subjective experience is unpleasant and the accompanying physiological signs such as sweating, rapid heart beat, and trembling are disturbing in themselves. Our language probably has more synonyms for the word fear than for any other emotion term. It also contains a number of expressions that seem to be related to fear.

"I feel butterflies in my stomach."
"I was scared stiff."
"My hair stood on end."

Fortunately, in the ordinary course of events, most dangerous situations that induce fear are transient, and the fear experience is brief. However, some unusual aspects of fear seem puzzling. Many people have intense fears of things—moths, insects, caterpillars, and birds, for example—that could not possibly hurt them. In the lives of most people, contacts with such creatures are rare events; yet people fear them more than such dangerous objects as electrical outlets, cars, and guns. These fears are so common that psychologists have given them special names and have compiled long lists of such phobias. Table 14.1 briefly defines 22 phobias, and the possibilities are endless.

Another puzzling thing about fear is the fact that some people experience uncontrollable panic attacks, usually without a clearly provoking incident. These panic attacks are often so severe that medication and psychiatric intervention may be necessary.

Clinicians are particularly interested in fear because they consider it to be the central ingredient of *anxiety*, a state that is believed to be the basis of neurosis and many psychiatric conditions. Depression rarely occurs without associated fear or anxiety, and anger and aggressive reactions in people are often a result of fear. Some clinicians have referred to the present time as the *Age of Anxiety*. Anxieties, in contrast to fears, tend to be more persistent, more generalized, and more a part of an individual's personality. The following illustration from the psychiatrists' *DSM III R Case Book* is associated with their manual of diagnostic concepts.

Illustration: A 27-year-old married electrician complained of dizziness, sweating palms, heart palpitations, and ringing of the ears. He had also experienced dry mouth and throat, periods of uncontrollable shaking, and a constant "edgy" and watchful feeling that had often interfered with his ability to concentrate. These feelings have been present most of the time over the previous two years; they have not been limited to discrete periods.

Because of these symptoms the patient had seen a family practitioner, a neurologist, a neurosurgeon, a chiropractor, and an ear, nose and throat specialist.

Table 14.1	Some Common Phobias
Phobia	**Fear of**
Acrophobia	High places
Agoraphobia	Open places
Algophobia	Pain
Astraphobia	Thunder and lightning
Claustrophobia	Confined places
Coprophobia	Excreta
Hematophobia	Sight of blood
Hydrophobia	Water
Lalophobia	Speaking
Mysophobia	Dirt or contamination
Necrophobia	Dead bodies
Nyctophobia	Darkness, night
Pathophobia	Disease, suffering
Peccatophobia	Sinning
Phonophobia	Speaking aloud
Photophobia	Bright lights
Sitophobia	Eating
Taphophobia	Being buried alive
Thanatophobia	Death
Toxophobia	Being poisoned
Xenophobia	Strangers
Zoophobia	Animals

He had been placed on a hypoglycemic diet, received physiotherapy for a pinched nerve, and told he might have "an inner ear problem."

He also had many worries. He constantly worried about the health of his parents. His father, in fact, had had a myocardial infarction two years previously, but was now feeling well. [The patient] also worried about whether he was "a good father," whether his wife would ever leave him (there was no indication that she was dissatisfied with the marriage), and whether he was liked by coworkers on the job.

For the past two years the patient has had few social contacts because of his nervous symptoms. Although he has sometimes had to leave work when the symptoms became intolerable, he continues to work for the same company he joined for his apprenticeship following high school graduation. He tends to hide his symptoms from his wife and children, to whom he wants to appear "perfect," and reports few problems with them as a result of his nervousness (*DSM III R Casebook,* 1987, p. 262).

Clinical Descriptions of Anxiety Disorders

Because of the theoretical and practical importance of anxiety to clinicians, clinicians have attempted to identify the many different faces of anxiety disorders with the hope that such distinctions may be of value in deciding on appropriate treatments. For example, in the 1987 *Diagnostic and Statistical Manual,* psychiatrists identify the following types of anxiety disorders: panic disorders, social phobia, simple phobia, obsessive-compulsive disorder, posttraumatic stress disorder, and generalized anxiety disorder.

Sheehan (1983) has proposed another schema for describing anxiety disorders. In his model, there are basically two kinds of anxiety states, reactive or exogenous anxiety, and endogenous anxiety. Panic states are the most obvious example of endogenous anxiety, while fear of dogs, for example, is more likely to be of a reactive type. Clinicians have identified a number of differences between these two types of anxiety, which will be described shortly .

Let us consider in some detail two anxiety disorders, social phobia and panic disorder. The social phobic has an unusually strong fear of other people's scutiny or evaluation. The fear of embarrassment or humiliation is overwhelming and leads the individual greatly to restrict his or her interactions with others. Sometimes the fear is limited to such things as being unable to speak in a group, or to urinate in a public lavatory, or write in front of people without trembling. In other cases the fear may be general and involve many of the above signs in the same person.

When the phobic person is faced with the need to enter into the feared situation, strong anticipatory anxiety occurs. If the individual forces him- or herself to enter the phobic situation, he or she usually experiences intense anxiety. Typically, most such individuals go to great lengths to avoid the situation that creates such unpleasant feelings.

Social phobias usually begin in late childhood or early adolescence. The disorder is often chronic, and appears more frequently in males than females. Because the phobic recognizes that his or her fear is unreasonable and sometimes tries to cope with the problem by means of alcohol or drugs, the danger of substance abuse is great.

Panic Disorder

The most dramatic expressions of anxiety disorders are panic attacks. These experiences usually occur spontaneously without an obvious cause, although sometimes the sense of being trapped in an elevator, an airplane, or a tunnel triggers them. The central feature of a panic attack is an overwhelming feeling of terror. In addition, many physical sensations occur such as chest pains and dizziness, as well as certain characteristic thoughts such as fear of dying or going crazy. An illustration follows:

> *Illustration:* Marie had been dating Adam for about six months. She had always felt nervous in restaurants so when Adam invited her to a good restaurant for her birthday she was upset but, in order not to disappoint him, decided to go. As they entered the restaurant she had the urge to turn and run. She sat down with her back to the window. As she faced the crowded room she felt out of control. Her breathing was too fast. Everything around her was becoming strange and unreal. She ordered a double scotch straight in the hope that the drink would relieve her anxiety. All of a sudden her heart started beating faster. She could feel the pounding in her chest; then a flushing sensation in her face. Her throat tightened and Marie felt that she was going to choke. Beads of sweat broke out on her forehead; a rushing sensation rose from her stomach up through her chest, then came a sinking sensation in the bottom of her stomach. She felt dizzy, lightheaded, and panicky. As she stood up her hands were shaking and her legs felt like rubber. She staggered to the ladies' room. Gradually the symptoms diminished (Sheehan, 1983).

Epidemiology of Anxiety Disorders

Several studies in Europe and the United States have tried to determine the prevalence of various types of anxiety disorders. When researchers compared three cities in the United States with cities in Switzerland, Germany, and Korea, they found the prevalence of panic disorders over a six-month period to vary over the small range of 0.6% to 1.5%, or approximately 1 person in 100 (Humble, 1987). The prevalence of agoraphobia in these cities was somewhat higher, with 3 to 6 persons in 100 reporting this problem. In all these investigations, women had a higher prevalence of anxiety disorders than did men, ranging from one and one-half to four times higher. In a comparison of two American and three European cities, the likelihood that a person would experience any type of anxiety disorder during a lifetime was between 10 and 20%. Here again, women had about twice the lifetime prevalence as compared to men.

Family studies have raised the possibility of genetic factors in anxiety. In one such study, researchers compared the first degree relatives (that is, father, mother, siblings and children) of 41 patients with panic disorders with the first degree relatives of 41 normal control subjects. It was found that the patients' relatives had a lifetime risk of panic disorders of 24.7%, while relatives of controls had a lifetime risk of 2.3%. Of great interest is the fact that the risk of generalized anxiety disorder was about the same in the relatives of both groups (Crowe, Noyes, Pauls, et al., 1983). This observation suggests that panic disorder may have a different etiology and course than do other forms of anxiety disorder. It is also noteworthy that alcoholism is twice as common in families of panic patients than in families of the controls (Harris, Noyes, Crowe, et al., 1983). This finding is consistent with the belief that alcohol is a common self-prescribed remedy for symptoms of anxiety.

In order to evaluate further genetic factors in anxiety and depression, researchers in Australia carried out a twin study involving 3,798 pairs of identical and fraternal twins. They asked each twin about current symptoms of anxiety and depression, including such things as insomnia, loss of interest, and feelings of panic. Using a mathematical model, the researchers estimated the relative importance of genetic and environmental factors with regard to each symptom. They found that genetic factors accounted for 34 to 46% of the causes, with specific life events accounting for the rest. These findings were interpreted as implying that genetic factors have a large effect in determining vulnerability to anxiety, and that traumatic life events trigger specific anxiety symptoms (Kendler, Heath, Martin, and Eaves, 1986).

When one considers the onset and cause of anxiety disorders, the findings are different for the subtypes of anxiety. Social phobias tend to appear first in childhood or adolescence and very rarely thereafter. The onset of panic disorders and agoraphobias tends to occur in late adolescence or early adulthood, with an average age of onset of about 26 years (Humble, 1987).

▌Theories of Anxiety

Psychoanalytic Theories

Freud based his first major theory of anxiety on the assumption that pathological anxiety represents a failure of repression. The individual represses normally painful or unacceptable sexual thoughts, but when the intensity of these thoughts increases or illness or other life experiences reduce the capacity to repress them, the signs and symptoms typical of sexual feelings break into consciousness. Along with anxiety are such symptoms as palpitations, dizziness, and difficulty in breathing.

Later, Freud introduced another theory, which psychoanalysts still accept today. Anxiety is seen as a signal to the ego that a dangerous situation has developed. Danger can result from concious or unconscious threats of injury or loss, forbidden wishes, and painful emotions. Further, agoraphobia is interpreted as an avoidance reaction to an unconscious conflict.

Biological Theories

Klein (1981) has pointed out that there seems to be two kinds of anxiety. One is a feeling of panic that occurs at unpredictable times. The second is called anticipatory anxiety which is a fear that the panic attack will recur. One reason for the distinction is that anticipatory anxiety may be temporarily reduced by sedatives that have little or no effect on panic attacks. At the same time, antidepressant medications seem to be able to block panic attacks but have no effect on anticipatory anxiety.

Klein proposed that the development of panic disorder and agoraphobia was linked to disturbed separation experiences in children. His studies found that about one-third to one-half of all adult patients with panic disorder or agoraphobia had histories of intense separation anxiety as children. Many of them exhibited school refusal, or developed nausea and stomachaches when expected to go to school. If they could be induced to go to school they suffered from worries that some disaster would occur to their parents or that their home is burning down. Many such children can be successfully treated with the same medications that reduce panic attacks in adults.

Endogenous and Exogenous Anxiety

The theory developed by David Sheehan, a psychiatrist, is based on the idea that there are two kinds of anxiety, exogenous and endogenous. The first type is simply a reaction to danger, and is typically provoked by a particular situation or incident. Endogenous anxiety appears to arise from within one's own body, and is what is usually called a panic attack. According to Sheehan (1983), anxiety as a disease usually starts with a group of symptoms that occur suddenly, spontaneously, without warning, and for no apparent reason. Initially these symptoms may occur without mental anxiety. The individual may feel as if some part of the body has briefly lost control of itself.

In this early stage of the anxiety disease, the individual may feel lightheaded, dizzy, and unbalanced; he or she may have difficulty breathing, palpitations, chest pain, choking feelings, tingling or numbness in some part of the body, hot flashes, nausea, diarrhea, headaches, and a feeling of being outside of or detached from one's own body. At some point, the individual enters the second stage of the illness, which consists of subjective feelings of panic and terror that occur, apparently at random, "out of the blue." Because of the great variety of symptoms that occur, diagnosis is sometimes difficult, and the patient often develops hypochondriacal attitudes about his or her own body. If the panic attacks persist, most patients develop one or more phobias depending on where the person happens to be when the panic attacks occur. (This does not imply that all phobias in the general population develop this way.)

One of the most common phobias to develop is social phobia, the fear of social situations such as eating, drinking, or writing in public, being watched, or being the focus of attention. As the phobias become extreme, they may take the form of agoraphobia, a fear of public places, crowds, cars, tunnels, and highways. Anticipatory anxiety develops as the individual begins to feel frightened in anticipation of a panic attack. And finally, as the individual finds it difficult to cope with the ordinary events of everyday life, as well as normal family responsibilities, he or she becomes pessimistic and depressed. The depression may include strong feelings of guilt, as well as suicidal thoughts.

In summary, Sheehan's theory tries to account for the varied symptoms of anxiety as a disease as well as the natural progression of the disorder. It implies that there is a biological abnormality (possibly a dysfunction of the locus ceruleus), a process of psychological conditioning, and a role for life stresses. Environmental stress can make any disease worse.

The Treatment of Anxiety

Therapists who have a behavioral orientation toward psychotherapy generally believe that they can effectively treat ordinary fears and phobias by systematic desensitization. This procedure requires the client to learn to relax the muscles at will, and to then confront the feared object or situation in graded steps in imagination. Sometimes the graded exposure to the feared object is carried out in vivo, that is, in an actual series of graded encounters. Researchers have reported this procedure to be more effective than desensitization performed in imagination (Janssen and Ost, 1982). Further research has apparently shown that gradual desensitization is not needed. Any therapy seems to work that encourages the client to confront the phobic situation (Klein, Zitrin, Woerner, et al., 1983).

In recent years, therapists have found a number of medications to be useful in the treatment of panic attacks and agoraphobia. Most effective in blocking panic attacks are the tricyclic antidepressants. When the attacks have been eliminated, levels of anticipatory anxiety usually decrease. Some research has demonstrated that behavioral desensitization treatment is more effective if the client is simultaneously receiving an antipanic medication (Zitrin, Klein, Woerner, et al., 1983).

▌The Function of Fear and Anxiety

A number of years ago, English ethologist Desmond Morris (1967) asked children viewing a zoo program on television which animal they liked most and which they disliked most. Of the 12,000 replies that Morris analyzed, Table 14.2 summarizes the top 10 likes and dislikes.

Table 14.2		Animals Liked Most and Disliked Most by 12,000 British Children Aged 4 to14	
Animals Liked Most	**Percent**	**Animals Disliked Most**	**Percent**
Chimpanzee	13.5	Snake	27.0
Monkey	13.0	Spider	9.5
Horse	9.0	Crocodile	4.5
Bush baby	8.0	Lion	4.5
Panda	7.5	Rat	4.0
Bear	7.0	Skunk	3.0
Elephant	6.0	Gorilla	3.0
Lion	5.0	Rhinoceros	3.0
Dog	4.0	Hippopotamus	2.5
Giraffe	2.5	Tiger	2.5

Source: D. Morris, 1967.

The characteristics of the most-liked animals is that they all have hair, rather than feathers or scales; most have flat faces, facial expressions, the capacity to manipulate small objects, and a more-or-less vertical posture. Morris suggests a law of animal appeal: "The popularity of an animal is directly correlated with the number of anthropomorphic features it possesses."

The animals the children disliked most shared one important feature: they are dangerous to humans. When one examines the reasons they gave for disliking snakes and spiders, the two highest ranked responses focus on "slimy and dirty" and "hairy and creepy." Morris proposes that this response implies either that snakes and spiders have a strong symbolic significance, or that humans have a powerful inborn response to avoid these animals. Consistent with this second idea is the fact that both monkeys and chimpanzees appear to have a strong aversion to snakes. This aversion is true even in young animals who have had little opportunity to learn how dangerous snakes can be (Seyforth, Cheney, and Marler, 1980a; 1980b,).

From an evolutionary point of view, the development of phobias (avoidance reactions) to dangerous animals has obvious survival value. The fact that some individuals have a lower threshold of reaction is consistent with the likelihood of a normal distribution of sensitivity thresholds to danger. Humble (1987) suggests the possibility that some individuals with an unusual sensitivity to anxiety reactions may be of value to the community threatened by vague or hidden dangers (such as predators lying in wait), despite the distress it may cause these individuals. It is also likely that brain mechanisms evolved to handle dangerous emergency situations as rapidly as possible, and that the existence of panic disorders reflects a dysfunction in this brain system.

It is probable that at least two different fear mechanisms have evolved to deal with threats to survival. One mechanism is to organize the body for flight and to focus all attention on this one goal. The second way the primitive brain system protects the individual from danger is to shut off briefly consciousness, inhibit reflex action, and cause fainting. This passive reaction to danger is likely when running away is impossible, but passivity may also decrease the chances of discovery and attack, and thus have some survival value (Smith, 1977).

Trower and Gilbert (1989) have suggested another way of looking at the function of fear and anxiety. Most mammals and especially primates live in social groups that are organized and stabilized by means of dominance hierarchies. That each individual enacts a role that defines his or her position within the hierarchy maintains cohesiveness of the group. If someone else of higher dominance status threatens another group member, escape from the group is rarely possible if the individual is to survive without the group's support. The result is usually some form of submissive ritual or gesture that allows the threatened individual to remain in the group. Thus, researchers assume that social anxiety evolved as a method for maintaining group cohesion. According to this theory, the socially anxious person has an appraisal and coping style that focuses on threats and loss of status in a hostile and competitive world. One way to change this pattern is to try to establish friendship networks. Another is to attempt to modify the perception of the world as dangerous. A third is to increase one's ability to negotiate within dominance hierarchies.

▎Anger and Violence

Anger is an emotion that almost everyone feels at one time or another. A wide variety of incidents can provoke it, from waiting in a long line, to hearing someone advocating abortion rights (or its opposite), to having your property stolen or your body violated. Anger generates an impulse to retaliate, attack, or injure the source of the provocation. People do not always act on such impulses, and when most people try to assess the possible results of retaliation, it may (or may not) inhibit the action. Thus, researchers consider anger to be an inner feeling that people do not necessarily express in overt behavior.

Although we usually think of a specific event triggering anger, we also recognize that individuals can sometimes appear to be angry or irritable most of the time, regardless of the situations in which they find themselves. In such cases, we think of the individual as exhibiting a personality trait or as having a disposition based on anger. We give a variety of names to such traits: hostile, irritable, spiteful, aggressive, quarrelsome, cantankerous, and sarcastic; but all have the common element of implied anger or attack.

In a questionnaire study dealing with the antecedents of emotions, Wallbott and Scherer (1989) obtained data from 779 subjects in eight countries. They found that the most common antecedents of anger were problems with relationships, interactions with strangers, injustice, and inconveniences. An extension of this same questionnaire study based on 2,235 subjects in 27 countries also revealed the types of symptoms that tended to be associated with anger. In order of frequency of report, these symptoms were a faster heartbeat; muscles tensing; change in facial expression; change in breathing; feeling hot; changes in voice; speech tempo change; lengthy utterance; and moving against someone.

Blanchard and Blanchard (1984) carried out another survey in Hawaii with several thousand college students, finding that a small number of situations seem to trigger angry reactions. Apparently anger occurs when individuals perceive a challenge to something they regard as symbolically or actually belonging to them or to a group with which they identify. A loss of status, dominance, or authority also generates anger. Property damage and injury are also likely to elicit anger, at least to some degree. Blanchard and Blanchard interpret these findings as indicating that conflicts between individuals over dominance relations and conflict over control of important resources such as food and sex are most likely to initiate anger.

The specific ways that humans express angry feelings may take indirect forms such as playing aggressive sports like football or tennis, challenging opponents to games of chess or backgammon, criticizing friends and enemies alike, and doing difficult tasks such as rock climbing and parachute jumping.

It is thus evident that anger in its various expressions enters into almost every aspect of life. In extreme form, it creates major problems both for the individual and for society. When other persons are the object of the anger, we speak of violence that needs to be controlled. Parents are the initial agents of control for all children, but if the expressions of violence became too strong in adolescents or adults, the legal institutions of society may become involved in a punitive way. If, however, the object of the violence is oneself, we describe this as suicide or a suicide attempt, and the mental health profession is likely to be called on.

Psychoanalysts have often pointed out that suicide attempts and violence toward other people are two sides of the same coin, consistent with many clinical observations. For example, about 30% of violent individuals have a history of self-destructive behavior, and about 20% of suicidal persons have a history of violent behavior (Bach-Y-Rita and Veno, 1974; Skodal and Karasu, 1978; Tardiff and Sweillam, 1982; Tardiff and Konigsberg, 1985). (In the following pages the word *violent* refers to overt acts committed against other people with intent to harm or kill.) Social statistics indicate that both suicide and violence are prevalent in America, and have been increasing in frequency over the years. For example, in a recent 10-year period, the American population increased by 3% while crimes of violence increased by 130% (Johnson, 1972). Suicides in adolescents over a recent decade have increased from about 12 deaths per 100,000 population to about 20 deaths per 100,000 people (Hendin, 1986).

An overview follows of some factors that contribute to violent behavior in individuals. First will be a review of studies on variables that contribute to the risk of suicide. Following this section is a review of factors that contribute to the risk of violent behavior directed toward other people.

Suicide as an Expression of Anger Directed at Oneself

Sometimes suicide expresses anger at oneself, as the following example illustrates:

Illustration: Steve is a 17-year-old senior in high school. Although he has been evaluated as having above average intelligence, his work this year has been very poor and he is failing in several subjects. His parents were divorced when he was quite young. His older sister bosses him around producing much resentment and occasional angry fantasies about killing her. One day after an argument with his sister he punched the wall. This made his mother lose her temper and throw a soda can at him. Steve ran out of the house and wandered the streets for hours. That night he could not sleep. In the morning he left a note saying "I can't stand it anymore" and went to school. When he got to his classroom, he climbed out onto the fourth floor ledge and threatened to jump. He was gradually coaxed back into the room and sent to a local emergency room for evaluation.

Illustration: Marnie is an 18-year-old college freshman at a large university 400 miles from her home. The first month or two was exciting but then she began to feel increasingly lonely. She was not comfortable with her roommates, and felt dominated by them. When each of her roommates found boyfriends, she felt even more depressed. Although she had been a good student in high school, she didn't seem to be doing well at college. She was ashamed to tell her parents about her sad feelings and her loneliness.

Table 14.3	Death Rates by Suicide in the United States in 1982
	Rates per 100,000/yr.
White Males	19.4
Black Males	10.8
White Females	5.8
Black Females	2.2
Nevada (Highest State)	29.0
Connecticut (Lowest State)	7.7
Age 20–24 Years	16.0
Age 40–44 Years	17.5
Age 60–64 Years	25.5

Source: R. Plutchik & H. M. van Praag, 1990.

Marnie found that she felt better after drinking a lot of beer and she began to spend more of her time in the local pubs. One night she met a male student at the bar who offered to drive her home. He stopped at a deserted place and cajoled her into having sex with him. When he did not call or see her again she became increasingly depressed and one night ingested about 20 aspirin tablets. Her roommates discovered her in a groggy condition and got her to the nearest hospital in time to have her stomach pumped.

Interestingly, the demographics of suicide show a great diversity of rates, Table 14.3 illustrates. White people in America commit suicide about two to three times more frequently than African Americans; and males commit suicide three to four times more frequently than females. Suicide rates tend to increase with age, and they vary greatly with area. In Connecticut, for example, the rate is approximately 7.7 deaths per 100,000 while in Nevada the rate is 29 per 100,000 (Pokorny, 1983). In Finland the rate is 40 per 100,000 and in Hungary it is 55 per 100,000. At one time, investigators believed there was a simple inverse relation between suicide and violence so that countries high in suicide were likely to be low in homicide. This theory is not true; in countries like Ireland and Norway, both the suicide and homicide rates are low, and in countries like the United States, both the suicide and homicide rates are quite high.

Table 14.4	Incidence of Suicide by Diagnostic Category*
Diagnosis	**Suicide Rate per 100,000/yr.**
Affective Disorder	695
Schizophrenia	456
Drug Abuse	194
Alcoholism	187
Personality Disorder	187
Neurosis	150
Organic Brain Syndrome	71
All Veterans	23
U.S. as a Whole	12

*Based on a 5-year follow-up of 4,800 veterans
Source: A. Pokorny, 1983.

Suicidal thoughts are also common. In a survey of 694 college freshmen, 44% of the males and 62% of the females had thought of taking their own lives; 4.7% of the males and 15.2% of the females had actually made suicide attempts (Meehan, Lamb, et al., 1992).

In addition to broad sociological variables such as race, age, and culture are individual or personal variables that researchers have identified. Psychologists generally accept that depression is a risk factor for suicide, as are various other psychiatric diagnoses. Table 14.4 shows the suicide rates for a large group of 4,800 male veterans followed prospectively for five years. Patients with affective disorders had 32 times the likelihood of committing suicide compared to veterans in general. Patients diagnosed as schizophrenic had 20 times the likelihood of suicide of veterans in general. In fact, patients with any psychiatric diagnosis at all had from 3 to 32 times greater probability of suicide than veterans as a whole. It is thus evident from this prospective study following large numbers of patients that any psychiatric diagnosis indicates an increased risk for suicide.

Two recent studies give some idea of what variables might determine the probability of suicide. Motto, Heilbron, and Juster (1985) evaluated

Table 14.5	Major Risk Factors for Suicide*

1. A family history of depression, alcoholism or other emotional disorders

2. An active bisexual, or an inactive homosexual life-style

3. Severe impairment in physical health in the past year

4. Previous psychiatric hospital admissions

5. Previous efforts to obtain help have been unsuccessful

6. Severe special stress (other than health or job)

7. Presence of suicidal impulses

8. Presence of ideas of persecution or reference

9. Sleeps too much

10. Has made a recent suicide attempt

*Based on a 2-year follow-up of 2,753 depressed or suicidal patients
Source: J. A. Motto, D. C. Heilbron, and R. D. Juster, 1985.

2,753 patients who had been hospitalized for depression and/or suicidal state. In a two-year follow-up, approximately 5% of the group had committed suicide. Table 14.5 shows major variables that were correlated with the likelihood of a suicide. They include a family history of alcoholism, depression and other psychiatric illnesses, severe impairment in physical health, special stresses, ideas of reference, and suicidal impulses.

In a review of 15 rating scales used for the estimation of suicide risk, Burk, Kurz, and Moller (1985) identified nine general categories of variables as predictors. The most important ones are evidence of emotional illness, previous suicidal behavior, antisocial behavior, social isolation, and a recent loss. All these characteristics clearly relate to the presence of certain emotions.

Despite the fact that many risk factors for suicide are known, it is extremely difficult to make accurate predictions about any particular individual. The most important reason for this is that suicide is rare, and rare events are inherently difficult to predict. To state this idea another way, prediction of rare events generally produces many false positives. For example, let us assume that suicide occurs to one person in 10,000 and we have a predictive test that is 99% accurate. If we test 10,000 people, we might still miss the one person who is going to commit suicide, but we will falsely identify as suicide risks approximately 100 people who are in fact not likely to commit suicide (i.e., 1% of 10,000 people = 100).

Violence as an Expression of Anger Directed at Others

The following illustration indicates that anger may not only be a transient reaction to a frustrating situation, but may be a chronic condition somewhat like a personality trait:

Illustration: George was examined at 3 1/2 years of age and had an episode of uncontrolled rage. When the doctor tried to get near him he screamed and held his breath. In his early years in school George was unusually destructive and violent. He gradually gave up holding his breath when he got irritated, but he was easily angered and provoked. When he was 8 he was observed to take some baby birds from a nest and torture them. In his preadolescent years his outbursts of temper continued and he was highly resistant to being interviewed by adults. At 12 he was very rough when playing with other boys but was rebellious and openly resentful toward adults. In his 20s he remained easily angered and frustrated, and often verbally attacked his wife, child, and strangers. He felt that being tough and aggressive was the only way to get anywhere in the world (Johnson, 1972).

An early study of violence (Climent et al., 1973) examined medical and psychiatric correlates of violent behaviors in 95 women prisoners in a Massachusetts prison. Climent and colleagues used a number of different ways of measuring violence in these women, including a self-rating of how frequently the individual showed certain types of violent behaviors. The study also included a rating a correctional officer made, based on observed behavior in the prison, and an estimate of the degree of violence involved in the crimes for which the women had been incarcerated. Based on these indices, some prisoners were defined as violent and others as not-violent.

When investigators compared the violent and not-violent women prisoners on all variables, they found that 12 variables significantly discriminated between the two groups, as Table 14.6 shows. The overall picture that emerges is that violent inmates were higher on loss of parents at an early age, on medical and neurological problems in their immediate families, and on easy access to weapons. They also tended to have made more suicide attempts, and to have had more menstrual problems (Climent et al., 1974).

In an extension of this type of study, researchers gave a battery of tests to 11 different groups (a total of 309 individuals) that included self-referred violent persons, male and female prisoners, psychiatric outpatients, college students, neurology patients, and epileptics. The self-referred violent patients scored highest on a scale designed to measure violent behavior. They were significantly higher than all other groups except the prisoners.

Table 14.6	Variables Significantly Correlated with Violence

Violent Prisoners Are Higher On:

1. Mean number of neurological disorders in the family

2. Mean number of medical disorders in the family

3. Number of episodic dyscontrol symptoms

4. Self-reported homosexuality

5. Percent who suffered loss* of mother before age 10

6. Percent who reported severe punishment from their parents

7. Percent who reported easy access to weapons

8. Percent who reported a suicide attempt in the past

9. Percent who reported menstrual problems

Violent Prisoners Are Lower On:

1. Mean age at loss* of father (approximately 10 vs. 16 years)

2. Mean age at loss* of mother (approximately 9 vs. 20 years)

3. Mean number of miscarriages

4. Number of symptoms of neurotic depression

5. Percent who reported having had outpatient psychiatric care

*Loss defined as any permanent separation of child from parent due to death, desertion, or separation.
Source: R. Plutchik, C. Climent, and F. Ervin, 1976.

The male and female prisoners also scored high on the violence scale. College students fell near the middle of the distribution of groups, and the temporal lobe epileptics' scores were toward the low end of the scale.

In every group, the violence measure and other variables showed high correlations between a history of family violence (frequent spankings, fights, and observation of parental quarrels and fights) and the extent of violence in the subjects. Other highly significant correlations with violence were the total number of life problems, signs of schizoid thinking, and intense sex drive.

The Interaction of Suicide and Violence

Newspapers periodically remind us of the close connection between violence and suicide. Headlines frequently tell us of people who commit murder and then commit suicide. The Guyana incident with Jim Jones is one well-known example, and a more recent one occurred in Oklahoma where a postman shot 14 co-workers and then killed himself.

A few reports have looked at the statistics of homicide followed by suicide. The classic study by West (1966) examined data in England and Wales for the period from 1954–1961. He reported that the murder-suicide rate was 33%. In contrast, it was 42% in Denmark, 22% in Australia, 4% in Philadelphia, 2% in Los Angeles (Allen, 1983), and 1 to 2% in North Carolina (Dalmer and Humphrey, 1980). The Los Angeles study found that in the majority of the homicide-suicide cases, the reason for the murder seemed to be an unbalanced, quarrelsome love relationship between husband and wife, or lovers. The following newspaper account is an example:

Illustration: Man shoots ex-lover, kills her fiancé. Former suitor commits suicide after shooting 3. Monticello—A groom-to-be was slain early yesterday—his wedding day—and his fiancée and brother were both shot by a spurned lover in the house where the couple were to be married, authorities said. The assailant later shot himself to death, police said. Manuel Saldana, 36, was to marry Emily Rodriguez at Saldana's home in a working-class neighborhood in Monticello, about 75 miles northwest of New York City. But Saldana was shot to death outside his raised-ranch house about 3 a.m. after arguing with Rodriguez's ex-boyfriend Eusbio Torres. Rodriguez told police that Torres, 34, entered Saldana's yard and triggered an alarm light. Saldana and his 34-year-old brother, Jose, went outside to talk to Torres, who was distraught over the upcoming marriage. Torres shot the brothers with a .22 caliber rifle, killing Manuel Saldana and wounding Jose Saldana in the shoulder and back, police said. Torres then shot Rodriguez twice through a storm door before fleeing into woods behind the house. Torres committed suicide soon after the shootings. Police found Torres' body about 4 a.m. in his apartment off the village's main street. Torres had been arrested in an assault on an ex-wife about three years ago (New Rochelle, New York, *Standard Star*, April 19, 1992).

Other evidence of a connection between violence and suicide comes from the literature on the effects of crowding in prisons (Cox, Paulus, and McCain,1984). A major review indicates that population increases in prisons are associated with increased rates of suicide, disciplinary infractions (violence), psychiatric commitment, and death. Decreases in prison populations are associated with decreases in assaults, suicide attempts, and death rates. The authors of this review suggest that the underlying reasons for these effects of crowding are the increases in uncertainty, goal interference, and cognitive load.

In the early part of this century, "epidemics of insanity" were reported among rubber and rayon workers accidentally poisoned by carbon disulfide. These workers showed symptoms of depression, extreme irritability, uncontrolled anger, and acute mania, and there were many cases of attempted suicide as well as homicide.

A Theoretical Model of Suicidality and Violence

The old psychoanalytic idea that suicide is violence turned inward has some validity, but it does not help us understand why some violent people are suicidal and others are not. In order to answer this question, one must consider aggression from a broad social and biological viewpoint.

Ethologists have pointed out that aggressive behavior serves to increase the probability of access to resources, helps deal with conflict among individuals, and increases the chances of successful courtship and mating. In addition, neurophysiological research over many decades has established the existence of brain structures that organize patterns of aggressive behavior (e.g., lateral hypothalamus, ventral tegmental areas, midbrain central gray area, and the central and anterior portions of the septum). Recent research has also shown that various neurotransmitter systems are involved in the expression of aggression. For example, animals fed a tryptophan-free diet became increasingly aggressive, implying that low serotonin levels are associated with a risk of violent behavior (Gibbons, Barr et al., 1979).

Finally, the recent literature on behavioral genetics has revealed that many, if not most, emotional characteristics are heritable. Studies show that aggressivity is heritable in mice and dogs (Fuller, 1986), and human studies of personality and temperament also indicate significant genetic components in assertiveness, extraversion, and dominance (Loehlin, Horn, and Willerman, 1981; Loehlin and Nichols, 1976; Wimer and Wimer, 1985).

A recent review of the literature on predation within species (i.e., cannibalism) has demonstrated that the killing and eating of an individual of one's own species is widespread. Researchers have observed it in about 1,300 species, including humans (Polis, 1981), and it appears to have a strong genetic component, although the availability of food supplies can affect its frequency. In some species, cannibalism has a major influence on population size. It has been observed in at least 14 species of carnivorous mammals: lion, tiger, leopard, cougar, lynx, spotted hyena, golden jackal, wolf, coyote, dingo, red fox, arctic fox, brown bear, and grasshopper mouse. In most such cases, adults prey on immature animals and cubs. Schankman (1969) also reports cannibalism in 60 human cultures.

This brief overview suggests that aggressive behavior has fundamental importance for survival and for regulation of populations in humans and lower animals. The evidence clearly indicates that neurological structures and biochemical processes are intimately connected with aggressive behavior, and that there are genetic contributions to the individual differences one sees in aggressive traits.

Ethological research further indicates what classes of events tend to trigger aggressive impulses. Generally speaking, threats, challenges, changes in hierarchical status, and various losses tend to increase aggressive impulses (Blanchard and Blanchard, 1984). However, we need to distinguish between aggressive impulses and aggressive behavior (or violence). Whether or not an individual expresses the aggressive impulse in the form of overt action, such as violent behavior, depends on the presence of a large number of forces, some of which act as amplifiers of the aggressive impulse and others act to attenuate the impulse. Examples of amplifiers are extensive school problems in the history of the individual, a history of assaultive acts, pervasive feelings of distrust, easy access to weapons, and a tolerant attitude toward the expression of violence. Examples of attenuators are a timid personality style, close family ties, and social support. These variables interact in complex ways and determine the probability that an individual will express the aggressive impulse in overt violent behavior.

▍The Function of Anger and Aggression

It is evident that experiences of anger are commonplace and expressions of aggression widespread. Why is this true? What functions do anger and aggression have in human life?

The literature dealing with aggression is vast. It deals with aggression in both animals and humans and covers the range from reef fish fighting over territories to human societies battling one another over ideologies and plunder. Controversies abound over the question of how best to interpret the diversity of observations concerning aggression.

Psychoanalysts have had much to say about aggression. Freud (1922) suggested that aggression is the oldest impulse of all and can be seen even in primitive organisms. Jackson (1954), another psychoanalyst, writes that "its source appears to be the emotion of anger, and its aim the destruction of the object which arouses this emotion." Sullivan (1956) points out that "anger is one of the ways of handling anxiety that we learn early. . . . Its purpose presumably is not to enable us to escape threatening or injurious situations, but to destroy them or drive them away." Anger is most likely to occur in connection with situations that contain barriers to reaching goals.

Psychoanalysts assume that both sex and aggression express biological drives. Freud theorized that individuals could express inhibited sexual impulses either in anxiety or aggression.

Ethologists and other biologists have also written extensively about aggression. For example, Cannon (1929) wrote:

> The rage response (crouching body, frowning brow, firm lips, clenched or grinding teeth, growled threats, tightened fists, etc.) is a complex attitude which we do not have to learn—its occurrence is a part of our native inheritance. It is a constant and uniform type of behavior, having features in common in widely scattered races of men and even in lower animals so that the nature of the attitude is at once understood without the necessity for words. It is a permanent mode of reaction; whether in childhood or old age, it differs only in minor details. . . . Any hampering or checking of activity, or opposition to one or another primary impulse brings it out. . . .These are the properties of a simple reflex, such as sneezing or coughing.

Scott (1980) has described aggression as one of nine basic adaptations that almost all organisms make. Aggression is one aspect of agonistic behavior; the other aspect is flight or avoidance.

Despite the fact that these patterns are widely distributed, the intensity of expression of each pattern may vary greatly both within and between species. We readily see this variance through the efforts of countless generations to domesticate wild animals. For example, Siamese fighting fish and Paradise fish belong to the same family, and in the wild both types are known for their aggressiveness. However, unlike the Siamese fighting fish, the Paradise fish have been bred for docility so they can be kept together and sold commercially to fish hobbyists.

Similarly, the brown Norway rat appeared in the United States about the time of the American Revolution, and was recognized as a fierce animal with high readiness to attack other animals or humans. As biologists and psychologists became interested in using these animals for research, animal suppliers began to develop new strains that would be domesticated, timid, and easy to handle. This inbreeding was successful within 8 to 10 generations. Researchers have shown that 70% of wild rats will attack and kill mice, while only about 12% of domesticated rats will do the same (Karli, 1956).

One sees this same process in domestic chickens. Most are bred for passivity and productivity, but a small group of roosters were bred for fighting ability. These specially bred roosters are so aggressive they will fight to the death in cockfights that are still prevalent in parts of the United States and many other countries.

Similarly, just as dogs were bred for herding of animals, for pointing at prey, for work, or for cuteness and cuddliness, others were selected in the past for their ability to fight. This trait is true of all the terriers, which are relatively insensitive to pain, with tough skin on their necks and shoulders, and strong jaws and teeth. In the fox hunts of England, beagles would be used in packs to locate a fox until the fox ran into a hollow tree trunk or a

hole in the ground, when a terrier would drag the terrified but still dangerous fox out of the hole.

These examples illustrate the fact that aggressiveness in animals is
based on genetic predispositions that selective breeding can modify.
However, the fact that the overt, or phenotypic, expression of aggression
can be modified does not mean that the capacity for aggression is eliminated. It is necessary to distinguish between the capacity to destroy and actual
destructive behavior. Selective breeding changes the average threshold for
reacting aggressively to a stimulus, but it does not do this uniformly for all
members of a group. Some animals will remain aggressive (or passive, as
the case may be). In any case, once someone or something has exceeded the
threshold for provoking aggression, even in a passive animal, the pattern
of evoked aggression will take much the same form as in an animal with a
low threshold for aggression. A peaceful pussycat can be provoked into a
screeching rage under certain conditions.

These observations about the genetics of aggressive behavior are consistent with other types of evidence. In Chapter 12, we saw how neural systems in the brain organize and control the expression of aggressive behavior. Researchers have often demonstrated that electrical stimulation of certain hypothalamic and amygdaloid nuclei in the brain will evoke attack
behavior in humans as well as lower animals. Some brain tumors, particularly in the temporal lobe, may be associated with increased levels of irritability and with unprovoked destructive outbursts. In most cases, if the
tumor is successfully removed, the aggressive outbursts subside. Diffuse
head injuries, rabies, and some kinds of epilepsy may also produce irritable
and aggressive behaviors. Increases in hormones such as testosterone will
increase aggressiveness in animals and, to some degree, in humans as well
(Moyer, 1986). The following example describes a case in which temporal
lobe disease figured:

> Illustration: A very capable young engineer gradually became increasingly
> aggressive toward his wife and other people. On many occasions, and apparently
> with little provocation, he would exhibit extreme forms of aggressive behavior.
> He broke down doors in his house, threatened to stab his wife, and threatened to
> shoot his neighbors. He was referred to a psychotherapist for treatment who
> came to the conclusion that the patient's impulsive attacks were irrational and
> out of proportion to the precipitating events and to his neurotic problems. The
> patient was referred for medical evaluation and was discovered to have temporal
> lobe disease which was treated successfully by medication.

All this evidence for the *innate* character of aggressive reactions raises
the question of purpose. From an evolutionary point of view, what is the
function of anger and violent behavior? Or, to put this another way, what
survival functions does it serve?

Konrad Lorenz, the well-known ethologist, discusses this issue at
length (1966). He points out that Darwin's expression, "The struggle for

existence," is sometimes erroneously interpreted as the conflict between different species. The struggle Darwin meant was the competition between members of the same species. Typical prey-predator relations exemplify conflicts between different species (interspecific conflict). In nature, a balance typically develops between the weapons of attack and those of defense. Fights between prey and predator never go so far as to cause extinction of the prey; a state of equilibrium is always established between them.

Lorenz also points out that fights between predator and prey do not generally involve overt expressions of emotion in the predator (that is, growling, laying the ears back, erection of hair or fur, and so on). However, many animals will attack ferociously if an enemy surprises them at less than a certain critical distance. This observation suggests the first function for aggressive behavior, that is, to space out a given population of animals in order to avoid exhausting all sources of nutrition in a given area. This function, basically true for nutritional competitors of the same species, is found in fish, birds, and many mammals including primates. Colors of coral fish function to identify members of each species so that the spatial distribution of competitors is easy to accomplish. The songs of birds play a similar role in acoustically defining territories, while the scent of urine or feces tends to mark the territories of many mammals.

A second function of aggression is to select the strongest male animals for reproduction through rival fights. Zebras, bisons, antelopes, and other grazing animals form large herds but do not engage in territorial aggression since there is enough food for all. Nevertheless, males of these species fight each other violently. Winners of the fights play a major role in fathering future generations. The survival value of herd defense results in selective breeding for size and strength in males.

A third function of aggression is in defense of offspring, readily seen in many animals and particularly in humans. In this case, aggressiveness is not limited to one sex, and females may be more aggressive than males.

A fourth function of aggression is in establishing a dominance or hierarchical structure within a group. Such a social structure acts to stabilize relations among members of a group and thus maintains group cohesion, undoubtedly a property that contributes to the likelihood of survival of members of the group. A dominance hierarchy also has another function. In such systems, tension usually exists between individuals who hold immediately adjoining positions in the rank order. When conflicts occur between two or more low-ranking individuals, high-ranking ones usually intervene to protect the weaker ones. Observers have also seen that members of primate groups tend to pay most attention to older, high-ranking individuals and will imitate and learn from such individuals only (Lorenz, 1966).

In summary, ethologists suggest at least four functions of aggression: It tends to space the members of a group within an environment in accordance with the food resources that are available. It selects strong males for the protection of the group and for the fathering of future generations. It serves to protect offspring under conditions of danger or threat. And it creates a hierarchical system within a social group that provides stability for the group. These are obviously important contributions of aggression, and they help to explain the persistence of aggression in living organisms.

Novaco (1976) describes another way of looking at the adaptive functions of anger and aggression when he points out that anger has a number of useful functions. First, it increases the energy or intensity with which we act to accomplish our goals. It is interesting to see normally quiet, friendly people marching in front of an abortion center, shouting, threatening, and sometimes fighting with police and picketers on the other side of this controversial issue. Anger arousal induces a sense of power that may facilitate the attainment of personal goals. Second, anger displays serve an expressive function; they quickly reveal how an individual feels and an intention to quarrel or fight. Third, individuals often use anger expressions to intimidate others and to give the impression of a strong, threatening presence. The success of such expressions in determining an individual's reputation may increase his or her ability to gain resources and survive in the face of threats. Fourth, Novaco suggests that anger reduces anxious feelings of vulnerability. Anger blunts feelings of personal insecurity and prevents feelings of helplessness from reaching levels of conscious awareness. And last, recognition of signs of anger in others and in oneself may alert the individual to use coping strategies that may be effective in resolving conflicts.

The fact that anger has so many positive values for individuals helps to explain what sometimes seems like a puzzling fact: many people enjoy getting angry. It is therefore misleading to describe anger as a negative emotion. It is probably more accurate to think of anger and fighting as potentially creating pleasant feelings of arousal and excitement, triumph, and joy if victorious, and sadness and pain if unsuccessful.

▌The Control of Anger

When anger occurs in extreme form, it is likely that someone will be injured. This fact is the basis for the many forms of social control that are used in an effort to limit the overt expression of anger.

The oldest and most common method for reducing anger and violence is the use of punishment. Punishment may be either physical, as in spankings, or psychological, as the following incident illustrates:

Illustration: A mother was waiting in a cashier's line in a department store. Her seven-year-old son was restlessly walking along the nearby aisle, touching everything he passed.

The mother became increasingly agitated and finally began to talk loudly to her son. She began with the following remark.

"Stop touching everything."

Her son ignored her and continued to touch the merchandise. She then said, "You're stupid. I can't wait for you to go back to school. Boy, am I going to go out and celebrate."

The son said nothing, but continued to touch things on the counters. The mother then said, "If you don't stop touching things I'm going to hit you so hard your teeth will rattle."

The boy ignored the mother, made no remarks, and continued to wander along the aisles. After a brief hesitation the mother said, "When we get home, if your room is clean I may let you go out and play."

This threat finally roused the son to respond. He looked at his mother and said, "But my room is clean."

The mother answered, "Well, it didn't look clean to me. When we get back I'll look at it and decide if I want to let you go out and play (Plutchik et al., 1990).

Many people believe that punishment reduces violent behavior, but evidence suggests that it has undesirable effects as well. The punishing parent may be a role model for the punished child, who learns that violence is a good technique for getting what one wants. This observation is consistent with various studies that have shown that angry parents tend to produce angry children.

Another technique for dealing with anger and its offshoot, violence, is the use of time-out from social reinforcement when certain clearly defined violent behaviors occur. Such behaviors include tantrums, self-injury, attacks on other children or teachers, screaming, biting, and destruction of property. When a child engages in such behavior, he or she is placed in a time-out room for a relatively short period. This procedure, when used consistently, is quite successful in reducing incidents of outbursts of anger.

Rewarding behavior that is incompatible with anger and violence is another approach to reducing anger. Children or patients are given tokens that may be exchanged for desirable rewards at a later time. If the tokens reward behavior that is incompatible with violent behavior, the violence is likely to gradually decrease.

Pharmacotherapy

A number of psychotropic drugs are widely used as a way to reduce violent behavior in psychiatric patients. Clinicians have used antianxiety agents for this purpose, but certain neuroleptics are more effective in quieting a violent patient. A major problem with such medications is that, long term, they often induce severe motor side effects. In recent years, investigators have directed considerable research toward finding a new class of psychiatric medications that reduce anger and violence and have few side effects. These new drugs, called *serenics,* are a type of serotonin receptor inhibitor.

Psychotherapy

Psychotherapy is widely used in an effort to reduce feelings of anger and to reduce the likelihood of violent acting out. Most therapies attempt to identify the probable causes of feelings of anger and then use one or more of several approaches to mitigate their effects.

One popular idea is to express the anger toward the offending person in imagination, through the use of psychodrama, for example. Another is to abreact the anger by yelling and screaming and punching a pillow in the comparative safety of the clinician's office. Another approach is to try to increase the individual's tolerance of frustration by talking about it, or through the use of homework assignments. Sometimes, the clinician encourages forgiveness. Finally, the clinician may teach the client new coping styles for dealing with problems. For example, instead of seeing a criticism of oneself as requiring revenge or attack, one tries to see it as a problem requiring a solution that minimizes any violent encounters.

In 1932, Albert Einstein sent a letter to Sigmund Freud asking him if he had any ideas about how to reduce the risk of war. In his interesting letter of response, Freud presented the following idea:

> If willingness to engage in war is an effect of the destructive instinct, the most obvious plan will be to bring Eros, its antagonist, into play against it. Anything that encourages the growth of emotional ties between men must operate against war. These ties may be of two kinds. In the first place they may be relations resembling those toward a loved object, though without having a sexual aim. There is no need for psychoanalysis to be ashamed to speak of love in this connection, for religion itself uses the same words: "Thou shalt love thy neighbor as thyself." This, however, is more easily said than done. The second kind of emotional tie is by means of identification. Whatever leads men to share important interests produces this community of feeling, these identifications. And the structure of society is to a large extent based on them.

Summary ■

A true understanding of emotions should provide insight into disorders of emotion. It appears that we can recognize emotional disorders in several different ways: (1) when some emotions are extreme or persistent; (2) when some emotions are absent or too limited; (3) when strong emotions are in conflict; and (4) when there are disconnections between cognitions and feelings, or cognitions and behavior.

Two of the most troubling emotions that clinicians see in practice are anxiety and anger. Individuals express anxiety in social phobias and panic disorders as well as in other ways. Epidemiological studies indicate that anxiety disorders are more likely to occur in women and to have a possible genetic component. The treatment of anxiety disorders often utilizes medication and a variety of psychological procedures such as psychotherapy, systematic desensitization, and confrontation. Various studies suggest that fear and anxiety have certain adaptive functions and in many dangerous circumstances may contribute to the possibility of survival.

Anger is a frequent emotional experience, but in extreme form it may lead to violence toward oneself in the form of suicide attempts, or it may lead to violence toward others. In fact, there is a persistent belief among clinicians that suicide and violence are two sides of the same issue. Various studies, in fact, show that many of the same variables influence the risk of both suicide and violence. For example, crowding in prisons increases both homicide and suicide rates. There are also many reports of individuals who murder someone and then commit suicide.

Ethological studies of aggression in animal populations suggest that such behavior has a role in regulating conflicts and populations, and thus has survival value. Genetic studies and brain stimulation studies (cited in an earlier chapter) imply that innate factors have an influence on aggression systems in the brain. Despite this tendency, it is possible to control the overt expression of violent behavior by a number of methods including punishment, time-out, catharsis, psychodrama, psychotherapy, and medication.

The Future
Emotions

▌The Future of Emotions

Some writers have suggested that emotions were once important to human beings who lived in caves and whose lives were constantly in danger. When these humans were threatened, their emotions would energize them to run or to attack. According to this view, in the modern world where laws and systems of justice regulate stable societies, emotions are no longer needed. Only logic and rationality are necessary.

Such a view of emotions is not in accord with the facts that this book describes. Emotions are not just feelings that sometimes trigger action. Rather, emotions are complex states that tend to be provoked by important external events that signal danger, blocking of goals, loss of rewards, and sources of pleasure. The complex reactions are not learned, but are part of our biological inheritance. One sees many parallel reactions in lower animals, in primates, and in humans. Infants and children with little or no opportunity to learn social signals show certain easily interpretable emotional reactions that are the same as those we see in adults. Cross-cultural studies reveal that fears develop in the same way and at the same rate in widely diverse human groups. Certain facial expressive patterns are similar and recognizable in different preliterate groups who have had little

th other societies. Electrical and chemical studies of the
at there are brain systems that organize emotional expres-
it is possible for suitable electrical or chemical stimuli to gen-
nal feelings as well as behaviors. Pharmacological studies
appropriate medications can reduce extreme emotional states
nxiety, depression, and anger in a selective fashion. From an evo-
ry point of view, emotions are phylogenetically ancient complex
of reactions that communicate information from one individual to
ther, that regulate the reactions among individuals, and that contribute
the likelihood of survival. Emotions in this broad sense have been an
aspect of living organisms since living things began to evolve. It is unlikely
that this condition will change in the foreseeable future.

It this is true, how are we to explain the diversity of expression of emotions in different individuals and cultures? There are several possible
answers to this question.

Although the basic emotions connected with impulses to fight, flee,
mate, attach, and so on will always be present, the thresholds that determine how easily each of these reactions may be evoked will vary. Some
individuals as well as groups will be more easily aroused to violent action,
or avoidance behavior, or attachment, than others. Such variation presumably reflects historical events, environmental events, and variations in
genetic potentials. In addition, social and cultural events will influence the
degree to which a particular individual in a specific subcultural group
expresses each emotion. In a society in which there are many police relative
to the population as a whole, as well as severe penalties for crimes, there
will be less overt aggression. In a society in which parents are abusive and
rejecting, children are more likely to show depression, anxiety, and irritability. When parents are more socially involved with their children and more
accepting of them, emotions of cheerfulness and joy are more likely to prevail. The particular form of expression of an emotion is always the result of
an interaction of a variety of universal biological predispositions with social
experiences, social rules, and social sanctions.

Another aspect of the problem of individual differences in emotional
expression is related to the fact that most emotional states are mixtures,
compound, of blends of the basic ones. Depending upon one's life experiences interacting with strong or weak dispositions, an individual may
develop a unique blend of emotions that may be difficult to classify or capture in a single word. This characteristic is also true of specific cultures,
where particular social experiences may produce blends of emotions rarely
seen in other cultures, so that simple dictionary translations are often
mpossible. But the fact that a single word may not exist for a particular
notional compound does not mean that strong emotions are not present.
re is no limit to the number of mixtures that are possible, just as one can
e countless melodies from the same basic set of musical notes, or

The Future of
Emotions

∎ The Future of Emotions

Some writers have suggested that emotions were once important to human beings who lived in caves and whose lives were constantly in danger. When these humans were threatened, their emotions would energize them to run or to attack. According to this view, in the modern world where laws and systems of justice regulate stable societies, emotions are no longer needed. Only logic and rationality are necessary.

Such a view of emotions is not in accord with the facts that this book describes. Emotions are not just feelings that sometimes trigger action. Rather, emotions are complex states that tend to be provoked by important external events that signal danger, blocking of goals, loss of rewards, and sources of pleasure. The complex reactions are not learned, but are part of our biological inheritance. One sees many parallel reactions in lower animals, in primates, and in humans. Infants and children with little or no opportunity to learn social signals show certain easily interpretable emotional reactions that are the same as those we see in adults. Cross-cultural studies reveal that fears develop in the same way and at the same rate in widely diverse human groups. Certain facial expressive patterns are similar and recognizable in different preliterate groups who have had little or no involvement with other societies. Electrical and chemical studies of the brain indicate that there are brain systems that organize emotional expressions, and that it is possible for suitable electrical or chemical stimuli to generate emotional feelings as well as behaviors. Pharmacological studies reveal that appropriate medications can reduce extreme emotional states such as anxiety, depression, and anger in a selective fashion. From an evolutionary point of view, emotions are phylogenetically ancient complex types of reactions that communicate information from one individual to another, that regulate the reactions among individuals, and that contribute to the likelihood of survival. Emotions in this broad sense have been an aspect of living organisms since living things began to evolve. It is unlikely that this condition will change in the foreseeable future.

It this is true, how are we to explain the diversity of expression of emotions in different individuals and cultures? There are several possible answers to this question.

Although the basic emotions connected with impulses to fight, flee, mate, attach, and so on will always be present, the thresholds that determine how easily each of these reactions may be evoked will vary. Some individuals as well as groups will be more easily aroused to violent action, or avoidance behavior, or attachment, than others. Such variation presumably reflects historical events, environmental events, and variations in genetic potentials. In addition, social and cultural events will influence the degree to which a particular individual in a specific subcultural group expresses each emotion. In a society in which there are many police relative to the population as a whole, as well as severe penalties for crimes, there will be less overt aggression. In a society in which parents are abusive and rejecting, children are more likely to show depression, anxiety, and irritability. When parents are more socially involved with their children and more accepting of them, emotions of cheerfulness and joy are more likely to prevail. The particular form of expression of an emotion is always the result of an interaction of a variety of universal biological predispositions with social experiences, social rules, and social sanctions.

Another aspect of the problem of individual differences in emotional expression is related to the fact that most emotional states are mixtures, compound, of blends of the basic ones. Depending upon one's life experiences interacting with strong or weak dispositions, an individual may develop a unique blend of emotions that may be difficult to classify or capture in a single word. This characteristic is also true of specific cultures, where particular social experiences may produce blends of emotions rarely seen in other cultures, so that simple dictionary translations are often impossible. But the fact that a single word may not exist for a particular emotional compound does not mean that strong emotions are not present. There is no limit to the number of mixtures that are possible, just as one can create countless melodies from the same basic set of musical notes, or countless hues from the same basic colors. The difficulties that occasionally arise in translating emotion terms from one subculture to another do not mean that the basic underlying structure of emotions is different in different cultures.

Every century and every society will have its spectrum of emotions. The exact shadings will vary somewhat, but the basic emotions will always be present. There will be times and places where there will be more anger, more sadness, more sadism, and more indifference to the feelings of others. But there will also be times when people will be more sensitive, more joyful, more friendly, and more loving. The study of emotion, in all its varied forms and colors, may help us discover the social and environmental conditions that produce the most harmonious blends of emotion for all people.

References

Aggleton, J. P., & Mishkin, M. (1986). The amygdala: Sensory gateway to the emotions. In R. Plutchik & H. Kellerman (Eds.), *Biological foundations of emotion* (Vol. 3). New York: Academic Press.

Ainsworth, M. D. S., and Bowlby, J. (1991). An ethological approach to personality development. *American Psychologist, 46,* 333–341.

Alessi, N. E., McManus, M., Brickman, A., & Grapentine, L. (1984). Suicidal behavior among serious juvenile offenders. *American Journal of Psychiatry, 141,* 286–287.

Allen, B., & Potkay, C. R. (1981). On the arbitrary distinction between states and traits. *Journal of Personality and Social Psychology, 4,* 916–928.

Allen, N. H. (1983). Homicide followed by suicide: Los Angeles, 1970–1979. *Suicide and Life-Threatening Behavior, 13,* 155–165.

American Psychiatric Association. (1980). *Diagnostic and statistical manual of mental disorders* (3rd ed.). Washington, D.C., APA Press, 1980.

American Psychiatric Association. (1987). Diagnostic and statistical manual of mental disorders. Washington, D.C.: Author.

American thesaurus of slang: A complete reference book of colloquial speech. (1953). New York: Crowell.

Andrew, R. J. (1963). The origin and evolution of the calls and facial expressions of the primates. *Behavior, 20,* 1–109.

Andrew, R. J. (1974). Arousal and the causation of behavior. *Behavior, 51,* 135–136.

Arnold, M. B. (1960). *Emotion and personality* (2 vols.). New York: Columbia University Press.

Aronoff, J., Barclay, A. M. , & Stevenson, L. A. (1988). The recognition of threatening facial stimuli. *Journal of Personality and Social Psychology, 54,* 647–655.

Averill, J. R. (1975). A semantic atlas of emotional concepts. *JSAS Catalog of Selected Documents in Psychology, 5,* 330. (Ms. No. 421)

Bach-Y-Rita, G., & Veno, A. (1974). Habitual violence: A profile of 82 men. *American Journal of Psychiatry, 131,* 1015–1017.

Bastock, M. (1967). *Courtship: An ethological study.* Chicago: Aldine.

Beck, A. T. (1983). Cognitive therapy of depression: New perspectives. In P. J. Clayton & J. E. Barrett (Eds.), *Treatment of depression: Old controversies and new approaches.* New York: Raven Press.

Bednar, R. L., Wells, M. G., & Peterson, S. R. (1989). *Self-esteem.* Washington, D.C.: American Psychological Association Press.

Bendig, A. W. (1956). The development of a short form of the Manifest Anxiety Scale. *Journal of Consulting Psychology, 20,* 384–387.

Benton, D. (1989). Measuring animal aggression. In R. Plutchik, & H. Kellerman (Eds). *The measurement of emotions* (Vol. 4). New York: Academic Press.

Berrey, E., & van den Bark (Eds.). (1953). *American thesaurus of slang: A complete reference book of colloquial speech.* New York: Crowell.

Bibring, E. (1941). The development and problems of the theory of the instincts. *International Journal of Psychoanalysis, 22,* 102–131.

Birch, H. G., Thomas, A., Chess, S., & Hertzig, M. E. (1962). Individuality in the development of children. *Developmental Medicine and Child Neurology, 4,* 370–379.

Blanchard, D. C., & Blanchard, R. J. (1984). Affect and aggression: An animal model applied to human behavior. In R. J. Blanchard & D. C. Blanchard (Eds.), *Advances in the study of aggression* (Vol. I). New York: Academic Press.

Block, J. (1957). Studies in the phenomenology of emotions. *Journal of Abnormal and Social Psychology, 54,* 358–363.

Bonner, J. T. (1962). *The ideas of biology.* New York: Harper & Row.

Boucher, J. D. (1973). *Facial behavior and the perception of emotion: Studies of Malays and Temuanorang Asi.* Paper presented to the Conference on Psychology and Related Disciplines in Malaysia.

Boucher, J. D. (1974). Culture and the expression of emotion. *International and Intercultural Communication Annual, 1,* 82–86.

Boucher, J. D., & Ekman, P. (1975). Facial areas and emotional information. *Journal of Communication, 25,* 21–29.

Bowlby, J. (1960). Grief and mourning in infancy and early childhood. In R. Eissler (Ed.),. *Psychoanalytic study of the child.* (Vol. 15). New York: International Universities Press.

Bowlby, J. (1969). *Attachment and loss: Vol. 1, Attachment.* New York: Basic Books.

Bowlby, J. (1979). *The making and breaking of affectional bonds.* London: Tavistock.

Brain, P. F. (1981). Differentiating types of attack and defense in rodents. In P. F. Brain & D. Benton (Eds.), *Multidisciplinary approaches to aggression research.* Amsterdam: Elsevier/North-Holland.

Brazelton, T. B. (1976). Early parent-infant reciprocity. In V. C. Vaughan III & T. B. Brazelton (Eds.), *The family: can it be saved?* New York: Year Book Medical.

Brazelton, T. B. (1983). Precursors for the development of emotions in early infancy. In R. Plutchik & H. Kellerman (Eds.), *Emotions in early development* (Vol 2). New York: Academic Press.

Breland, K., & Breland, M. (1966). *Animal behavior.* New York: Macmillan.

Brenner, C. (1974). On the nature and development of affects: A unified theory. *Psychoanalytic Quarterly, 43,* 532–556.

Brenner, C. (1975). Affects and psychic conflict. *Psychoanalytic Quarterly, 44,* 5–28.

Brenner, C. (1982). The concept of the superego: A reformulation. *Psychoanalytic Quarterly, 51,* 501–525.

Bright, M. (1984). *Animal language.* Ithaca: Cornell University Press.

Brody, C., Plutchik, R., Reilly, E., & Peterson, M. (1973). Personality and problem behavior of third-grade children in regular classes. *Psychology in the Schools, 10,* 196 –199.

Brown, G. W., & Harris, T. O. (1978). *Social origins of depression.* London: Tavistock.

Brunner, L. J. (1979). Smiles can be back channels. *Journal of Personality and Social Psychology, 37,* 728–734.

Buck, R. (1984). *The communication of emotion.* New York: Guilford Press.

Buckley, P., Conte, H. R., Plutchik, R., Wild, D. V., & Karasu, T. B. (1984). Psychodynamic variables as predictors of psychotherapy outcome. *American Journal of Psychiatry, 141,* 742–748.

Buechler, S., & Izard, C. E. (1983.) On the emergence, functions, and regulation of some emotion expressions in infancy. In R. Plutchik & H. Kellerman (Eds.), *Emotions in early development* Vol. 2. New York: Academic Press.

Buirski, P., Kellerman, H., Plutchik, R., Weininger, R., & Buirski, N. (1973). A field study of emotions dominance, and social behavior in a group of baboons (Papio anubis). *Primates, 14,* 67–78.

Buirski, P., & Plutchik, R. (1991). Measurement of deviant behavior in a Gombe Chimpanzee: Relation to later behavior. *Primates, 32,* 207–211.

Burk, F., Kurz, A., & Moller, H. J. (1985). Suicide risk scales: Do they help to predict suicidal behavior? *European Archives of Psychiatry and Neurological Sciences, 235,* 153–157.

Campos, J., Barrett, K., Lamb, M., Goldsmith, H., & Sternberg, C. (1983). Socioemotional development. In P. H. Mussen (Ed.), *Handbook of child psychology Vol. 2. Infancy and developmental psychology.* New York: Wiley.

Camras, L. A. (1977). Facial expressions used by children in a conflict situation. *Child Development, 48,* 1431–1435.

Camras, L. A., & Allison, K. (1985). Children's understanding of emotional facial expressions and verbal labels. *Journal of Nonverbal Behavior, 9,* 84–94.

Cannon, W. B. (1929). *Bodily changes in pain, hunger, fear and rage*. New York: Appleton.

Carpenter, M. B., & Sutin, J. (1985). *Human neuroanatomy*. Baltimore: Williams & Wilkins.

Cattell, R. B. (1957). *Personality and motivation: Structure and measurement*. New York: Harcourt Brace Jovanovich.

Chamove, A. S., Rosenblum, L.A., & Harlow, H. F. (1973). Monkeys (macaca mulatta) raised only with peers: A pilot study. *Animal Behaviour, 21*, 316–325.

Charlesworth, W. R. (1982). An ethological approach to research on facial expressions. In C.E. Izard (Ed.), *Measuring emotions in infants and children*. New York: Cambridge University Press.

Chevalier-Skolnikoff, S. (1973). Facial expression of emotion in nonhuman primates. In P. Ekman (Ed.), *Darwin and facial expression*. New York: Academic Press.

Chiera, E. (1938). *They wrote on clay*. Chicago: University of Chicago Press.

Clancy, J., & Noyes, R., Jr. (1976). Anxiety neurosis: A disease for the medical model. *Psychosomatics, 17*, 90–93.

Clarke, D. J., & Brown, N. S. (1990). Kluver-Bucy syndrome and psychiatric illness. *British Journal of Psychiatry, 157*, 439–441.

Climent, C. E., Raynes, A., & Plutchik, R. (1974). Epidemiological studies of female prisoners II. Biological, psychological and social correlates of drug addiction. *International Journal of the Addictions, 9*, 345–350.

Climent, C. E., Rollins, A., Ervin, R. R., & Plutchik, R. (1973). Epidemiological studies of women prisoners I: Medical and psychiatric variables related to violent behavior. *American Journal of Psychiatry, 130*, 985–990.

Clore, G. L., Ortony, A., & Foss, M. A. (1987). The psychological foundations of the affective lexicon. *Journal of Personality and Social Psychology, 53*, 751–766.

Coleman, J. C. (1949). Facial expressions of emotion. *Psychological Monographs, 63*. (Whole No. 269)

Conte, H. R., & Plutchik, R. (1981). A circumplex model for interpersonal personality traits. *Journal of Personality and Social Psychology, 40*, 701–711.

Conte, H. R., Plutchik, R., Wild, C. V., & Karasu, T. B. (1986). Combined psychotherapy and pharmocotherapy for depression: A systematic analysis of the evidence. *Archives of General Psychiatry, 43*, 471–479.

Cox, V. C., Paulus, P., & McCain, G. (1984). Prison crowding research: The relevance for raising prison standards and a general approach regarding crowding phenomena. *American Psychologist, 39*, 1148–1160.

Crowe, R. R., Noyes, R., Pauls, D. L., & Slymen, D. (1983). A family study of panic disorder. *Archives of General Psychiatry, 40*, 1065–1069.

Dalmer, S., & Humphrey, J. A. (1980). Offender-victim relationships in criminal homicide followed by offender's suicide. North Carolina 1972–1977. *Suicide and Life-Threatening Behavior, 10*, 106–118.

Darwin, C. (1965). *The expression of the emotions in man and animals*. Chicago: University of Chicago Press. (Original work published 1872)

Darwin, C. (1987). *The autobiography of Charles Darwin and selected letters*. F. Darwin (Ed.). New York: Dover, 1958.

Davis, R. C. (1934). The specificity of facial expressions. *Journal of Genetic Psychology, 10*, 42–58.

Davitz, J. R. (1969). *The language of emotions*. New York: McGraw-Hill.

Davitz, J. R. (1970). A dictionary and grammar of emotion. In M. Arnold (Ed.), *Feelings and emotions: The Loyola Symposium*. New York: Academic Press.

Delgado, J. M. R. (1960). Emotional behavior in animals and humans. In L. J. West & M. Greenblatt (Eds.), *Explorations in the physiology of emotions* (Psychiatric Research Report No. 12). Washington, D.C.: American Psychiatric Association.

Delgado, J. M. R. (1964). Free behavior and brain stimulation. In C. C. Pfeiffer & J. R. Smythies (Eds.), *International Review of Neurobiology* (Vol. 6). New York: Academic Press.

Delgado, J. M. R. (1966). *Emotions*. Dubuque, Iowa: Brown.

Dethier, V. G. (1964). Microscopic brains. *Science, 143,* 1138–1145.

DSM III R Casebook (1987). American Psychiatric Association. Washington, D.C.

Duchenne de Boulogne, G. B. (1990). *The mechanism of human facial expression.* New York: Cambridge University Press. (Original work published 1862)

Edelstein, M. G. (1990). *Symptom analysis: A method of brief therapy.* New York: W. W. Norton.

Eibl-Eibesfeldt, I. (1971). *Love and hate.* New York: Holt, Rinehart, and Winston.

Eibl-Eibesfeldt, I. (1973). The expressive behavior of the deaf-and-blind-born. In M. von Cranach and I. Vine (Eds.), *Social communication and movement.* New York: Academic Press.

Eibl-Eibesfeldt, I. (1975). *Ethology: The biology of behavior* (2nd ed.). New York: Holt.

Eibl-Eibesfeldt, I. (1979). *The biology of peace and war.* New York: Viking.

Eibl-Eibesfeldt, I., & Sutterlin, C. (1990). Fear, defense and aggression in animals and man: Some ethological perspectives. In P. F. Brain & S. Parmigiani (Eds.), *Fear and defense.* London: Harwood.

Ekman, P. (1970). Universal facial expressions of emotion. *California Mental Health Research Digest, 8,* 151–158.

Ekman, P. (1993). Facial expression and emotion. *American Psychologist, 48,* 384–392.

Ekman, P., & Friesen, W. V. (1971). Constants across cultures in the face and emotion. *Journal of Personality and Social Psychology, 17,* 124–129.

Ekman, P., & Friesen, W. V. (1976). Measuring facial movement. *Environmental Psychology and Nonverbal Behavior, 1,* 56–75.

Ekman, P., & Friesen, W. V. (1986). A new pan-cultural facial expression of emotion. *Motivation and Emotion, 10,* 159–168.

Ekman, P., Friesen, W. V., & Ancoli, S., (1980). Facial signs of emotional experience. *Journal of Personality and Social Psychology, 39,* 1125–1134.

Ekman, P., Friesen, W. V., & Simons, R. C. (1985). Is the startle reaction an emotion? *Journal of Personality and Social Psychology, 49,* 1416–1426.

Ekman P., & Oster, H. (1979). Facial expressions of emotion. *Annual Review of Psychology, 30,* 527–554.

Ekman, P., Sorenson, E. R., & Friesen, W. V. (1969). Pan-cultural elements in facial displays of emotion. *Science, 164,* 86–88.

Enquist, M. (1985). Communication during aggressive interactions with particular reference to variation in choice of behavior. *Animal Behavior, 33,* 1152–1161.

Epstein, S. (1979). The ecological study of emotions in humans. In P. Pliner, K. R. Blankstein, & I. M. Spigel (Eds.), *Advances in the study of communication and affect: (Vol. 5), Perception of emotions in self and others.* New York: Plenum.

Epstein, S. (1984). Controversial issues in emotion theory. In P. Shaver (Ed.), *Review of Personality and Social Psychology* (Vol. 5). Beverly Hills, California: Sage.

Ervin, F. R., & Martin, J. (1986). Neurophysiological bases of the primary emotions. In R. Plutchik & H. Kellerman (Eds.), *Emotion: Theory, research and experience Vol. 3, Biological foundations of emotion.* New York: Academic Press.

Feleky, A. M. (1914). The expression of the emotions. *Psychological Review, 20,* 33–41.

Fenichel, O. (1946). *The psychoanalytic theory of neurosis.* Boston: Routledge and Kegan Paul.

Feyereisen, P. (1986). Production and comprehension of emotional facial expressions in brain-damaged subjects. In R. Bruyer (Ed.), *The neuropsychology of face perception and facial expression.* Hillsdale, New Jersey: Lawrence Erlbaum.

Fisher, G. A., Heise, D. R., Bohrnstedt, G. W., & Lucke, J. Z. (1985). Evidence for extending the circumplex model of personality trait language to self-reported moods. *Journal of Personality and Social Psychology, 49,* 233–242.

Flynn, J. P. (1967). The neural basis of aggression in cats. In D. C. Glass (Ed.) *Neurophysiology and emotion.* New York: Rockefeller University Press.

Fraiberg, S. (1971). Smiling and stranger reactions in blind infants. In J. Hellmuth (Ed.),

Exceptional abnormalities. New York: Brunner/Mazel.

Freedman, D.G. (1974). *Human infancy: An ethological perspective.* Hillsdale, New Jersey: Erlbaum.

Freud, S. (1922). *Beyond the pleasure principle.* London: Hogarth Press.

Freud, S. (1932). Why war? In J. Strachey (Ed.), *Collected papers.* New York: Basic Books.

Freud, S. (1936). *Studies on hysteria* (A. A. Brill, Trans.). New York: Nervous and Mental Disease Publications. (Original work published 1915)

Freud, S. (1949a). On narcissism: An introduction. In S. Freud, *Collected papers* (Vol. 4). London: Hogarth Press. (Original work published 1915)

Freud, S. (1949b). Repression. In S. Freud, *Collected papers* (Vol. 4). London: Hogarth Press. (Original work published 1915)

Freud, S. (1959). Fragment of an analysis of a case of hysteria. In S. Freud, *Collected papers* (Vol. 3). New York: Basic Books.

Fridlund, A. J. (1988). Evolution and facial action in reflex, social motive, and paralanguage. In P. K. Sickles, J. R. Jennings, & M. G. H. Coles (Eds.), *Advances in psychophysiology* (Vol. 4). Greenwich, CT: JAI Press.

Frijda, N.H. (1986). *The emotions.* New York: Cambridge University Press.

Frodi, A. N., Lamb, M. E., Leavitt, L. A., Donovan, W. L., Neff, C., & Sherry, D. (1978). Fathers' and mothers' responses to the faces and cries of normal and premature infants. *Developmental Psychology, 14,* 190–198.

Fulcher, J. S. (1942). "Voluntary" facial expressions in blind and seeing children. *Archives of Psychology, 38,* Whole No. 272.

Fuller, J. L. (1986). Genetics and emotions. In R. Plutchik & H. Kellerman (Eds.), *Emotion: Theory, research and experience: Vol. 3, The biological foundations of emotions.* New York: Academic Press.

Fuller, J. L., & Thompson, W. R. (1960). *Behavior genetics,* New York: Wiley.

Gallup, G.G., Jr. (1977). Self-recognition in primates: A comparative approach to the bidirectional properties of consciousness. *American Psychologist, 32,* 329–338.

Gardner, B. T., & Gardner, R. A. (1974). Comparing the early utterances of child and chimpanzee. In A. Pick (Ed.), *Minnesota symposium in child psychology* (Vol. 8). Minneapolis: University of Minnesota Press.

Gardner, R. A., & Gardner, B. T. (1978). Comparative psychology and language acquisition. *Annals of the New York Academy of Sciences, 309,* 37–76.

Gardner, R. A., & Gardner, B. T. (1984). A vocabulary test for chimpanzees (pan troglodytes). *Journal of Comparative Psychology, 98,* 381–404.

Gautier-Hion, A., Bourliere, F., Gautier, J. P., & Kingdom. J. (1988). *A primate radiation: Evolutionary biology of the African guenons.* New York: Cambridge University Press.

Gehm, T. L., & Scherer, K. R. (1988). Factors determining the dimensions of subjective emotional space. In K. R. Scherer (Ed.), *Facets of emotion: Recent research.* Hillsdale, NJ: Lawrence Erlbaum Associates.

Gellhorn, E., & Loofbourrow, G.N. (1963). *Emotions and emotional disorders.* New York: Hoeber Durscon, Harper & Row.

Gewirtz, J. L. (1965). The course of infant smiling in four child-rearing communities in Israel. In B. M. Foss (Ed.), *Determinants of infant behavior.* New York: Wiley.

Gibbons, J. L., Barr, G. A., Bridger, W. H., & Leibowitz, S. F. (1979). Manipulation of dietary tryptophan: Effects on mouse killing and brain serotonin in the rat. *Brain Research, 169,* 139–153.

Gilbert, A. N., Fridlund, A. J., & Sabini, J. (1987). Hedonic and social determinants of facial displays to odors. *Chemical Senses, 12,* 355–363.

Gluhbegovic, N., & Williams, T. H. (1980). *The human brain: A photographic guide.* New York: Harper & Row.

Goddard, M. E., & Beilharz, R. G. (1985). A multivariate analysis of the genetics of fearfulness in potential guide dogs. *Behavior Genetics, 15,* 69–89.

Goodall, J. (1987). *The chimpanzees of Gombe: Patterns of behavior.* Cambridge, Mass; Belknap.

Goodenough, U. W. (1991). Deception by pathogens, *American Scientist, 79,* 344–355.

Goodman, L. S., & Gilman, A. (1960). *The pharmacological basis of therapeutics,* (2nd ed.). New York: Macmillan.

Goodwin, F. K. (1985). Epidemiology and clinical description of depression. In S. H. Snyder (Ed.), *Biopsychiatric insights on depression.* Summit, New Jersey: Psychiatric Diagnostic Laboratories of America.

Gorman, J. M., Liebowitz, M. R., & Klein, D. F. (1984). *Panic disorder and agoraphobia.* Kalamazoo, MI: The Upjohn Company.

Gough, H. G. (1960). The Adjective Checklist as a personality assessment research technique. *Psychological Reports, 6,* 107–122.

Gray, J. A. (1988). *The psychology of fear and stress* (2nd ed.). New York: Cambridge University.

Green, D. P., Goldman, S. L., & Salovey, P. (1993). Measurement error masks bipolarity in affect ratings. *Journal of Personality and Social Psychology, 64,* 1029–1041.

Green, S. (1975). Communication by a graded vocal system in Japanese monkeys. In L.A. Rosenblum (Ed.), *Primate behavior* (Vol. 4). New York: Academic Press.

Griffin, D. R. (1976). *The question of animal awareness.* New York: Rockefeller University Press.

Guilford, T., & Dawkins, M. S. (1991). Receiver psychology and the evolution of animal signals. *Animal Behavior, 42,* 1–14.

Guthrie, R. D. (1973). The evolution of menace. *Saturday Review of the Sciences, 1,* 22–260.

Harkavy-Friedman, J. M., Asnis, G. M., & DiFiore, J. (1987). The prevalence of specific suicidal behaviors in a high school sample. *American Journal of Psychiatry, 144,* 1203–1206.

Harlow, H. F., Gluck, J. P., & Suomi, S. J. (1972). Generalization of behavioral data between nonhuman and human animals. *American Psychologist, 27,* 709–716.

Harlow, H. F., & Harlow, M. K. (1972). The language of love. In T. Alloway. L. Krames, & P. Pliner (Eds.), *Communication and affect: A comparative approach.* New York: Academic Press.

Harlow, H. F., & Mears, C. E. (1983). Emotional sequences and consequences. In R. Plutchik and H. Kellerman (Eds.), *Emotions in early development* (Vol. 2). New York: Academic Press.

Harris, E. L., Noyes, R., Crowe, R.R., & Chaudry, D. R. (1983). Family studies of agoraphobia: Report of a pilot study. *Archives of General Psychiatry, 40,* 1061–1064.

Harris, V. A., & Katkin, E. S. (1975). Primary and secondary emotional behavior: An analysis of the role of autonomic feedback on affect, arousal and attribution. *Psychological Bulletin, 82,* 904–916.

Harter, S., & Whitesell, N. R. (1989). Developmental changes in children's understanding of single, multiple, and blended emotion concepts. In C. Saarni & P. L. Harris (Eds.), *Children's understanding of emotion.* New York: Cambridge University Press.

Harvard, S. R., Steklis, H. D., & Lancaster, J. (Eds.). (1977). Origins and evolution of language and speech. *Annals of the New York Academy of Sciences, 280.*

Haskins, R. (1979). A causal analysis of kitten vocalizations: An observational and expermental study. *Animal Behavior, 27,* 726–736.

Heath, R. G. (1986). The neural substrate for emoton. In R. Plutchik & H. Kellerman (Eds.), *Biological foundations of emotion* (Vol. 3). New York: Academic Press.

Hebb, D. O. (1946). Emotion in man and animal: An analysis of the intuitive processes of recognition. *Psychological Review, 53,* 88–106.

Hebb, D. O. (1949). *The organization of behavior.* New York: Wiley.

Hebb, D. O. (1958). The motivating effects of exteroceptive stimulation. *American Psychologist, 13,* 109–113.

Hebb, D. O. (1972). *Textbook of psychology.* Philadelphia: Saunders.

Heider, F. (1958). *The psychology of interpersonal relations.* New York: Wiley.

Hendin, M. H. (1986). Suicide: A review of new directions in research. *Hospital and Community Psychiatry, 37,* 148–154.

Hendrick, C., & Hendrick, S. (1986). A theory and method of love. *Journal of Personality and Social Psychology, 50,* 392–402.

Henry, J. P. (1986). Neuroendocrine patterns of emotional response. In R. Plutchik & H. Kellerman (Eds.), *Biological foundations of emotion.* New York: Academic Press.

Herrick, C. J. (1956). *The evolution of human nature.* Austin: University of Texas Press.

Hill, D. C. (1955). *The communication of emotions by facial expressions in the light of a new theory.* Unpublished master's thesis. Hofstra College, Hempstead, NY.

Hinde, R. (1982). Endocrine behavior-environment interaction. In *Ethology* (pp. 162–166). A Fontana Paperback Masterguide.

Hinde, R. A. (1966). *Animal behavior: A synthesis of ethology and comparative psychology* New York: McGraw-Hill.

Hjortsjo, C. H. (1970). *Man's face and mimic language.* Malmo, Sweden: Nordens Boktrycheri.

Hofer, M. A. (1983). On the relationship between attachment and separation processes in infancy. In R. Plutchik & H. Kellerman (Eds.), *Emotions in early development* (Vol. 2). New York: Academic Press.

Hofer, M. A. (1984). Relationships as regulators: A psychobiologic perspective on bereavement. *Psychosomatic Medicine, 46,* 183–197.

Hoyt, D. P., & Magom, T. M. (1954). A validation study of the Taylor Manifest Anxiety Scale. *Journal of Clinical Psychology, 10,* 357–361.

Huizinger, J. (1950). *Homo ludens: A study of the play element in culture.* New York: Roy.

Humble, M. (1987). Aetiology and mechanisms of anxiety disorders. *Acta Psychiatrica Scandanavica, 76,* (Suppl. 335), 15–30.

Inamdar, S. C., Lewis, D. O., Siomopoulous, G., Shanok, S. S., & Lamela, M. (1982). Violent and suicidal behavior in psychotic adolescents. *American Journal of Psychiatry, 139,* 932–935.

Izard, C. E. (1971). *The face of emotion.* New York: Appleton-Century-Crofts.

Izard, C. E. (1972). *Patterns of emotions: A new analysis of anxiety and depression.* New York: Academic Press.

Izard, C. E. (1979). *MAX training manual.* Unpublished manuscript, University of Delaware, Newark, Delaware.

Izard, C. E. (1983). Emotions in personality and culture. *Ethos, 11,* 305–312.

Izard, C. E. (1990). Facial expressions and the regulation of emotions. *Journal of Personality and Social Psychology, 58,* 487–498.

Izard, C. E. (1991). *The psychology of emotions.* New York: Plenum Press.

Izard, C. E., & Buechler, S. (1980). Aspects of consciousness and personality in terms of differential emotions theory. In R. Plutchik & H. Kellerman (Eds.), *Theories of emotion* (Vol. 1). New York: Academic Press.

Izard, C. E., & Tomkins, S. S. (1966). Affect and behavior: Anxiety as a negative affect. In C. D. Spielberger (Ed.), *Anxiety and behavior.* New York: Academic Press.

Jackson, L. (1954). *Aggression and its interpretation.* London: Methuen.

James, W. (1884). What is emotion? *Mind, 19,* 188–205.

James, W. (1890). *The principles of psychology.* New York: Holt, Rinehart and Winston.

Janssen, L., & Ost, Z. (1982). Behavioral treatments for agoraphobia: An evaluative review. *Clinical Psychology Reviews, 2,* 311–336.

Johnson, R. N. (1972). *Aggression in man and animals.* Philadelphia: W. B. Saunders.

Jolly, A. (1985). The evolution of primate behavior. *American Scientist, 73,* 230–239.

Jurgens, U. (1979). Vocalization as an emotional indicator: A neuroethological study in the squirrel monkey. *Behavior, 69,* 88–117.

Kabnick, K. S., & Peattie, D. A. (1991). Giardia: A missing link between prokaryotes and eukaryotes. *American Scientist, 79,* 34–43.

Kaplan, H. I., & Sadock, B. J. (1988). *Synopsis of psychiatry: Behavioral sciences, clinical psychiatry* (5th ed.). Baltimore: Williams & Wilkins.

Karli, P. (1956). The Norway rat's killing response to the white mouse: An experimental analysis. *Behaviour, 10*, 81–103.

Kellerman, H. (1979). *Group psychotherapy and personality: Intersecting structures.* New York: Grune and Stratton.

Kellerman, H. (1987). Nighmares and the structure of personality. In H. Kellerman (Ed.), *The nightmare: Psychological and biological formulations.* New York: Columbia University Press.

Kellerman, H. (1990). Emotion and the organization of primary process. In R. Plutchik and H. Kellerman (Eds.), *Emotion psychopathology and psychotherapy* (Vol. 5). San Diego, CA: Academic Press.

Kellogg, W. N., & Kellogg, L. A. (1967). *The ape and the child.* New York: Macmillan (Hafner Press). (Original work published 1933)

Kelly, K. L., & Judd, D. B. (1955). *The ISCC-NBS method of designating colors and a dictionary of color names.* (National Bureau of Standards Circular 553). Washington, D.C.: U.S. Government Printing Office.

Kemper, T. D. (1987). How many emotions are there? Wedding the social and the autonomic components. *American Journal of Sociology, 93*, 263–289.

Kendler, K. S., Heath, A., Martin, & Eaves, I. J. (1986). Symptoms of anxiety and depression in a volunteer twin population. *Archives of General Psychiatry, 43*, 213–221.

Kernberg, O. F. (1990). New perspectives in psychoanalytic affect theory. In R. Plutchik and H. Kellerman (Eds.), *Emotion, psychopathology, and psychotherapy* (Vol. 5). New York: Academic Press.

Kinsey, A. C., Pomeroy, W. B., & Martin, C. E. (1948). *Sexual behavior in the human male.* Philadelphia: Saunders.

Klein, D. F. (1981). Anxiety reconceptualized. In D. F. Klein & J.G. Robkin (Eds.), *Anxiety: New research and changing concepts.* New York: Raven Press.

Klein, D. F., Zitrin, C. M., Woerner, M. G., & Ross, D. C. (1983). Treatment of phobias: II Behavior therapy and supportive psychotherapy: Are there any specific ingredients? *Archives of General Psychiatry, 40*, 139–145.

Klinnert, M. D., Campos, J. J., Sorce, J. F., Emde, R. N., & Svejda, M. (1983). Emotions as behavior regulators, social referencing in infancy. In R. Plutchik & H. Kellerman (Eds.), *Emotions in early development* (Vol 2.). New York: Academic Press.

Kushner, M. G., & Beitman, B. D. (1990). Panic attacks without fear: An overview. *Behavior Research and Therapy, 28*, 469–479.

Lacey, J. I., & Lacey, B. C. (1962). The law of initial value in the longitudinal study of autonomic constitution: Reproducibility of autonomic responses and response patterns over a four-year interval. *Annals of the New York Academy of Sciences, 98*, 1257–1326.

Lamb, M.E., Thompson, R.A., Gardner, W., & Charnov, E.L. (1985). *Infant-mother attachment.* Hillsdale, N. J.: Lawrence Erlbaum.

Landis, C. (1924). Studies of emotional reactions: II General behavior and facial expression. *Journal of Comparative Psychology, 4*, 447–509.

Lazarus, R., & Folkman, S. (1984). *Stress, appraisal and coping.* New York: Springer.

Lazarus, R. S. (1966). *Psychological stress and the coping process.* New York: McGraw-Hill.

Lazarus, R. S. (1975). A cognitively oriented psychologist looks at feedback. *American Psychologist, 30*, 553–561.

Lazarus, R. S. (1991). *Emotion and adaptation.* New York: Oxford University Press.

LeDoux, J. E. (1984). Cognition and emotion: Processing functions and brain systems. In M. S. Gazzeniga (Ed.), *Handbook of cognitive neuroscience.* New York: Plenum.

LeDoux, J. E. (1988). Emotion. In *Handbook of phsysiology—The nervous system V.* Bethesda, MD: American Physiological Society.

Lee, J. A. (1988). Love styles. In R. J. Sternberg & M. Barnes (Eds.), *The psychology of love.*

New Haven, CT: Yale University Press.

Lester, D., Beck, A. T., & Mitchell, B. (1979). Extrapolation from attempted suicides to completed suicides: A test. *Journal of Abnormal Psychology, 88,* 78–80.

Levine, H. G. (1981). The vocabulary of drunkenness. *Journal of Studies on Alcohol, 42,* 1038–1051.

Leyhausen, P. (1956). In R. A. Hinde, *Animal behavior: A synthesis of ethology and comparative psychology.* New York: McGraw-Hill, 1966.

Lieberman, P. (1975). *On the origins of language.* New York: Macmillan.

Lobel, B. & Hirschfeld, R. M. A. (1984). *Depression: What we know.* U.S. Department of Health & Human Services. (NIMH Publication No. ADM 85–1318). Rockville, MD: U.S. Government Printing Office..

Loehlin, J. C., Horn, J. M., & Willerman, L. (1981). Personality resemblance in adoptive families. *Behavior Genetics, 11,* 309–330.

Loehlin, J. C., & Nichols, R. C. (1976). *Heredity, environment, and personality: A study of 850 sets of twins.* Austin, TX: University of Texas Press.

Loomis, W. F. (1988). *Four billion years.* Sunderland, MA: Sinauer Associates.

Lorenz, K. (1952). In Eibl-Eibesfeldt, I., *Love and hate,* New York: Holt, Rinehart & Winston.

Lorenz, K. (1966). *On aggression.* New York: Harcourt Brace Jovanovich.

Lorr, M. & McNair, D. M. (1984). *Manual: Profile of mood states: Bipolar form.* San Diego, CA: Educational and Industrial Testing Service.

Lumsden, C. J., & Wilson, E. O. (1981). *Genes, mind, and culture: The coevolutionary process.* Cambridge, MA: Harvard University Press.

Lutz, C. (1982). The domain of emotion words on Ifaluk. *American Ethnologist, 9,* 113–128.

Lyman, B., & Waters, J. C. E. (1986). The experiential loci and sensory qualities of various emotions. *Motivation and Emotion, 10,* 25–37.

MacLean, P. D. (1963). Phylogenesis. In P. H. Knapp (Ed.), *Expressions of the emotions in man.* New York: International Universities Press.

MacLean, P. D. (1984). Evolutionary psychiatry and the triune brain. *Psychological Medicine, 14,* 1–3.

MacLean, P. D. (1986). Ictal symptoms relating to the nature of affects and their cerebral substrate. In R. Plutchik & H. Kellerman (Eds.), *Biological foundations of emotion (Vol.3).* New York: Academic Press.

Mandler, G. (1975). *Mind and emotion.* New York: Wiley.

Mark, V. H., & Ervin, F. R. (1970). *Violence and the brain.* New York: Harper and Row.

Marler, P. (1977). Primate vocalization: Affective or symbolic? *Progress in ape research.* New York: Academic Press.

Marler, P., & Tenaza, R. (1977). Signaling behavior of apes with special reference to vocalization. In T. A. Sebeok (Ed.), *How animals communicate.* Bloomington, IN: Indiana University Press.

Marsh, P. (1988). *Eye to eye: How people interact.* Topsfield, MA: Salem House.

Marshall, G., & Zimbardo, P. S. (1979). Affective consequences of inadequately explained physiological arousal. *Journal of Personality and Social Psychology, 37,* 970–988.

Maslach, C. (1979). Negative emotional biasing of unexplained arousal. *Journal of Personality and Social Psychology, 37,* 953–969.

Mason, W. A. (1976). Environmental models and mental modes: Representational processes in the great apes and man. *American Psychologist, 31,* 284–294.

Mathews, R. T., & German, D. C. (1984). Electophysiological evidence for excitation of rat ventral tegmental area dopamine neurons by morphine. *Neuroscience, 11,* 617–625.

Matsumoto, D., Kudoh, J., Scherer, K., & Wallbott, H. (1988). Antecedents of and reactions to emotions in the United States and Japan. *Journal of Cross-Cultural Psychology, 19,* 267–286.

McDonald, M. V. (1989). Function of song in Scott's seaside sparrow Ammodramus Mantimus peninsulae. *Animal Behavior, 38,* 468–485.

McDougall, W. (1921). *An introduction to social psychology.* Boston: Luce.

McFarland, W. L., Morgane, P.J., & Jacobs, M.S. (1969). Ventricular system of the brain of the dolphin, Tursiops truncatus, with comparative anatomic observations and relations to brain specializations. *Journal of Comparative Neurology, 135,* 275–368.

McGrath, E., Keita, G. P., Strickland, B. R., & Russo, N. F. (Eds.). (1990). *Women and depression: Risk factors and treatment issues.* Washington, D.C.: American Psychological Association.

Meehan, P. J., Lamb, J. A., Saltzman, L. E., & O'Carroll, P. W. (1992). Attempted suicide among young adults: Progress toward a meaningful estimate of prevalence. *American Journal of Psychiatry, 149,* 41–44.

Menzel, E. W. (1971). Communication about the environment in a group of young chimpanzees. *Folia Primatologica, 15,* 220–232.

Miller, R. E., Caul, W. F., & Mirsky, I. R. (1967). Communication of affects between feral and socially isolated monkeys. *Journal of Personality and Social Psychology, 7,* 231–239.

Millodot, M., & Riggs, L. A. (1970). Refraction determined electrophysiologically. *Archives of Opthalmology, 84,* 272–278.

Monroe, R. R. (1970). *Episodic behavioral disorders.* Cambridge, MA: Harvard University Press.

Moody, R. A., Jr. (1979). Laughter and humor in medical practice. *Behavioral Medicine,* February, 25–29.

Moore, T. V. (1948). *The driving forces of human nature.* London: Heinemann.

Morris, D. (1967). *The naked ape.* New York: McGraw-Hill.

Morris, D. (1977). *Manwatching: A field guide to human behavior.* New York: Harry N. Abrams.

Morris, D., Collett, P., Marsh, P., & O'Shaughnessy, M. (1979). *Gestures: Their origins and distribution.* New York: Stein and Day.

Morris, D. J. (1954). The reproductive behavior of the zebra finch [Peophila guttata] with special reference to pseudofemale behavior and displacement. *Behaviour, 6,* 271–322.

Morton, E. S. (1977). On the occurrence and significance of motivation: Structural rules in some bird and mammal sounds. *American Naturalist, 111,* 855–869.

Moss, H. A., and Robson, K. S. (1968, August). *The role of protest behavior in the development of the mother-infant attachment.* Paper presented at the meeting of the American Psychological Association, San Francisco.

Motto, J. A., Heilbron, D. C., & Juster, R. D. (1985). Development of a clinical instrument to estimate suicide risk. *American Journal of Psychiatry, 142,* 1061–1064.

Moyer, K. E. (1983). Biological bases of aggressive behavior. In R. Plutchik and H. Kellerman (Eds.), *Biological foundations of emotion* (Vol. 3), New York: Academic Press.

Murstein, B. I. (1974). *Love, sex and marriage through the ages.* New York: Springer.

New Rochelle *Standard Star* (April 19, 1992). New Rochelle, New York.

Nihara K., Foster, R., Shellhaas, M., & Leland, H. (1970). *AAMD Behavior Scales.* Washington, D.C.: American Association on Mental Deficiency.

Nolen-Hoeksema, S. (1987). Sex differences in unipolar depression: Evidence and theory. *Psychological Bulletin, 101,* 259–282.

Novaco, R. W. (1976). The functions and regulation of the arousal of anger. *American Journal of Psychiatry, 133,* 1124–1128.

Olds, J., & Milner, P. (1954). Positive reinforcement produced by electrical stimulation of septal area and other regions of rat brain. *Journal of Comparative and Physiological Psychology, 47,* 419–427

Oppenheimer, R. (1956). Analogy in science. *American Psychologist, 11,* 127–135.

Ortony, A., Clore, G. L., & Collins, A. (1988). *The cognitive structure of emotions.* New York: Cambridge University Press.

Ortony, A, & Turner, T. J. (1990). What's basic about basic emotions? *Psychological Review, 97,* 315–331.

Osgood, C. E., Suci, G. J., & Tannenbaum, P. H. (1957). *The measurement of meaning.*

Urbana: University of Illinois Press.

Oster, H., & Ekman, P. (1978). Facial behavior in child development. In W. A. Collins (Ed.), *Minnesota symposium on child psychology* (Vol. 11). Hillsdale, NJ: Erlbaum.

Pam, A., Plutchik, R., & Conte, H. R. (1975). Love: A psychometric approach. *Psychological Reports, 37,* 83–88.

Panksepp, J. (1982). Toward a general psychobiological theory of emotions. *The Behavioral and Brain Sciences, 5,* 407–468.

Panksepp, J. (1986). The anatomy of emotions. In R. Plutchik & H. Kellerman (Eds.), *Biological foundations of emotion* (Vol. 3). New York: Academic Press.

Panksepp, J. (1989). The neurobiology of emotions: Of animal brains and human feelings. In H. Wagner & A. Manstead (Eds.), *Handbook of social psychophysiology.* New York: John Wiley & Sons.

Panksepp, J., Siviy, S., &.Normansell, L. (1984). The psychobiology of play: Theoretical and methodological perspectives. *Biobehavioral Reviews, 8,* 465–492.

Papez, J. W. (1937). A proposed mechanism of emotion. *Archives of Neurology and Psychiatry, 38,* 725–743.

Phoenix, C. H. (1974). Effects of dihydrotestosterone on sexual behavior of castrated male rhesus monkeys. *Physiology and Behavior, 12,* 1045–1055.

Piersma, T., & Veen, J. (1988). An analysis of the communication function of attack calls in little gulls. *Animal Behavior, 36,* 773–779.

Platman, S. R., Plutchik, R., Fieve, R. R., & Lawlor, W. G. (1969). Emotion profiles in mania and depression. *Archives of General Psychiatry, 20,* 210–214.

Ploog, D. (1986). Biological foundations of the vocal expressions of emotions. In R. Plutchik & H. Kellerman (Eds.), *Biological foundations of emotion* (Vol. 3). New York: Academic Press.

Ploog, D. (1989). Psychopathology of emotions in view of neuroethology. In K. Davison & A. Kerr (Eds.), *Contemporary themes in psychiatry.* London: Royal College of Psychiatrists.

Ploog, D. W., & MacLean, P. D. (1963). Display of penile erection in squirrel monkey (saimiri sciureus). *Animal Behavior Monographs, 11,* 32–39.

Plutchik, R. (1958). Outlines of a new theory of emotion. Transactions of the New York *Academy of Sciences, 20,* 394–403.

Plutchik, R. (1962). *The emotions: Facts, theories and a new model.* New York: Random House.

Plutchik, R. (1966). The psychophysiology of individual differences, with special reference to emotions. *Annals of the New York Academy of Sciences, 134,* 776–781.

Plutchik, R. (1970). Emotions, evolution and adaptive processes. In M. Arnold (Ed.), *Feelings and emotions.* New York: Academic Press.

Plutchik, R. (1971). Individual and breed differences in approach and withdrawal in dogs. *Behaviour, 40,* 302–311.

Plutchik, R. (1977). Cognitions in the service of emotions. In D. K. Candland, J. P. Fell, E. Keen, A. I. Leshner, R. Plutchik, & R. M. Tarpy (Eds.), *Emotion.* Monterey, CA: Brooks/Cole.

Plutchik, R. (1980). *Emotion: A psychoevolutionary synthesis.* New York: Harper and Row.

Plutchik, R. (1980). Universal problems of adaptation: Hierarchy, territorality, identity and temporality. In J.B. Calhoun (Ed.), *Environment and population: Problems of adaptation.* New York: Praeger.

Plutchik, R. (1983). Emotions in early development: A psychoevolutionary approach. In R. Plutchik & H. Kellerman (Eds.), *Emotion: Theory, research, and experience:* Vol. 2, *Emotions in early development.* New York: Academic Press.

Plutchik, R. (1984). Emotions: A general psychoevolutionary theory. In K. R. Scherer, & P. Ekman (Eds.), *Approaches to emotion.* Hillsdale, NJ: Erlbaum.

Plutchik, R. (1985, August). *Emotion and temperament.* Paper presented at meeting of the American Psychological Association, Los Angeles, California.

Plutchik, R. (1987). Evolutionary bases of empathy. In N. Eisenberg and J. Strayer (Eds.), *Empathy and its development.* New York: Cambridge University Press.

Plutchik, R. (1989). Measuring emotions and their derivatives. In R. Plutchik & H. Kellerman (Eds.), *Emotion: Theory, research, and experience: Vol. 4, The measurement of emotions.* San Diego, CA: Academic Press.

Plutchik, R. (1990). Emotions and psychotherapy: A psychoevolutionary perspective. In R. Plutchik & H. Kellerman (Eds.), *Emotion: Theory, research, and experience Vol. 5, Emotions, psychopathology and psychotherapy.* New York: Academic Press.

Plutchik, R., Climent, C., & Ervin, F. (1976). Research strategies for the study of human violence. In W. L. Smith & A. Kling (Eds.), *Issues in brain/behavior control.* New York: Spectrum.

Plutchik, R., Conte, H. R., Weiner, M.B., & Teresi, J. (1978). Studies of body image IV. Figure drawings in normal and abnormal geriatric and nongeriatric groups. *Journal of Gerontology, 33,* 68–75.

Plutchik, R., & Kellerman, H. (1974). *Emotions profile index manual.* Los Angeles: Western Psychological Services.

Plutchik, R., Kellerman, H., & Conte, H. R. (1979). A structural theory of ego defenses. In C.E. Izard (Ed.), *Emotions, personality and psychopathology.* New York: Plenum.

Plutchik, R., McCarthy, M., and Hall, B. H. (1975). Changes in elderly welfare hotel residents during a one-year period. *Journal of the American Geriatrics Society, 23,* 265–270.

Plutchik, R., & Plutchik, A. (1990). Communication and coping in families. In E. A. Blechman (Ed.), *Emotions and the Family* (pp. 35–51). Hillsdale, N. J.: Lawrence Erlbaum.

Plutchik, R., & van Praag, H. M., (1990). Psychosocial correlates of suicide and violence risk. In H. van Praag, R. Plutchik, & A. Apter (Eds.), *Violence and suicidality: Perspectives in clinical and psychobiological research.* New York: Brunner/Mazel.

Pokorny, A. D. (1983). Prediction of suicide in psychiatric patients. *Archives of General Psychiatry, 40,* 249–257.

Polis, G. A. (1981). The evolution and dynamics of intraspecific predation. *The Review of Ecology and Systematics, 12,* 225–252.

Poole, J. H. (1989). Announcing intent: The aggressive state of musth in African elephants. *Animal Behavior, 37,* 140–152.

Premack, D. (1976). Language and intelligence in ape and man. *American Scientist, 64,* 674–683.

Pribram, K. H. (1967). Emotion: Steps toward a neuropsychological theory. In D. C. Glass (Ed.), *Neuropsychiatry and emotion.* New York: Rockefeller University Press.

Pribram, K. H. (Ed.). (1970). Feelings as monitors. *Feelings and emotions: The Loyola Symposium.* New York: Academic Press.

Prince, J. H. (1975). *Languages of the animal world.* New York: Thomas Nelson.

Rado, S. (1969). *Adaptational psychodynamics: Motivation and control.* New York: Science House.

Rado, S. (1975). *Psychoanalysis of behavior.* New York: Grune and Stratton.

Rapaport, D. (1950). *Emotions and memory.* New York: International Universities Press.

Redican, W. K. (1982). An evolutionary perspective on human facial displays. In P. Ekman (Ed.), *Emotion in the human face* (2nd ed.) (pp. 212–282). New York: Cambridge University Press.

Reisenzein, R. (1983). The Schachter theory of emotion: Two decades later. *Psychological Bulletin, 94,* 239–264.

Ricci, N. (1990). The behavior of ciliated protozoa. *Animal Behavior, 40,* 1048–1069.

Richards, T. W., & Simons, M. P. (1941). The Fels child behavior scales. *Genetic Psychology Monographs, 24,* 259–309.

Riggs, L. A. (1976). Human vision: Some objective explorations. *American Psychologist, 31,* 125–134.

Rinn, W. E. (1984). The neuropsychology of facial expression: A review of the neurological and psychological mechanisms for producing facial expressions. *Psychological Bulletin, 95*, 52–77.

Rothstein, S. I., Yokel, D. A., & Fleischer, R. C. (1988). The agonistic and sexual functions of vocalizations of male brown-headed cowbirds, Molothrus ater. *Animal Behavior, 36*, 73–86.

Rowell, T. E. (1962). Agonistic noises of the rhesus monkey (Macaca mulatta). *Symposium Zoological Society of London, 8*, 91–96.

Rozin, P., & Fallon A. (1987). A perspective on disgust. *Psychological Review, 94*, 23–41.

Rubin, Z. (1973). *Liking and loving: An invitation to social psychology.* New York: Holt, Rinehart, and Winston.

Russell, J. A. (1983). Two pan-cultural dimensions of emotion words. *Journal of Personality and Social Psychology, 45*, 1281–1288.

Russell, J. A. (1989). Measures of emotion. In R. Plutchik and H. Kellerman (Eds.), *The measurement of emotions* (Vol. 4). New York: Academic Press.

Russell, J. A., & Mehrabian, A. (1977). Evidence for a three-factor theory of emotions. *Journal of Research in Personality, 11*, 273–294.

Saarni, C. (1978). Cognitive and communicative features of emotional experience, or do you show what you think you feel? In M. Lewis and L.A. Rosenblum (Eds.), *The development of affect.* New York: Plenum.

Savitsky, J. C., Izard, C. E., Kotsch, W. E., & Christy, L. (1974). Aggressor's response to the victim's facial expression of emotion. *Journal of Research in Personality, 7*, 346–357.

Schachter, S., & Singer, J. E. (1962). Cognitive, social and psychological determinants of emotional state. *Psychological Review, 69*, 379–399.

Schankman, P. (1969). Le roti et le bouilli: Levi-Strauss' theory of cannibalism. *American Anthropologist, 71*, 54–69.

Scherer, K. R. (1986). Vocal affect expression: A review and a model for future research. *Psychological Bulletin, 99*, 143–165.

Scherer, K. R. (1989). Vocal measurement of emotions. In R. Plutchik and H. Kellerman (Eds.), *The measurement of emotions* (Vol. 4). New York: Academic Press.

Scherer, K. R., Wallbott, H.G., & Summerfield, A.B. (Eds.) (1986). *Experiencing emotion: A cross-cultural study.* Cambridge, England: Cambridge University Press.

Scott, J. P. (1958). *Animal behavior.* Chicago: University of Chicago Press.

Scott, J. P. (1980). The function of emotions in behavioral systems: A systems theory analysis. In R. Plutchik and H. Kellerman (Eds.), *Theories of emotion* (Vol. 1). New York: Academic Press.

Scoville, R. & Gottlieb, G. (1980). Development of vocal behavior in Peking ducklings. *Animal Behavior, 28*, 1095–1109.

Seyfarth, R. M., Cheney, D. L., & Marler, P. (1980a). Monkey responses to three different alarm calls: Evidence of predator classification and semantic communication. *Science, 210*, 801–803.

Seyfarth, R. M., Cheney, D. L., & Marler, P. (1980b). Vervet monkey alarm calls: Semantic communication in a free-ranging primate. *Animal Behavior, 28*, 1070–1094.

Scarr, S., & Salapatek, P. (1970). Patterns of fear development during infancy. *Merrill-Palmer Quarterly of Behavior and Development, 16*, 53–90.

Schaefer, E. S., & Plutchik, R. (1966). Interrelationships of emotions, traits, and diagnostic constructs. *Psychological Reports, 18*, 399–410.

Schlosberg, H. (1941). A scale for the judgment of facial expressions. *Journal of Experimental Psychology, 29*, 497–510.

Shafii, M., Carrigan, S., Whillinghil, L., & Derrick, A. (1985). Psychological autopsy of completed suicide in children and adolescents. *American Journal of Psychiatry, 142*, 1061–1064.

Shapiro, D. (1989). *Psychotherapy of neurotic character.* New York: Basic Books.

Shaver, P., Schwartz, J., Kirson, D., & O'Connor, C. (1987). Emotion knowledge: further explorations of a prototype approach. *Journal of Personality and Social Psychology, 52,* 1061–1086.

Shaver, P. R., & Hazan, C. (1988). A biased overview of the study of love. *Journal of Social and Personal Relationships, 5,* 473–501.

Sheehan, D. V. (1983). *The anxiety disease.* New York: Scribner.

Shields, S. A. (1984). Distinguishing between emotion and nonemotion: judgments about experience. *Motivation and Emotion, 8,* 355–369.

Simpson, G. G. (1972). The evolutionary concept of man. In B. Campbell (Ed.), *Sexual selection and the descent of man: 1871–1971.* Chicago: Aldine.

Skinner, B. F. (1953). *Science and human behavior.* New York: Macmillan.

Skinner, B. F. (1963). Behaviorism at fifty. *Science, 140,* 951–958.

Skodal, A. E., and Karasu, T. B. (1978). Emergency psychiatry and the assaultive patient. *American Journal of Psychiatry, 135,* 202–205.

Sletten, I. W., Evenson, R. C., & Brown, M. L. (1973). Some results from an automated statewide comparison among attempted, committed, and non-suicidal patients. *Life-Threatening Behavior, 3,* 191–197.

Smiley, P., & Huttenlocher, J. (1989). Young children's acquisition of emotional concepts. In C. Saarni & P. L. Harris (Eds.), *Children's understanding of emotions.* New York: Cambridge University Press.

Smith, J. L., McDougal, C., & Miquelle, D. (1989). Scent marking in free-ranging tiger, Panthera tigris. *Animal Behavior, 37,* 1–10.

Smith, M. J. (1977). *Kicking the fear habit.* New York: Dial Press.

Smith, M. L., & Glass, G. V. (1977). Meta-analysis of psychotherapy outcome studies. *American Psychologist, 32,* 752–760.

Smith, W. J., Chase, J., & Lieblich, A. K. (1974). Tongue showing: a facial display of humans and other primate species. *Semiatrica, 11,* 201–246.

Spielberger, C. D., Gorsuch, R. L., & Lushene, R. E. (1970). *STAI Manual for the State-Trait Inventory.* Palo Alto, CA: Consulting Psychologist Press.

Spitz, R. A. (1946). Anaclitic depression. *Psychoanalytic Study of the Child, 2,* 313–342.

Sroufe, L. A. (1979). Socioemotional development. In J.D. Osofsky (Ed.), *Handbook of infant development.* New York: Wiley.

Stanley-Jones, D. (1966). The thermostatic theory of emotion. A study in kybernetics. *Progress in Biocybernetics, 3,* 1–20.

Stanley-Jones, D. (1970). The biological origin of love and hate. In M. Arnold (Ed.), *Feelings and emotions.* New York: Academic Press.

Stenberg, C. R., & Campos, J. J. (1990). The development of anger expressions in infancy. In N. L. Stein, B. Leventhal, & T. Trabasso (Eds.), *Psychological and biological approaches to emotion.* Hillsdale, N.J.: L. Erlbaum.

Sternberg, R .J. (1986). A triangular theory of love. *Psychological Review, 93,* 119–135.

Sternglanz, S. H., Gray, J. L., & Murakami, M. (1977). Adult preferences for infantile facial features: An ethological approach. *Animal Behaviour, 25,* 108–115.

Stevenson-Hinde, J., & Simpson, A. E. (1982). Temperament and relationships. In R. Porter and G.M. Collins (Eds.), *Temperamental differences in infants and young children.* London: Pitman.

Storm, C., & Storm, T. (1987). A taxonomic study of the vocabulary of emotions. *Journal of Personality and Social Psychology, 53,* 805–816.

Strongman, K. (1987). *The psychology of emotion.* New York: Wiley.

Strum, S. C. (1988). *Almost human: A journey into the world of baboons.* New York: Random House.

Sullivan, H. S. (1956). *Clinical studies in psychiatry.* New York: Norton.

Tardiff, K., & Koenigsberg, H. W. (1985). Assaultive behavior among psychiatric outpatients. *American Journal of Psychiatry, 142,* 960–963.

Tardiff, K., and Sweillam, A. (1982). Assaultive behavior among chronic inpatients. *American Journal of Psychiatry, 159,* 212–215.

Taylor, J. (1953). A personality test for manifest anxiety. *Journal of Abnormal and Social Psychology, 48,* 285–290.

Terrace, H. S. (1979). Is problem-solving language? *Journal of the Experimental Analysis of Behavior, 31,* 161–175.

Theodorson, G. A. (1965). Romanticism and motivation to marry in the United States, Singapore, Burma, and India. *Social Forces, 43,* 17–27.

Thompson, J. (1941). Development of facial expressions of emotion in blind and seeing children. *Archives of Psychology, 37,* No. 264.

Thompson, R. F. (1967). *Foundations of physiological psychology.* New York: Harper & Row.

Tomkins, S. S. (1962). *Affect imagery consciousness: (Vol. 1), The positive affects.* New York: Springer.

Tomkins, S. S. (1970). Affect as the primary motivational system. In M. Arnold (Ed.), *Feelings and emotions.* New York: Academic Press.

Tomkins, S. S. (1980). Affect as amplification: Some modifications in theory. In R. Plutchik & H. Kellerman (Eds.), *Emotion: Theory, research and experience: Vol. 1, Theories of emotion.* New York: Academic Press.

Tomkins, S. S., & McCarter, R. (1964). What and where are the primary affects? Some evidence for a theory. *Perceptual and Motor Skills, 18,* 119–158.

Trevarthen, C. (1977). Descriptive analysis of infant communicative behavior. In H. R. Schaffer (Ed.), *Studies in mother-infant interaction.* New York: Academic Press.

Trower, P., and Gilbert, P. (1989). New theoretical conceptions of social anxiety and social phobia. *Clinical Psychology Review, 9,* 19–35.

Tuttle, R. H. (1986). *Apes of the world.* Park Ridge, NJ: Noyes Publications.

Valins, S. (1966). Cognitive effects of false heart-rate feedback. *Journal of Personality and Social Psychology, 4,* 400–408.

van Hooff, J. A. R. A .M. (1973). A structural analysis of the social behaviour of a semi-captive group of chimpanzees. In M. von Cranach and I.Vine (Eds.), *Social communication and movement.* New York: Academic Press.

Van Lawick-Goodall, J. (1973). The behavior of chimpanzees in their natural habitat. *American Journal of Psychiatry, 130,* 1–12.

Wallbott, H. G., & Scherer, K. R. (1989). Assessing emotion by questionnaire. In R. Plutchik and H.Kellerman (Eds.), *Emotion: Theory, research and experience: Vol 4. The measurement of emotions.* New York: Academic Press.

Watson, D., Clark, L. A., & Tellegen, A. (1988). Development and validation of brief measures of positive and negative affect: The PANAS Scales. *Journal of Personality and Social Psychology, 54,* 1063–1070.

Watson, D., & Tellegen, A. (1985). Toward a consensual structure of mood. *Psychological Bulletin, 98,* 219–235.

Watson, J. B., 1919 (1st ed.), 1924 (2nd ed.), and 1929 (3rd ed.). *Psychology from the standpoint of a behaviorist.* Philadelphia: Lippincott.

Wentworth, H., & Flexner, S. B. (Eds.). (1975). *Dictionary of American slang.* New York: Crowell.

West, D. J. (1966). *Murder followed by suicide.* London: Heinemann.

Whissell, C. M. (1989). The dictionary of affect in language. In R. Plutchik and H. Kellerman (Eds.), *Emotion: Theory, research and experience: Vol. 4, The measurement of emotions.* New York: Academic Press.

White, T. H. (Ed.) (1960). *The bestiary: A book of beasts.* New York: Capricorn Books.

Wiggins, J. S., & Broughton, R. (1985). The interpersonal circle: A structural model for the integration of personality research. *Perspectives in Personality, 1,* 1–47.

Wilder, J., & Plutchik, R. (1982). Preparing the professional: Building prevention of burnout into professional training. In W. Payne (Ed.), *Job stress and burnout.* Beverly Hills, CA: Sage.

Wilson, E. O. (1975). *Sociobiology: The new synthesis.* Cambridge: Harvard University Press.

Wimer, R. E., & Wimer, C. C. (1985). Animal behavior genetics: A search for the biological foundations of behavior. *Annual Review of Psychology, 36,* 171–218.

Wise, R. A. (1988). The neurobiology of craving: Implications for the understanding and treatment of addiction. *Journal of Abnormal Psychology, 97,* 118–132.

Woerdeman, M. W. (1960). *Atlas of human anatomy: nervous system.* New York: Excerpta Medica Foundation.

Wolff, P. H. (1987). *The development of behavioral states and the expression of emotions in early infancy.* Chicago: University of Chicago Press.

Wortman, C. B., & Laftus, E. F. (1985). *Psychology.* New York: Alfred A. Knopf.

Young, G., & Decarie, T. (1977). An ethology-based catalogue of facial/vocal behavior in infancy. *Animal Behavior, 25,* 95–107.

Young, P. T. (1927). Studies in affective psychology. *American Journal of Psychology, 38,* 157–193.

Young, P. T. (1967). Affective arousal: Some implications. *American Psychologist, 22,* 32–40.

Zajonc, R. B., and Moreland, R. L. (1982). Exposure effects in person perception: Familiarity, similarity, and attraction. *Journal of Experimental Social Psychology, 18,* 395–415.

Zajonc, R. B., Murphy, S. T., & Inglehart, M. (1989). Feeling and facial efference: Implications of the vascular theory of emotion. *Psychological Review, 96,* 395–416.

Zitrin, C. M., Klein, D. F., Woerner, M. G., & Ross, D. C. (1983). Treatment of phobias. I. Comparison of imipramine hydrochloride and placebo. *Archives of General Psychiatry, 40,* 125–138.

Zuckerman, M., & Lubin, B. (1965). *Manual for the multiple affect adjective check list.* San Diego: Educational and Industrial Testing Service.

Acknowledgments

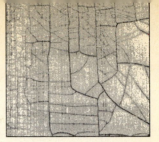

Chapter 1

Figure 1.1 From "The Expressive Behavior of the Deaf-and-Blind Born" by I. Eibl-Eibesfeldt. In M. von Cranach and I. Vine (Eds.), *Social Communication and Movement*. New York: Academic Press, 1973. Reprinted by permission.

Figure 1.2 From "The Behavior of Chimpanzees in Their Natural Habitat" by J. van Lawick-Goodall. *American Journal of Psychiatry*, 1973, *130*, 1–12. Reprinted by permission.

Figure 1.3 From *The Bestiary: A Book of Beasts*. T. H. White (Ed.), New York: G. P. Putnam's Sons, 1960. Reprinted by permission.

Chapter 3

Table 3.1 From "A Taxonomic Study of the Vocabulary of Emotions" by C. Storm and T. Storm. *Journal of Personality and Social Psychology*, 1987, *53*, 805–816. Reprinted by permission.

Table 3.2 From "How Many Emotions Are There? Wedding the Social and the Autonomic Components" by T. D. Kemper, *American Journal of Sociology*, 1987, *93*, 263–289. Reprinted by permission.

Table 3.4 From "The Dictionary of Affect in Language" by C. M. Whissell. In R. Plutchik and H. Kellerman (Eds.), *The Measurement of Emotions*. New York: Academic Press, 1989. Reprinted by permission.

Figure 3.1 From "Studies in the Phenomenology of Emotions, by J. Black. *Journal of Abnormal and Social Psychology*, 1957, *54*, 358–363. Reprinted by permission.

Table 3.5 From *Emotion: A Psychoevolutionary Synthesis* by R. Plutchik. New York: Harper and Row, 1980. Reprinted by permission.

Figure 3.2 From *Emotion: A Psychoevolutionary Synthesis* by R. Plutchik. New York: Harper and Row, 1980. Reprinted by permission.

Figure 3.3 From "Measures of Emotion" by J. A. Russell. In R. Plutchik and H. Kellerman (Eds.), *The Measurement of Emotion*. New York: Academic Press, 1989. Reprinted by permission.

Chapter 4

Table 4.1 From "On the Nature and Development of Affects: A Unified Theory" by C. Brenner. *Psychoanalytic Quarterly*, 1974, *43*, 532–556. Reprinted by permission.

Figure 4.2 From "Emotions in Early Development" by R. Plutchik. In R. Plutchik and H. Kellerman (Eds.), *Emotions in Early Development*. New York: Academic Press, 1983. Reprinted by permission.

Figure 4.3 From *Emotion: A Psychoevolutionary Synthesis* by R. Plutchik. New York: Harper and Row, 1980. Reprinted by permission.

Table 4.3 From "Emotions and Their Vicissitudes" by R. Plutchik. In M. Lewis and J. M. Haviland, *Handbook of Emotions*. New York: Guilford Press. Reprinted by permission.

Chapter 5

Table 5.2 From "Measuring Emotions and Their Derivatives" by R. Plutchik. In R. Plutchik and H. Kellerman (Eds.), *The Measurement of Emotions*. New York: Academic Press, 1989. Reprinted by permission.

Figure 5.1 From "Emotion Profiles in Mania and Depression" by S. R. Platman, R. Plutchik, R. R. Fieve, and W. G. Lawlor. *Archives of General Psychiatry*, 1969, *20*, 210–214. Reprinted by permission.

Table 5.3 From "Assessing Emotion by Questionnaire" by H. G. Wallbott and K. R. Scherer. In R. Plutchik and H. Kellerman (Eds.), *The Measurement of Emotions*, New York: Academic Press, 1989. Reprinted by permission.

Table 5.4 From "Assessing Emotion by Questionnaire" by H. G. Wallbott and K. R. Scherer. In R. Plutchik and H. Kellerman (Eds.), *The Measurement of Emotions*, New York: Academic Press, 1989. Reprinted by permission.

Table 5.5 From "Anxiety Neurosis: A Disease for the Medical Model" by J. Clavey and R. Noyes. *Psychosomatics*, 1976, *17*, 90–93. Reprinted by permission.

Table 5.6 From "A Structural Analysis of the Social Behavior of a Semicaptive Group of Chimpanzees" by J. A. R. A. M. van Hooff. In M. von Cranach and I. Vine (Eds.), *Social Communication and Movement*. New York: Academic Press, 1973. Reprinted by permission.

Figure 5.2 From "Measuring Animal Aggression" by D. Benton. In R. Plutchik and H. Kellerman (Eds.), *The Measurement of Emotions*. New York: Academic Press, 1989. Reprinted by permission.

Table 5.7 From "Measuring Animal Aggression" by D. Benton. In R. Plutchik and H. Kellerman (Eds.), *The Measurement of Emotions*. New York: Academic Press, 1989. Reprinted by permission.

Figure 5.4 From "Studies of Body Image, IV. Figure Drawings in Normal and Abnormal Geriatric and Nongeriatric Groups" by R. Plutchik, H. R. Conte, M. B. Werner, and J. Teresi. *Journal of Gerontology*, 1978, *33*, 68–75. Reprinted by permission.

Chapter 6

Figure 6.1 From *The Mechanism of Human Facial Expression* by G. B. Duchenne de Boulogne. New York: Cambridge University Press, 1990/1862. Reprinted by permission.

Figure 6.2 From *The Expression of the Emotions in Man and Animals* by Charles Darwin. Chicago: University of Chicago Press, 1956/1872. Reprinted by permission.

Table 6.1 From "Measuring Facial Movement" by P. Ekman and W. V. Friesen. *Psychology and Nonverbal Behavior*, 1976, *1*, 56–75. Reprinted by permission.

Figure 6.4 From *Man's Face and Mimic Language* by C. H. Hjortsjo. Malmo, Sweden: Nordens Boktrycheri, 1970. Reprinted by permission.

Figure 6.5 From *Manwatching: A Field Guide to Human Behavior* by D. Morris. New York: Harry N. Abrams, 1977. Reprinted by permission.

Figure 6.6 From "The Recognition of Threatening Facial Stimuli" by J. Aronoff, A. M. Barclay, and L. A. Stevenson. *Journal of Personality and Social Psychology*, 1988, *54*, 647–655. Reprinted by permission.

Figure 6.7 From *Love and Hate* by I. Eibl-Eibesfeldt. New York: Holt, Rinehart and Winston, 1971. Reprinted by permission.

Figure 6.8 From "Fear, Defense, and Aggression in Animals and Man: Some Ethological Perspectives" by I. Eibl-Eibesfeldt and C. Sutterlin. In P. F. Brain and S. Parmigiani (Eds.), *Fear and Defense*. London: Harwood, 1990. Reprinted by permission.

Figure 6.9 From "Fear, Defense, and Aggression in Animals and Man: Some Ethological Perspectives" by I. Eibl-Eibesfeldt and C. Sutterlin. In P. F. Brain and S. Parmigiani (Eds.), *Fear and Defense*. London: Harwood, 1990. Reprinted by permission.

Table 6.2 From "The Expressive Behavior of the Deaf-and-Blind Born" by I. Eibl-Eibesfeldt. In M. von Cranach and I. Vine (Eds.), *Social Communication and Movement*.

New York: Academic Press, 1973. Reprinted by permission.

Figure 6.10 From *Gestures: Their Origins and Distribution* by D. Morris, P. Collett, P. Marsh, and M. O'Shaugnessy. New York: Stein and Day, 1979. Reprinted by permission.

Table 6.3 From *Gestures: Their Origins and Distribution,* by D. Morris, P. Collett, P. Marsh, and M. O'Shaugnessy. New York: Stein and Day, 1979. Reprinted by permission.

Chapter 7

Figure 7.1 From *Almost Human: A Journey into the World of Baboons* by S. C. Strum. New York: Random House, 1988. Reprinted by permission.

Figure 7.2 From *A Primate Radiation: Evolutionary Biology of the African Guenons* by A. Gautier-Hion , F. Bourliere, J. P. Gautier, and J. Kingdom. New York: Cambridge University Press, 1988. Reprinted by permission.

Figure 7.3 From "Facial Expression of Emotion in Nonhuman Primates" by S. Chevalier-Skolnikoff. In P. Ekman (Ed.), *Darwin and Facial Expression.* New York: Academic Press, 1973. Reprinted by permission.

Chapter 8

Table 8.1 From "An Ethogy-Based Catalogue of Facial/Vocal Behavior in Infancy" by G. Young and T. G. Decarie. *Animal Behavior,* 1977, *25,* 95–107. Reprinted by permission.

Figure 8.2 From *The Development of Behavioral States and the Expression of Emotions in Early Infancy* by P. H. Wolff. Chicago: University of Chicago Press, 1987. Reprinted by permission.

Table 8.2 From "Relationships as Regulators: A Psychobiologic Perspective on Bereavement" by M. A. Hofer. *Psychosomatic Medicine,* 1984, *46,* 183–197. Reprinted by permission.

Figure 8.3 By courtesy of J. J. Campos.

Figure 8.4 From "Adult Preferences for Infantile Facial Features: An Ethological Approach" by S. H. Sternglanz, J. L. Gray, and M. Murakami. *Animal Behavior,* 1977, *25,* 108–115. Reprinted by permission.

Figure 8.5 From "Adult Preferences for Infantile Facial Features: An Ethological Approach" by S. H. Sternglanz, J. L. Gray, and M. Murakami. *Animal Behavior,* 1977, *25,* 108–115. Reprinted by permission.

Figure 8.6 From *Psychology* by C. B. Wortman and E. F. Loftus. New York: Alfred A. Knopf, 1985. Reprinted by permission.

Chapter 9

Figure 9.1 From "The Evolution of Primate Behavior" by A. Jolly, *American Scientist,* 1985, *73,* 230–239. Reprinted by permission.

Chapter 10

Table 10.1 From *Animal Language* by M. Bright. Ithaca: Cornell University Press, 1984. Reprinted by permission.

Table 10.2 From "Primate Vocalization: Affective or Symbolic?" by P. Marler. In *Progress in Ape Research.* New York: Academic Press, 1977. Reprinted by permission.

Figure 10.1 From "The Reproductive Behavior of the Zebra Finch (Peophia guffata) with Special Reference to Pseudofemale Behavior and Displacement Activities" by D. J. Morris. *Behavior,* 1954, *6,* 271–322. Reprinted by permission.

Figure 10.2 From *Animal Behavior: A Synthesis of Ethology and Comparative Psychology* by R. A. Hinde. New York: McGraw-Hill, 1966. Reprinted by permission.

Figure 10.3 From *Love and Hate* by I. Eibl-Eibesfeldt. New York: Holt, Rinehart, and Winston, 1971. Reprinted by permission.

Figure 10.4 From *The Psychology of Fear and Stress* by J. A. Gray. New York: Cambridge University Press, 1988. Reprinted by permission.

Figure 10.6 From "A Structural Analysis of the Social Behavior of a Semicaptive Group of Chimpanzees" by J. A. R. A. M van Hooff. In M. van Cranach and I. Vine (Eds.), *Social Communication and Movement.* New York: Academic Press, 1973. Reprinted by permission.

Chapter 11

Figure 11.1 From *The Ideas of Biology* by J. T. Bonner. New York: Harper and Row, 1962. Reprinted by permission.

Figure 11.2 From *The Evolution of Human Nature* by C. J. Herrick. Austin: University of Texas Press, 1956. Reprinted by permission.

Table 11.2 From *Foundations of Physiological Psychology* by R. F. Thompson. New York: Harper and Row, 1967. Reprinted by permission.

Figure 11.3 From *Atlas of Human Anatomy: Nervous System* by M. W. Woerdeman. New York: Excerpta Medica Foundation, 1960. Reprinted by permission.

Figure 11.4 From "Ventricular System of the Brain of the Dolphin, Tursiops Truncatus, with Comparable Anatomic Observatoins and Relations to Brain Specializations" by W. L. McFarland, P. J. Morgane, and M. S. Jacobs. *Journal of Comparative Neurology,* 1969, *135,* 275–368. Reprinted by permission.

Figure 11.5 From *Atlas of Human Anatomy: Nervous System* by M. W. Woerdeman. New York: Excerpta Medica Foundation, 1960. Reprinted by permission.

Figure 11.6 From *The Human Brain: A Photographic Guide* by N. Gluhbegovic and T. Williams. New York: Harper and Row, 1980. Reprinted by permission.

Figure 11.7 From "Core Text of Neuroanatomy" by M. B. Carpenter and J. Sutin. Baltimore: Williams and Wilkins, 1985. Reprinted by permission.

Figure 11.8 From *Foundations of Physiological Psychology* by R. F. Thompson. New York: Harper and Row, 1967. Reprinted by permission.

Figure 11.9 From "Display of Penile Erection in Squirrel Monkeys (Saimiri sciureus)" by D. W. Ploog and P. D. MacLean. *Animal Behavior Monographs,* 1963, *11,* 32–39. Reprinted by permission.

Chapter 12

Table 12.1 From *Emotion* by J. M. B. Delgado. DuBuque, Iowa: William C. Brown, 1966. Reprinted by permission.

Figure 12.1 From "Neurocrine Patterns of Emotional Response" by J. P. Henry. In R. Plutchik and H. Kellerman (Eds.), *Biological Foundations of Emotion.* New York: Academic Press, 1986. Reprinted by permission.

Figure 12.2 From "Neurocrine Patterns of Emotional Response" by J. P. Henry. In R. Plutchik and H. Kellerman (Eds.), *Biological Foundations of Emotion.* New York: Academic Press, 1986. Reprinted by permission.

Table 12.2 From "The Anatomy of Emotions" by J. Panksepp. In R. Plutchik and H. Kellerman (Eds.), *Biological Foundation of Emotion.* New York: Academic Press, 1986. Reprinted by permission.

Figure 12.3 From "Emotion" by J. E. LeDoux. In *Handbook of Physiology: The Nervous System,* V. Bethesda, Maryland: American Physiological Society, 1988. Reprinted by permission.

Figure 12.4 From *Foundations of Physiological Psychology* by R. F. Thompson. New York: Harper and Row, 1967. Reprinted by permission.

Chapter 13

Table 13.2 From "A Biased Overview of the Study of Love" by P. R. Shaver and C. Hazan. *Journal of Social and Personal Relationships,* 1988, *5*, 473–501. Reprinted by permission.

Table 13.3 From *Women and Depression: Risk Factors and Treatment Issues* by E. McGrath, G. P. Keita, B. R. Strickland, and N. F. Russo (Eds.). Washington, D.C.: American Psychological Association, 1990. Reprinted by permission.

Chapter 14

Table 14.2 From *The Naked Ape* by D. Morris. New York: McGraw-Hill, 1967. Reprinted by permission.

Table 14.3 From "Prediction of Suicide in Psychiatric Patients" by A. D. Pokorny. *Archives of General Psychiatry,* 1983, *40,* 249–257. Reprinted by permission.

Table 14.4 From "Prediction of Suicide in Psychiatric Patients" by A. D. Pokorny. *Archives of General Psychiatry,* 1983, *40,* 249–257. Reprinted by permission.

Table 14.5 From "Development of a Clinical Instrument to Estimate Suicide Risk" by J. A. Motto, D. C. Heilbron, and R. D. Juster. *American Journal of Psychiatry,* 1985, *142,* 1061–1064. Reprinted by permission.

Table 14.6 From "Research Strategies for the Study of Human Violence" by R. Plutchik, C. Climent, and F. Ervin. In W. L. Smith and A. Kling (Eds.), *Issues in Brain/Behavior Control.* New York: Spectrum, 1976. Reprinted by permission.

Author Index

Subject Index